The Museological Unconscious

VICTOR TUPITSYN

Communal (Post)Modernism in Russia

THE MIT PRESS CAMBRIDGE, MASSACHUSETTS LONDON, ENGLAND

MIT Press books may be purchased at special quantity discounts for business or sales promotional use. For information, please email special_sales@mitpress.mit.edu or write to Special Sales Department, The MIT Press, 55 Hayward Street, Cambridge, MA 02142.

This book was set in Sabon and Univers by Graphic Composition, Inc., Bogart, Georgia. Printed and bound in Spain.

Library of Congress Cataloging-in-Publication Data

Tupitsyn, Viktor, 1945–
The museological unconscious : communal (post) modernism in Russia / Victor Tupitsyn.
p. cm.
Includes bibliographical references and index.
ISBN 978-0-262-20173-5 (hard cover : alk. paper)
1. Avant-garde (Aesthetics)—Russia (Federation)
2. Dissident art—Russia (Federation) 3. Art and state—Russia (Federation) 4. Art, Russian—20th century.
5. Art, Russian—21st century. I. Title.
N6988.5.A83T87 2009
709.47′09045—dc22
2008031026

10 9 8 7 6 5 4 3 2 1

To Margarita

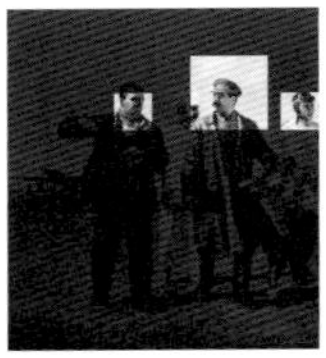
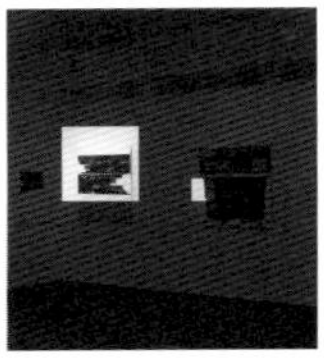
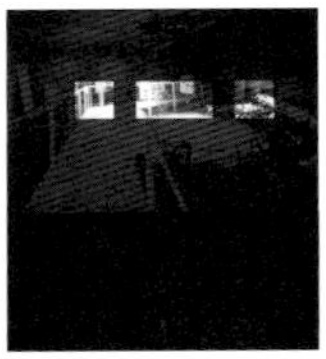
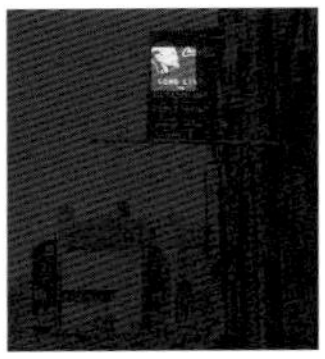
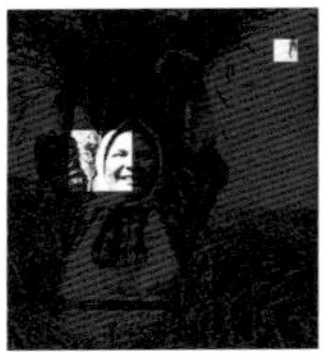
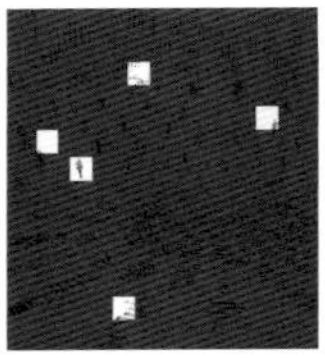
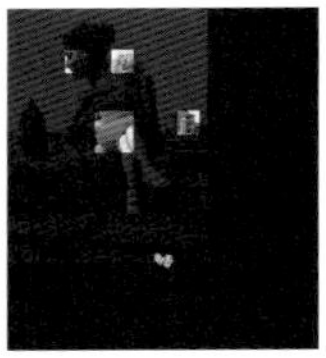
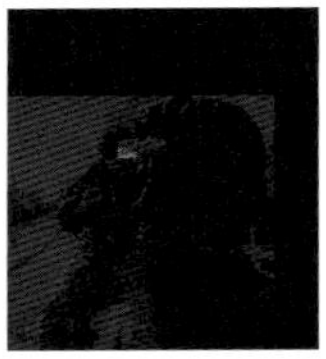
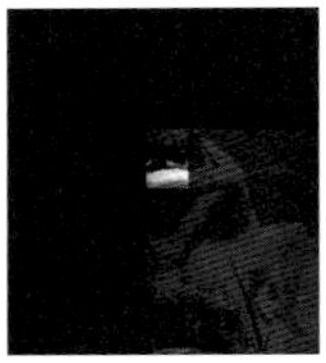
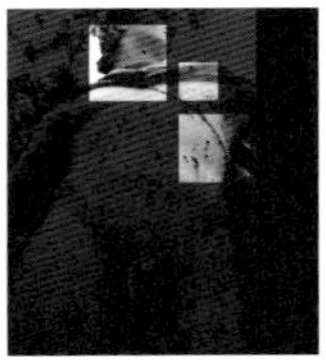
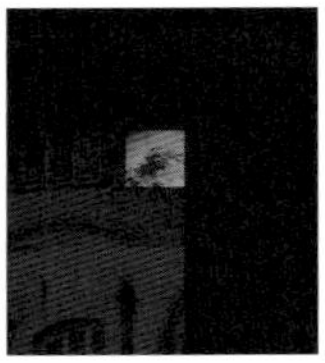
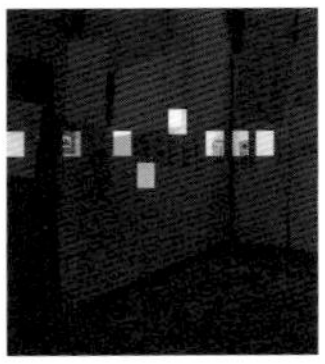
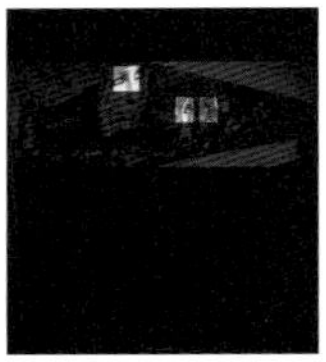

CONTENTS

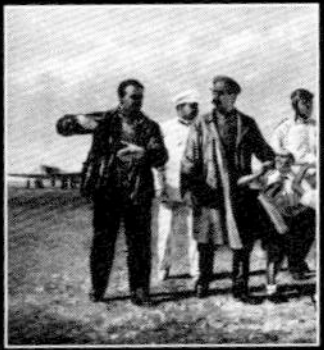

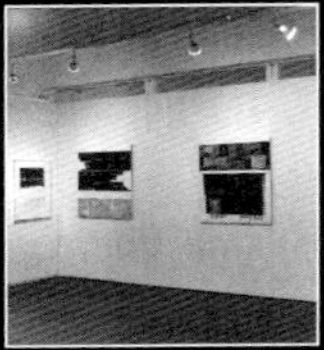

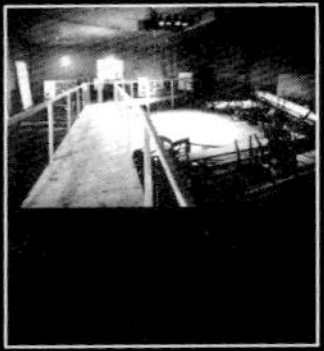

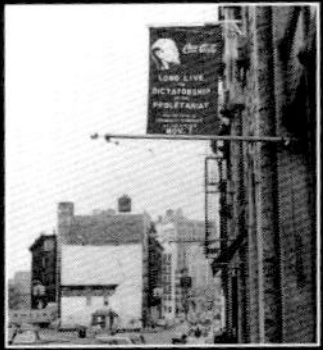
LONG LIVE
DICTATORSHIP
PROLETARIAT

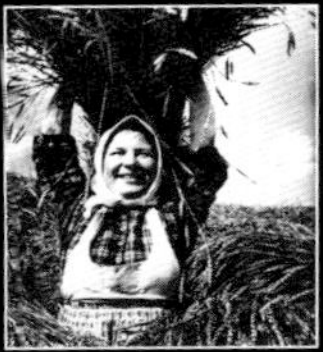

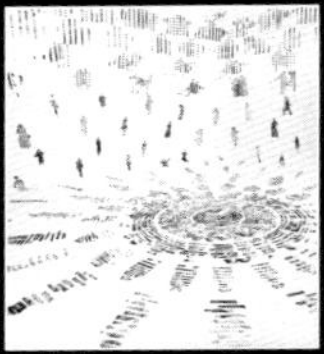

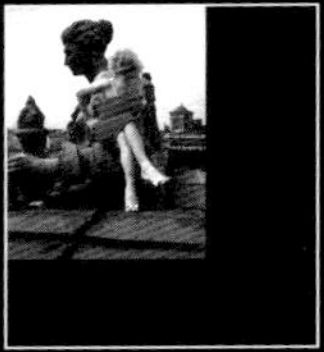

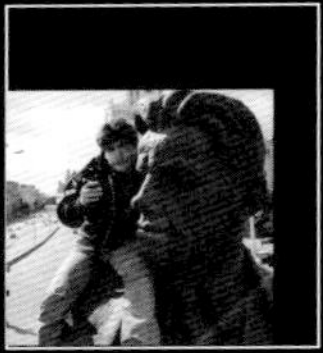

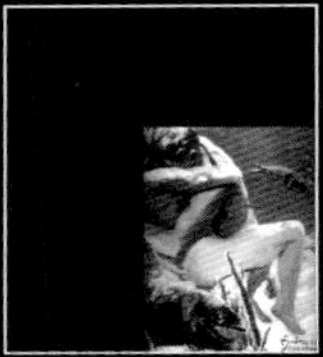

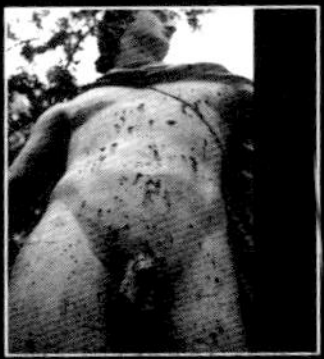

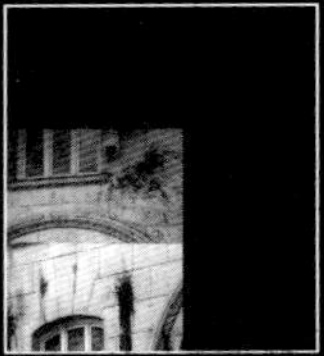

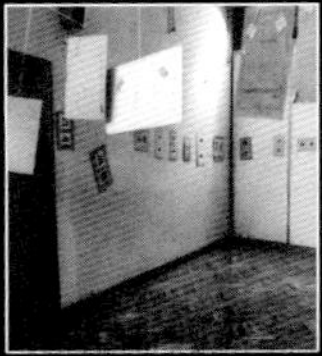

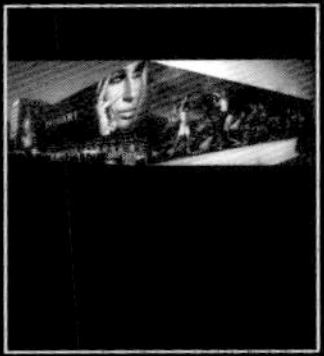

PREFACE

This book presents the history of contemporary Russian art as a communal paradigm—a model that grants the opportunity to discuss and analyze seemingly disconnected and incompatible events as effected by a number of communal phenomena, such as communal living, communal perception, and communal speech practices. Because of this "communalizing" approach, many artists and art movements are brought together for the first time, as if they were the tenants of one large communal apartment.

This common approach to a variety of issues is based on the theory that the optical unconscious of the Soviet people was structured like communal speech. Admittedly, all texts in this publication have been guided by a look-alike principle—the analogy between communal speech and communal vision is linked to the imperative of seeing through the eyes or on behalf of the "collective other." Everything that appealed to the communal eye in post–World War II Russia is critically scrutinized in *The Museological Unconscious,* including the reproductions of up to one hundred artworks from both Soviet and post-Soviet periods. The reference to "communal postmodernism" in the title of the book reflects the fact that instead of fully abandoning their frustrating heritage, the alternative Russian artists of the post-Stalin era have turned their "vices" into "virtues," thereby creating a new postmodern language.

Whereas chapter 1 lays the ground for a coherent theoretical treatment of a variety of issues discussed in the subsequent chapters of this book, chapter 2 surveys the history of the alternative (unofficial) Russian art. Here, the conceptual matrix developed in the late 1980s and elaborated in chapter 1 comes to play on the level of recollecting, sorting out, and interpreting a vast historical material that stretches from the late 1950s to the present. In chapter 10, the conditions of seeing, discussed in the first chapter, are subjected to a different approach, focused on the phenomenon of compulsive museification, through which the "museological unconscious" manifests itself.

The rest of the book deals with specific issues (e.g., feminism, body politics) or artistic phenomena (e.g., sots art, apt art). Predictably, the final chapters are dedicated to the latest stage of the post-Soviet cultural metamorphoses—the art of the new millennium. One may hope, however, that some of the interpretive and critical strategies spelled out in *The Museological Unconscious* will transcend the specificity of its "domestic context" and prove to be useful for socially engaged artists and intellectuals from all over the world (including Eastern Europe and Third World countries). All photographic images belong to Victor and MargaritaTupitsyn's archive. Every effort has been made to contact the rights holders, but in the event that I have missed any, I welcome hearing from those artists.

I have been writing about contemporary Russian art since 1975, the year of my emigration to the United States. In 1976 I defended my Ph.D. thesis at SUNY Stony Brook, and in 1988, thanks to glasnost and perestroika, was able to spend a sabbatical year in Moscow, thereby renewing my access to its alternative art milieu, with which I had kept up an intense epistolary contact. Since then trips to Moscow and St. Petersburg have been regular, and I have frequently contributed to the artistic life of these cities as a writer and critical observer. The arguments outlined in this book originate from that period. Much of that writing was instigated by the sustained support of a number of magazine editors that include Joanne Morra and Marquard Smith of *Parallax;* Chantal Pontbriand, Jim Drobnik, and Eduardo Ralickas of *Parachute;* Rasheed Araeen and Jean Fisher of *Third Text;* Pierre Restany of *D'Ars;* Tim Griffin of *Artforum;* Aleksandr Ivanov of *Ad Marginem;* Nikolai Sheptulin of *Mesto pechati;* Viktor Mazin and Olesia Tourkina of *Kabinet;* Viktor Misiano of *Kh/Zh;* Arsenii Meshcheriakov of *WAM;* and Irina Prokhorova of *NLO*. I would also like to thank the artists for sharing their insights with me in more than forty interviews and conversations, printed in a number of museum catalogues and in two books published in Moscow in 1997 and 2006. Special thanks to Susan Buck-Morss for discussing several chapters of this book with me in the introductory piece. I am grateful to Roger Conover for being receptive to *The Museological Unconscious,* and to my daughter Masha, the author of *Beauty Talk & Monsters,* for her incisive editorial interventions. Lastly, I want to express my gratitude to Margarita Tupitsyn, with whom I have been privileged to engage in brainstorming "seminars" on a daily basis.

Victor Tupitsyn

INTRODUCTION: SUSAN BUCK-MORSS IN CONVERSATION WITH VICTOR TUPITSYN

SUSAN BUCK-MORSS **In chapter 1 ["Civitas Solis: Ghetto as Paradise"], you state that "socialist realism is not transportable." You argue that it is necessary to interpret this artistic phenomenon within the context of Soviet experience, and you provide a blackly humorous description of communal life under Stalin. When you describe the infantilism of this communalism, I could not agree with you more. I am fully convinced by what you say. But it immediately raises the question: Why is this case unique? Why only socialist realism? Why not other artistic movements—surrealism, say, or conceptualism, or even abstract expressionism? This leads to the second question: Isn't art recontextualized every place it is shown?**

VICTOR TUPITSYN Socialist realism is not transportable because—unlike surrealism—it was more than just an art movement or a sensibility shared by a limited number of individuals. It was the representation of the Soviet identity addressed to a nationwide audience that was extremely receptive. The high level of reciprocation that existed between the communal subject and socialist realist imagery presents enough evidence to believe that socialist realism does not work without communal perception. It is an integral part of an immense system that is too difficult to fit into crates. Such "crating" is at the expense of socialist realism's identificatory dimension. You can travel the paintings to Kassel or Long Island City, but you cannot transport the optical conditions required for adequate communication with those paintings. For that you need to communalize the viewer and radically change his or her sense of visual identity. There's nothing new about recontextualization, except for our desire to museify it. In this sense we have become truly postmodern. Now, let me respond to your second question: "Isn't art recontextualized every place it is shown?"

Yes, but simply because recontextualizing is an art medium. Take, for example, Duchamp's *Fountain,* or Darwinian theory, according to which *Homo sapiens* is a recontextualized ape. As for the correlation between conditions pertaining to recontextualization of a "text" and its translatability, it is too vague to be based on Husserl's conviction that "as heterogeneous as the essential structures of several constituted languages or cultures may be, translation in principle is an always possible task."[1] Husserl believed in the existence of the irreducible horizon, common to all empirical contexts, and it seems to me that the trust you put into recontextualization is based on the same kind of "inaccessible infra-ideal." This is precisely what Derrida (in his introduction to Husserl's *Origin of Geometry*) called "consciousness of a pure and precultural *we*."[2] I share his skepticism when he asks: "Are not non-communication and misunderstanding the very horizon of culture and language?"[3] I might as well argue that unlike socialist realist painting or any other "work of art in the age of communal perception," a theoretical account of it cannot be exempt from "transportability." I am absolutely convinced that because of their susceptibility to eidetic determination, interpretive strategies and intellectual reflections are perfectly convertible, even if the corresponding referents are not. Chances are that sooner or later socialist realism will become recontextualized beyond recognition. But will it be possible fully to appreciate the "true nature" of this "symbolic expenditure" without surrendering to the affective force of the communal eye?

SBM Is the so-called "art world" territorially or temporally located? Is it sociohistorically specific?

VT I certainly hope so. Also, the ways in which art worlds are temporally and territorially dislocated can be viewed as sociohistorically specific. That is why in "Civitas Solis: Ghetto as Paradise," I shift attention from totalitarian culture to its "dangerous supplement," the communal—communal perception, communal optics, communal (post)modernism, etc. On the other hand, art has the potential to come forth as an ersatz of time. Temporality is being museologized through our thinking of history in terms of artworks that we see (or imagine) on museum walls. We assume that if we have a sense of culture, we have a sense of time.

SBM How best to explain the "communal vision" of Soviet art? In fact, I think you convey it excellently through your humorous criticism of daily life. It seems to me that you accomplish linguistically what the sots artists [Erik Bulatov, Komar & Melamid, etc.][4] did visually. Your criticism not only condemns the Soviet experience, but makes us almost long for it—like memories of a bad childhood which, however miserable, keeps us grateful.

VT In the USSR, where "collective monologue" and "collective seeing" became reciprocal ways of life, one could easily translate images or even brush strokes into words. In the communal world,[5] this horizon of seeing is linked to the phenomenon of cathartic merging with an identificatory icon, i.e., it is not visuality, but psychedelia. I am talking about *perestroika zrenia* (optical restructuring) of immense proportions. It was an A-bomb of communal vision[6] that exploded in Russia in the 1930s. Given the scale of this "explosion" (and the impact it made on the Soviet cultural mentality), there are hardly any nonnuclear ways to recontextualize this "Hiroshima."

Massive or petite, recontextualization pins its hopes on (a) a change of identity, and (b) an ideology to justify it. In this sense ideology is a byproduct of recontextualization.

Frankly, the idea of criticizing daily life or condemning the Soviet experience has never been high on my agenda. I'd rather be blamed for sympathizing with the Soviet (post)revolutionary avant-garde or socialist modernism ("sots modernism," in my terminology). I am referring to the specific texts "Civitas Solis: Ghetto as Paradise," and "Icons of Iconoclasm" [chapter 4], which also expose the duality between socialist realism and the communal world as well as some other issues—such as, for example, anti-alienation treatments administered to communal subjects to resolve their identificatory dramas.

SBM You want us to believe that in Soviet life "reality was annulled." One lived in a myth. But where is it different? At Disneyland?

VT Disneyland is, indeed, a Civitas Solis (American-style). Thus, it comes as no surprise that Walt Disney was an informer . . .

SBM What do you think of the work of younger scholars like Christina Kiaer who have written on Arvatov, Rodchenko, and early theories of the "socialist commodity"?

VT Christina's interpretation of the constructivist *veshch* (thing) is limited to the NEP period,[7] the time when capitalist objects were reintroduced within the socialist context. She also discusses the reverse situation—Rodchenko's construction of his Workers' Club interior in Paris (1925). In this respect, one can talk about an object in its transition (and its division)—a dichotomized object still hesitant to quit its horizontal axis but already exploring the vertical one.

The notion of "socialist commodity" has nothing to do with the items of everyday use—kitchenware, furniture, clothing, etc. Such items were habitually dismal; they lacked any sense of pleasure, any hope for prestige or comfort. The ways in which the communal psyche connected itself to communal objecthood were completely defetishized. In 1922, Aleksei Gan theorized the so-called *obshchestvennaia veshch* (public thing)—an indexical sign-object from the inventory of photographic, sculptural, or architectural agitprop.[8] During the NEP years, posters for Western movies as well as billboards that advertised cookies, cigarettes, or household goods used images of attractive women. In such instances, when the consumer's gaze moved from the erotic image to the political one, it still retained (by dint of inertia) its libidinal intensity. As a result, what occurred was a transfer of libidinal interest from one iconographic context to another. In this manner, a consumer optic facilitated the eroticization of political imagery. The communal Eros was redirected to the sphere of public (socialist) objecthood.

You once mentioned an analysis of socialist realism that you found insightful in emphasizing that regardless of the propaganda content, the utopian effect of these artworks was sensual: the paintings are full of light, warmth, and an atmosphere of bodily pleasure. In certain cases repression is, indeed, a prerequisite of bodily pleasure. Since 1934, following [Andrei] Zhdanov and [Karl] Radek's campaign against sexuality in arts and literature, the only acceptable kind of physical pleasure—acceptable for totalitarian imagery—has been the pleasure of transcending sexuality, an androgynous "bodily" pleasure, so to speak. The problem with androgyny, however, is that its physique and its senses are entirely constituted.

Terms like "warmth" and "sensuality" may well be used to characterize the energy discharged by the communal psyche as it pulls itself through the symbolic network of seeing. Sometimes, when we touch a wire, we notice how warm (or even hot) it is. But the next moment, we realize that what we are holding in our hands is connected to a refrigerator . . . which produces the ice.

SBM In the solar myth that you describe, there were two extremes: on the one hand a kind of hubris of human technology: the thematics of the opera *Victory over the Sun,* where the sun was actually captured by humans. But on the other hand, the early Soviet era experimented with solar energy, and had a kind of ecological unconscious that was never allowed to challenge the dominance of the Stalinist superego (why do you use the French term, *sur-moi*?), but existed nonetheless. Does [Andrei] Tarkovsky's movie *Solaris* speak to this thematics?

VT I doubt very much that Stanisław Lem, whose book inspired Tarkovsky's movie, was interested in pursuing any kind of heliocentric or helioclastic agenda. Lem was clearly fascinated with surrealism: his *Solaris* is a huge psychomimetic enterprise, a brain capable of materializing unconscious representations—fears, desires, images of dead lovers, etc.

SBM Let me make a small critique. I am not so sure concepts like Deleuze's "oral mother" or Lacan's "family complex" are any more easily "transportable" than socialist realism. Do you feel that evoking these theorists helps translate the Soviet experience into a Western one? Or do you have other motives?

VT Affirmative concepts like "mother" and "family" are likely to be reaffirmed by equally positive experiences, unless you're an orphan. During the time of perestroika, there was a pop music group called Laskovyi Mai. The fact that this group consisted of orphans made all of Russia fall in love with them. Among their most appealing songs was "Diadia Misha" (Uncle Misha). In it, the performer insisted he was Mikhail Gorbachev's nephew. This innocent lie prompted the KGB to challenge and subsequently dismiss the alleged family ties. As for the orphan, a team of therapists was assigned to help him translate his experience from one realm to the next. I might need the same treatment. Otherwise, I will keep "evoking these theorists" ...

And yet there are people who tell me that the "truth" would have been much better served if I—in my writings about Russia—had referred exclusively to local sources and local (not Western) theorists. This creates an impression that the books of certain authors (particularly French and German) are privately owned by a group of self-appointed guardians of academic wisdom, the connoisseurs of Occidental thought.

My texts are written in English and printed outside of Russia. Also, as they are being addressed to an audience with its own allegories of reading, I have to evoke these allegories in order to invoke the corresponding reactions. The goal is to maximize receptiveness. Needless to say, I overdo it: too many proper names, too many references, too many theories. They all interfere with one another like tenants in an overcrowded Moscow apartment. The whole scenario fits the definition of the communal (not the "ideal") speech situation. Noise results. However deafening, this noise enables me to reactivate (within my own textual limitations) sedimental memories of the communal environment I am writing about.

SBM Maybe it is because I was trained as a theorist that I find "theory" so problematic. I don't trust it.

VT As with everything else, these issues are not without a prehistory. In the 1960s and 1970s, I was under the spell of *Znaika* (Knows-It-All), a familiar character of Soviet children's literature. As I write in chapter 7 ("Pushmi-pullyu: St. Petersburg-and-Moscow"), the mission of *Znaika* was taken by the party-state ideocracy, while the label of *Neznaika* (Know-Nothing) was pinned on the adversarial artistic intelligentsia. All *Neznaikas* (and I was one of them) had to fake or veil their identity and to embrace the Knowledge. Not for the sake of "unveiling the truth," but as an adequation with reality. Such adequation attests to the fact that Knowledge—besides being an instrument of repression—is a protective agency . . .

As in any repressive enterprise, Knowledge results in fear. Fear of not being able to answer fully and correctly when taking an exam or arguing with someone more knowledgeable. Fear that haunts us regardless of age, achievements, etc. That is why I am still trying to read—out of fear and panic, of course—the texts of all the theorists under the sun and refer to them in my own writings.

Most likely, I will never be able to pull off the image of *Znaika.* Nor would I be willing to deny my conspiratorial identity—*Neznaika. Neznaika*'s body of knowledge is a showcase of part-objects. No wonder that the references are vague and the quotes are nominal. For *Neznaika,* these props are all he needs to appear on stage as *Znaika.* This is like Dionysus wearing the mask of Apollo in Greek tragedy. Such a cover-up, combined with Freudian "self-splitting in repression," has resulted in a comic attitude to Knowledge as such, manifested in the tendency to emphasize its decorative (baroque) and exterior features—proper names, pompous quotes and epigraphs, worn-out phrases of famous thinkers, and so forth.

At times, to know nothing is an advantage, because keeping distance from Knowledge allows us to fantasize about it, unknowingly to misread it and partially to replace it with "allegories of [our] own lived experience"—as you put it in your book about Walter Benjamin's *Passagen-Werke.*[9] As for the distance from Knowledge, it gives way to a Brechtian (rather than Aristotelian) "companionship" between *Neznaika* and *Znaika.* At the same time, the place of the author-as-producer of Knowledge remains vacant and can be filled by anyone or anything. In Russia, for example, it can be filled by many people at once, since authorship in that country is still a communal property. That is why the game of acknowledging, quoting, and referencing is not as ritualized there as it is here.

In *Neznaika*'s case, residing on the margins of Thought is in harmony with the circular model of learning: the more we know, the longer the length of the circle that separates Knowledge from the Unknown. *Neznaika*'s desire to learn more (sometimes, even more than *Znaika*) and to stretch the circle of Knowledge has to do with the fact that the expansion of this circle is rife with the expansion of its margins. Likewise, some people buy additional acres of land in order to be better protected (or isolated) from their neighbors. But it would be too far-fetched to assume that margin-widening enables *Neznaika* to contemplate his "true self": the process of such widening deframes his identity to the extent that it becomes too vague even to use the term "identity." To conclude, I will point out that *Neznaika* is doomed to always present himself as *Znaika.* Every time he takes the stage as a custodian of Knowledge, he feels terrible afterward, regardless of the outcome (success or failure). That is what I feel when I am presented (in some publications) as a theorist or a philosopher.

SBM I want to move to your text "Negativity Mon Amour" (chapter 11), which is in fact my favorite (although "Batman and the Joker: the Thermidor of the Bodily" [chapter 8] is also terrific). You begin with a visual montage, the wall of the American embassy in Moscow, splattered with paint in protest against the NATO bombing of Serbia, spring 1999, juxtaposed to the Greenberg-approved, paint-splattered canvases of abstract expressionism. The humorous shock of this montage is your way of contextualizing art socially. This method is itself theory—better than theory, it is critical practice. The effect is not merely to urge respect for cultural "difference" in some vaguely liberal, relativistic way. Rather, yours is a practice of resistance against the homogenization of any culture. You are equally at home (or should I say, equally alienated) in both "cultures," Moscow (or St. Petersburg) and New York. That is what makes your perspective so valuable, both inside and outside, both lived experience and critical reflection. There is none of the anthropologist's sentimental glorification of the "other." Your observations show humorous affection for the Soviet-Russian culture of your birth, through the lens of a New Yorker's urbane tolerance.

To give another example: in chapter 9, "The Body-without-a-Name," you compare Clinton's presidency as "a mess" with Yeltsin as "the entirely sick leader." That's great because it does not set up any moralistic, good-bad binaries. And then you make the entirely astute observation that this is just what makes people identify with these leaders, it accounts for their popularity. I love that. Where others would see difference, you find similarities. But in other contexts, where others would argue for universals, you fight against the hegemonic and homogenizing project of globalization. That's negative dialectics and one does not have to even mention the name of Theodor Adorno to make this point.

This brings me back to our earlier discussion of theory. Of course, I accept your *Neznaika* explanation, and its specifically Russian meaning. First-year students of Russian in my college went around the dormitories singing, to the tune of "Frère Jacques": "Ya ne znaiu, ya ne znaiu, nichevo, nichevo, nichevo ne znaiu, nichevo ne znaiu, horosho, horosho"(I don't know, I don't know, anything, anything, absolutely nothing, absolutely nothing, which if fine, which is fine). That reveals something about the Russian soul, maybe the figure of the "holy fool" belongs here too. But your own cultural space is one of hybridity, not Russianness, and it is the vital ground for your spirit of freedom. Your topic is the art world. That is a global space. But the political hope of this space is precisely the hybridity that you yourself embody. To put it sociologically: global capitalism produces the "art world," which constantly tries to escape being absorbed into the culture industry that capitalism knows best. (You say as much in "The Body-without-a-Name.") But Western theory is also in danger of being absorbed into the culture industry, nowhere more so than when the big names are dropped in texts like so many authority markers. "Reification" is what Lukács called it. Cultural figures become fetishized, and sometimes I want to criticize you for that. But then it seems like you are up to something else. Let me give a specific example. In "Negativity Mon Amour," you let us see what is going on in Boris Mikhailov's photographs of post-Soviet citizens, that his "negative optics" depict the abject not as a critique of the beautiful in art, but in order to evoke the affirmative images of socialist realism. That sets up very interesting resonances with, say, Diane Arbus in this country (as you yourself note in

chapter 5 ["The Sun without a Muzzle"]). But just when we might be thinking along these lines, you as a writer dodge behind the figure of Lacan or Bataille, Barthes and Benjamin. You become invisible, and so does the point. You come out again and give us what we need, however, with a critique of the uncritically affirmative nature of identity politics (or identity art) that parallels Mikhailov's critique of socialist realism's affirmativity, and you apply it to intellectuals today. Even today's negatively critical intellectuals, you say—rightly, I think—are all the same, craving from the sidelines the very mass culture that they attack. Their alliances, you write, can be compared to NATO jets, "whose purpose is to seek more and more places where they can drop their discursive bombs and subsequently return to their prior (moralizing or melancholically detached) image." That's great. But are not your own critical forays also bomb-dropping, exploding Western theory with its own concepts? Is not your own intellectual role that of an evasive "deframer" of identity? Evasiveness—or "goblinry," as you describe the folktale figure of Leshyi in "Pushmi-pullyu: St. Petersburg-and-Moscow"?

Similarities emerge in unusual places in your texts, and the similar suddenly looks different. Or, the marginal suddenly looks central. The method is montage, juxtaposing pieces of the past and present, East and West. The tactic is anarchistic, which suits me fine. But there are still difficult issues, where simply to mimic the strategy of negativity seems insufficient. How, for example, would you address these multiple layers of cultural negativity: the performance artist Avdei Ter-Oganian, whom you discuss in "Negativity Mon Amour," offered visitors to Manezh Square a chance to chop a copy of a Russian Orthodox icon to pieces with an axe. You compare this "testing of the boundaries" of official culture to Andres Serrano's piece *Piss Christ.* We can add now Chris Ofili's painting of the Madonna with elephant dung that evoked such threat of censorship in the "Sensations" show at the Brooklyn Museum. But what about the graffiti-spirited seventy-two-year-old man who dared to defy the museum's sanctity and spray the Madonna with white paint? Was he a "deframer" of identity? And what of the museum's staff who ran in immediately to "clean up" the painting and restore it to its original state which had the art world seal of approval? Who stopped the play of meaning, the contextual deferral? What is at stake here? Where is *la différance*?

VT Neither of us underestimates the danger of fetishistic reification. But I am equally afraid of being hypocritical about it. One cannot call for protecting theoretical thoughts from inflation (or "sacred" from "profane") without admitting that all widely published Western thinkers are active players in the culture industry. I agree that dodging behind the figures of Lacan, Bataille, Barthes, or Benjamin makes me invisible as a writer. In this sense, the author does disappear. But definitely not the point. I simply see no connection here. To make such a connection—either in my case or beyond—one needs to be more resourceful in demonstrating that pointlessness and nobodiness are one and the same thing. The fact that X criticizes Y directly rather than on behalf of Z does not necessarily spare X's criticism from being groundless. At the same time, anonymous or undisclosed "sources" are perfectly capable of hinting at vital issues as vocally as those individuals who think that they are identical to their names. To tell you the truth, I wonder if any author can ever be cured from misrecognizing him- or herself for someone else. If you sense such a potential in my texts, the problem then lies in my literary skills, not elsewhere. Given my background as writer and poet, there are certain ways in which I perceive critical texts—my own or authored by others. For me, every name that you have just mentioned is the name of a "character" in a play I "wrote." Sometimes, I hide behind such a character, use him or her as a screen. By throwing someone else's name in my place, I engage in subterfuge, hoping that I will be able to prolong my own de-reified critical activity. In other words, I take a step back, leaving the heroes of my narratives in the foreground. This does not mean that I take no responsibility for what they do or think. Just the opposite: no matter what Uncle Vanya says or how the other characters react to it, the play of meaning (in the final analysis) will still be attributed to Chekhov.

When the Big Names (the names of authority makers, etc.) are constantly referred to, it not only attests or contributes to affirmation, but is also rife with subversion. The lineup of names (comparable in fate to the *Titanic* and *Lusitania*) in my texts spurs on our efforts to figure out "who will be the next to sink?" There is yet another explanation—the "bail-hunting" analogy. Since the meaning of what I write is deferred and thus unavailable to me, I instinctively search for it in the texts of others. In the course of chasing a renegade meaning, lots of addresses, phone numbers, clues, and tips come to play. Including the names.

It is hardly debatable that name-oriented practices are the worst possible manifestations of logocentrism. "I love logocentrism," admits Derrida in an interview.[10] But why? And what is that chthonic faculty which the pleasure of logocentrism is based on? There are things attributable to the anal drive or characterized as anal erotic. These can be detected in the early childhood when infants take pleasure from deferring the moment of defecation, i.e., from having the sensation of rectal presence. The color of a young child's feces is yellow or yellowish. Later, in a mature age, these gilded memories of childhood contribute to our fascination with gold. That is how some people become bankers and coin collectors. Intellectuals are knowledge collectors; instead of collecting precious metals, they collect precious thoughts. For them, anal pleasures are extended to names and titles printed on the cover of books. This twist of the Symbolic function partially explains why we constantly make references to "paradigmatic individuals," eroticize and fetishize them. Big Names are big chunks of pleasure in one's ass.

The longer we play Scrooge, the more generous we are at the time of defecation. I am talking about compulsive spending and dissemination of assets—be it a pension fund or a repository of ideas, names, etc. Also, the soil becomes more fertile after we finally let this stuff go. In rural Europe, it is not unusual to see a peasant riding a horse with a bag attached to its ass. As a centauric author (half poet, half critic), I might still rely on my instincts and continue to fertilize the field of writing—unless you give me a really good reason not to.

As for the second part of your question, I am convinced that our efforts to facilitate art's interaction with life are either aimed at deframing or caused by it. As applied by the intellectuals, deframing appears to be negatively defined. It is true that certain acts of "deframing" are performed on behalf or in the name of some other (familiar) frames. In such acts, negativity is a "hired gun," an accomplice of the affirmative. What is really at stake here is the politics of deframing vis-à-vis the deframing of politics.

SBM **When are similarities in artistic practice not a response to common objective conditions, but merely imitation? For example, Oleg Kulik and Aleksandr Brener's**

simulations of sexual intercourse with animals or biting a passerby seem to allow for an easy comparison with Vito Acconci's work, like *Seedbed,* where the artist masturbated underneath the gallery floor.

VT We usually emphasize similarities in artistic practice when there is nothing else to talk about. Simulation of sexual intercourse with animals and masturbation "beneath the bar" might look alike here and there, before and after, but to highlight this kind of likeness without paying attention to social dynamics and historic circumstances would be an example of "wishful seeing." Repetition is hardly a "perfect match," unless it is seen through the lens of desire. You cannot enter the same river twice, not only because it changes but also because you do too. This makes sameness or simulacrum doubly coincidental. In order to register them as cultural phenomena, one needs to artificially alter the context, to disregard its fluidity, its Protean nature. The observation that is being made here is applicable to both questions in which you juxtapose cutouts from two distant realities. It is fun to be a quilt maker, but I'd rather be more informed about the circumstances, especially in the case of the graffiti-spirited seventy-two-year-old man whose motives are totally unknown to me.

SBM You are like a goblin, in leading your reader into the forest of theory, threatening her with abandonment if she cannot jump as fast as you do.

VT And you are like a Snow White, whose situation is not that bad, because the forest of theory is full of kindly dwarfs.

SBM Your "pushmi-pullyu" diagrams are a parody of Lacan. You love Freudian concepts and sexual analogies. But where is visual art in this discussion? If literally mediated pain is bearable, if it cannot be judged in the same way as real bodily pain, then what of artistic representations? You seem to be saying that their task is to create a sensory "real" that can be experienced in the gap between literary culture and actually lived life, and that this is done more successfully by the "bodily" optics of St Petersburg's artists, with their "aesthetics of blind spots," than by the intellect-driven "aesthetics of transparency" of Moscow's conceptual artists. Now, that makes me nervous. It reminds me of Michel Foucault's praise of capitalism, the "invisible hand" which resists governmentality, he writes approvingly, because it cannot be seen. But systems of power are no less oppressive when they are invisible. Not all power is manifest, just as not all desire is manifest. Latent power loves an aesthetics of blind spots. Might not the reverse be true, that the artists who revel in blind spots thrive on latent power?

VT Your comment is very much to the point. Sometimes (which is basically what happened in "Pushmi-Pullyu") I try to adopt my opponent's position in order to understand what it is based on. The world would be too banal if all "blind spots," without exception, were hotbeds of latent power. We have no right to accuse every such microcosm, a priori, of secretly hatching the egg of power. Perhaps such "spots" are nothing more than temporary shelters from the boundless power of text. Besides, there is no need to mix up different kinds of resistance. Resistance to the governmentality of Text is not always rife with the will to dominate. At the same time, testing "blind spots" for symptoms of "power-centrism" is one of the tasks of the critical function. In the fabric of Brezhnev-era Soviet society, there were, despite the totality of ideological control, various rips and folds in which "nonidentity" was either freed from the power of "identity" or maintained certain illusions of freedom. It is also unclear to what extent power is identical to itself. That is why I prefer the concept of "powercentrism" to that of "power." These are equally dangerous: even if the nests of power have no eggs, the birds are still hatching. Hatching is an unalienable part of any political ritual, its ornithological dimension, so to speak.

SBM Tupitsyn at his typical best: "After the October Revolution, Russian women were liberated to the degree that they were required to serve not only their husbands, but also the government" [chapter 6]. From your discussion of contemporary women artists in Russia, it seems that they are being liberated within the art world only to serve the art world better ("The men got together and conceived an idea. Then the girls came and fulfilled it"). Is there any evidence of libidinal freedom—I mean real bodily pleasure and not just nakedness—in their work, or that of the male Russian artists?

VT No, I do not think so. But on the other hand, libido contains—within it—another term, *ibid,* which is intrinsic to desire. Speaking of "undressed" (naked) libido, i.e., libido with no beginning (*l*) and no end (*o*), I've seen it quite repeatedly, especially in scholarly publications. I wish I knew what *l* and *o* really stand for. Laius and Oedipus, Laertes and Odysseus, Law and Order? Your guess is as good as mine.

SBM In your text on photography [chapter 5], you adopt Lyotard's distinction between Kant's "sublime" and Freud's "sublimated." Certainly there were "official" Soviet photographers who captured this sublimeness in their work. It is staged almost exclusively in public space. In contrast, "alternative" Russian photography, as a "factography of resistance," troubles the boundary between public and private, collective and individual. The result is demythification. How does sublimation in the Freudian sense play a role in the process?

VT In my text on photography, "The Sun without a Muzzle," I wrote about the prospects for unearthing private memory, and the corresponding factographic archive, from under the mass of officially sanctioned information about what the past was "really" like. I was fully aware of the hopelessness of such a phenomenological rescue; yet, in contrast to mathematics, for instance, where a hopeless approach to solving a problem has no value, in the humanities (where truth is not as rigidly determined) aberrancy of the navigational tools sometimes turns out to be an advantage. Aberrant and unjustified methods have something to do with what you defined as the creation of the "sensory real." When organized-crime murders are committed in Russia, the bodies are rarely found because they are buried in cemeteries, under the old graves. How do you like this version of the Archeology of Knowledge, this model of the Archive: the present buried beneath the past? Curiously, when I began the story, I thought it had to do with the distinction between the sublime and the sublimated. Now I see that the episode I have described refers to something else. Here, you've got a typical example of the aberrancy mentioned previously.

SBM I think the problem with Lacanian and Freudian theory within your texts is this: one can be either a humorist or a psychoanalyst, not both simultaneously. In *Jokes and Their Relation to the Unconscious,* one of his earliest texts, Freud exposes the unconscious, demonstrating its existence precisely in the gap between manifest and latent

content which is invaded by the surprised spasm of laughter. But as soon as he fills that gap with theory, the humor disappears. One cannot have it both ways. It strikes me that there is too little observation of the fact that as the theory of psychoanalysis has ascended to astounding heights within contemporary intellectual discourse, the practice of psychoanalysis has been in decline. And yet the practice is everything. The theory of the dream's interpretation is nothing without the dream. Liberatory libidinal power lies in the latter, not the former, which is secondary process thought, and tries to pin things down.

Your own writing seems to become increasingly libidinal. It appears to document the historical opening up of a new space for your own commentary. You begin writing about the late Soviet artists for a Western audience and end by describing this new space, encouraging us to join the artists as pioneers in inhabiting it. Would that be too optimistic a reading? Is your own vision more catastrophic?

VT I am always tickled by statements like "one can't combine the facetious level with the theoretical." I don't know how to respond to these taboos and prohibitions. It is precisely such prohibitions that make one want to break them. One feels a need for anarchy, for the carnivalization of the theoretical text. Žižek, who is a Lacanian, cracks jokes all the time. And it works. I think that interpretations of our old dreams, as well as the dreams of others, play a significant role in the formation of our subsequent dreams. These interpretive "clips" (etiological representations) can be inscribed, in a variety of ways, within the liberatory dreams that we portray as purely empirical, "devoid of all theory" and so forth. I am not sure that with time my texts become more and more libidinal. In a sense, the economy of writing is libidinal economy. The problem is that in the works of some authors, the libido is deliberately repressed to prevent opaqueness (related to the proliferation of ecstatic "blind spots") and to enhance the transparency of the argument. In my view, the outwardly modest and extremely de-ecstaticized texts of Descartes, Kant, or Husserl possess far greater libidinal tension than, say, the texts of Nietzsche, Bataille, or Barthes. The sublime terror which academic thinkers inflict on their own writings appears to be libidinally mediated. In Husserl's work, for instance, the act of undressing the truth looks like a gynecological checkup. Barthes, on the other hand, is less interested in undressing than in dressing up. For him, truth is a drag queen to be ecstatically draped in the veil of writing. That is what he means by "pleasure of the text." It is possible that the libidinality of my own writing is a form of camouflage, an attempted denial of the age-related testosterone drop on the nether horizons of writing. Some writers are undoubtedly influenced by this, in that their vision becomes "more catastrophic." Others, on the contrary, feel relief—such as the famous Stalin-era crooner Leonid Utesov. When he became completely impotent in old age, he uttered a much-repeated line addressing, as it were, his flaccid organ: "Finally I'll get a chance to live for myself."

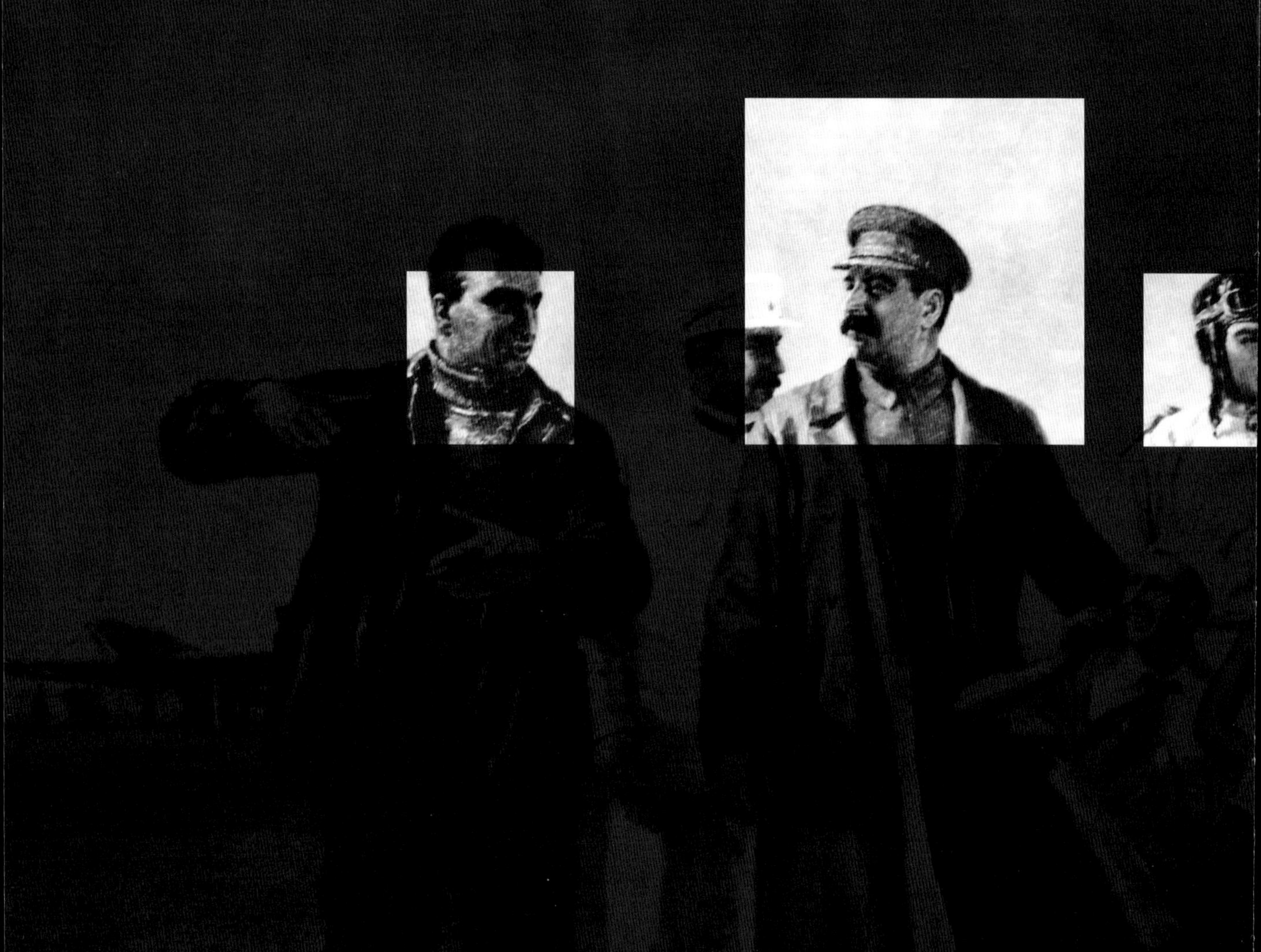

CHAPTER 1

Civitas Solis: Ghetto as Paradise

When I get tired of myself
I'll fling myself into the golden sun.
Velimir Khlebnikov

In November of 1993 two exhibitions of socialist realist art were organized in Europe and America. The first one, "Stalin's Choice: Soviet Socialist Realism, 1932–1956," opened in New York at the Institute for Contemporary Art, P.S. 1 Museum; the second one, "Agitation zum Gluck: Sowjetische Kunst der Stalinzeit," took place in Kassel, Germany, at Documenta-Halle (fig. 1.1). From Kassel the exhibition went back to the State Russian Museum in St. Petersburg where it was open until midsummer of 1994. Without getting into details, one may conclude that while trying to promote their treatise of Soviet society as a spectacle viewed through a historicist lens, the organizers of the two exhibitions were incapable of reconstructing the most crucial element of the socialist realist enterprise—the communal perception. The thought that socialist realism is not transportable without it apparently did not cross their minds. Regardless of being banal both semantically and aesthetically, socialist realism was nonetheless an integral part of the structure in which it was expected to perform its duties. Therefore an adequate staging of the socialist realist "spectacle" on alien territory is impossible without the transformation of this territory beforehand. This would require an instant optical revolution that switched from an individualized vision to a communal one. But since restructuring "the gaze of the beholder" by shifting its "optics" from individual to collective takes years (as was the case in the USSR), any attempt to become instantly accustomed to the "heritage" of a totalitarian past or "to perform a total and immediate reactivation"[1] of its referents is likely to end up being a failure. On the other hand, one can hardly succeed in replaying collective language games (Soviet-style), unless the attention is evenly spread between both sides of the "medal"—Stalinist "psychedelic commodity"[2] (i.e., socialist realism) and its ultimate consumer, the Communal.[3] The unwillingness on the part

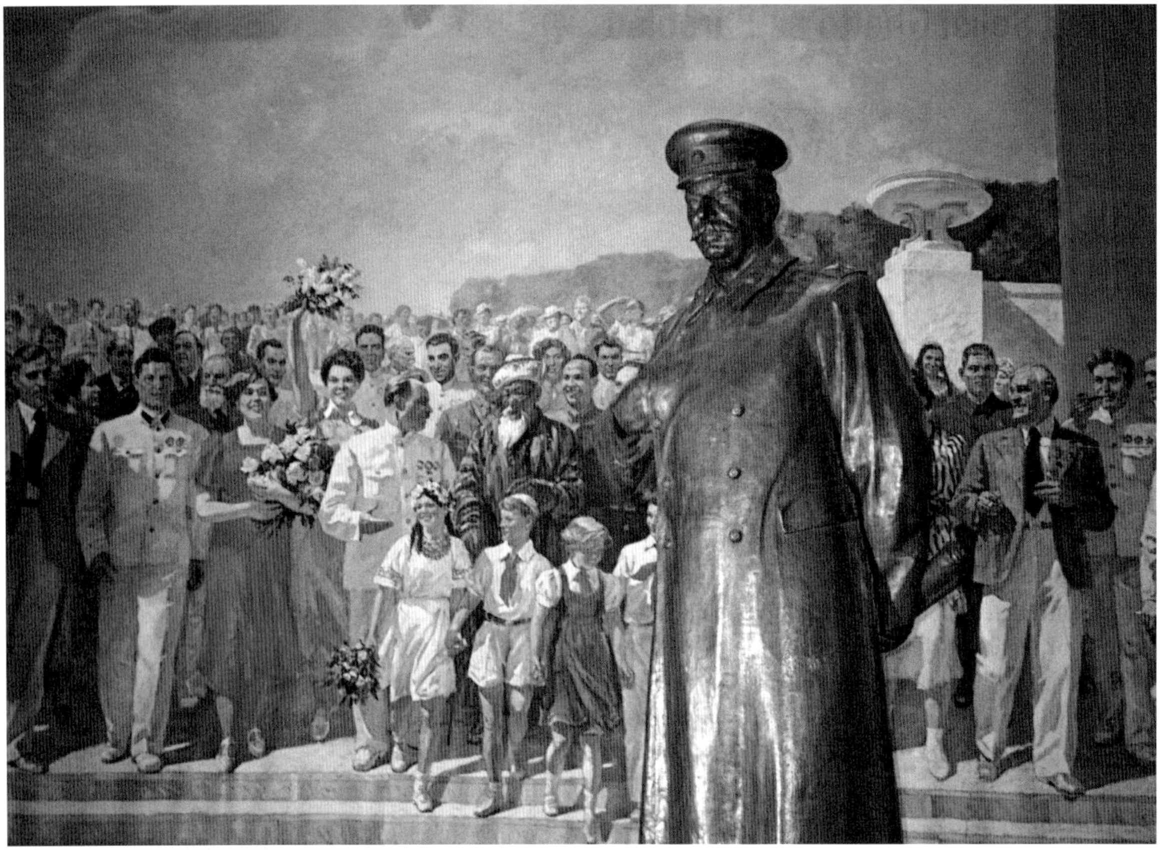

1.1
Installation view, "Agitation zum Gluck: Sowjetische Kunst der Stalinzeit," Documenta-Halle, Kassel, Germany, 1994.

of the curators to realize this, is, perhaps, the greatest weakness of both exhibitions. To compensate for this flaw is the main purpose of this essay.

In psychoanalysis, *imagoes* are unconscious representations that give form to our bodily and emotional reactions toward the outside world. In his early works, Jacques Lacan emphasized "family" complexes as those which are responsible for the imaginary replication of the environment in the psyche of an individual. Given the living conditions in urban Russia after the October Revolution, it seems apt to stretch the notion of the family even further and to treat "family complexes" as communal. The aforementioned unconscious representations are frequently at odds with the official version of reality (falsified representations). To compensate, the officialdom assumes the role of "analyst," thereby imposing a therapy upon an individual ("analysand") in order to adjust his or her relations with "reality." This adjustment usually results in identification with characters populating image-making media (from television to pornography), i.e., those "others," whom the viewer misrecognizes as him- or herself (e.g., a personage, a role model, etc.). However, the identificatory efforts fail to prevent the subject's alienation from his *jouissance,* which—according to Lacan—belongs to an *other.*[4] Only the hero of visual representation is "blessed" with the opportunity to be exempt from alienation, to hold on to his or her *jouissance* on a permanent basis. Despite the fact that two of the models portraying the "Marlboro Man" died of lung cancer, we can still see him—on the corporate billboards or in our memory—experiencing the moment of ecstasy (the ecstasy of smoking). But outside the realm of representation, the rules are different. The Real (*le réel*) is manifested in the viewer's impossibility to appropriate *jouissance* through imitation of a hero's experiences without losing tempo. This hysterogenic factor was subjected to a different treatment in the Soviet Union, where the emphasis was placed on "ideological *jouissance*" as opposed to sexual satisfaction, or the enjoyment of high living standards, or commodity-oriented pleasures.

The treatment administered to the communal subject in the form of socialist realism's mesmerizing narratives—regardless of the technical signifier—aimed at identification without alienation. Communal sight was equipped with the cathartic optics necessary to decrease the distance between the viewer and the hero, whose ideological *jouissance*[5] was supposed to be instantly, without delay, shared by the audience. To those familiar with the communal environment, the preference for ideological over sexual *jouissance* is not accidental. According to the artist Ilya Kabakov, who is the chronicler of the communal world order, "illicit sex in *kommunalka* [i.e., a communal dwelling space] is considered tantamount to theft and therefore invites the severity of collective sanction."[6]

And this is despite the fact that "everything which is discussed in a communal apartment is camouflage for what is really going on, that is to say, the copulation of words, a logogyration."[7] It suffices to remember Andrei Zhdanov and Karl Radek's 1934 campaign against sexuality, which made erotically explicit representations unacceptable for Soviet artists. In this respect, we can apply to the Soviet case Michel Foucault's assessment that sexuality in Victorian times was "so rigorously repressed, because it was incompatible with a general and intensive work imperative."[8] There was also another motive behind Zhdanov and Radek's discomfort with sexual imagery. The viewer's alienation from the protagonist's libidinal pleasure seemed not to be affected by the cathartic optic as effectively as in cases of ideological orgasm.[9] Lately, the never-ending attempts to master identification without alienation have taken a new turn—virtual reality, a three-dimensional techno-ersatz of communal optics. To those familiar with Emmanuel Levinas's writings, virtual reality is synonymous with an ironic downplaying of the philosopher's belief that "one sees and hears like one touches. . . . It is like caressing: the caress is the unity of approach and proximity."[10]

In all likelihood, the true cause of the jealousy of communal speech toward conventional sexual practices is the fact that speech is itself a form of sex,[11] an orgy of chatter, "texturbation." The latter, regardless of its denial by the very participants of the communal exchange, attests to the bodily nature of speech rituals. This, in combination with "the presence of some lofty [extracommunal] imperative,"[12] contributes to what Georges Bataille—in his analysis of Sade—noted as a hypocritical appeal to the language of power and authority. Speech, consequently, is both the torturer and the ecstatically quivering victim. But who, then, is *homo communalis*? And what about his or her drama, fears, pain, and suffering? Could it be that communal apartment-dwellers are nothing more than audio props, a podium for the protagonist whose name is speech?

In chapter 4 I argue that the portraits of Soviet leaders functioned as mirrors (screens or reflectors) responsible for redirecting the identificatory waves of the communal subject from some images to others; that is, they functioned de facto as instruments of synchronicity. The idea of the screen or the reflector also extends to other identificatory schemes related, for example, to the postrevolutionary New Economic Policy (NEP, 1921—1928) in Russia. During the NEP years, posters for Western movies as well as billboards that advertised cookies, cigarettes, or household goods used images of attractive women. Next to these commercial advertisements, one could also see propaganda posters and photographic displays that represented images of "model" citizens and their deeds that were worthy of imitation. In such instances, when the consumer's gaze moved from the erotic image to the political one, it still retained (by dint of inertia) its libidinal intensity. As a result, what occurred was a transfer of libidinal interest from one iconographic context to another. Thus the erotic context turned out to be a screen or a reflector in relation to the political one. In this manner, a consumer optic facilitated eroticization of political imagery. Later, the libidinal economy of socialist realism and of Soviet mass media came to be dominated by two aspects: ideological perception of the body and bodily perception of ideology.[13]

Parallel to the NEP's aim to reintroduce capitalist commodities to a country swept by communalism,[14] there was yet another process that had been developing on a much larger scale. I am referring to the production of socialist commodities—things that can be characterized as both psychedelic and didactic. These things had nothing to do with the items of everyday use—kitchenware, furniture, clothing, etc. Such items were habitually dismal; they lacked any sense of pleasure, any hope for prestige or comfort. The ways in which the communal psyche connected itself to communal objecthood were completely defetishized. The communal Eros was redirected to the sphere of public (read socialist) objecthood which—for the most part—consisted of indexical sign-objects from the inventory of photographic, sculptural, or architectural agitprop.[15] These also included "cine-forms" through which one could "perceive a tempestuous and incessant flow of people as an interrupted moving form of never stopping content."[16] Even if they looked tangible, they were still images and traces of something else. Thus, the socialist commodity had a repeatedly postponed presence—an object in its pure potentiality. However elusive, especially as seen through the lens of individual (i.e., noncommunal) optics, the socialist commodity (*obshchestvennaia veshch* in Aleksei Gan's terminology) has never failed to be perceived as an object. By this I mean that the indexical and anticipatory nature of the socialist commodity has tended to be objectified by turning the representation of its presence into the presence of representation. As was mentioned earlier, many socialist objects functioned as instruments of synchronicity (they were "in charge" of channeling the waves of communal desire in the "proper" direction). The fact that the socialist commodity had a postponed presence was in harmony with the deferral of individual subjectivity.[17] With this double deferral, the capitalist subject/object dichotomy was subjected to the same fate.

▪▪

Philosophers and historians are familiar with the concept of the "solar" myth,[18] both its connection with the cults and religions of antiquity and its use, in various modifications, in secular cultural tradition. "Were the eye not sunlike, how could we behold light?" asked Goethe in his *Zur Farbenlehre*.[19] Clearly, the pathos of sun imitation—creative (or civic) fire lighting the road to the truth—is inseparable from the image of both the artist and the statesman, the "father of nations" who can not only warm his subjects in the glow of paternal generosity, but also reduce them to ashes in the pitiless rays of his "just" wrath. The Soviet *Ozhegov* dictionary (1953) indicates that, in the figurative sense, the sun is "that which is a source and a concentration of something valuable, lofty, and vitally important." An example: "the sun of the Stalin constitution." Phenomena of a reverse character include (I quote): "sunstroke—the affliction of brain centers by the heat of the sun."

The projection of a paradise on earth, made in the image of the solar referent, was reflected in Tommaso Campanella's utopian work of 1623, *Civitas Solis* (City of the sun), which Lenin recommended to Anatolii Lunacharskii as early as 1918 as a source of ideas for the improvement of monumental propaganda. For many Russian thinkers, artists, and poets—from the Slavophiles to cosmists and futurists—heliotrop(ism) was a sense-of-life metaphor, a means for understanding the artistic image of history within the framework of some unifying principle, however illusory. Here one can also recall Hegel, for whom (as, incidentally, for the theorists of socialist realism, Georg Lukács and Mikhail Lifshits) unity and totality were identical to truth, while fragmentation, which undermines faith in the "indubitability" of this identification, contained the virus of heliomachy, rife with the emancipation of the individual (the ray) from the whole (the light).

Ancient sun cults are known to have practiced human sacrifice. In this context, it is appropriate to interpret the recurrence of mass slaughter in Stalin's Russia and in Nazi Germany as a revival of solar traditions.[20] As previously noted, the solar myth is characterized by the hegemony of metaphor, "the rights and obligations" of which are essentially reduced to the synchronization of fragments under the aegis of a single meaning, which in turn, legitimizes the means of sacrificing the Other in the name of the triumphant Same. However, we should not forget that the widespread notion of socialist realism as a collective artistic practice is correct only under the condition that the Collective tends not to be "identical to itself." This practice was the implementation of the extremely individualistic *Gedankenformen* (thought forms) of party leaders and theoreticians who personified the Cartesian model of subjectivity, while the communal subject was bound to confessional-cathartic relationships with organs of power and mass repression. To turn these relationships into an imperative, the population was subjected to a shock therapy of Great Purges and exemplary trials or doomed to socialist realists' anti-alienation treatment. Traumatic neuroses, unavoidable under such circumstances, were relieved through neuroleptic events—holiday demonstrations, mass celebrations, military and sport parades.

In socialist realist paintings, Stalin was often portrayed in the presence of Lenin's statue: the monument to the dead leader was needed to legitimize the viewers' inscription into the image of the one alive. However, the masses were not thus inscribed to imitate him—this would be a sacrilege—but rather to enable them to experience the sense of wholeness in the astral body of the "Father." Among such paintings are Aleksandr Gerasimov's *Stalin's Speech at the XVI Party Congress* (1935), Grigorii Shegal's *Leader, Teacher and Friend* (1937), and Mikhail Khmel'ko's *To the Great Soviet People* (1949). The role of these artists, however, was not solely artistic, which is in fact true of all the official artists—members of the Moscow Union of Soviet Artists (MOSKh).

In the beginning of the 1930s, it became clear that Lenin's behest "to be as radical as reality itself" was not going to be fulfilled: reality was annulled. Soviet art criticism described socialist realism in the spirit of its own mythological traditions.[21] This was not just myth about myth, but also a form of cathartic adhesion of mythographer and mythology, a situation that radically contradicted the definition of the critical function as defined by Bertolt Brecht and the Frankfurt School. Brecht's "alienation effect" was experienced by Soviet critics only in relation to bourgeois art; in conformity with the domestic situation, it was replaced by an undistanced (and, consequently, uncritical) relation to what took place. For this we may, rephrasing Max Horkheimer and Herbert Marcuse,[22] bring the phrase "the affirmative culture of socialist realism" into practice.

Right after the revolution, Lenin issued the requisition of the city apartments (especially in the central areas) in order to divide them among the poor: the "norm" was set up to be one room per person. By 1924 this norm was reduced to 8 square meters per person.[23] In the beginning, the authorities were busing workers to the outskirts of the city, where major plants and factories were located. That is how the program of proletarianization of the center was conducted. Following the death of Lenin in 1924 and the concurrent curtailing of the NEP in Soviet Russia, there began a period of collectivization identifiable with the initial steps of the so-called Stalinist revolution. The peasantry, which in prerevolutionary Russia had constituted the overwhelming majority of the population, was, for the most part, forcibly recruited into collective farms or, in smaller numbers, wiped out or banished to distant regions of the country to perform forced labor. A significant number of others were compelled to migrate to urban areas. This phenomenon engendered a housing problem of enormous proportions—one that even today awaits a solution.

Stalin's course was to exploit the situation so as to further his project of "de-individualizing" the consciousness and daily life of the Soviet people. City apartments, as provided by law, became as populous as anthills and beehives.[24] Such *uplotnenie*[25] reached its climax when two or three different tenants had to live in one room.[26] Families of every variety, belonging to various social, national, and cultural-ethnic groups, were forced to cleave together in a single communal body. Toilets, baths, and kitchens became the site of this "great experiment" in mass communalization. Thin walls and partitions afforded no guarantee of what Westerners call "privacy." Losing attachment to themselves-as-individuals, the inhabitants of the communal *thermae* were becoming prisoners of each other (an example of alienation from oneself in favor of the collective).

The frustration inherent in such an Orwellian living arrangement was exacerbated by a hysterogenic contrast between the communal interior and the ideological facade, between the overcrowded apartment and the myths of the extracommunal space. According to Kabakov's (sarcastic) assessment,

> The world beyond the communal walls is beautiful and whole. Only *we* live divvied up, we're shit. That's the way it was under Stalin. Radio was very important—the announcer Iurii Levitan, whose voice personified the state for thirty years, and all those other hearty voices. The song "Morning paints the ancient Kremlin / oh so softly with its brush, / and the mighty Soviet nation / is awake with dawn's first blush . . ." would fill the apartment. It is really on the subconscious level that this takes effect. Out there is paradise, out there healthy young creatures are off to display their athletic prowess in the May Day parade through the Red Square. While in here, you, sucker, live like a dog.[27]

Going to work in the morning, the toiling Soviet citizens would leave the squalid communal ghetto to descend—like Orpheus—into the "underground kingdom" of the Moscow subway system, with whose pharaonic architectural grandeur and imperial splendor their pitiful communal existence, naturally, could not withstand comparison.[28] Stalin's kitschy skyscrapers and architectural ensembles, such as the pavilions of the All-Union Agricultural Exhibition (VSKhV, later called VDNKh) in Moscow,[29] played the same role. Derrida's term "being-in-construction"[30] comes to mind once we realize that all megalomaniac projects (propagandized under the aegis of the "pillars for the people" campaign) were, in effect, aimed at creating an unprecedented psycho-ideological pressure resulting from the state's imposition on its subjects, the signs and codes of status and authority.[31] The paradox, however, lies in the fact that, despite these internal hysterogenic factors, the officialdom always managed to convince its communal counterpart that the source of the latter's troubles and miseries resided abroad.

In communal life there were no actions other than speech acts: everyone was drawn into a process of "serial" talking (be it relatively harmless gossip or extreme cases of verbal abuse). As a result, "with the passage of time, the monstrous dough of spoken kitsch rose,"[32] leavened with the yeast of the Dionysian sensibility characteristic of relations within peasant families, collectives, and agrarian sects—relations marked with autochthony of collective somatics and ruled by speech rituals. This echoes Leopold von Sacher-Masoch's "Law of the Commune" (which Gilles Deleuze identifies with the so-called oral mother).[33] Being involved in the pan-Slavic movement, Masoch (whose favorite poets, besides Goethe, were Aleksandr Pushkin and Mikhail Lermontov) was undoubtedly familiar with the writings of the Russian Slavophiles (notably Aleksei Khomiakov and Ivan Kirievskii) who, long before him, idealized and promoted an orthodox version of the "Law of the Commune" under the aegis of the lofty concept of *sobornost'* (ecclesiastical communality).[34] Thus, it should come as no surprise that after haunting Europe for such a long time, the specter of communality had finally come to settle on Russian soil.

The concept of communalism can be traced back to the Petrashevtsy of the 1840s or to Mikhail Chernyshevsky's *What Is to Be Done?* (1863). In this book we learn about people who—in addition to working together—are also voluntarily engaged in communal living. In *Revolutionary Dreams*, Richard Stites writes that long before the revolution there had been cooperative-communal apartments (*artel'nye kvartiry*) rented by people of the lower classes who hired themselves out for temporary work in the city: "Groups of workers [usually peasants, brought into the towns by rapid industrialization] would hire a communal apartment, share the rent, buy food and dine together, and even attend leisure events in groups."[35] According to Stites, fifteen people in one large room, with their beds circling a table, was a common "residential pattern."

Utopian projects aiming at the creation of communes were popular in the 1920s. The members of OSA (Union of Contemporary Architects)[36] saw the residential commune (*dom-kommuna*) as the only solution to the housing shortage. But this was not their only goal. OSA theorists insisted that in order to have communist consciousness, one had to live communally. In Lunacharskii's words, "communal life is based not on compulsion and the need to herd together for mere self-preservation, as it had been in the

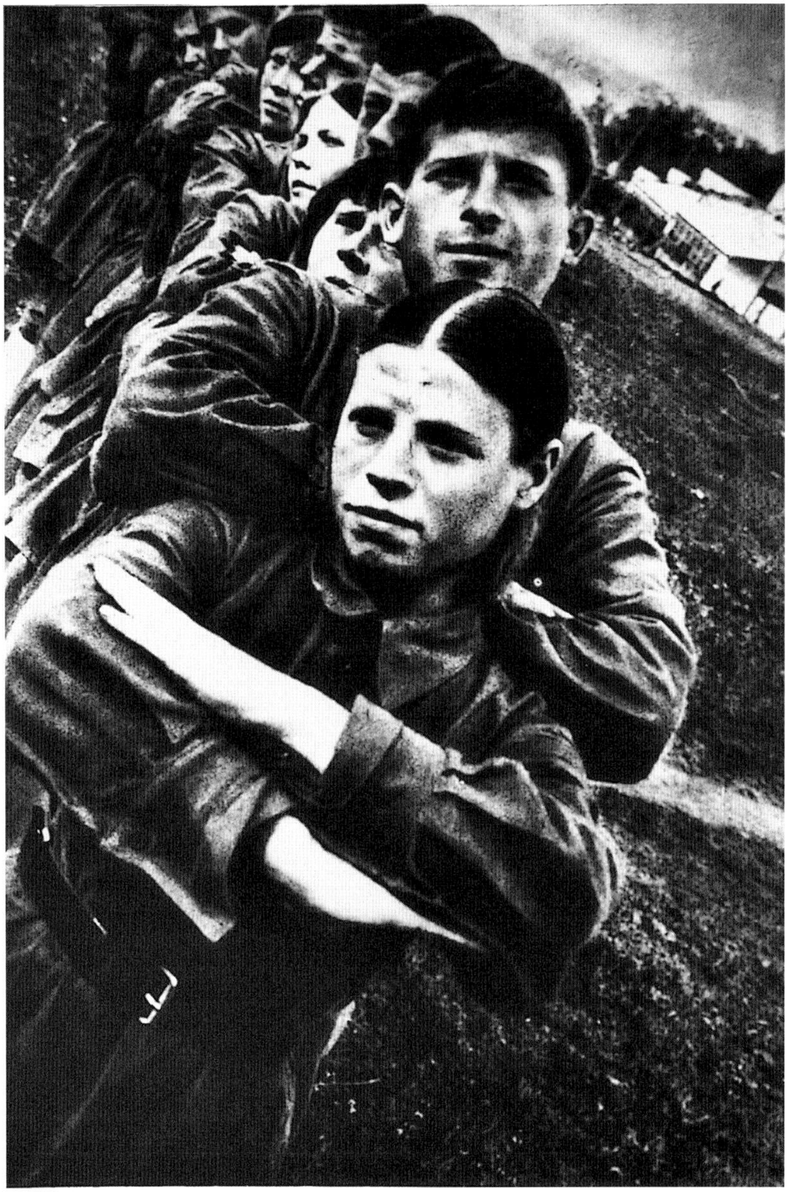

1.2
Aleksandr Rodchenko, page from the magazine *USSR in Construction,* no. 12, 1933.

past, but on a free and natural merging of personalities into superpersonal entities" (fig. 1.2).[37]

In 1921 there were 865 house communes in Moscow. Three years later the Bakhmetevskaia Commune was organized, and in 1928 the AMO (automotive workers) Commune. In 1931, Stalin voiced his hostility to *uravnilovka* or *obezlichka* (leveling). The epoch of communal egalitarianism came to a halt. After the Sixteenth Communist Party Congress, Lazar' Kaganovich was mandated to cancel the projects linked to utopian living, and by 1932 communes ceased to exist. As Stites points out, "The actual housing system of the 1930s, still persisting in the center of large Soviet towns, was a parody of communalism. The *kommuna* gave way to the so-called communal apartment (*kommunalnaia kvartira* or *kommunalka*). And between the *kommuna* and the *kommunalka,* the social and psychological gap was enormous."[38]

In summary, the urban peasantry of Stalin's epoch not only swallowed and assimilated other forms of class identity (such as proletariat and intelligentsia), but also built their own "house of being," known as communal speech (or "communal-speech-corporeality"). The very notion of difference had gradually dissolved into the swamp of the Same, and the wizardry of the political language game triumphed over the rhetoric of class consciousness. Thus, the thesis of Stalin's book *Marxism and Questions of Linguistics*—that language is politically predetermined but class-free—literalizes the ultimate "ends" of Stalinist "means." And since the (post) revolutionary avant-garde had initially associated itself with the proletariat, the dissolution of the latter is part of what prompted the former to "fling [it]self into the sun" or (which is the same thing) to commit suicide by becoming a vehicle for the glorification of Stalinism. Evidently, the phenomenon of dissolution of class consciousness in the "lower depth" of urban peasantry and the retreat of the proletariat "beneath its bar" (as Lacanians would put it)[39] is what appears to be in agreement with the Benjaminian notion of "unconscious proletariat" or, for that matter, the "political unconscious." In his *Critique of Cynical Reason,* Peter Sloterdijk argues that "since proletarian existence is defined negatively, . . . positive ego can only be achieved by de-proletarization."[40] This offers an additional explanation why the proletariat had to wither in the USSR (as revolutionary negation gave way to Stalinist affirmation).

The language of communal apartments is both the national disaster and the national heritage of Russia.[41] Whereas in the West communal dwelling usually means the ghetto, in the Civitas Solis (Soviet-style) almost everyone lived in the same sort of ghetto. And inasmuch as communal living is a phenomenon of a minority in Europe and America, communal speech has not fallen within the purview of elitist theories, whether mainstream or marginal, which focus on discourses of power or resistance but not on the lexicon of what has been defeated, broken, or reduced to the level of verbal garbage.[42] Alongside communal speech, *homo communalis* also knew another ("Apollonian") tongue, that is, the voice of power blaring from Soviet radio. On the one hand, this voice can be referred to as the vocalization of *sur-moi* (superego). On the other hand, to fully equate the Soviet regime (and its vocal cords) with *sur-moi* would be too hasty. This entity is constituted due to interiorization of "parental" demands and prohibitions. The means of such an interiorization is at times conscious, but mostly it is unconscious. And yet, considering the tremendous scale of communalization in Russia and how deeply the communal sensibility was rooted in all segments of Soviet life, one may—with some reservations, of course—perceive the authoritarian ego of the state as the communal *moi*'s upper bound, that is, *sur-moi*.

The perplexity of a case study of the relationships between the *kommunalka* and the extracommunal mythical machine is reflected, for example, in my conversation with Kabakov, who argues that:

> In one or another form, any figure of communal speech is—on the automatic, subconscious level—saturated with . . . [an] enormous quantity of impersonal constructions that so stagger foreigners. All the impersonal pronouns and verb forms for which English has, in most cases, no equivalent—a large quantity of locutions in principle unconnected to the concrete inhabitants of the apartment, locutions expressive of insufficiency, uncertainty, hope, and so on. The outside world, in short, appears in the form of indeterminate texts. For example: "Today they did not deliver any fresh bread; I stood in line for nothing." This is a classical construction: "They did not deliver." Or: "The radiators are cold again today. But yesterday I saw the coal get dumped smack in the middle of the yard." The external world, that is, appears only via passive verbs. Which is to say nothing of expressions for eviction or making repairs, all of which are accomplished by the neuter *ono* (it). The degree of communal life's helplessness before the outside world, is on the whole, horrifying. No one in *kommunalka* hammers nails into board or repairs faucets, because all these functions are performed by "it."[43]

This observation shows that the communal verbal exchange—especially when it refers to the extracommunal superego—is reduced to predicates. On the one hand, it reminds us that "simple predicative sentences are called affirmative,"[44] for they endorse the acts of synthesis. On the other hand, it shows a tendency toward what Lev Vygotsky defined as "inner speech" or endophasy.[45] Using as an example Kitty's conversation with

Levin in Tolstoy's *Anna Karenina,* Vygotsky insists that when the speakers' thoughts are the same, their speech becomes condensed at the expense of omitting the subject of a sentence: "In inner speech, the 'mutual' perception is always there, in absolute form; therefore, . . . it becomes governed by an almost entirely predicative syntax."[46] Vygotsky continues, "Between people who live in close psychological contact, communication . . . in the fewest words, . . . is the rule, rather than exception."[47] In his opinion, the child's speech—especially "under the condition of the insufficient isolation"—is "a collective monologue," because it "occurs in the presence of other children engaged in the same activity, and not when the child is alone."[48] The same terms can be used to describe life in the communal apartments, in which "insufficient isolation" and "collective monologue" were the way of life. This, in fact, may fit the notion of the communal unconscious, not in a Jungian sense, but rather as that which has been conditioned by the extraordinary scale of stereotyping characteristic of the communal ghetto. The notion (introduced above) echoes Félix Guattari's concept of "collective subjectivity"[49] as well as the Crimean psychiatrist Viktor Samokhvalov's statement that "a human being functions in ways similar to an orchestra: different personalities (enclosed within one's 'I') act like musical instruments."[50] To make Lacan concrete,[51] we may assert that the communal unconscious is structured like communal speech, and on the strength of the clichédness of the latter, almost everything that is displaced into the unconscious—save for the prelingual (the infantile period of life)—coincides to a significant degree for the majority of communal dwellers.

But the peculiarity of the language practiced in the communal "lower depths" of Civitas Solis lies in the fact that the decreasing vocalization in endophasy turns into its increasing in communal speech. An explanation can be found in Piaget's description of egocentric speech, which begins to develop at the age of three and disappears on the threshold of school age. At this point it becomes silent and turns into inner speech. As Vygotsky points out, "The decreasing vocalization of egocentric speech denotes . . . the child's new faculty to think words instead of pronouncing them."[52] The reason for this decreasing vocalization is the child's growing acceptance of the fact that the content of his or her thinking is different from that of the listener. But the case of *kommunalka* appears to be the exact opposite: stereotypization makes egocentric thought comprehensible to others. This is why utterance fails to be repressed in the communal mode of self-expression.[53] To be precise, the latter—given that it always remains incomplete and transitory—is not reducible to either egocentric speech (with its "influx of sense") or inner speech (with its reduction to predicates), nor could it qualify as one-hundred-percent external (social) speech.[54] Curiously, the phenomenon of nondecreasing vocalization is compensated in communal speech by a decrease of visuality. To clarify this matter, it would be helpful to quote Kabakov, who does not believe that a "genuine visual art exists in Russia." "Speech," he says, "is behind everything, I do not see, I speak. I can paint a jackrabbit only because I have a story to tell about it."[55] To those who are familiar with the mythological content of socialist realist painting, it turns out to be faultlessly readable: one can easily translate images or even brush strokes into words. The painterly palette of Soviet easel art is fraught with the incarnation of speech referents; therefore, it is not visuality, but psychedelia or "visionary visuality," as Kabakov puts it. From this viewpoint, visualized messages of the Politburo (i.e., the extracommunal) cannot be adequately analyzed without paying attention to its exclusive addressee and its neglected Other (i.e., the communal).

Like Peter Pan, communal speech never achieves maturity. Its failure to grow up becomes synonymous with eligibility for salvation on the ark of solar-centric metaphor. Thus, in Petr Mal'tsev's painting *Meeting of a Heroic Crew* (1936), we see Stalin and other Politburo members taking a walk with the pilots at an airdrome (fig. 1.3). They are accompanied by children ("young pioneers") who—on a closer look—appear to have adult faces. The artist's sloppiness turns out to be a revelation: *homo communalis* is a child, and Civitas Solis is the homeland of eternal youth. Such infantilism stems from the fact that the land of the Soviets persistently propagandized itself as a paradise, and therefore Christ's admonition to be "as children" could be suitably reproduced in the paradisiacal rhetoric of the Fathers of the State. They would always claim that "children are the only privileged class in the Soviet Union" and that "children are our future." The reward for not growing up was a trip not to Disneyland, as is the case for many American children, but to Civitas Solis; yet because it belongs to the realm of representation, the City of the Sun was unfit to dwell in. In order to move in, one had to build it first. And as long as such projects—and modernism was among them—remain uncompleted, the enthusiastic builders will have to huddle in the barracks at the construction site—on the territory of the temporary, not permanent paradise.[56] Thus, the only vacant place left to serve as heaven-on-earth is the communal ghetto.

The mythographers of Civitas Solis have always managed to ignore its counterpart, the communal. An exception to this rule was the writer Mikhail Zoshchenko, and everyone in Russia knows what happened to him.[57] For socialist realists, *kommunalka* was unpresentable, opaque, and impenetrable to the rays of representation. Throughout Stalin's reign,

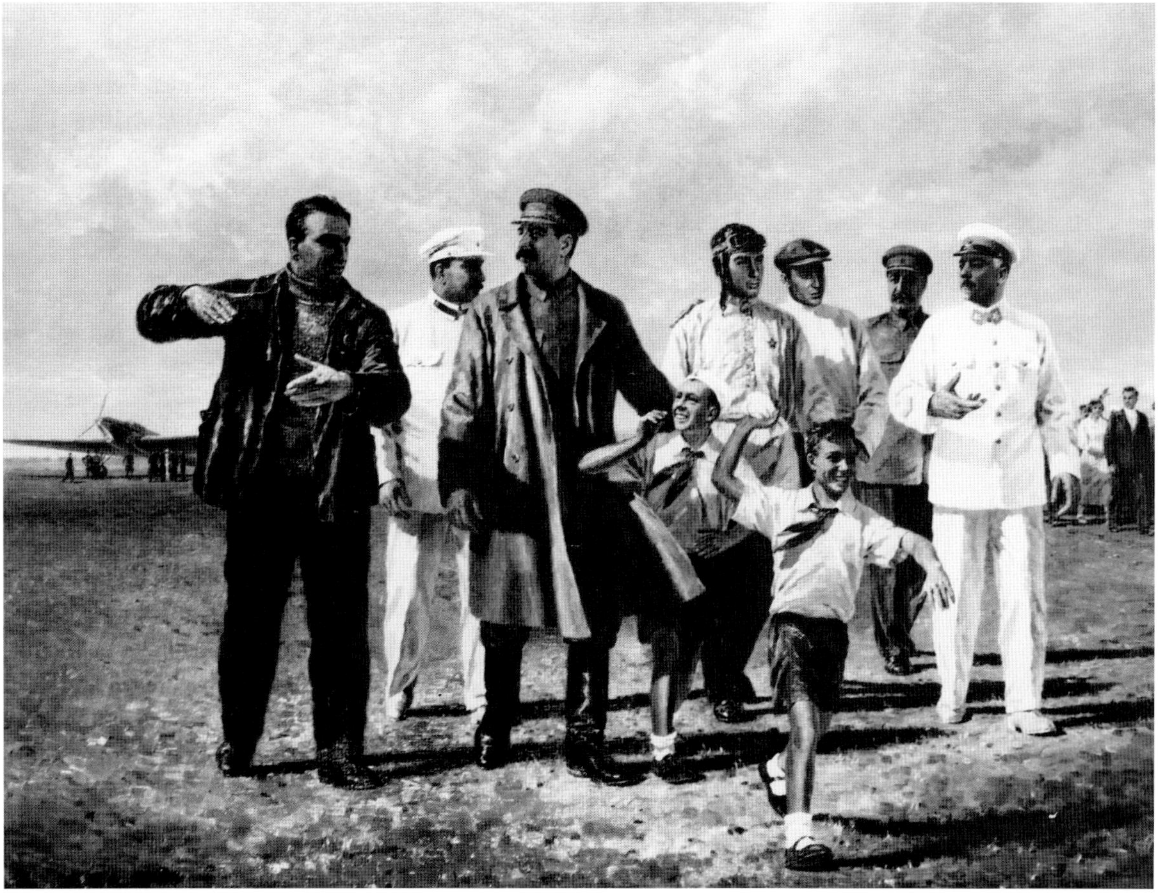

1.3
Petr Mal'tsev, *Meeting of a Heroic Crew,* 1936.

communal speech was perceived and treated by the USSR's cultural establishment as the serpent hidden in the "house of being." But in spite of (and simultaneously due to) the sharpness of contrast between the solar-centric and the ghetto-centric, the latter played an affirmative role in signifying the triumph of the former. In this sense the entire communal body of urban Russia can be referred to as an affirmative (or signifying) corporeality.

▪▪

Communal chat stands comparison with the cicadas' buzzing at night in the Crimea or in the Caucasus. The rubbing of their wings and legs, as orgiastic as incessant "logogyration" in communal speech practices, suggests associations with the "magic word" *tieret'* (the act of rubbing), which evokes the case study of Sergei Pankeiev, a Russian émigré artist and one of the Freud's patients.[58] To Pankeiev, or the "Wolf Man" (as the therapists called him because he had hallucinations of "white wolves sitting on the big walnut tree in front of the window"), the word "rub" (*tieret'*) appeared as the most unspeakable of all crypted pleasures, and therefore was not to be mentioned. As a small child, Pankeiev had witnessed either an episode (*Urszene*) of parental love-making or, possibly, a pedophilic act (between his sister and their father), which both frightened and fascinated him. What shocked him was the connection between rubbing and erection, as well as the sight of the pedophile's sexual organ, in the posture of a wolf sitting on its hind legs. But in Russian, the capital "Я" (i.e., "I") written on a white sheet of paper—the "I" of textophilia and the "I" of logocracy—has the same posture as well. The psychosis of individual subjectivity, such as Pankeiev's traumatic experience, differs from the psychosis of communal subjectivity in that the inability to pronounce, in his case the word *tieret'*, is compensated in the communal case by the act of logogyration itself (that is, a partaking in orgiastic talk). Thus, the rubbing involved in masturbation can be equated with the rubbing of word against word, since, in the latter case, it is symbolic constructs (logos, phallus, and their modifications which assume an anthropomorphic shape or, in Pankeiev's nightmares, the shape of inhabitants of a psychedelic bestiary) that become erect. Russian history is the best illustration of the dependency between communal "texturbation" and the reign of the authoritarian "I" of the state. The verbal frictions of the communal body can be interpreted as a mass ritual aimed at "caressing" the organs of state power, which "grow" to turn into organs of violence and repression. Without this collective bodily function (verbal "rubbing"), the priapism of the pedophilic father (read the Fatherland) could never materialize.

Curiously, even in Soviet poetry of the Stalin era, the themes of the "wolf" and the "sister" seem inextricably linked with the fear of metastasizing communal word exchange. When Osip Mandel'shtam asserted that "the wolfhound-century leaps on [his] shoulders, but [he is] not a wolf by [his] blood,"[59] an echo of the communalization of the subject of repression can already be heard in the metaphor. Boris Pasternak's poetics is drawn to a different pole: the spell-casting reference to life as a close relative ("my sister life, you are overflowing today")[60] hints at the author's nostalgic striving to put the traits of a family iconostasis (read intimate, humane) back into the "wolfhound-century."[61]

In Pankeiev's vocabulary, an appeal to one's "sister life" is seen as a veiled evocation of the verb *tieret,'* for it alludes to the noun *tierka* (grater) and, subsequently, to *sis-tierka* (sis-the-grater).[62] The latter is the Wolf Man's portrayal of Vagina Dentata, linked to castration anxiety and thus detrimental to the "organs" of male power. A monument to this petrifying threat is Vera Mukhina's *The Worker and the Female Collective Farmer* (1937), an enormous sculptural composition, whose characters look like siblings caught off guard while joining their tools (the hammer and sickle) into a dangerously close proximity, thus contributing to the aforementioned anxiety. Combined, these tools fit the allegory of the Clashing Rocks with the narrow passage between them through which a bird of autonomous art once flew (read the full story in chapter 2).

It is no secret that total communality and total power are essentially forms of social perversion. Being sado-masochistic utopias, at times they compensate for the qualitative side of matters quantitatively, as was the case with the USSR. Given this, the "retreat" of communality or individualism in no way guarantees us that one or the other will not resume (or "return"). In nontotalitarian societies, communality and individualism balance one another, forming odd combinations, including so-called neutral and complex terms. *Corpo*rate structures of a postindustrialist type are associated with the latter. Moreover, in countries where fragmentation and individualism seem to have reached the limit, a nostalgia for collective *corpo*reality is most sharply felt. In the United States, for example, this is manifested in the interest in talk shows, which make up a substantial part of television programming and serve as a school for confessional-cathartic communality. In such instances, however, communality takes a contractual form as opposed to an institutional one (known in Russia as *kommunalka*).[63]

An urge to encounter communal speech "ritual" has always driven Westerners (from Lee Harvey Oswald to Jacques Derrida) to the USSR's "speech zones"—be it a workers' hangout in Minsk or the Moscow Institute of Philosophy. Apparently, this is the ultimate form that Orientalism has taken since the time of perestroika.

▪▪

In *The Eclipse of Solar Mythology,* Richard Dorson shows how deeply "solarism" was rooted in the Victorian mentality, which had an unfailing appetite for Eastern myths, religions, and folklore. The connections between Orientalism and the "solarized" psyche of nineteenth-century Europeans unfold themselves in Hegel's *Lectures on the Philosophy of History:* "The History of the World travels from East to West, for Europe is absolutely the end of History, Asia the beginning. . . . Here rises the outward physical Sun, and in the West it sinks down: here rises the sun of self-consciousness, which diffuses a nobler brilliance."[64]

The hubbub concerning Gorbachev's Russia, which reached its zenith in 1988, may be termed an instance of Orientalism.[65] In the 1920s and 1930s, Western intellectuals like Walter Benjamin, René Etiemble, Louis Aragon, and André Gide invested their Orientalist aspirations into the Russian revolutionary (read communal) experiment, for they perceived it as the model for the universal future. A diametrically opposite ideologeme emerged in the late 1980s, when it became clear that the promise of the communal future was not going to be fulfilled. Instead, contemporary Russia is beginning to resemble the historic past of Western Europe and America, in particular the moment of "wild" capitalism at the turn of the century.

This new image of Russia has led to a dramatic reversal of the previous Orientalist paradigm: the utopian worldview has given way to a nostalgic one in which the communal is identified with "yesterday" rather than with "tomorrow." At the end of the 1980s, Russia became for the West what the Orient had been for it in Victorian times: a target and object of sublimated desires, fantasies, intrigues, and self-deceptions. Speaking of Orientalist ventures, one should mention the "success" of Sotheby's 1988 auction in Moscow, which—to the naked eye—seemed completely dreamlike, because almost everything that was "sold" at this auction in point of fact (due to the absence of a Western market for the local art) did not possess an "exchange value." Rather, it had to do with *potlatch* (archaic expenditure). As in the period when anthropological expeditions were undertaken to the jungles of the Amazon River to study the Baroro or Nambikwara Indians, *potlatch* continues to be present—albeit partially—in the processes of converting signs and symbolic values (e.g., East/West exchange). Being an integral part of Orientalism's symbolic economy, *potlatch* is endowed with a potential that in the early 1970s enabled Henry Kissinger to strike a deal with Leonid Brezhnev, who—according to a story I heard from a friend—agreed to give exit visas to 20,000 Jews in exchange for ... an American car, a Chevrolet Monte Carlo. If true, such an exchange between the superpowers would be the most outstanding example of geopolitical "potlatch." Years later, on April 29, 2000, after dinner at the American Academy in Berlin, I asked Kissinger if the story was true. He confirmed it, but added that the car was a Cadillac, not a Chevrolet.

The embryo of disintegration of Civitas Solis was conceived in 1961, when Stalin's mummy was carried out of Lenin's mausoleum. Ironically, the "dispersal" of the mausoleum's inhabitants cannot be regarded as anything other than the "master plot" of decommunalization.[66] The still pending question is what the communal will turn into while authoritarian power is being replaced by the power of money. Everyone who visits Russia regularly notices the intensive growth of real estate prices in hard currency. The reason for this lies not in the foreigners' desire to buy apartments there, but that in Russia there are only two "prestigious" cities, Moscow and St. Petersburg. Everyone who becomes rich in Siberia, the northern regions, or anywhere else buys apartments in the best areas of these two cities. Here is an example of how this occurs. Let us say that somewhere in the center of Moscow three different families live in one big communal apartment. A *nouveau riche* buys (through an agent) three small private apartments in peripheral areas. He then offers each of the three families the ownership of an individual living space. As a rule, they accept such deals. Meanwhile, the family of the wealthy person moves to the now vacant communal apartment. As a result, the rich gradually settle into the center of the city and the poor move to the outskirts. Thus, the Soviet dichotomy of power/communal is turning into the Western dichotomy of center/periphery. The Soviet city ghetto, which hitherto was not aware of the differences between the center and the periphery, must face this new reality.

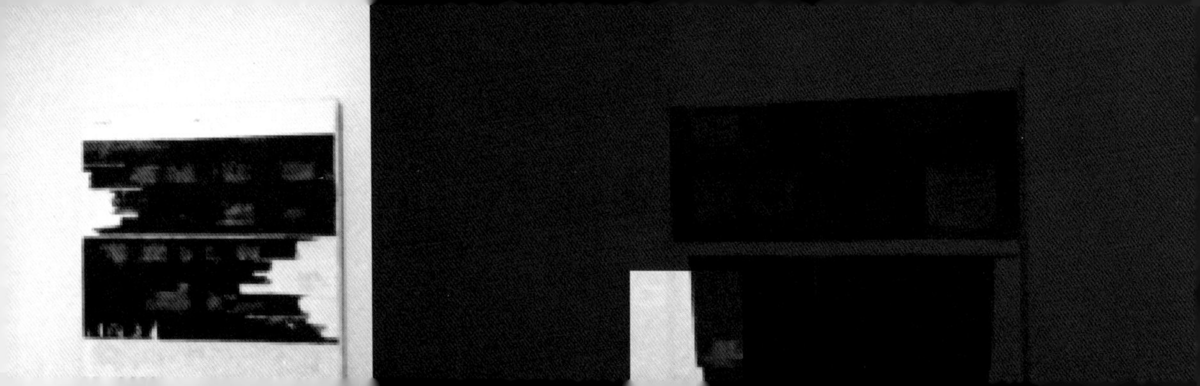

CHAPTER 2

Communal (Post)Modernism: A Short History

Nonidentity is the secret telos of identification.
Theodor W. Adorno

1. THE END OF THE 1950S, THE BEGINNING OF THE 1960S

If the artists' works featured in this chapter fall under the category of "dereified activity," it is not by virtue of their solidarity with Lukács or Adorno, but due to the political climate in the USSR that prevented such activities from being institutionalized and culturally processed in due time. This resulted in both positive and negative outcomes—positive in that the Soviet culture industry of the postwar period did not attempt to absorb unofficial (i.e., non–socialist realist) art, and negative in that for many years its body of works, still partially unaccounted for, constituted the would-be contents of an indefinitely deferred museum. The failure to obtain a museum niche made artists feel anxious and prompted them to compete collectively for inclusion, thereby triggering the formation (around this void) of a compensatory symbolic structure that alludes to the notion of "museological unconscious" discussed in chapter 10.

After the death of Stalin in 1953, a few more years were needed for the fresh air of the Khrushchev thaw to become perceptible in the art world. In the spring of 1956, immediately following the Twentieth Congress of the Soviet Communist Party, the artists Ullo Sooster, Boris Sveshnikov, and Lev Kropivnitskii returned from confinement. As a result of the Central Committee's resolution "On Overcoming the Cult of Personality and Its Consequences" (passed that same year on June 30), the exclusive right to the status of individuality, which had be usurped by the party's upper echelons, lost its earlier "infallibility." Now, for the first time, the creative intelligentsia—which had oscillated, until this point, between the Scylla of communality and the Charybdis of socialist realism—had a chance to decommunalize, to cease being solely the "ancient choir" in a typically Soviet "optimistic tragedy." Several exhibitions of Western modernist art

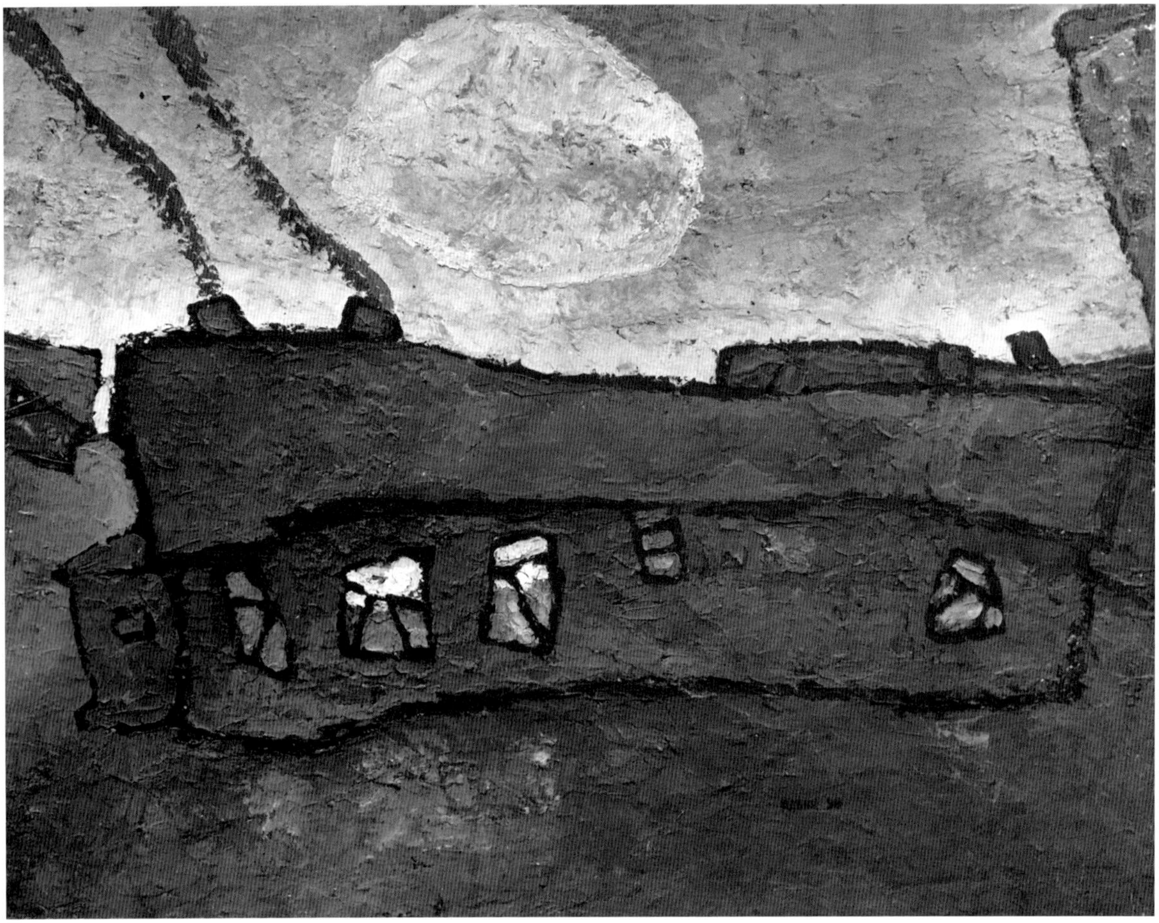

2.1
Oskar Rabin, *Barrack*, 1959.

held at the end of the 1950s[1] left an ineradicable trace on the collective psyche of Muscovite visual culture, and finally allowed Soviet artists (official and unofficial alike) to become acquainted with paradigms of individual authorship, paradigms devoid for the most part of the authoritarian individualism of the party elite.

To avoid ambiguity, a distinction should be made between the terms "unofficial" and "alternative." Unofficial artists were individuals who did not belong to the Moscow Union of Soviet Artists (MOSKh) or other official structures controlled by socialist realists. "Unofficials" (*neofitsial'nye khudozhniki*) had no right to studios or any legal means to sell their art. As for "alternative" artists, they could be either unofficial or official; to be official, they had to be silent in their refusal to adhere to socialist realism, while remaining on the margins of MOSKh as graphic designers or illustrators of children books.[2]

In 1958, the Studio School for the Improvement of Qualifications at the Moscow School of Printing, which had existed since 1954 under the direction of Eli Beliutin, passed to the protection of the Committee of Graphic Designers. In his speech at the opening of the studio, Beliutin had criticized the "wingless realism" of official art. Instead, he called for a passage through "the entire worldwide history of human culture," including modernity. At the end of 1959, having become the first private educational institution in the history of Soviet art, the Studio School found a home on Taganskaia Street. Among those who taught or were educated there were Vladimir Iankilevskii, Viktor Pivovarov, Boris Zhutovskii, and Ernst Neizvestnyi.

At about the same time, the Lianozovo group emerged, consisting of the artist/poet Evgenii Kropivnitskii and the artists Ol'ga Potapova, Valentina Kropivnitskaia, Oskar Rabin, Lev Kropivnitskii, Lidiia Masterkova, Vladimir Nemukhin, and Nikolai Vechtomov, as well as the poets Vsevolod Nekrasov, Genrikh Sapgir, and Igor' Kholin. These people did not manifest any particular unanimity on the plane of aesthetic values; their coherence as a group was based on their shared search for a new sociocultural identity. In other words, they sought to create a neocommunal body, but in a voluntary and noncoercive way.

While no aesthetic consensus could be observed among the members of the Lianozovo group, Rabin's paintings and drawings betray their debt to the poetry of Evgenii Kropivnitskii, Kholin, Sapgir, and Nekrasov. Rabin shared with these poets a taste for the social grotesque bordering on the aestheticization of misery, which is precisely what distinguishes the representatives of the declassed communal intelligentsia of the thaw era from their predecessors (the socialist realists), who created a paradisiac image

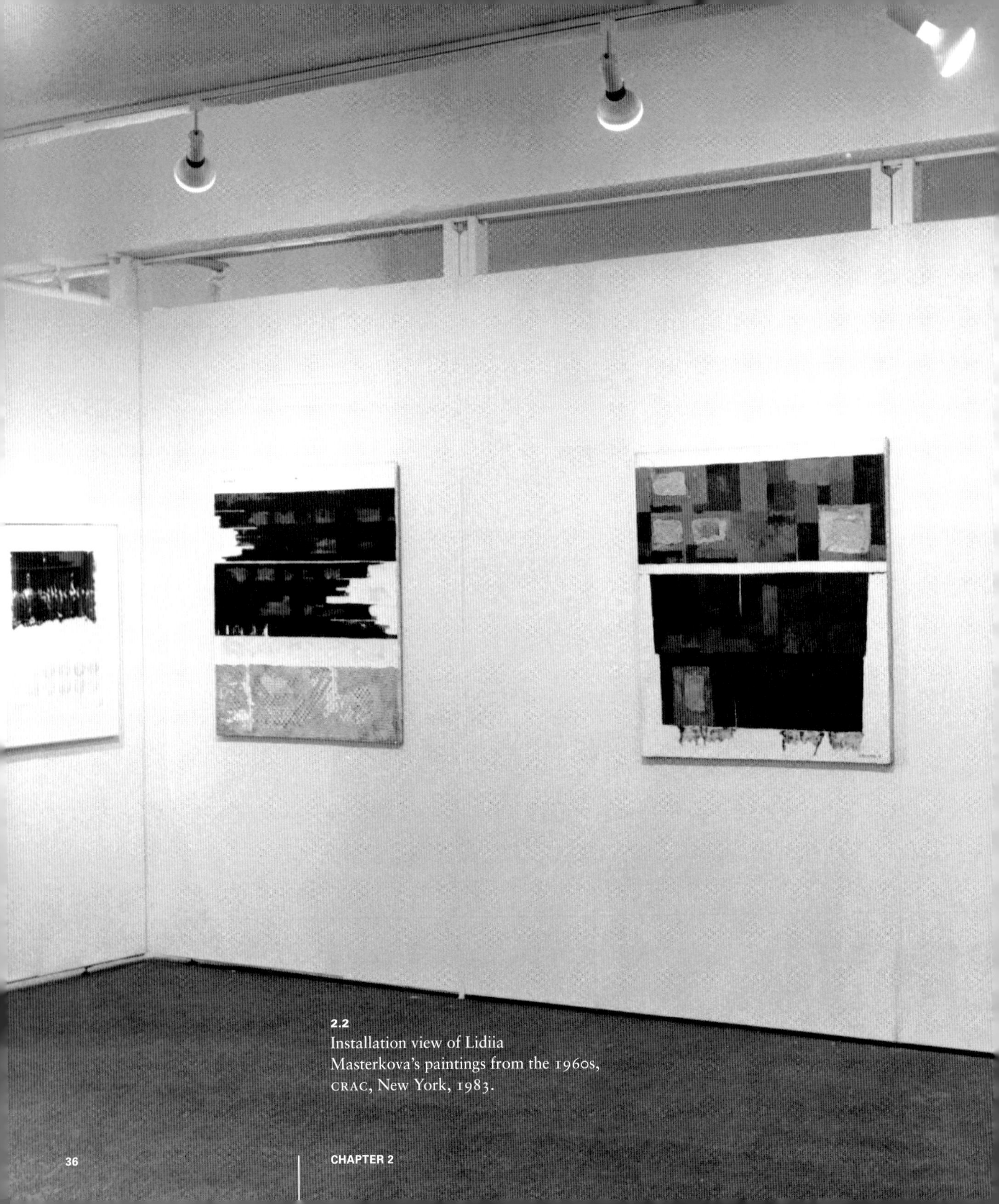

2.2
Installation view of Lidiia Masterkova's paintings from the 1960s, CRAC, New York, 1983.

of history. Stamped upon Rabin's works are crooked Moscow streets with ramshackle homes and barracks, hungry cats on roofs and beneath gates, and the claustrophobia-filled "living" spaces of communal apartments (fig. 2.1). Blame for these miserable living circumstances is laid on the absurdity of existence, or on some anonymous character who appears before communal consciousness as simply "it." This faceless, formless "it" is the chief dramatis persona of the ghetto-centric narrative championed by the forefathers of "nonconformism"—from Rabin and Ilya Kabakov to the artists of the Leningrad "Barracks School."[3] Rushing ahead of myself, I will say that it took no fewer than fifteen years for this extra-communal "it" to find, at last, the recognizable features of state and party bureaucracy. It's unmasking (the unmasking of "it") found a place in sots art,[4] whose adherents were inspired by Rabin's painting *Passport* (1964), as well as by his still lifes containing *Pravda*'s front page.

Masterkova and Nemukhin did not share Rabin's appetite for social transgression and for "talking back" to the Soviet authorities. They espoused indifference as a virtue, and with this attitude, plunging into abstraction was their logical choice. A visit in the summer of 1959 to the "National American Exhibition," displayed in the pavilions of Sokol'niki Park, and featuring works by Jackson Pollock and Willem de Kooning, guaranteed their initial preference for abstract expressionism. Not long after, however, both artists committed themselves to semiabstract compositions. In her first abstractions, distinguished by the passion for organic forms and vivid color fields colliding with one another, Masterkova began to glue old bits of lace and fragments of ecclesiastical attire (chasubles and the like) to the surfaces of her canvases (fig. 2.2). The use of lace (which in the context of those years may be considered the antithesis of a "masculine" relation to *faktura* [texture] and to the "politics" of material selection)[5] placed the artist in an isolated position in the patriarchal world of Muscovite alternative art.

Nemukhin's choice of objects is observable in his numerous still lifes with playing cards, fighting cocks, and fragments of card tables (fig. 2.3). This entire iconography, borrowed from the sphere of competitive games, corresponds well with the vitality of his artistic character. In the majority of cases, this inventory bore a conditional semantic burden, intensifying the effect of chance, intrigue, indeterminacy—that is, everything that would contrast with the doctrines of "objectivity and the universal character of causality" espoused by the Soviet establishment. Later Nemukhin added "cuts" to his canvases in the manner of Lucio Fontana; in most cases, they were illusory, but occasionally (as, for example, in pieces executed in collaboration with Anatolii Zverev and damaged in an axe-throwing contest) they were real.

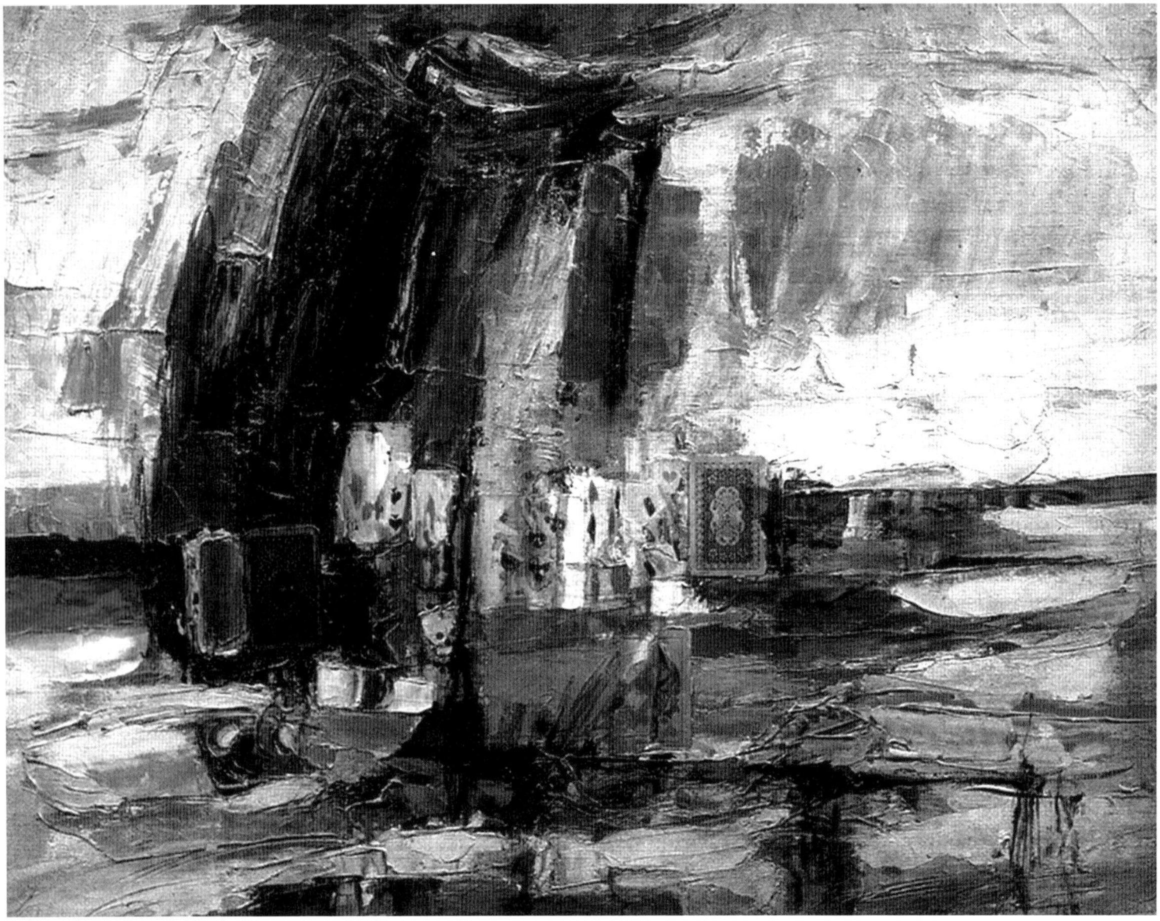

2.3
Vladimir Nemukhin,
Poker on the Beach, 1965.

The notion of being one of the "chosen" and of having a spiritual mission was not alien to many representatives of "dissident modernism."[6] Thus, for example, Oleg Tselkov considered (as he does to this day) that he "does not create, but simply executes."[7] Here, supernatural forces supplant the historic giver of orders: the party and government. Another candidate for the same post is the *Idealich* (*moi idéal*). Projected onto culture, the *Idealich* is the narcissistic ideal of omnipotence, that is, the artist as Zarathustra. At the end of the 1950s, this kind of heroic individualism was associated with the sculptors Vadim Sidur and Neizvestnyi. All "dissident modernists," to equal degrees, ignored the languages of communalism and power. They made these topics taboo and, consequently, displaced them, not only from the zone of consciousness but also (for the time being) from the sphere of the unconscious. The vacuum that was formed as a result was filled in, in Kabakov's words, "by the sweet visions, magical sights, and original worlds that had unfolded before one's eyes."[8]

However, the artists at this time knew no vision other than a cathartic one. Therefore, anything that envisaged an "alienation effect" or that might lead to the realization of the "critical function" was immediately crossed off the list of phenomena worthy of attention. This response was linked to the experience of communality, but also to memories of the Stalinization of culture. That is why in the late 1950s the very notion of a "critical function" was still identified with the verdictive language of Zhdanovism (in the 1930s, "criticism" of writers or artists often landed them in prison or labor camps). Soviet alternative art, alas, would frequently be run over by such "criticism," with some modifications, in the course of its thirty-year history.

▪▪

Reflecting on the first steps of Russian "dissident"—or, in my terminology, "communal"—modernism, one must necessarily look at such early representatives as Sveshnikov, Vladimir Veisberg, Dmitrii Krasnopevtsev, Mikhail Shvartsman, Dmitrii Plavinskii, Aleksandr Kharitonov, and Vladimir Iakovlev. After his return from the labor camps, Sveshnikov settled in Tarusa (130 kilometers from Moscow), and at the very beginning of the 1960s moved to Moscow. He brought with him from confinement a large number of sketches executed in the manner of the old masters (from Botticelli to Dürer) and in the spirit of Goya's *Los Caprichos*.

In these works, the theme of prison life acquires a certain atemporality; some of them might be confused with illustrations for Dante's *Inferno*. This type of apprehension of time and space was termed "Dantesque chronotope" or "the chronotope of vertical time" by literary theorist Mikhail Bakhtin.[9] Within such a framework, the temporal distinction between narration and what is narrated vanishes and—in exchange—the two are endowed with the status of simultaneity. And Sveshnikov's temporal response to the Stalin years was not isolated. In one of his poems, Boris Pasternak even refers to this period as "the years of timelessness." Many communal modernists applied precisely this interpretation to the period that succeeded the era of the Russian avant-garde, believing that Russia seemed to have "fallen out of culture" during that time.[10]

A similar eschatologism, which occurs in the work of a number of Sveshnikov's contemporaries, is "the death of time." Veisberg, having attempted—like Pushkin's Salieri—"to verify harmony with algebra," composed his meditative works (including his "white on white" series) from the most minuscule units of color. For the most part, he painted still lifes and portraits, reaching an ecstatic frenzy by cutting himself on his arms and chest. Veisberg admitted frequently that he selected as models only those whom he had seen in his nightmares lying in their coffins. It seems far from coincidental that, in 1973, the sculptor Sidur began to execute a series of works with the title *Coffin Art*.

Iakovlev, a painter valued in the unofficial milieu for his still lifes, abstractions, and distorted (at times, explicitly erotic) portraits, is yet another example of the paradigm of the "myth of originality"[11] (see fig. 10.3). From Goya and van Gogh to Egon Schiele and Antonin Artaud, the tradition of modernism not only legitimized but canonized the image of the madman-genius. In accordance with this tradition, insanity is considered a necessary correlate of artistic talent. In this sense, the mentally ill Iakovlev, who was almost deprived of his eyesight but "compensated" for this defect with creative vision, was and remains—for the Russians—a legendary figure.[12]

2. THE 1960S

When the lavishly reproduced books on Western modernism (the so-called coffee-table books) began to surface in the Soviet Union, it seemed that one had only to follow all of their commandments and a place in history would be guaranteed. In other words, Soviet nonconformists preferred the most modest position within the "genuine" and "pure" capitalist culture industry to the very highest pedestal in the pantheon of the "false" and "unsterile" domestic art situation. In the 1960s a number of Russian artists began to orient themselves toward foreign buyers, exhibitions outside of the USSR, and publication in the Western press. To be a member of MOSKh or embark on a career as a cultural bureaucrat ceased to be the sole means of attaining a "creative reputation" and an adequate standard of living, as had been the case previously.

In Federico Fellini's film *Amarcord* (1973), the inhabitants of a provincial seaside town learn that an American superliner is scheduled to pass within a few miles of the shore on the following night. In order to see it, the residents set off into the open sea. In the darkness there appears before them a sumptuous, twinkling giant, which at that moment—like a ghost—disappears, dissolving into the night. This allegory, similar to a hallucination, recalls the spirit of the late 1950s and early 1960s, when before the eyes of the underground artists the magic ship of modernism arose.[13]

It is worth remembering that, at one time, Western modernists (let alone postmodernists) digested and culturally processed the experience of the Russian avant-garde, adapting this experience to their own context and to their politics of the signifier. Having had no such luck, most communal modernists were barred from access to archives and museum storage rooms in which Russian works from the early twentieth century were kept. For them, access to this heritage was possible only "secondhand"—that is, through exposure to the works of those European and American artists (minimalists, for example) who were influenced by the experiments of the Russian avant-garde. Thus, their experience can be seen as yet another search for a *temps perdu* that is doomed from the start, just like, for instance, an attempt to recreate Vladimir Tatlin's context by looking at Dan Flavin's series of neon constructions titled *"Monument" for V. Tatlin*.[14]

As for the Soviet communal modernists of the late 1950s and early 1960s, the reaction to their art in the United States and in Western Europe was—for the most part—unfavorable. The artists were repeatedly criticized for *literaturnost'* (literariness) and for copying from the "original sources." Given the history of such twofold stereotypes (e.g., literariness and copying on par with "original sources"), the informed reader can trace the aforementioned criticism to Clement Greenberg who, in his famous essays "Avant-Garde and Kitsch" (1939) and "Towards a Newer Laocoön" (1940), failed to appreciate (or simply to face) the fact that art contaminated by literature cannot be separated from "pure" visuality: they are Romulus and Remus, nourished by the same she-wolf. Today, however, tirades about liberation from the dungeons of language are useless, in part because the verbal and the visual are to equal degrees clichéd, processed by the media or culture industry, and are largely coextensive. The media or culture industry is what we need to be liberated from, which is, of course, a utopian idea. But several decades ago it was still acceptable to rely on the existence of essential, extracted, and extremely pure forms of the verbal and the visual that were not blended with, or bound to, anything else.

A difference between the experiments of Soviet unofficial artists of the 1960s and the museo-commercial shrines of Western modernism was manifested, as a rule, on the register of the "secondary signs," or in the space of signification, in relation to which "primary signs" play the role of the signifier. Here one and the same visual stereotype, in the case of contextual change, transfer, or rupture, can become a springboard for dissimilar interpretations—literary, philosophical, and political. Thus, as a result of their brief, but "direct" encounter with European and American art, and also the stream of coffee-table books, Soviet artists suddenly began to project themselves onto the Other, thereby endowing "it" with a totally different content. The result turned out to be utterly estranged from its wellspring: for the local unofficial artists, who armed themselves with signifiers of Western modernism, its vital context and its living history remained incomprehensible, vague, and inessential. In the majority of cases they insisted on art's ritualistic dimension, hitherto "buried" by Tret'iakov and Benjamin, thereby attesting to the fact that the communal modernists epitomize not continuity, but a break with the postrevolutionary Soviet avant-garde ("socialist modernism") of the 1920s.

The above does not in any way diminish the significance of the artifacts of the post-Stalin underground. On the contrary, it gives them (from the standpoint of contemporary theories) a more interesting angle. Likewise, these artists' insufficient knowledge of the "original sources" should not be viewed as their greatest misfortune, for it left room for fantasy and creative distortion. Taking into account the aberrancy of their interpretation of Western (and, for that matter, of "their own," pre- and postrevolutionary) art, one must assume that this very aberrancy is the greatest contribution of communal modernists to what we (zealously) call "world culture." What's more, it is such a cliché to think of art in terms of a single contextual frame or a single descriptive narrative. The existing tendency to globalize artistic contexts, histories, and sensibilities is, in fact, suffocating and counterproductive. Luckily, many such contexts, including those which are considered to be "similar" and "synchronous," are both different and deferred.

▪▪

The 1960s mark the decommunalization of a remarkably broad mass of Soviet citizens. This was due to the sweep of Khrushchev's building programs, which were charged with resettling people from the communal apartments of Stalin's time. The "new lands" program (in Siberia and Kazakhstan)—which provided for the migration of "productive forces" to rural localities—also helped to lessen the population density in the nation's cities. A few years later, Khrushchev, already removed from power, admitted to a journalist that his chief service to the nation had been to improve housing conditions, in order to "let people live."[15]

The spread of decommunalization significantly affected the lives of alternative artists. At this time, many of them quit their communal abodes and began to work in studios, which became the incubators for developing new forms of relations in the art world. In the studios, shows were arranged, poems recited, theoretical texts presented, opinions and books—including those on Western art—exchanged. For the most part, these artists earned their living by making children's books (for example, Sooster, Kabakov, Pivovarov, Erik Bulatov, Oleg Vasil'ev, and Eduard Gorokhovskii) or by collaborating with popular-science journals (as did Sobolev and Nemukhin). Such a minimal form of participation in the Soviet culture industry at least gave the alternative painters and sculptors the right to studios. In the framework of these studios, all sorts of groupings took shape, held together if not by a unity of artistic purposes, then by shared opposition to the establishment. These fellowships served as laboratories for the rediscovery and recreation of the paradigms of individual authorship usurped (in the "years of timelessness") by the authoritarian "I" of state power.

Alongside the contacts in studios there arose other, previously unheard-of phenomena: the arrangement of shows of non–socialist realist art in clubs, scientific research institutes, youth cafés (such as the Aelita and the Blue Bird), and in private apartments (such as those of composer Andrei Volkonskii, art critic Il'ia Tsirlin, pianist Sviatoslav Rikhter, and dissident Aleksandr Ginzburg). Jazz clubs and literary or artistic salons arose, connected with the names of Sooster, Sobolev, Iurii Mamleev, Alena Basilova, and Mikhail Grobman. All of the musical performances, theatrical productions, and literary publications which helped to counter socialist realism's "symbol of faith" deserve their own investigations, as do other cultural phenomena from the early 1960s.

On December 1, 1962, an exhibition at the Manezh Exhibition Hall opened and displayed—amid typically Soviet productions—the works of Sooster, Sobolev, Neizvestnyi, Beliutin, Zhutovskii, and Iankilevskii. The leaders of official culture invited Khrushchev and the upper echelons of the party to the opening with the aim of stirring them up against their enemies, the alternative artists. The scandal that erupted at the opening and the subsequent persecution of "deviant" art marked a watershed in the history of unofficial art.[16] Like a mollusk extricating itself from its shell, the communal body of Muscovite dissident modernism worked itself free of the ghetto's limits for the first time. The infantile phase, or "mirror stage," of alternative art drew to a close. The artists recognized the utopianism of their hopes for linearity and continuity in the process of the convalescence of cultural life. To grasp the severity of the situation generated by Khrushchev's condemnation of the Manezh events, it suffices to cite his angry words at the show's opening: "Just give me a list of those of you who want to go abroad, to the so-called 'free world.' We'll give you foreign passports tomorrow, and you can get out. Your prospects here are zero. What's hung here is simply anti-Soviet. It's immoral. . . . Are you pederasts or normal people? . . . As long as I am Chairman of the Council of Ministers we are going to . . . maintain a strict policy in art."[17]

At the meeting of party and government representatives and the artistic intelligentsia in January 1963, at the House of Receptions in the Lenin Hills, Khrushchev summarized the discussion of the so-called nonconformists. He said, in effect, "They needn't be put in jail, but rather into the madhouse." Later, under Brezhnev, Khrushchev's words were made literal: madhouses became laboratories for the forcible "reeducation" and reformation of aesthetic views. As had once been the case in Stalin's camps, in the nuthouses, communal experiences were reinscribed: along with doses of insulin, patients received injections of communal psychology. In 1993, the St. Petersburg artist Afrika (Sergei Bugaev), having spent a month in a psychiatric hospital as part of an artistic project, informed me that he had "nowhere before experienced such a degree of imperativity to merge with the communal body."

■■

To the list of the characteristics that constitute the image of the communal modernist, I would like to add four more types: the hobo, the "holy fool," the hippie, and the schizoid. The first type, which was taking shape already at the end of the 1950s, is identified first and foremost with Anatolii Zverev, who became the talk of the town thanks to his spontaneity and knack for improvisation. These skills were demonstrated in many genres, styles, and tendencies, from animalism and impromptu portraits to abstract compositions (fig. 2.4). The chief novelty that Zverev introduced to the Moscow art world was his abolition of distinctions between life and the artistic act. Once, for instance, while working on a series of portraits, he used, along with paints squeezed from tubes, toothpaste and cigarette butts, and accompanied his "action painting" with medleys on the piano and improvising in verse. A fragment of one of these verses went, as I recall, "A Tatar boy shoots from a bow. 'Fu-u-u-ck' sings the bowstring after the arrow flies off." Drunkenness and vagrancy (which brought about his premature death in 1986), together with his gift for improvisation, won Zverev the reputation of the muse's beloved, and added a number of supplementary features to the Muscovite paradigm of the "myth of originality."

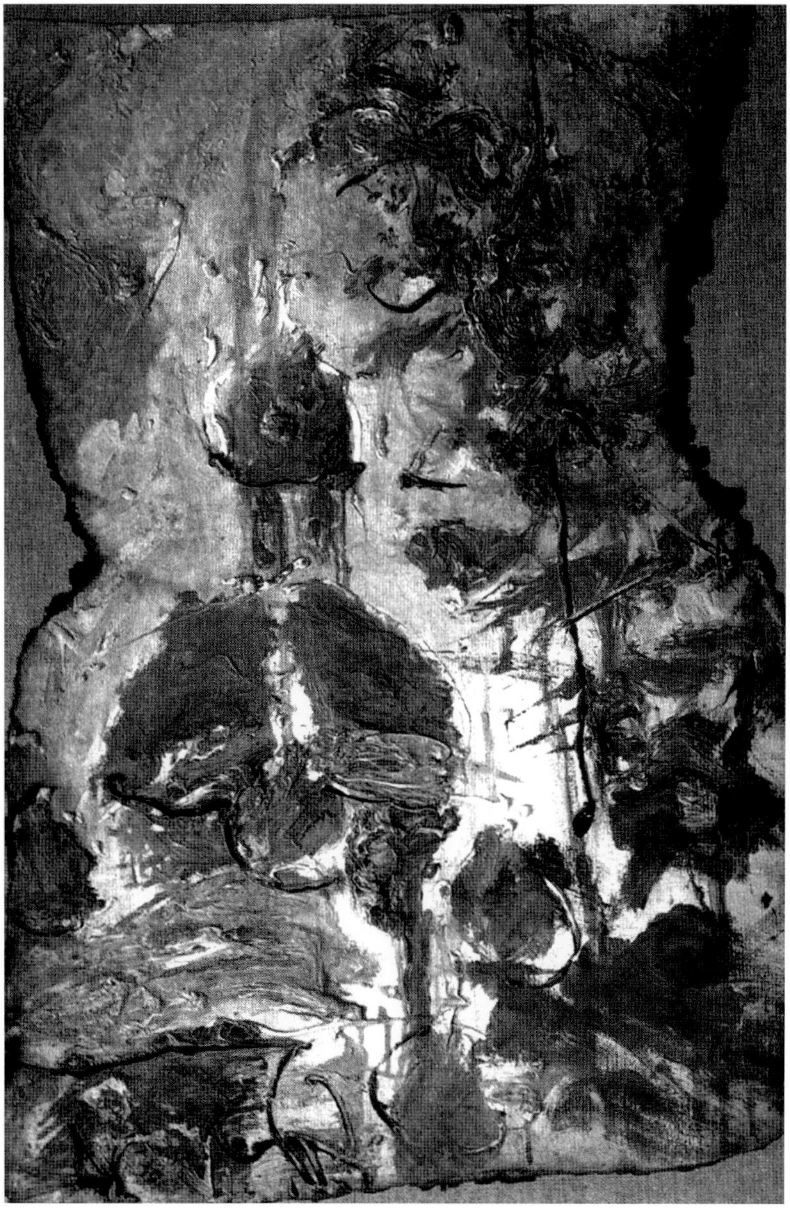

2.4
Anatolii Zverev, *Church in Peredelkino*, 1960.

The role of the holy fool, like that of the hobo, is inseparable from the Russian tradition of opposition to the establishment. An intolerance of power, characteristic of all periods of Russian history, developed to the point that alternative individuality was forced to resort to camouflage. The drunkard and the holy fool were permitted forms of social (or, to be precise, asocial) expression forbidden to ordinary members of society. Like Zverev, Vasilii Sitnikov had a virtuous command of methods of "playing the fool." His bag of holy fool's tricks included both jocular manners and a passion for folkloric articulations. Sitnikov wore an untucked shirt and work boots, collected icons, and gave painting lessons to numerous pupils, who were hypnotized by their teacher's Rasputinesque charm and intensity. Shocking his charges, he painted with a boot brush, attaining precise enough visual effects nonetheless. Sitnikov's subjects varied from folkish representations of Russian churches powdered with New Year's snow to caricatured nudes and grotesque genre scenes executed in a pale palette. In 1980—having emigrated to New York—Sitnikov made the acquaintance of two or three gallery dealers (with my help), promising that "for prison fare and accommodations in barracks" he would paint for them a number of epochal pictures over several years. It goes without saying that no contracts were signed. Not long before his death in 1987, I ran into him in the East Village. In his hands he held a huge brush for washing the floors of corporate lobbies. "Finally I have obtained a brush suitable for the scale of my painterly grandeur," he said in parting.

The artist Vladimir Piatnitskii, who died in 1978 of a drug overdose, can be considered the Russian incarnation of self-destructive tendencies in the mold of the Beat generation (Jack Kerouac and others). In his oils and works on paper, the swarms of communal freaks are subordinated to a psychedelic logic, which is also not alien to the heroes of the underground writer Mamleev's stories (see fig. 2.24). It's no accident, for example, that in one of Piatnitskii's paintings a character, resembling the artist himself, holds in his hands a then-unpublished volume of Mamleev's texts. In the 1960s, Mamleev's salon on Iuzhinskii Lane 13 was a crucial factor in the formation of yet another paradigm of artistic and bohemian behavior, the "schizoid." Interestingly, this concept arose and became popular in Moscow more than a decade before Deleuze and Guattari's *Anti-Oedipus*, in which "schizoidness" and "schizoanalysis" are developed into a means of theoretical enterprise.

As I have already noted, the 1960s were associated not only with artistic alternatives but with social experimentation. This was often connected to the search for new forms of camaraderie, intellectual and creative alike. Like the Lianozovo group, artists associated with Sretenskii Boulevard cannot be linked with any specific theoretical model or stylistic persuasion. Instead, it was another link in the reinterpretation and redefinition of communal language games and their rules. After all, every citizen of the USSR who has studied in a Soviet school, graduated from an institute, or served in the army, even if he was lucky enough to have his own apartment or studio, is nonetheless a product of this communal education. Kabakov was correct in stating that "he knows himself insofar as he is a communal dweller" and that "to transcend the boundaries of the communal is to become an angel."[18]

What took place in the unofficial art world in the 1960s was linked to a changeover from institutional forms of communality to "contractual" ones. It was "contractual" communality, or neocommunality, based on the principle of optional communalization, that became the ecological niche for Muscovite alternative art over the course of three decades—right up to perestroika. Among the artists generally borne in mind when the words "Sretenskii Boulevard" are pronounced, one may list Sooster, Kabakov, Bulatov, Pivovarov, Sobolev, Eduard Shteinberg, and Iankilevskii.

Iankilevskii's sketches, paintings, and triptychs may be considered incarnations of the communal unconscious, not in a Jungian sense, but rather as that which has been conditioned by *statistics*, including the unprecedented scope of stereotyping and depersonalization characteristic of speech acts and the perception thereof, of behavioral norms, and of the very tenor of Soviet life. And, on the strength of the clichéd nature of communal verbal exchange, almost everything that is displaced into the unconscious—save for the prelingual (the infantile period of life)—coincides to a significant degree for the majority of communal dwellers. When gazing at Iankilevskii's compositions, in which foreshortenings of a deformed anthropomorphism are laid atop a rigid structure of communications nets and aggregates in the spirit of Francis Picabia and Max Ernst, Nietzsche's words "Dionysus the crucified" spring to mind (fig. 2.5).

For Shteinberg, the "communal unconscious" revealed itself during his search for a symbolic father. This quest was preceded by a number of circumstances that emancipated consciousness but broke the familiar rhythm of unconscious identification. Among them was the unmasking of the cult of personality at the Twentieth Communist Party Congress and the removal of Stalin's mummy from Lenin's mausoleum in 1961; these were dramatic, national-scale examples of what psychoanalysis defines as "the death of the father." With Shteinberg, the lost paternal icon was supplanted by the patriarch of the Russian avant-garde, Kazimir Malevich. Shteinberg not only appropriated Malevich's visual language, but also to some extent "corrected" his legacy, developing the messianic potential of

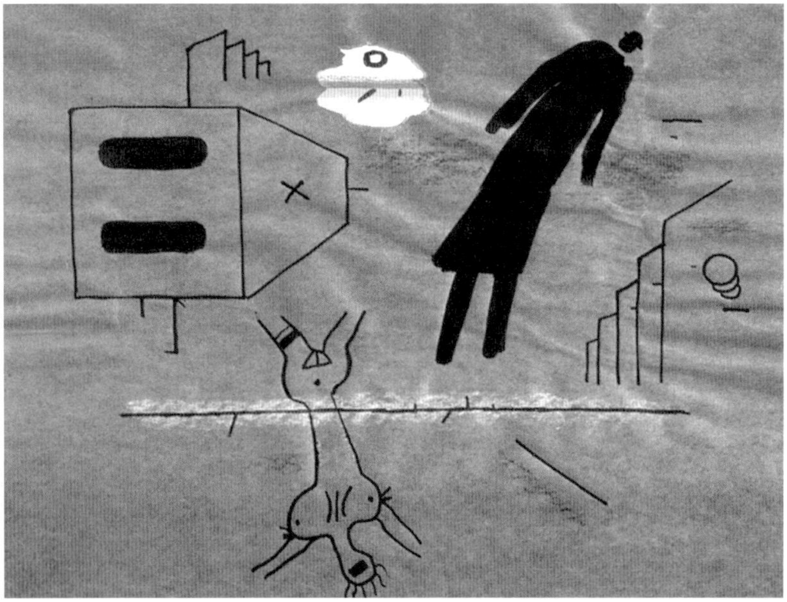

2.5
Vladimir Iankilevskii, *Kafkaesque Atmosphere*, 1969.

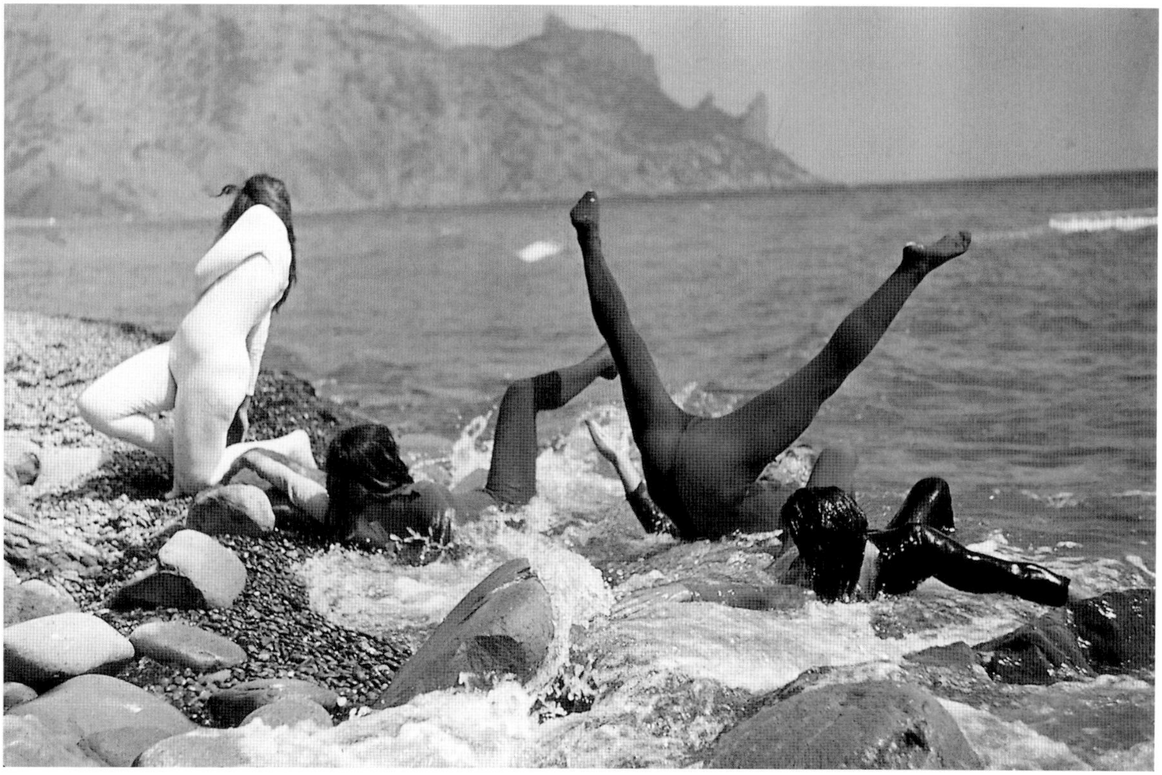

2.6
Lev Nussberg and Movement group,
Shift of Times, performance, 1971.

Malevich's abstractions to their extreme and truncating their secular signification. The Neoplatonists—Plotinus, Proclus, and others—did more or less the same with Plato's philosophy. In the 1980s, Shteinberg wrote a letter to "the beloved Kazimir Severinovich" (Malevich), which became a manifestation of symbolic authority delegated to the paternal metaphor. Since any symbolic father is a symptom ("the return of the repressed"), this Name-of-the-Father turns out to be "more father than father himself."[19]

Curiously, a few years before Shteinberg wrote his letter, Lev Nussberg, who founded the Movement group in 1962, had staged a similar correspondence with Malevich.[20] Besides Nussberg, the Movement group included Francisco Infante, Vladimir Akulinin, and Galina Bitt, among others. The group focused on the propagation and development of kinetic art, the design of artificial environments, and the staging of outdoor spectacles comparable with Western happenings and body art (fig. 2.6).

For Nussberg, the task of art boiled down to the symbiosis of the natural and the artificial; in the era of Sputniks and cosmic euphoria, he was able to convince Soviet officialdom of the actuality of his pop-science fantasies, which gravitated—at the level of design and architectural forms—toward the aesthetics of the 1920s (from Malevich and Lissitzky to Tatlin and Pevsner). Like many of his compatriots (for example, Neizvestnyi in *The Tree of Life*), Nussberg believed that the world's progress could be assured under the aegis of a single artistic project. Incidentally, he enriched the domestic version of the "myth of originality" with yet another Zarathustrian facet—the "will" to leadership and tutorship.

In 1970, Infante broke off from the Movement group, having created, along with Nonna Goriunova, his own collective under the name ARGO. The group's aim was, in Infante's words, "to bring to fruition planned projects for artificed spaces."[21] For many, Infante's "artefacts" are associated with fragments of nature reflected in mirrors. This doubling, like the installations with mirrors themselves, is somewhat reminiscent of the earlier works of Robert Smithson.

Among those who, along with Shteinberg, Nussberg, and Infante, had affection for geometric and organic abstraction were the students of Vladimir Sterligov in Leningrad and Mikhail Chernyshov in Moscow. Chernyshov socialized frequently with and exhibited works alongside Mikhail Roginskii, who included in his visual lexicon representations of everyday objects—primus stoves, irons, matchboxes, and the like. A few pieces merit special consideration: *Red Door,* a readymade from 1965, and *Fuck You* and *Ass,* 1966, both featuring pants hung off a stool (fig. 2.7).

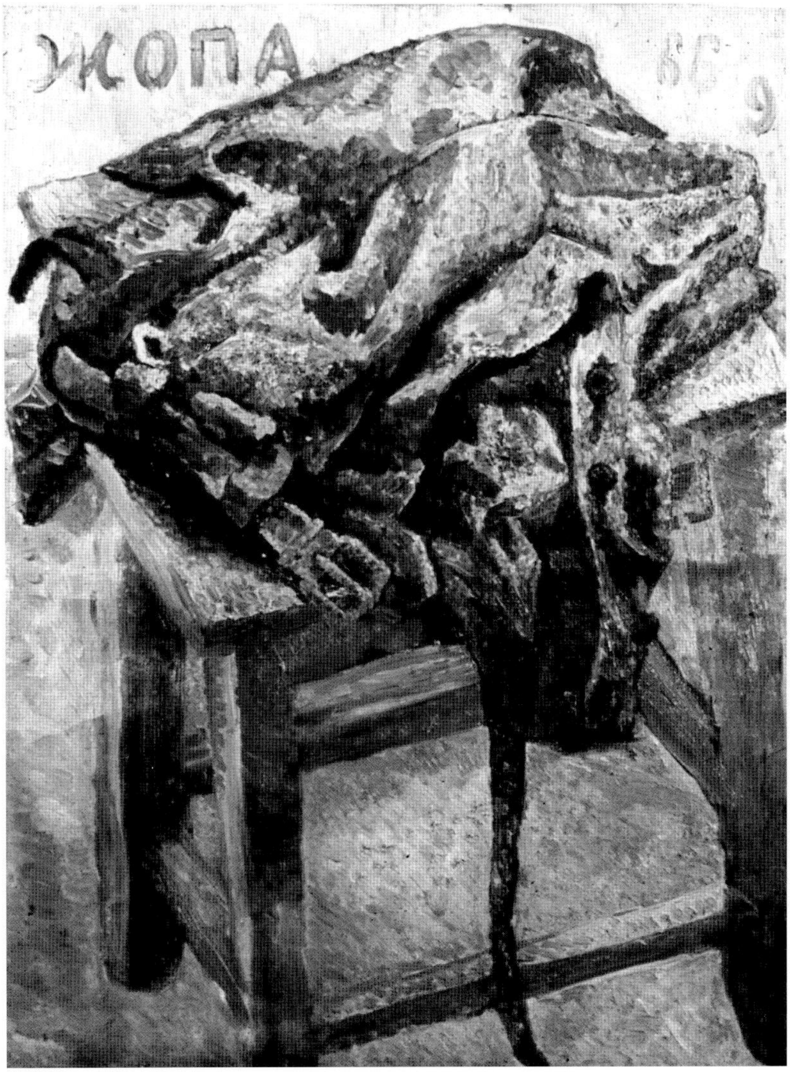

2.7
Mikhail Roginskii, *Ass*, 1966.

It might seem that this inventory of objects is similar to those employed by Rabin in his barracks motifs. In fact, however, Roginskii's works herald another apprehension of the selfsame iconography. If Rabin's objects serve as witnesses for the prosecution, wailing about the crimes of an extra-communal "it," then with Roginskii the objects' self-sufficiency is returned to them. In their unsightly everydayness, the artist found his own theme, amortized to no one else: the theme of coexistence with things, or—and this is just the same—the ability of the ghetto residents to relinquish their hostility toward things and to "accept their misery as your own."[22] The argument that Roginskii created a Russian version of pop art (i.e., "communal pop art") is mistaken: in contrast to the West, where the fetishization of consumer culture could not fail to be reflected in art, in the USSR, this fetishization remained utopian.

▪▪

In the 1960s, the first art collectors and art collections appeared. At the beginning, they included Aleksandr Rusanov, Evgenii Nutovich, Nina Stevens (the Russian wife of an American journalist), and Leonid Talochkin. Later came Aleksandr Glezer and Tat'iana Kolodzei. Georgii Kostakis filled an important role by collecting works of the earlier Russian avant-garde alongside works by contemporary artists. In the same decade, the American economics professor Norton Dodge began collecting unofficial Soviet art. Overall, the sale of works to foreigners became in the 1960s an economic factor that played an increasingly important role in the infrastructure of "communal modernism." However, as such sales were illegal, the purchasers—primarily diplomats and journalists accredited in Moscow—for the most part acquired works of small dimensions so they could export them in their suitcases. From this practice the term "suitcase style" arose to denote modestly scaled artworks destined for export.

Far from fulfilling a mission of "enlightenment," foreigners in the USSR, with rare exceptions, had only vague notions of the actual issues of vanguard art in their own countries. All they could offer their Russian friends in the guise of *Kulturträger* were books or catalogues of museum shows promoting art that had already become synonymous with *die Kulturindustrie*. Contemporary trends in American and European art proved to be beyond the reach of these types of publications. In those times almost no one in Russia knew about Beat culture, minimalism, Arte Povera, the Situationist International, or Fluxus, or about such artists as John Cage, Yves Klein, Joseph Beuys, Eva Hesse, Marcel Broodthaers, Gordon Matta-Clark, Edward Kienholz, and Hans Haacke, although precisely these artists constituted Western "nonconformism" of the 1960s. Thus, the Soviet "nonconformists" accidentally identified themselves not with marginal activities or iconoclastic gestures of their Western contemporaries, but with "ascendant" culture, that which had already been tamed, assimilated, and, in the final analysis, endorsed by the institutions of power. As a result, Soviet alternative artists, while remaining in opposition to domestic officialdom, served unwittingly as apologists for the Western cultural establishment. This circumstance to a certain extent explains the unfavorable reactions of leftist critics to exhibitions of the nonconformists' work abroad.

After Brezhnev came to power in 1964, the organization of alternative exhibitions in Moscow turned into its own sort of Russian roulette. Thus, for example, the exhibition of the Lianozovo group (with the addition of several pieces by Plavinskii, Shteinberg, and Zverev) at the Friendship Club on the Enthusiasts' Highway in 1967 was called off by the authorities two hours after it opened. This failed initiative was officially accused of "ideological sabotage" and provoked an irate reaction in the Soviet press. Meanwhile, other important shows of alternative art passed without any particular action by the authorities. Among these was a whole sequence of short-running events in the Blue Bird café, including Vitaly Komar and Aleksandr Melamid's exposition "Retrospectivism" (spring 1967), Kabakov and Bulatov's joint show (summer 1968), and solo shows by Vagrich Bakhchanian and Vasil'ev that followed right after.

By 1968, Vasil'ev had already turned out a number of key devices (such as pass keys) and "ramming" contrivances permitting a passage through the walls of planar "fortifications." Having reinterpreted the legacy of his teachers, Vladimir Favorskii and Robert Fal'k, Vasil'ev conceptualized painterly space by "positing axonometry as its sublation,"[23] that is, by embedding rectilinear surfaces in it and by supercharging the pressure of light. Vasil'ev's methods of creating "high and deep spaces" give rise to effects reminiscent simultaneously of X-rays and visual aids on spectral analysis. Even though some story is always told in Vasil'ev's pictures, narrative is optional in them. The true subject of these works is going through the purgatory of visuality. Years later, this approach was summed up in *Ogonek* (1980), in which streams of light epitomizing "pure visuality" and issuing from the painting's corners incinerate a source of speech, in this case an orator located in the center (fig. 2.8).[24]

3. THE 1970S

Understandably, the accenting of problems of visuality in a country enthralled by speech practices, whether communal speech or the language of power, is a classical example of Don Quixotism, which Vasil'ev's case definitely relates to. Nonetheless, a few other artists were able to realize

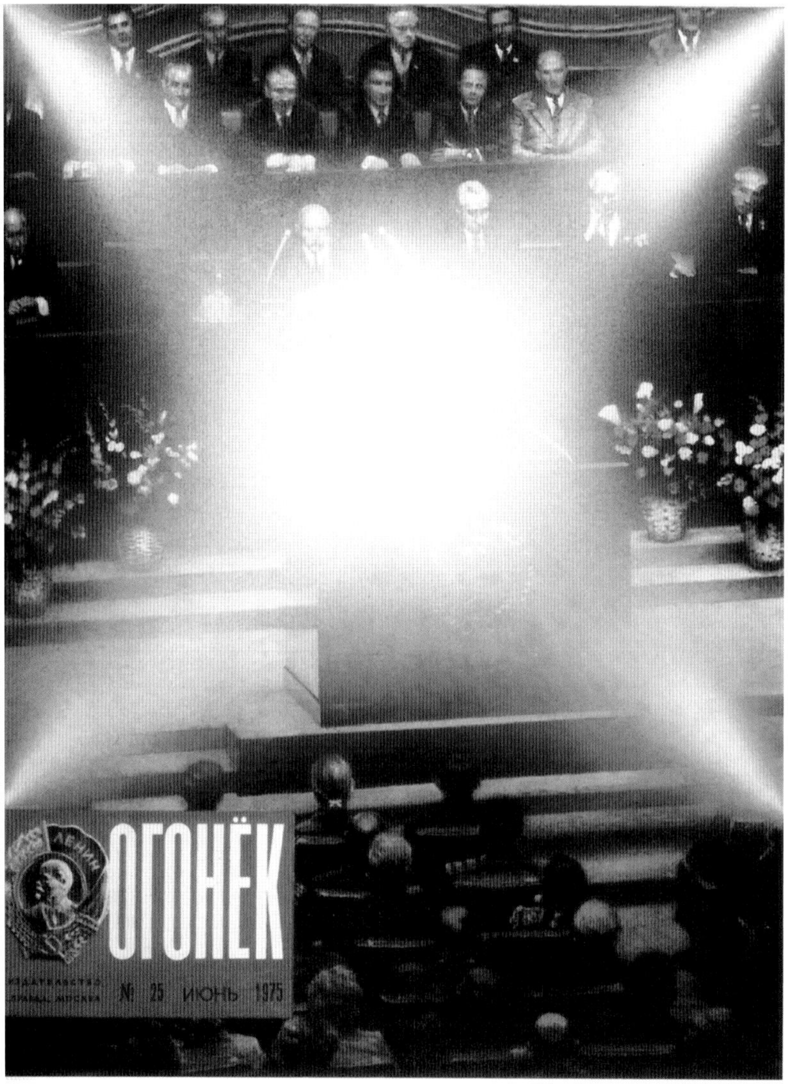

2.8
Oleg Vasil'ev, *Ogonek no. 25, 1975*, 1980.

the cost price of this problematic, including Bulatov and Ivan Chuikov. More than the others, Chuikov is concerned with the epistemological examination of the visual. For him, visuality is an antinomy arising from the "collision of reality and fiction."[25] In his words, it is "the result of the operation of turning the relations of the subject and object of apprehension inside out."[26] Chuikov is famed for his series of "window frames" with images drawn on them, which carry to its limit the conflict between the presumption of spatial reality (behind the window) and flat representation (on its surface) (fig. 2.9). Each of these representations, done in the mid-1970s, can be seen as a poster for a show that has been postponed—the show of contemplating *reality as it is*. "We'll ha't [the play] tomorrow night"—these words spoken by Hamlet could be endorsed by anyone for whom the delayed reality is replaced by its painted copy.

The place Bulatov has staked out for his easel in the sociocultural cosmos is the border between the "cave" (e.g., Plato's cave) and the light-bearing agency positioned outside it. "It is on this border that I work," he writes.[27] And even though vision, in his case, is guaranteed by the source of light positioned outside the picture, one can see it only from the inside (the "cave"). Concerning the nature of such extrapictorial radiance that imparts visibility to being, nothing is known except for the fact that identification with it (that is, with the "light of truth") is dangerous,[28] and Bulatov's canvas *Dangerous* (1972) warns us of the side effects of light-seeking (fig. 2.10).

▪▪

Curiously, every communal modernist of the 1960s or 1970s would always choose a famous artist from the past to identify with. For Kabakov, it was Vermeer; for Bulatov and Vasil'ev, it was Velázquez; for Masterkova, it was El Greco; and for Nemukhin, it was Zurbarán. Perhaps the experience of being socially displaced (discharged from the "now-and-here") prompted them to seek spiritual identification with past lives, thoughts, and things. The vacancy of their own situation was filled by a Western European past "displaced" (or deferred) by "natural causes," whether chronological, territorial, or historical. Allegorically speaking, communal modernists trapped themselves in the double bind of Milton's *Paradise Lost* and Proust's *Temps perdu:* they viewed art history as if it were a sort of paradise in which one could establish tenancy. This is understandable, considering that any museum of fine arts is—in a way—a *kommunalka,* where artists from different epochs end up "living" together.

In the 1970s, finally, the infantile play of the "it" came to a close. Its ubiquity and dominance were not in doubt, yet no one wanted to get into details. Nevertheless, the fact that the "it" was an authoritarian Other

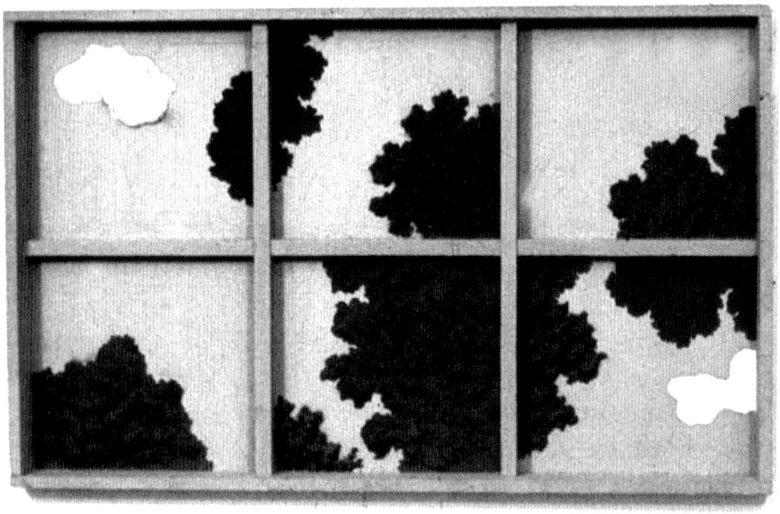

2.9
Ivan Chuikov, *Window IV,* 1974.

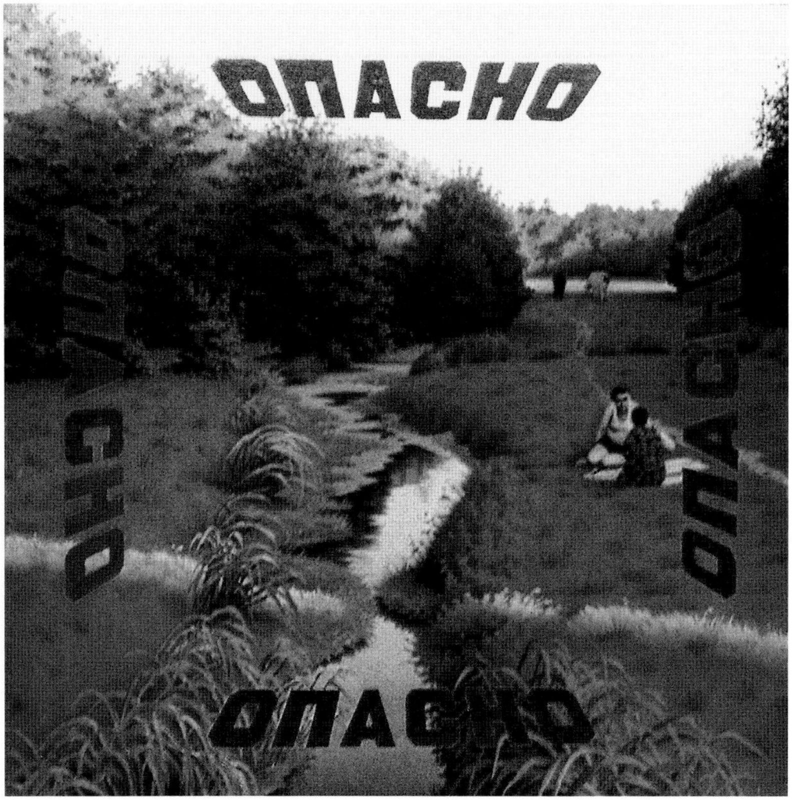

2.10
Erik Bulatov, *Dangerous,* 1972–1973.

whose language structured the communal unconscious attested to the necessity of studying the "it." In turn, the description of the authoritarian vocabulary—verbal or visual—was impossible without knowledge of the mechanisms of communal perception and communal communication through words or images. Moreover, without analysis and (in some cases) adaptation of the language of communality and the language of power (including artistic forms of adaptation and interaction with these languages), the chances of overcoming such languages were problematic.

Although Kabakov is the chief chronicler and challenger of the communal world order, it would be rash to suppose that his art is a punitive expedition or crusade against communality. There is a paradox in the fact that, being the destroyer of the Bastille of speech, he nevertheless did not cease to be its captive. His installations[29] can be interpreted as acoustic structures through which one may listen to the author's inner voice (which, in Bakhtin's opinion, acts as a surrogate of the unconscious). This "voice" is possessed by a passion for telling stories of an autobiographical nature, impersonating, through these narrations, legions of characters, populating a labyrinth of both personal and communal memory.

As an illustrator of children's books since the 1960s, Kabakov came to understand that this genre corresponded entirely with infantilism and the illustrational nature of the communal vision of the world. The devices and skills of illustrative drawing, probed and selected by Kabakov over ten years, proved acceptable for rereading in the context of a "grown-up" thematic. This discovery gave him a powerful stimulus to his evolution as a conceptual artist. Of course, to the informed reader this should appear as nothing other than a regular instance of the literariness proper to the Russian artistic tradition as such. However, one should not submit to the temptation of synopsizing (referring) communal-speech vision into the social realism of the Peredvizhniki (popular in the second part of the nineteenth century) or of socialist realism, the imagery of which corresponds either to the slogans of prerevolutionary egalitarianism or to the "mythical speech" of Stalinist culture. In contrast to both of these, the language of the communal apartment is based on psycholinguistics differing in kind.

In 1971, Kabakov started working on a series of albums with the title *Ten Characters;* these related the lives of various dwellers in a building partitioned into overcrowded communal apartments (fig. 2.11). Having ten heroes endows the author's imagination with a number of optical advantages (similar to the ones described by Leibniz in his *Monadology*). One of them is a variability of perspectives. The "monadic" optic makes it possible to cover the full spectrum of relational clichés, speech acts, and behavioral stereotypes, which sketch out an existential profile of

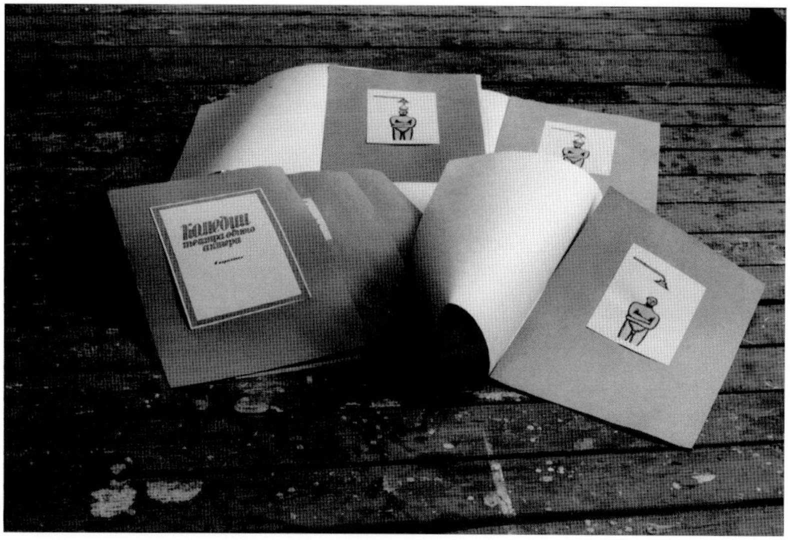

2.11
Pages from Ilya Kabakov's album *Shower, a Comedy,* late 1960s–early 1970s, displayed on the floor of his studio, Moscow, 1988. Photo Igor' Makarevich.

communality. In Kabakov's albums, the author himself is the eleventh character, possessed with the passion to tell stories of an autobiographical nature; the other ten are the artist's imaginary neighbors residing in the communal apartment of his memory and fantasy. It is interesting that the camouflaging of the authorial "I" behind a screen of characters became, thanks to Kabakov, Komar and Melamid, and also to Pivovarov, a phenomenon rather typical for Moscow communal conceptualism (fig. 2.12).[30]

▪▪

The term "sots art" was coined in 1972 by Komar and Melamid, who share responsibility with Kabakov, Bulatov, Pivovarov, and Chuikov for the initiation of Soviet ("communal") postmodernism. Sots art can be characterized by its striving toward a break with the familiar tradition of recontextualizing visual clichés of the early Russian avant-garde or Western modernism. In their search for a "new false identity," the choice fell to socialist realism—a gesture "of posing the problem of the status of the discourse which borrows from a heritage the resources necessary for the deconstruction of that heritage itself."[31]

In Komar and Melamid's conceptual project *A Circle, a Square, a Triangle—For Every Home, for Every Family* (1975), the artists construct a parallel between the Platonic eternal ideas "linked *a priori* to nothing" and the ideology of socialist realism, which—regardless of the fact that it operates with "sensible objects"—also dwells on nothing (fig. 2.13). The latter is an eidetic dimension of both conceptual and official art, their anonymous referent, hidden under the layers of myths, personages, slogans, and other representations of the transient and the relative. This eidetic dimension, according to "the famous artists of the beginning of the 1970s,"[32] is always vacant for communication (home delivery) of codes of status and authority, whose speech character is also commented upon in the 1975 work titled *The Essence of Truth (Grinding Pravda).*[33]

In winter 1976, Komar and Melamid became the first alternative artists to have a comprehensive exhibition at Ronald Feldman Fine Arts (New York). Titled "Color Is a Mighty Power," it allowed American viewers to familiarize themselves with Komar and Melamid's concept of sots art. Several years later, following their emigration from the USSR in 1977, these artists in 1981 announced their new version of sots art, which they termed "nostalgic socialist realism." Alongside a deconstruction, that is, "overturning and displacing the conceptual order"[34] of Stalinist art, "nostalgic socialist realism" renewed (on a postmodern level, of course) the search for "lost fatherhood" undertaken by Shteinberg and Nussberg in the 1960s.

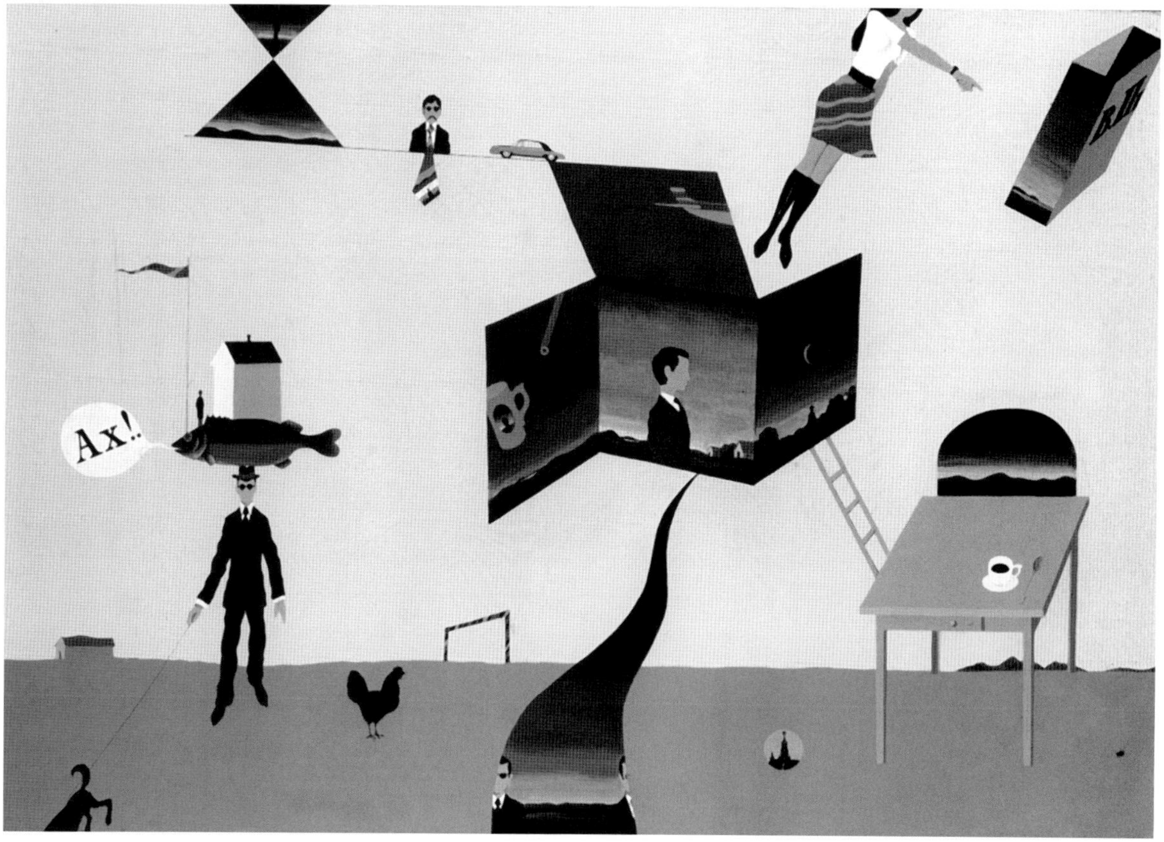

2.12
Viktor Pivovarov, *Ah!*, 1971.

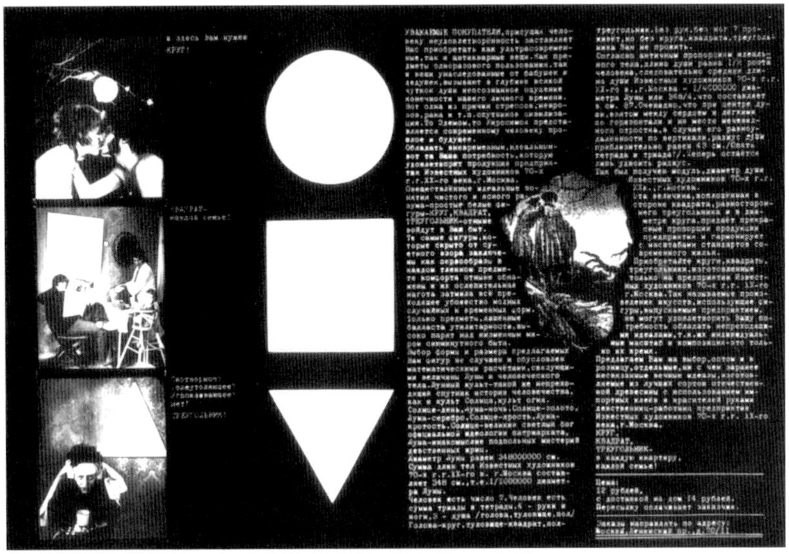

2.13
Vitaly Komar and Aleksandr Melamid,
A Circle, a Square, a Triangle, 1975.

Although borrowing phrases from the "verbarium" of an extracommunal "it" is characteristic of Bulatov's work, his approach differs from Komar and Melamid's sots art in that, from his point of view, the extracommunal "it" is not exhausted by "mythical speech" alone, but entails the presence of an ontological horizon. The specific character of his reading of the socialist realist representational canon lies in the discrediting of the ontological ambitions of authoritarian speech (e.g., its claim to the status of Ur-text). This takes place not in a fit of destructive fervor, as is sometimes the case with Komar and Melamid, but rather with the aim of sweeping away obstacles on the "path to truth." In Husserl's philosophy this sort of sweeping away is identified with the procedure of "bracketing" (the phenomenological *epoché*). In this connection, Bulatov's method may be termed phenomenological sots art.

Until the mid-1980s, Bulatov's visual inventory consisted of a limited number of textbook images: charming countrysides, cityscapes, blue skies, clouds, etc. These were culturally and ideologically processed clichés, indistinguishable from the familiar socialist realist representations, with the only difference being that they were no longer affirmative. Such transformations were due to the intrusion of words into pictorial space, a clash of the titans responsible for turning positively anxious images into negatively anxious pictures. In the end, anxiety—regardless of its role reversal—remained intact, as if reaffirming itself as an unalienable part of the Russian cultural tradition—visual or literary. One wonders whether the creator of *Dangerous* (1972–1973), *Caution* (1973), *and Glory to the Communist Party* (1975) was aware of yet another danger—the "condition of spectacle," which anxious pictures often epitomize or contribute to.

Apparently, all the aforementioned paradigms of deconstruction have suffered from one-sidedness. Whereas Kabakov, in his attempt to place the heritage of the ghetto-centric utopia under erasure, has never directly challenged the ambitions of the powers that be, sots art aimed at the subversion of the state's "mythical speech," but took a rather tolerant position toward the "speech-vision" of the communal.[35] The same is true of many conceptual artists from Kabakov's circle.[36]

Sots art is sometimes spoken of as a variety of pop art,[37] even though the latter was in large measure a reaction to the $14 billion that the United States government spent to create a "middle class" in the postwar years. I am referring to the G.I. Bill passed by Congress in 1944, which gave low-interest loans or subsidies to citizens who had been directly or indirectly involved in military action. Many members of the lower classes were able to receive a college education, as well as loans that enabled them to acquire comfortable homes. The growth of the middle class led to growth in the production of consumer goods, the sale of which required effective advertising. It was in this period that mass euphoria about material goods and high living standards reached its peak. A new round of consumer fetishism engendered new aesthetic clichés. The aesthetic of the elite gave way to the aesthetic of the middle class, with its interest in practical and convenient household items, inexpensive automobiles, kitchen sets, home design, clothes, and furniture. Great numbers of artists worked in advertising. Some of them were able to maintain an ironic distance from what they had to produce, while (nevertheless) retaining the external signs of fascination with such material. Andy Warhol was one of them.

Unlike pop art, socialist realism advertised political ideology rather than consumer products, even though narratives that pass off wishful thinking as reality are an essential ingredient of political and commercial rhetoric alike. If one forgets about the specificity of the product being advertised and considers solely the sphere of its representation, at this level sots artists can indeed be confused with pop artists. However, this is certainly not true of everyone. Just like pop art, sots art exhibited a fair amount of variety.

In fact, when Aleksandr Kosolapov showed his first experiments with ideological material to Komar and Melamid in 1973, he was surprised to hear them respond, "This is no sort of Sots art, but American consumer stuff." In Kosolapov's work *Study, Sonny* (1975), an assiduous schoolboy and a policeman who encourages him are depersonified to the level of comic book heroes or advertisement panels. From 1972 to 1975, along with appropriations of political iconography, Kosolapov produced pop objects in the spirit of Claes Oldenburg: padlocks sewn of rags, a hand pressing a doorbell button, and yogurt being poured into a glass (all executed in wood). Kosolapov's contribution to sots art lies in his discovery of points of resemblance between the mechanisms of depersonalization that Soviet power applied with regard to communality and those that are still used by capitalists with the aim of controlling the mass of consumers (fig. 2.14).

Leonid Sokov's sculptural baggage from the 1970s includes *Threatening Finger* (1975), a mobile which moves as if giving a warning (fig. 2.15), and *Project to Construct Glasses for Every Soviet Citizen* (1976), a painted wood sculpture that pays tribute (in a mock-heroic way) to viewing the world through red stars. Sokov wanted to connect sots art with folkloric thematics. In his sculptural compositions, executed in the genre of political *skazka* (fairy tale), the protagonists of socialist realist myth become crude toys, characters in medieval marketplace dramas, or heroes in a pulp novel bestiary. In one work, Stalin has a bear's paw and beastly claws, Khrushchev turns into a "weeble,"[38] and Andropov's ears start to move.[39] Like many of

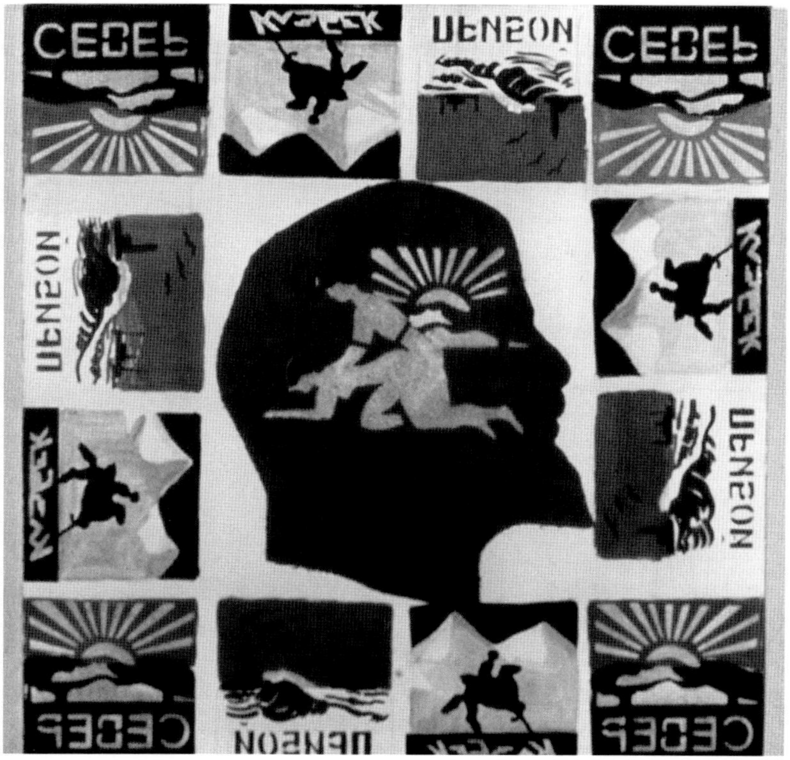

2.14
Aleksandr Kosolapov, from the series
North, 1974.

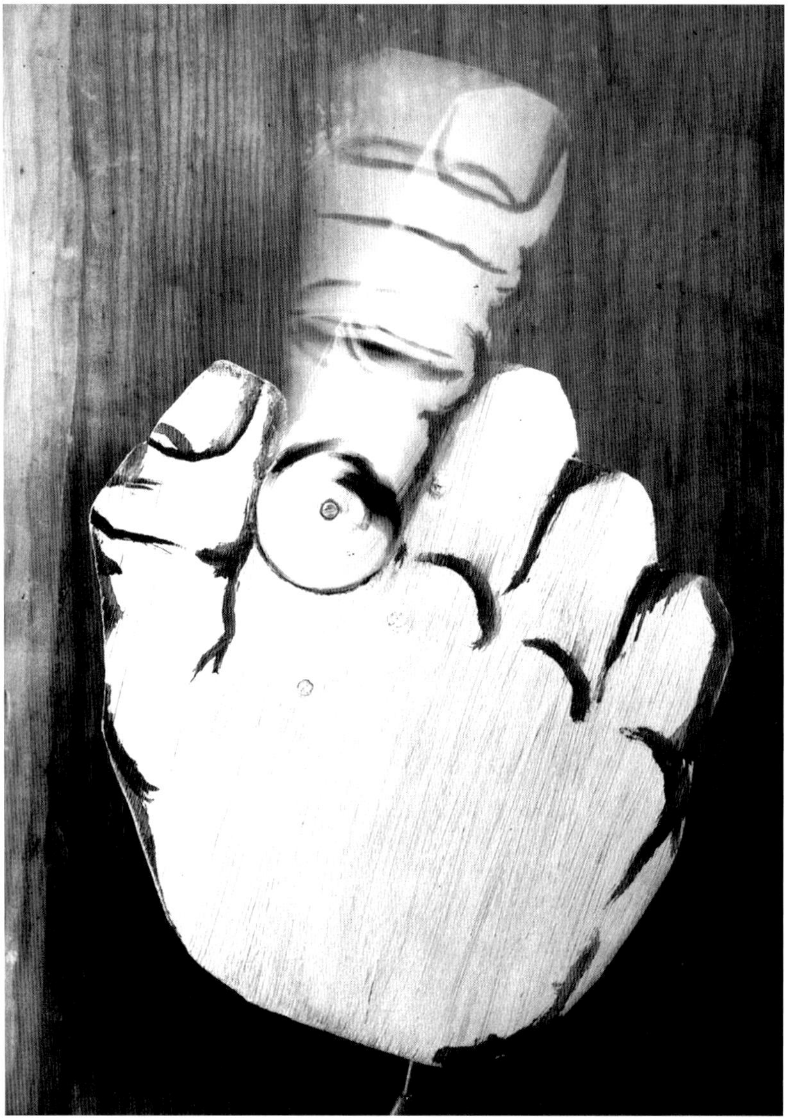

2.15
Leonid Sokov, *Threatening Finger*, 1974.

Sokov's works, this one takes up a tradition of popular humor and suggests that the version of sots art he favors derives from the heart of the "urban peasantry," from the depths of communality.

In the *Luriki* series (1971–1985), Boris Mikhailov appropriated the old-fashioned technique of making hand-colored prints, a skill he learned while working as a retoucher of family photographs. Snatched from communal debris or found in a garbage heap, these black-and-white pictures were not intended for public view. Thanks, however, to Mikhailov's intervention, they were made public. By coloring the faces of his "faceless" compatriots, the photographer added the zest of artificial festivity peculiar to the socialist realist palette. This brings to mind Kumar and Melamid's first piece of sots art, where the two artists decided to paint a portrait of Melamid's father in the bombastic style of Soviet visual propaganda. Unlike *Luriki,* which dwells on private memories, Mikhailov's *Sots Art* series (1975–1985) deals with "unauthorized" recollections of public events:[40] jubilant demonstrations, law-abiding citizens at the voting booth, military training routines, and so forth (fig. 2.16). There are also paired representations. For example, in one picture two young tennis players pose near a river with their racquets stretched high like the hammer and sickle in Vera Mukhina's *The Worker and the Female Collective Farmer.* In the second snapshot the same couple is shown playing tennis. The photographs look as if they could have been featured in the mass-circulated media, provided they had earned the approval of the authorities. The author's plot reveals itself in the metaphor of "bringing justice" back to politically loyal and "well-behaved" narratives bastardized by the "Great Myth." By toning and hand-coloring these slightly anemic prints, Mikhailov reenergizes them to the degree that they become (almost) acceptable to the mainstream of state mythology. Another aspect of Mikhailov's *Sots Art* series is that it functions as a meet commentary in regard to socialist realist praxes.

Sots art culminated in an exhibition in New York at the New Museum of Contemporary Art, organized by Margarita Tupitsyn in 1986 (fig. 2.17). The show included works by Komar and Melamid, Sokov, Bulatov, Kosolapov, Leonid Lamm, and the Kazimir Passion performance group (Aleksandr Driuchin, Kosolapov, Vladimir Urban, and Victor Tupitsyn) (fig. 2.18).[41] That this movement continued to agonize until the end of the 1980s is evidenced by Dmitrii Aleksandrovich Prigov's newspaper installations or the sculptures of Grisha Bruskin (fig. 2.19). From 1986 to 1988, Gorokhovskii, who earlier had been known for his semiconceptual silk screens, created a series of post–sots art paintings, including a divisionist portrait of Stalin in which each of the 2,488 elements of color ("strokes") prove to be, upon closer examination, a stenciled image of Lenin.

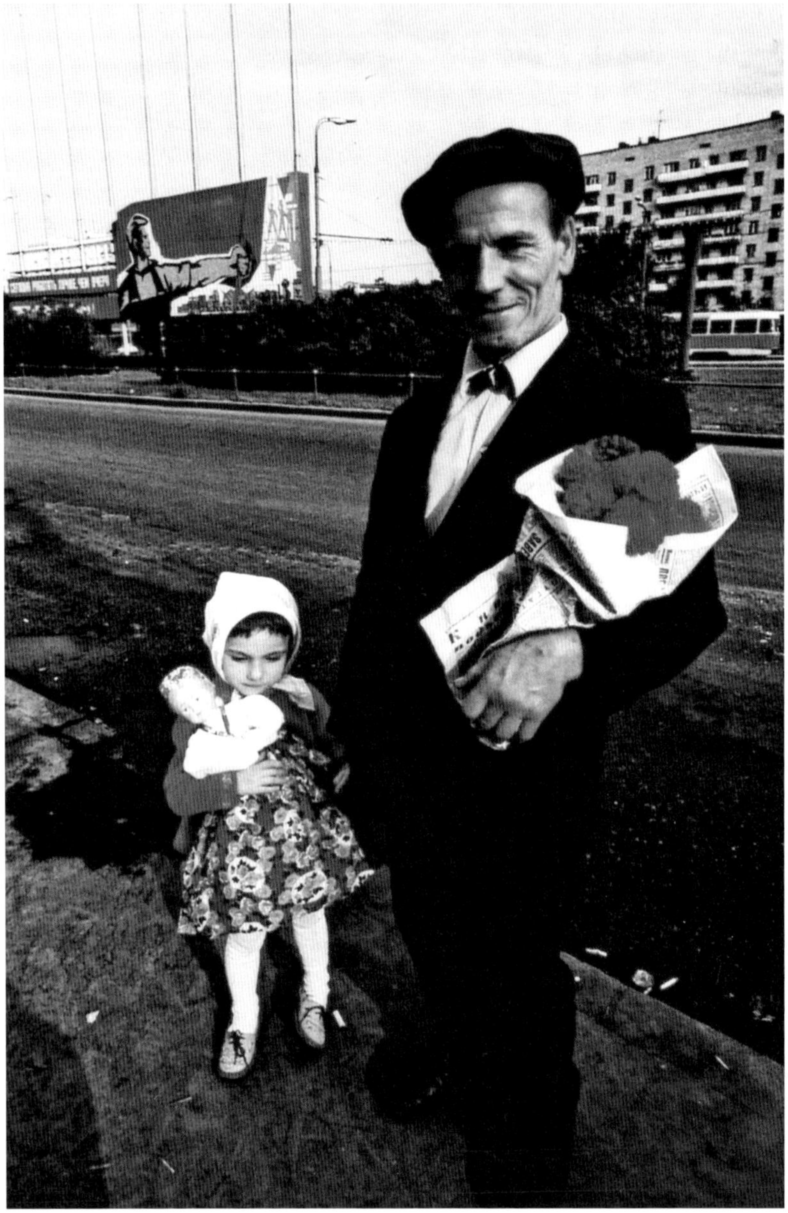

2.16
Boris Mikhailov, from the series *Red*, 1970s.

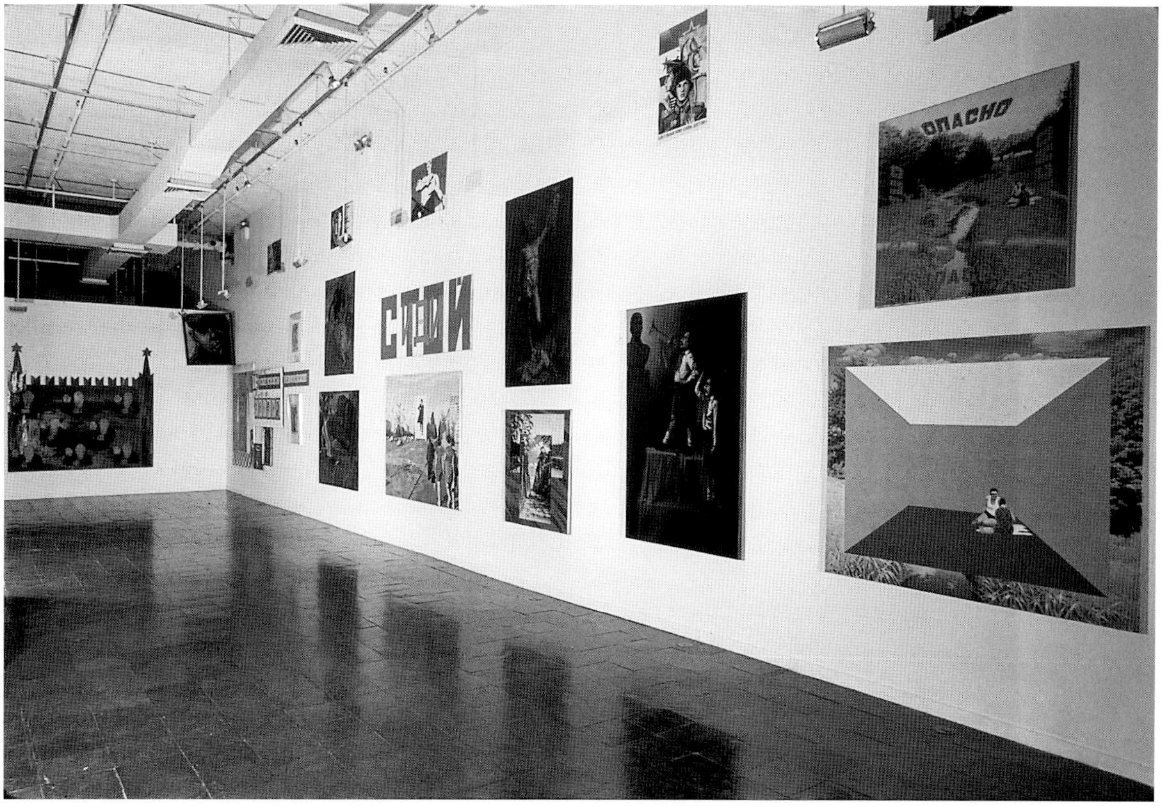

2.17
Installation view, "Sots Art,"
New Museum of Contemporary Art,
New York, 1986.

Andrei Monastyrsky and the Collective Actions group (CA), which formed in 1976, are linked with the concept of "trips outside the city."[42] Many representatives of the alternative art world were involved in numerous actions that resulted from these trips over the years, some as viewers, some as participants. Among the key group members, along with Monastyrsky, were artists Nikita Alekseev, Nikolai Panitkov, Georgii Kizeval'ter, Igor' Makarevich, and Elena Elagina, and philologists Sergei Romashko and Sabina Haensgen. These artists' search for a common alternative to both the language of communality and the language of power resulted in their escape from the urban environment. Staged outdoors, their performances greatly contributed to the formation of an alternative artistic milieu in Moscow. They demonstrated rather effectively that "contractual" (i.e., noninstitutional) aesthetic activity can be a unifying factor as well as a pastime for a number of individuals. The group's adherence to the so-called factographic discourse has been underscored repeatedly by the use of *photography* and *verbal* (tape-recorded) documentation. To fully appreciate the impact of the CA group's performances on the Moscow alternative art world, it is useful to cite Ilya Kabakov's recollection of those events. "From the moment I got on the train" (all viewers had to take a train to some country site to see the action), admits Kabakov, "my goals, the questions and affairs that constantly preoccupied me, my fears of myself and others, were all, as it were, taken away from me. The most remarkable thing, however, was that those who led us had no goals either! And, of course, there is something else: for the first time in my life, I was among 'my own'; we had our own world, parallel to the real one, and this world had been created and compressed by the CA group until it had achieved complete materiality, or, one might say, tangibility—if this notion is at all applicable to something absolutely ethereal and elusive."[43]

Monastyrsky and the CA group are discussed in more detail in chapter 3. I shall limit myself here to quoting from Monastyrsky's own description of CA's performance *For G. Kizeval'ter (The Slogan—1980)*, which took place on April 13, 1980 (fig. 2.20):

> Kizeval'ter, our group member in Iakutiia, receives a parcel from us containing a package with an accompanying letter. The letter tells Kizeval'ter that he has to go off to an isolated place out of town—to a field surrounded by forest, and it must be a pretty desolate place. Obviously, he has to take the package with him so as to open it there, in the middle of the field and completely alone. He'll find a ready-made slogan in the package, except that the surface of the slogan (where the caption is) is covered with a black cloth. This black cloth is attached to the

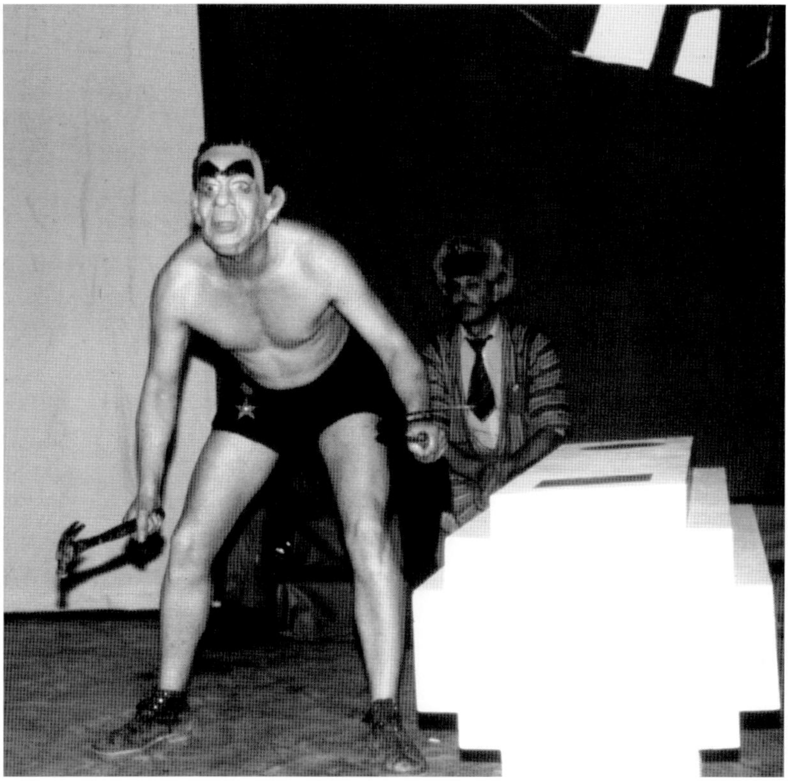

2.18
Kazimir Passion group, *The 28th Party Congress of the Union of Soviet Socialist Republics*, performance, The Kitchen, New York, November 7, 1982.

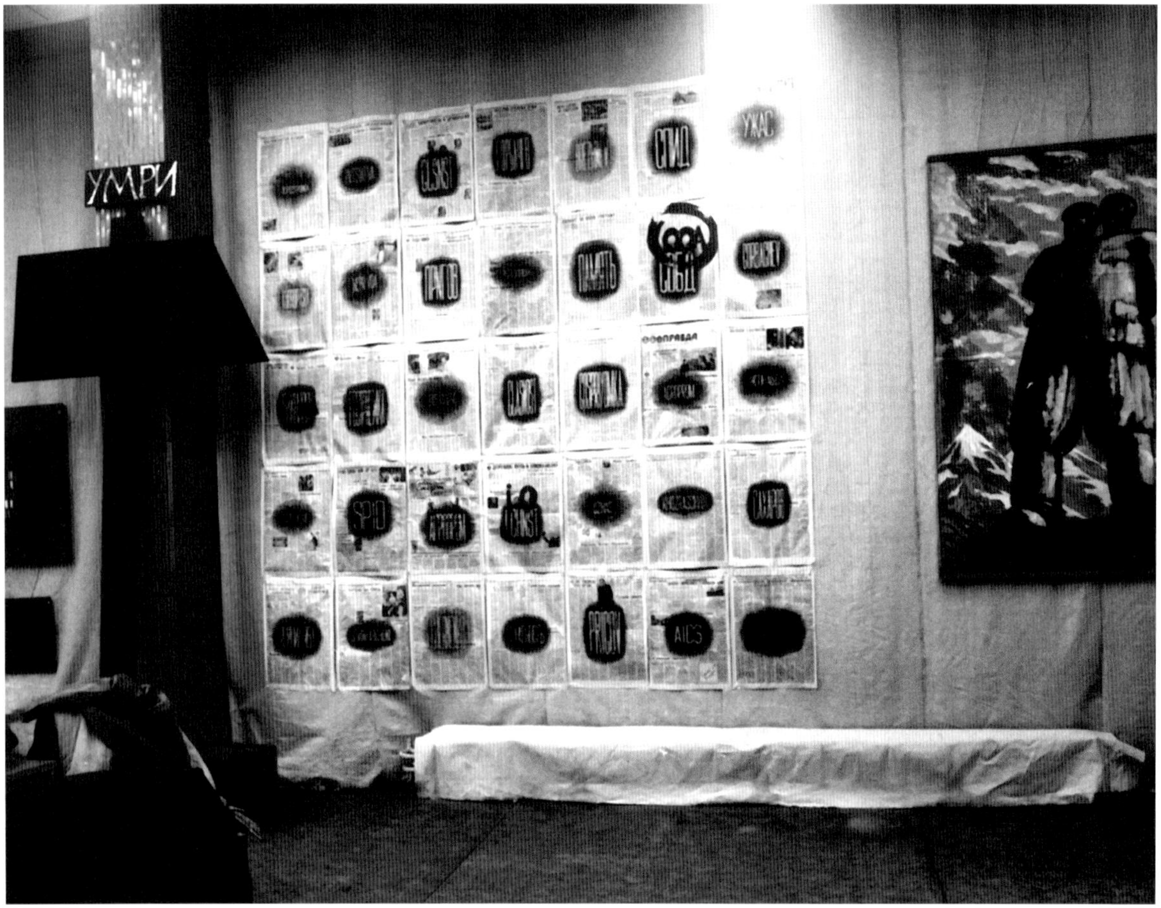

2.19
Installation view, "Perspectives of Conceptualism," Moscow, 1989. Left: work by Andrei Filippov; right: work by Dmitrii Prigov.

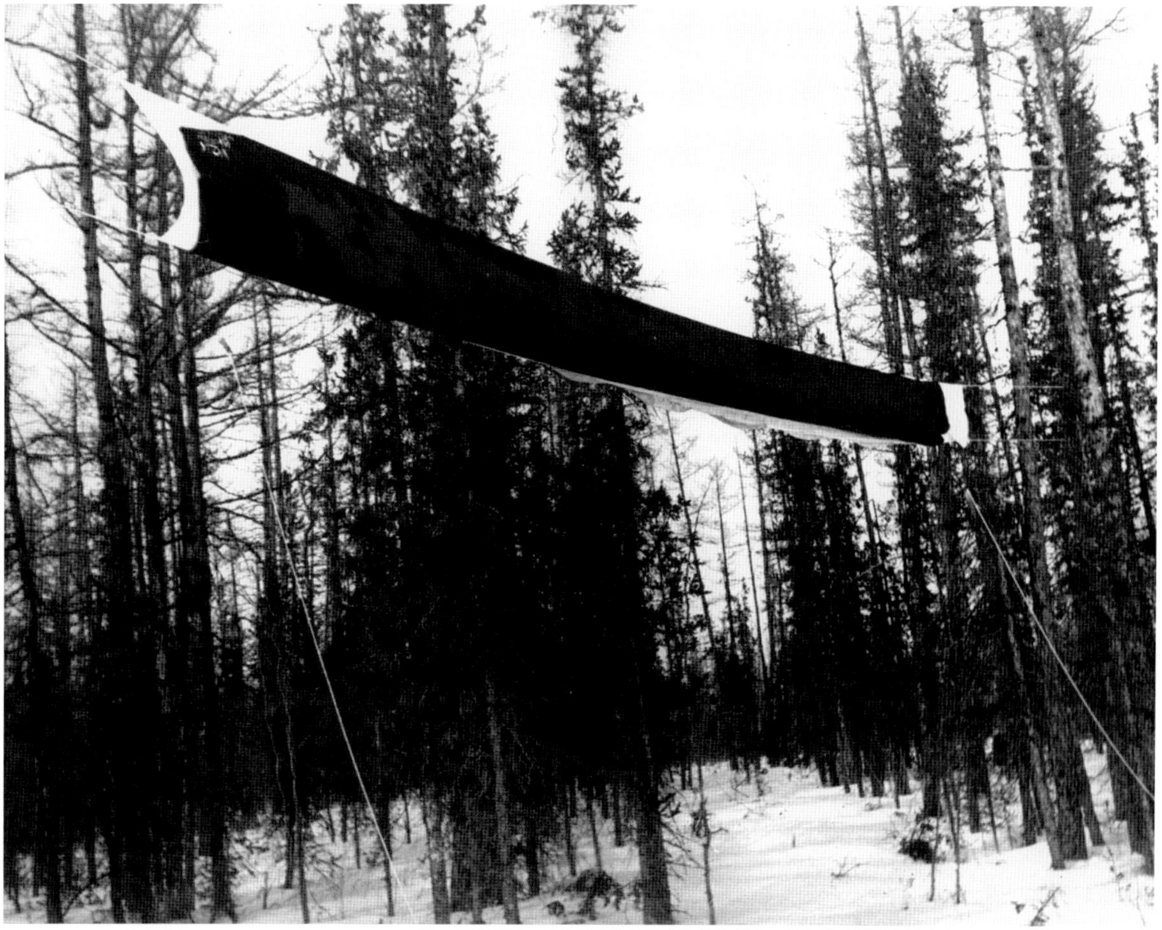

2.20
Collective Actions group, *For G. Kizeval'ter (The Slogan—1980)*, April 13, 1980.

> entire length of the slogan by two strings, top and bottom. The top string, which is on the left, is 70 meters long, the bottom string, on the right, is also 70 meters long. Kizeval'ter will also find instructions in the package telling him what to do: that he must hang up the slogan between two trees, facing the field and still uncovered, he mustn't remove the black cloth at any cost. He must then thread the top string behind the tree to the left of the slogan and do the same with the bottom string on the right tree; he must take hold of both ends and walk off into the field as far as the strings allow. After proceeding 70 meters from the slogan, he must face the slogan and first pull the bottom string towards him (it will stretch taut and loosen the bottom edge of the black cloth). He'll then have to pull the top string whereupon the black cloth will fall to reveal the caption on the slogan. But the whole point is that the caption will be visible, but it will be impossible to make it out (because of the distance). And here is the most important: the instructions will tell him that under no circumstances must he approach the slogan to try to read it. He must simply photograph it from where he is, turn round and go away, never to return. So the result must be a powerful psychological struggle with oneself . . . That's the general idea of this project. Still, what will be written on the slogan? A descriptive text: "In winter, on the edge of a field where he couldn't make out a thing, Kizeval'ter hung up a white, 10 x 1 meter sheet with a caption in red letters."[44]

▪▪

Several shows, which took place at the beginning of the 1970s, are of particular importance: the kineticists' exhibition in the Artist's House on Kuznetskii Most (1973); and—in the same year—Komar and Melamid's installation and performance entitled *Paradise* in a private apartment in Kolomenskoe (fig. 2.21). But the culmination of the exhibition activity of the 1960s and 1970s was the so-called "Bulldozer Show." On September 1, 1974, two weeks prior to the show, my wife Margarita and I were visited by Nemukhin, Masterkova, Evgenii Rukhin, and Rabin, who let us in on their plan to organize an outdoor exhibition. In their opinion, the empty lot alongside our house seemed the most suitable place for this type of event. In accordance with their plan, our apartment on Ostrovitianov Street (in Beliaevo) would become a repository for works to be exhibited, and also a place for the artists to sleep the day before the show so that they might avoid arrest on the way to the lot. Naturally, we had no objections, and everything went forward as planned, with one important exception.

In contrast to the primarily oral confrontations of the Manezh era, the show in the empty field on September 15 resulted in serious physical reprisals by the authorities, who used bulldozers, fire trucks, and policemen in civilian clothes (figs. 2.22, 2.23). Many of the works on display were destroyed or confiscated, while the artists and their sympathizers were

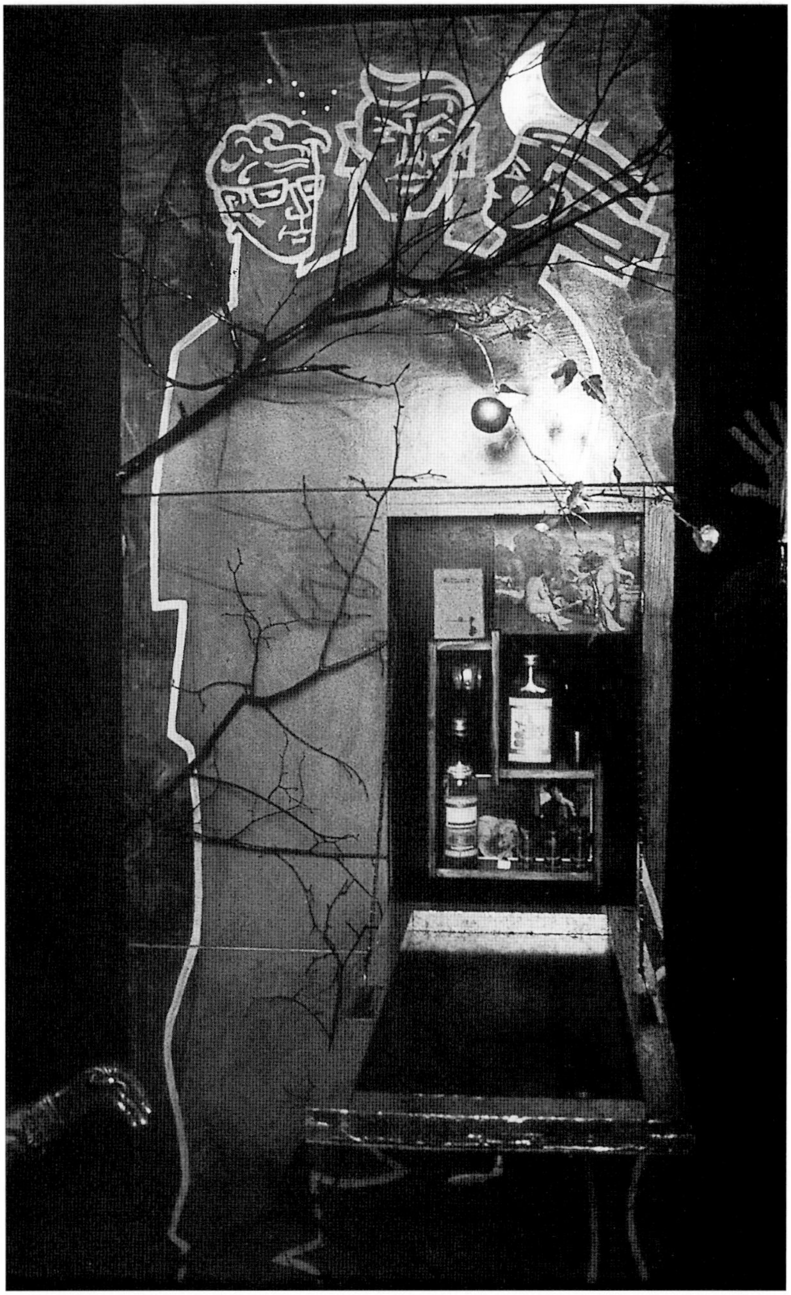

2.21
Vitaly Komar and Aleksandr Melamid, detail from the installation *Paradise*, private apartment, Moscow, 1973.

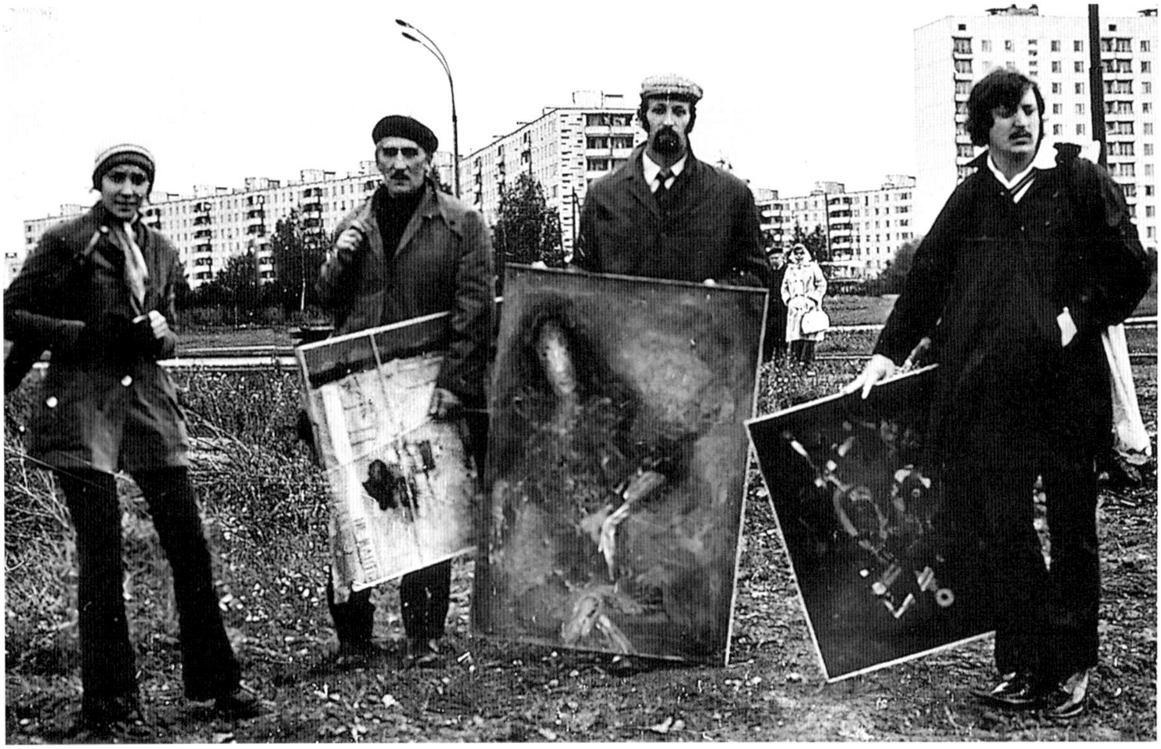

2.22
View of the "Bulldozer Show," Moscow, September 15, 1974. Left to right: Margarita Tupitsyn, Vladimir Nemukhin, Victor Tupitsyn, Sergei Bordachev. Photo Vladimir Sychev.

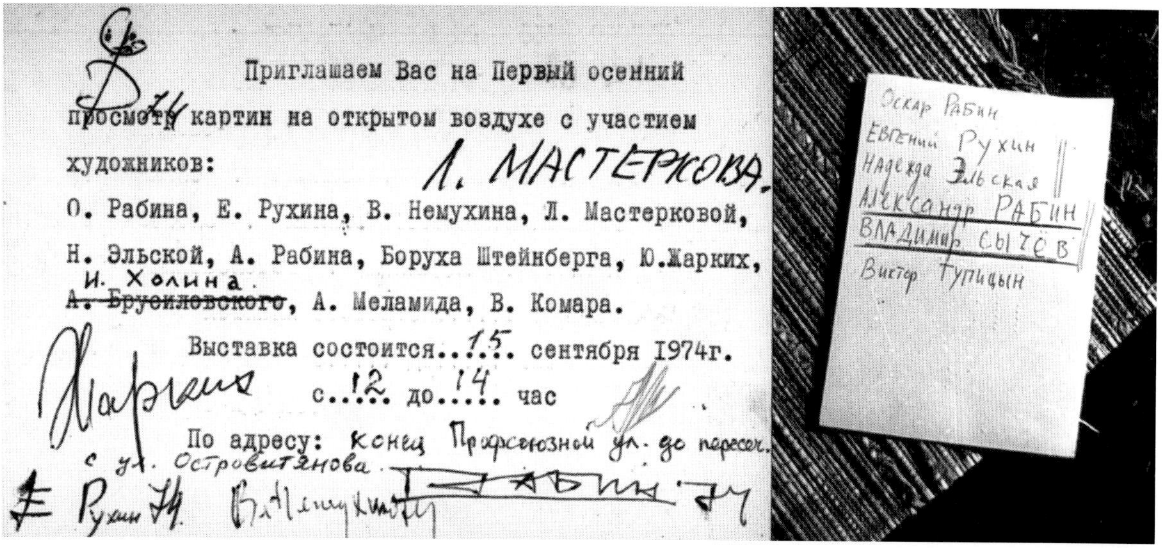

Приглашаем Вас на Первый осенний
просмотр картин на открытом воздухе с участием
художников: Л. Мастеркова.
О. Рабина, Е. Рухина, В. Немухина, Л. Мастерковой,
Н. Эльской, А. Рабина, Боруха Штейнберга, Ю.Жарких,
И. Холина
~~А. Брусиловского~~, А. Меламида, В. Комара.

Выставка состоится 15 сентября 1974г.
с 12 до 14 час

По адресу: конец Профсоюзной ул. до пересеч. с ул. Островитянова.

Оскар Рабин
Евгений Рухин
Надежда Эльская
Александр Рабин
Владимир Сычёв
Виктор Тупицын

2.23
Invitation to the "Bulldozer Show" and a note listing the arrested participants.

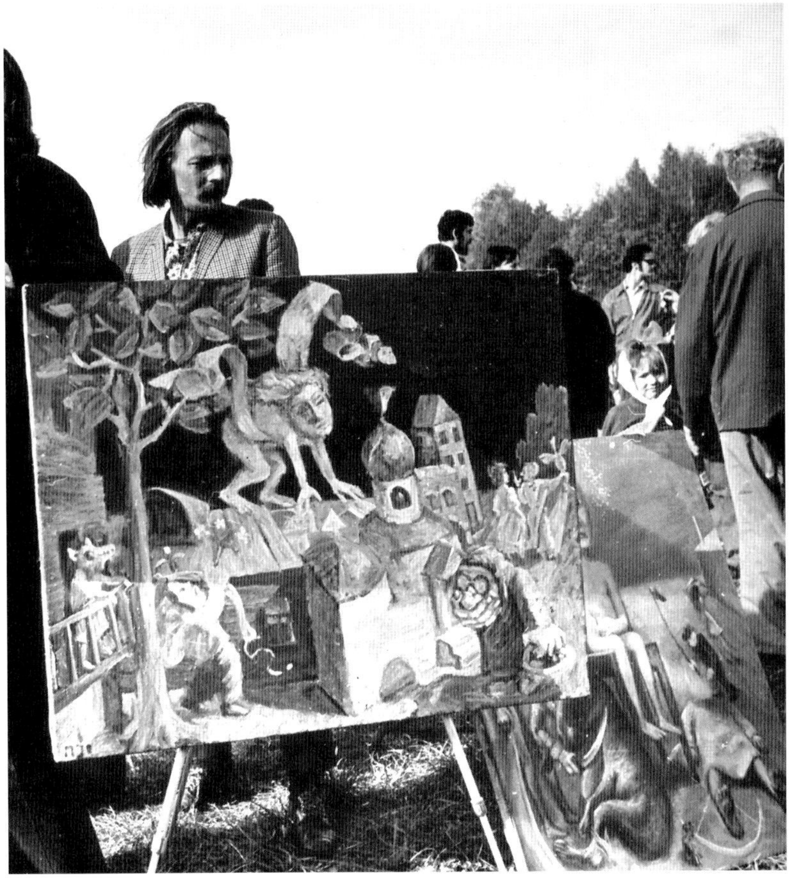

2.24
View of the exhibition at Izmailovskii Park with Vladimir Piatnitskii showing his paintings, September 29, 1974.

beaten, arrested, or subjected to administrative sanctions. The "Bulldozer" event, fraught with violations of the Helsinki Accords on Human Rights, seriously damaged the already dubious reputation of the Soviet government in the West.

A desire on the part of the party bureaucracy to set its image aright in the eyes of "world society" led to the organization of a second outdoor exhibition two weeks after the first one. Although this event was, in essence, foisted upon the artists by the government, the intensity of the negotiations and compromises connected with it had no precedent in the history of relations between unofficial culture and officialdom. In the fourteen-day period following the "Bulldozer Show," during which time its participants were subjected to unceasing pressure from the authorities, Rabin's organizational talents manifested themselves. He demonstrated not only an enviable sangfroid, but also a thorough knowledge of the Soviet system. However, his authoritarian inclinations were no less in evidence. Whenever a decision needed to be made, it was always articulated by Rabin. As I recall, only Nemukhin and I ever dared contradict him—and even then, not on the essential points but more to create the atmosphere of a democratic forum. In one such instance, Rabin declared that since I was not an artist, I did not have the right to cast a decisive vote. And he immediately put the issue to a vote. As a result, the possibility of a different opinion was nipped in the bud. None of this diminishes Rabin's merit. Like him, we are all products of a Soviet upbringing, in the sense that each of us is able to express himself or herself in either a communal way or an authoritarian one. This duality is difficult to overcome even for those who, like me, have lived abroad for many years.

However, Rabin's strategy was completely vindicated: the strong of this world made concessions, and an officially sanctioned "unofficial" exhibition took place on September 29, 1974, in Izmailovskii Park (fig. 2.24). No provisions were made for censorship, and no limitations on the number of participants were imposed. As for viewers, the four-hour exhibition broke all attendance records.

The events described above forced the party leadership to reconsider its interrelations with the artistic intelligentsia. A decision was reached to do away with unsolicited and uncensored art, but by peaceful means. To this end, the artists were quite literally "shoved" into official creative organizations, one of which turned out to be the Gorkom (Grafikov), otherwise known as MOGKh (the Moscow Joint Committee of Graphic Artists). An alternative to this type of job placement was enforcement of the law on "parasitism," and therefore few of the "venerable" unofficial artists were able to avoid recruitment into MOGKh.

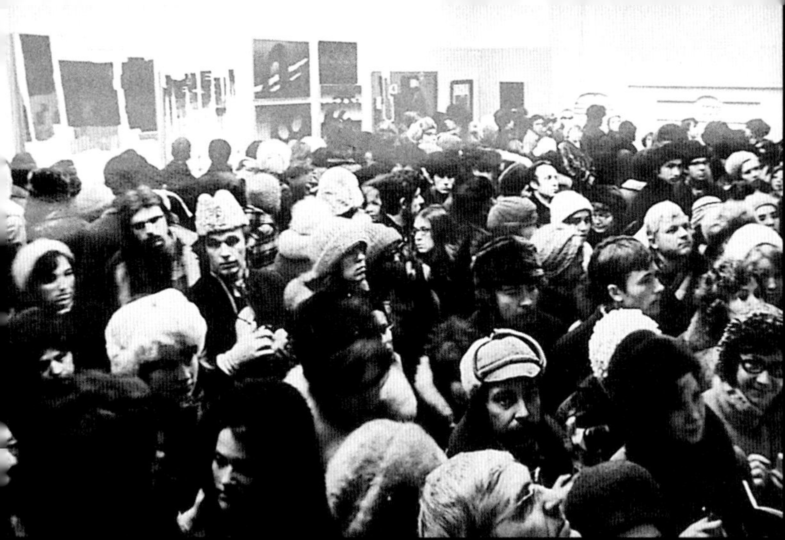

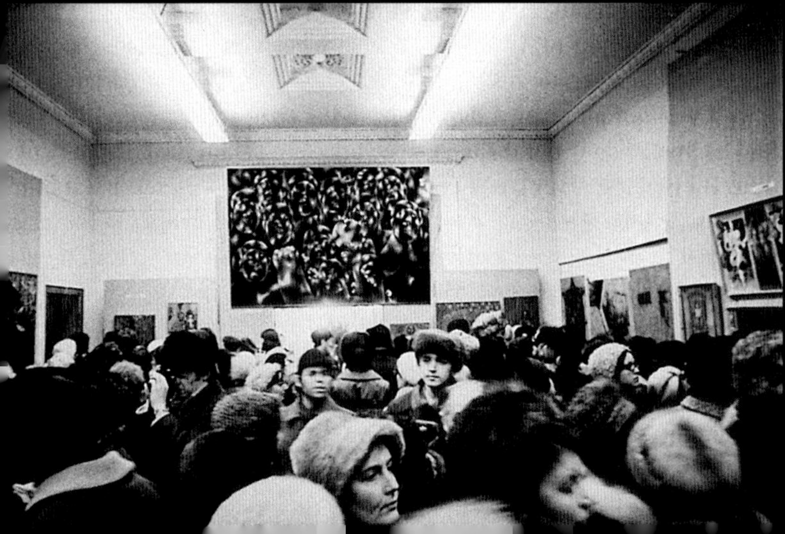

Besides the liquidation of unofficial art as a social phenomenon, the authorities also envisioned the establishment of control over alternative artists by means of the Gorkom and other similar institutions. In brief, the extracommunal "it" in due time set about institutionalizing "contractual" corporality. The next permitted exhibition under the aegis of Gorkom took place at the VDNKh's Beekeeping Pavilion in February 1975 (fig. 2.25).[45] A group show in the MOSKh Exhibition Hall on Kuznetskii Most in May 1976 can be listed along with other examples of the successful assimilation of communal modernism within the framework of official institutions. One should not, however, consider the cultural politics of the Soviet authorities one hundred percent effective. As Foucault has written, "There exists no concrete, fixed place which is the seat of rebellions, just as there is not a single formula of revolution. There are various points where all this arises, and various forms of resistance."[46]

The validity of this observation is supported by the unceasing apartment and studio shows at the end of the 1970s. Among them, a 1976 exhibition in Sokov's studio became a noteworthy event. Along with Sokov, artists of different generations including Chuikov, Igor' Shelkovskii, and the Gerlovins took part in the show. Rimma Gerlovina was represented there by her "cubelets" (fig. 2.26). Externally reminiscent of Petr Miturich's *Graphic Dictionary* of 1919 (fig. 2.27),[47] these cubes, on closer inspection, turned out to be agents of speech: on their faces (both from the outside and inside) could be read fragments of communal conversations in the spirit of Kabakov or the poet Lev Rubinshtein. Rephrasing an old definition of socialist realism, we may say that these art objects were modernist in form and communal in content. Valerii Gerlovin's metallic structures (like, for example, *Spermatozoid*) were put together from modules used by children in edifying play. The painted reliefs of Shelkovskii also made a strong impression; they skillfully managed to transfer divisionist technique from painting to sculpture. After emigrating to Paris, Shelkovskii put out—between the end of 1979 and the mid-1980s—seven issues of the art magazine *A-Ya,* which played a significant role in familiarizing Soviet and Western audiences with the history of alternative art.

Emigration from the USSR began in the early 1970s. Within ten years, the list of Soviet artists who emigrated included forty-five to fifty names.[48] Rabin's 1978 trip outside the country resulted in his expulsion: a decree from the president of the Supreme Soviet of the USSR deprived him of his Soviet citizenship.[49] As a result, he and his wife, artist Valentina Kropivnitskaia, received political asylum in France.

After moving to the West, many of these artists experienced the shock of dual "orphanhood" prompted by the simultaneous loss of both their

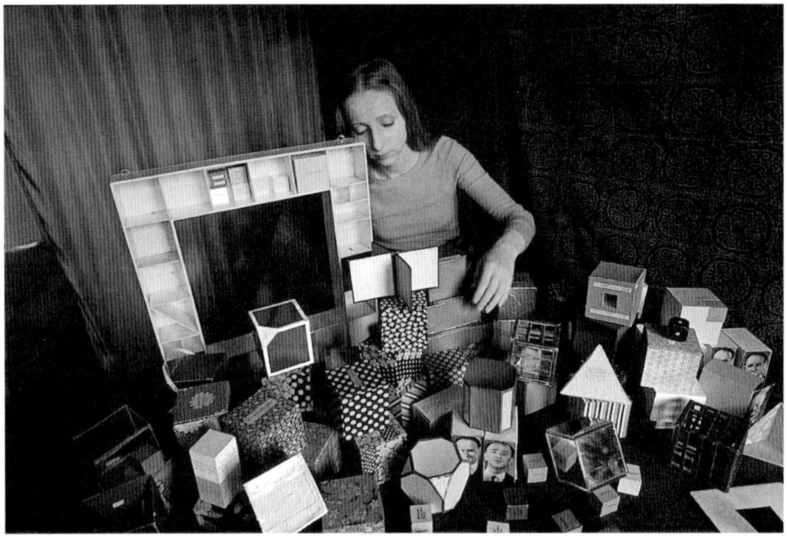

2.26
Rimma Gerlovina, *Cubes*,
1975–1976.

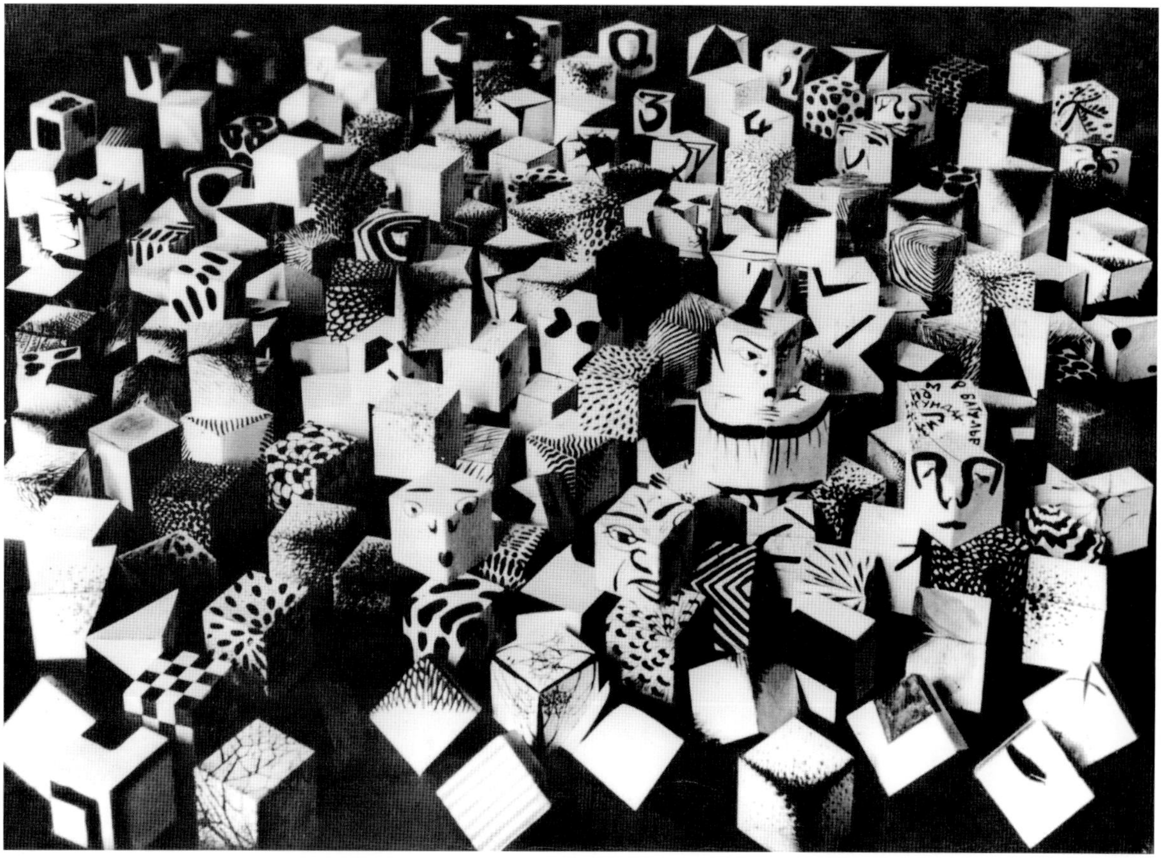

2.27
Petr Miturich, *Graphic Dictionary*, 1919.

2.28
Nest group, *Let's Become One Metre Closer*, 1976.

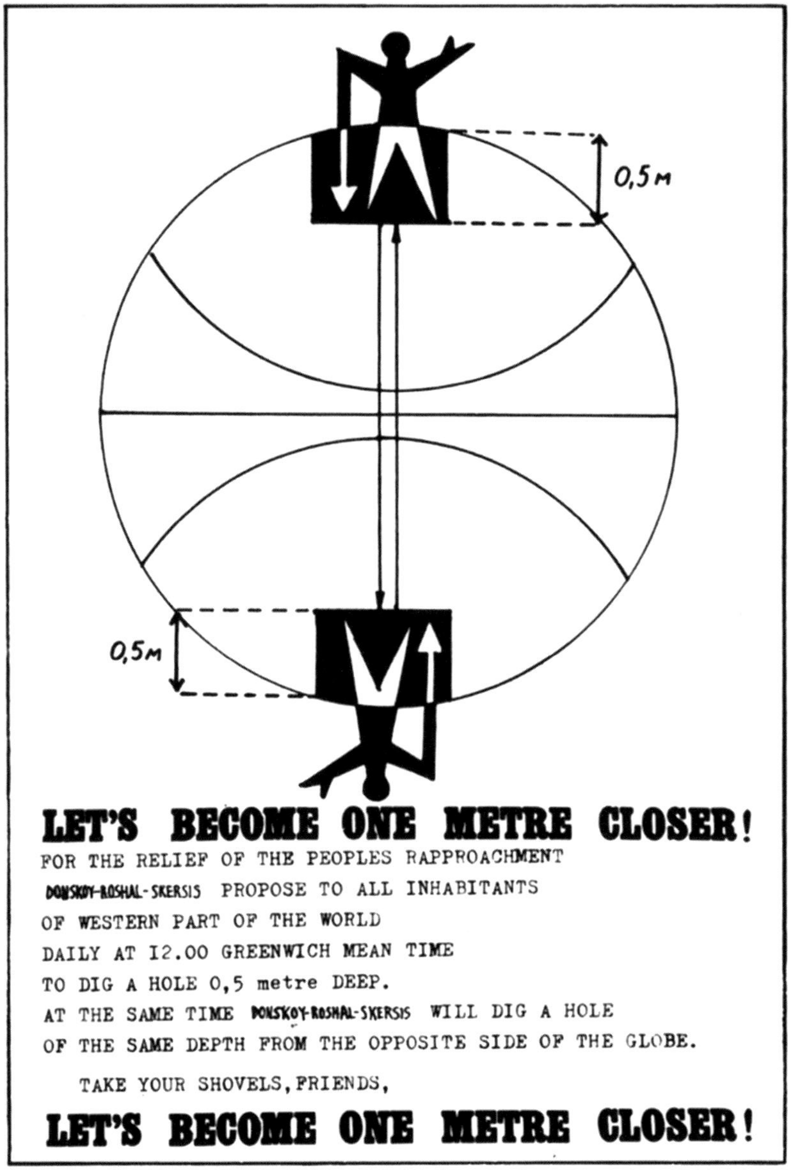

parental languages: the "paternal" (authoritarian speech) and the "maternal" (communal speech).[50] This psycholinguistic drama was sharply coexperienced by those who remained in the homeland. Correspondence and information exchanges reached an incredible incandescence in the 1970s and early 1980s,[51] which to a significant degree set aright the image of the West in the eyes of the Soviet intelligentsia. A performance by the Nest group (Gennadii Donskoi, Mikhail Roshal', and Viktor Skersis) titled *Let's Become One Metre Closer* (1976) may be considered a reaction to these circumstances (fig. 2.28), as might Makarevich's conceptual project *Traveling Gallery of Russian Artists*, in which the author asked emigrating artists for their fingerprints, which were then blown up and put on display, becoming a symbol of a sociocultural identity in the process of being lost.

4. THE 1980S

In 1979, the Mukhomor (Toadstools) group was started in Moscow. It consisted of recent art college graduates—Sven Gundlakh, Sergei and Vladimir Mironenko, Konstantin Zvezdochetov, and Aleksis Kamenskii. In the beginning, they were influenced by Monastyrsky, who described in a letter one of their early performances (fig. 2.29):

> The Mukhomors recently conducted the action *Pour.* The action was staged by dividing an empty room with a screen of white paper. The viewers took their seats, not knowing that the Mukhomors were on the other side, adjacent to the bathroom. Then the Mukhomors began to slowly cut openings in the screen—first with a razor and then with a needle. After that, they poured water through the slits and rips, and dropped pieces of paper and small objects through them. Simultaneously, while this was taking place, the water in the shower, which was on the same side as the Mukhomors, was turned on. Then, from their side, they projected a slide with the image of a seascape on the screen, and after a while, they began to cut the part of the screen where the slide was reflected so that the seascape would be projected directly onto the audience. Through the opening in the screen, one could see a table—it was obscured by the light from the projector and therefore looked like an altar. This table was littered with Pepsi-Cola bottles, dirty ashtrays, cigarettes butts, etc.—that is, no unique or distinct objects, but merely those which are used on a daily basis. At that point, the audience was invited into the bathroom where they saw that the faucet had been turned on, leaving the water running. Each audience member was presented with a jar labeled "containing this water." Afterwards, several boxes were made from the pieces of the screen and handed to the viewers. The entire performance was accompanied by a tape recording of different sounds like mooing, burping, huffing and puffing, and random, unrelated words. The sounds had been recorded at noon, while the two Mukhomors had sonorously basked in

2.29
Mukhomor group, *Pour,* performance, July 7, 1981.

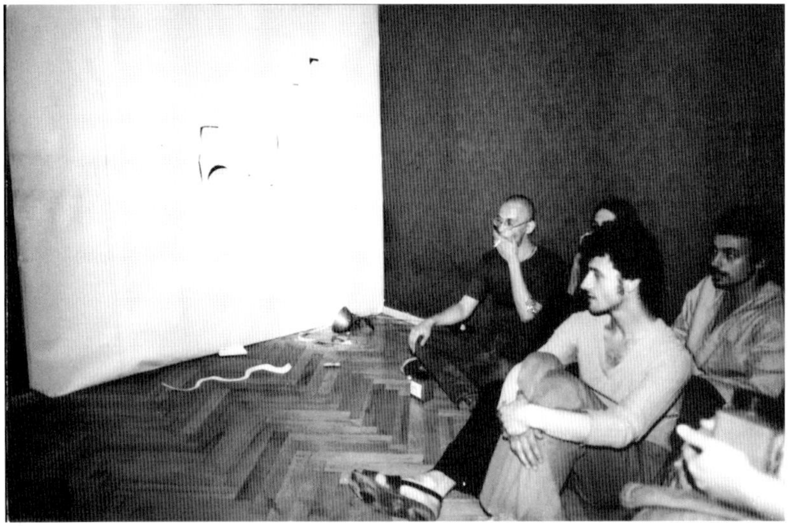

the heat. This mindless ocean was created on such a low key that it was pleasant to lose oneself in it.[52]

▪▪

In the 1980s, "contractual" communality ceased to be only a means of "subcultural survival" and became an object of aesthetic reflection as well. On this plane, apt art may be considered the most precise copy of its era. Apt art (a series of apartment shows as well as *plein air* exhibitions in and outside Moscow between 1982 and 1984) happened to be the next postmodernist strain which it made sense to speak of as a "movement." Although there had been apartment and studio shows previously, to exhibit under the aegis of apt art became a style and not simply a "grudging necessity,"[53] as it had been in the 1960s and 1970s. It also manifested a desire to reenact the *kommunalka,* but only as a playground instead of as a stage for "logical investigation."

Graffiti and a "Santa Claus aesthetics," together with a subversive appropriation of the accessories of the Soviet communal objecthood and an immeasurable carnival energy, were the baggage of this Soviet variety of the New Wave. Being an elemental rebellion against intellectualism, the new movement took on the same role that humor, in Kierkegaard's view, plays in relation to romantic irony. Apt artists did not share the eschatological anxiety of the communal modernists, the "fear of death" that, according to Kabakov, "shaped their consciousness." Having declared its "nonidentity within identity" (that is, its *otherness* within the alternative milieu as a whole), the new movement established its own neocommunal image by means of a "generational conflict." The best example is the photo series by Vadim Zakharov titled *I Have Made Enemies* (1982), in which the artist subjects the "patriarchy" of Moscow alternative art to what one may refer to as "kommunalnaia razborka" (the malicious dressing-down of one's neighbors in conversation). For instance, he confronts Bulatov with a slogan, stenciled on his palm, "Bulatov, you're bluffing. It is dangerous!" (fig. 2.30).

The first showing of apt art, called "Autumn Exhibition," opened in the Moscow apartment of Nikita Alekseev on October 20, 1982, and lasted for twelve days (fig. 2.31). Its participants included Monastyrsky, the Mukhomor group, Alekseev, Nataliia Abalakova, Anatolii Zhigalov, Zakharov, Skersis, Roshal', Sergei Anufriev, Kizeval'ter, Rubinshtein, and Nikolai Panitkov. In 1983 the artists organized two open-air exhibitions: "Apt Art en Plein Air" on May 29, and "Apt Art beyond the Fence" on September 25 (figs. 2.32, 2.33). In addition to all of the first apt art participants except Monastyrsky, these two included Iurii Al'bert, Iurii Leiderman, Larisa Rezun, Leonid Voitsekhov, and Andrei Filippov. At the same time as sots art was demythologizing the mythical speech

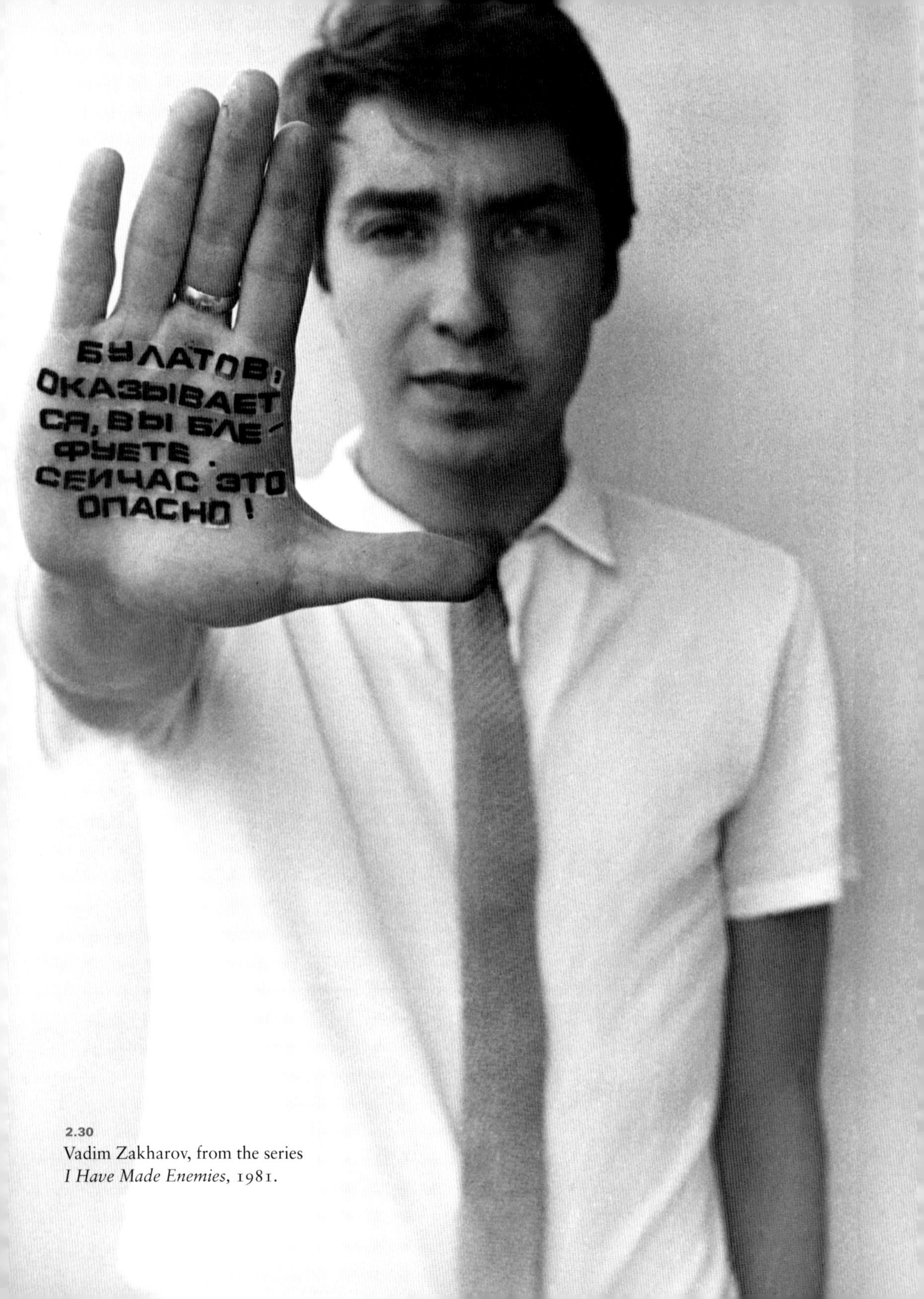

2.30
Vadim Zakharov, from the series
I Have Made Enemies, 1981.

of socialist realism, apt art was able to do the same thing in relation to the communal modernism of the 1960s and 1970s.[54] Moreover, the carnivalesque aspects of apt art hinted at the ability of its participants to acknowledge their communal heritage: unlike their predecessors—who lived and worked in denial of their communal psyche (i.e., in conflict with their communal sensibility)—the apt artists had finally come to terms with what (or who) they really were. The following excerpt from a 1987 conversation reveals their acceptance of communal speech as the *pharmakon* that provides the means to transfigure frustration into therapy and therapy into frustration:

> Zakharov: It is time to grow up, but instead, like before,
> we get together and yak ...
> Gundlakh: Yakking is our pastime ...
> Al'bert: That is what we are really good at, right?[55]

The authorities' assault on the "Apt Art Gallery" took place on February 18, 1983, and was violent. As Alekseev reported: "Early in the morning of that day, the employees of 'well-known' organization came with a search warrant and smashed the exhibition of Skersis and Zakharov, confiscated some of the works along with other materials.... From the employee's remarks it was clear that they tend to interpret all works if not as anti-Soviet then pornographic or both."[56]

Fortunately, the movement was able to escape disintegration, and was reborn under glasnost and perestroika. The so-called Kindergarten group,[57] which included Garik Vinogradov, Nikolai Filatov, and Andrei Roiter, together with the occupants of the Furmannyi Lane Studios, instigated a new phase of apt art activities, based on cooperation and mutual sympathy between young alternative artists (fig. 2.34). The youngest representatives of this coterie were Champions of the World (Guram Abramishvili, Boris Matrosov, Andrei Iakhnin, and Konstantin Latyshev)[58] (fig. 2.35) and the Medical Hermeneutics (Anufriev, Pavel Pepperstein, and Leiderman), who, in their texts, performances, and installations, relied on the strategy of "inspection"—an epistemological plot needed to detect and explore what they call "the Unknown" (fig. 2.36).

It is worth noting that the Furmannyi Lane Studios were situated in an abandoned building where there had earlier been a school for the blind, while the Kindergarten group was housed on premises where there had once been a kindergarten. These two facts, by some strange confluence of circumstances, bring together the psycholinguistic characteristics of communal corporality, its "blindness" (that is, the speech rather than visual

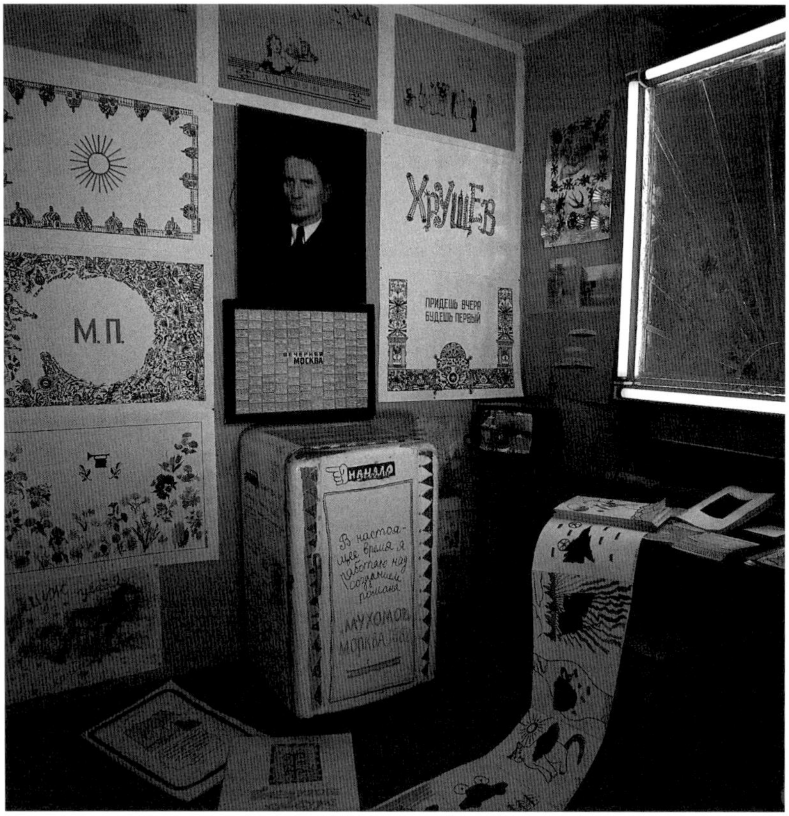

2.31

Installation view, first "Autumn Exhibition" of apt art, 1982.

character of its "vision") and its infantility. By 1990, the Furmannyi Lane Studios had ceased to exist, and their denizens migrated to the deserted communal apartments on Trekhprudnyi Lane. In the late 1980s, there were several important exhibitions involving members of these groups both in Russia and abroad (figs. 12.1, 2.37).[59] The first (and only) issue of the Russian edition of *Flash Art* appeared in 1989.[60] The exhibitions at the famous Sandunov steam baths (1988) and at the notorious Butyrskaia prison (1992) were the last echoes of communalism.

▪▪

I would also like to draw attention to the fates of some of those artists who emigrated from the USSR. As I have already noted, they were forced to experience the shock of dual orphanhood connected to the loss of that which structured their lives in their homeland, namely, the will to communality and the will to authoritarian power. Having turned up abroad, many tried at first to reproduce one or the other structure, cohering into communal bodies and simultaneously attempting to totally control (in the spirit of Soviet leaders) the process of the West's familiarization with the alternative "image" of Soviet culture. The publication of the journal *A-Ya* constitutes an exception to this rule: it was made possible for the most part by the resources of Moscow communal conceptualism. For instance, Bulatov's painting *Dangerous* was acquired by Norton Dodge in 1984, and this profit covered the publication of four issues of the journal.

The activities of Russian émigrés in New York reached their peak in 1981, when Dodge opened the Contemporary Russian Art Center of America (CRAC) at 599 Broadway in Soho. Margarita Tupitsyn became this institution's curator. In the two and a half years of its existence, the CRAC organized a number of important group exhibitions. These exhibitions attracted swarms of viewers and generated a significant number of reviews in the New York art press, as did the catalogues the CRAC published. As a result of the CRAC's efforts, the American public was able to receive a fuller understanding of both the Moscow communal modernism of the 1960s and 1970s and (more importantly) the Russian postmodernism of the 1980s. Following the loss of its home in Soho at the end of 1983, the CRAC's activities were reoriented: it began to sponsor Russian shows in other exhibition spaces. Of particular note are two sots art exhibitions in New York at the Semaphore Gallery in January 1984 and at The New Museum of Contemporary Art in April 1986 (fig. 2.17). In the latter show, apt art was displayed alongside sots art. Throughout the 1980s, a solid groundwork was laid for a theoretical discourse focusing on Russian art using various (at times, even conflicting) methodologies, such as critical theory (Frankfurt School) and the French poststructuralism of the 1960s

2.32

Installation view, "Apt Art en Plein Air," Kalistovo, 1983. Left: work by Iurii Al'bert; right: work by Konstantin Zvezdochetov.

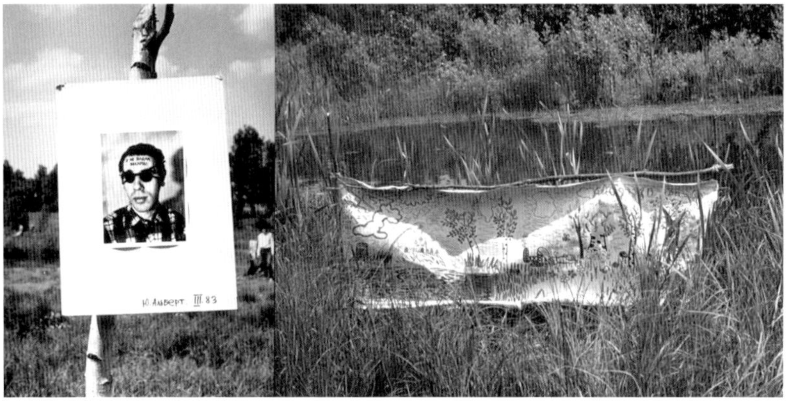

2.33

Installation view, "Apt Art beyond the Fence," 1983. Left: work by Andrei Filippov; right: work by Larisa Rezun-Zvezdochetova.

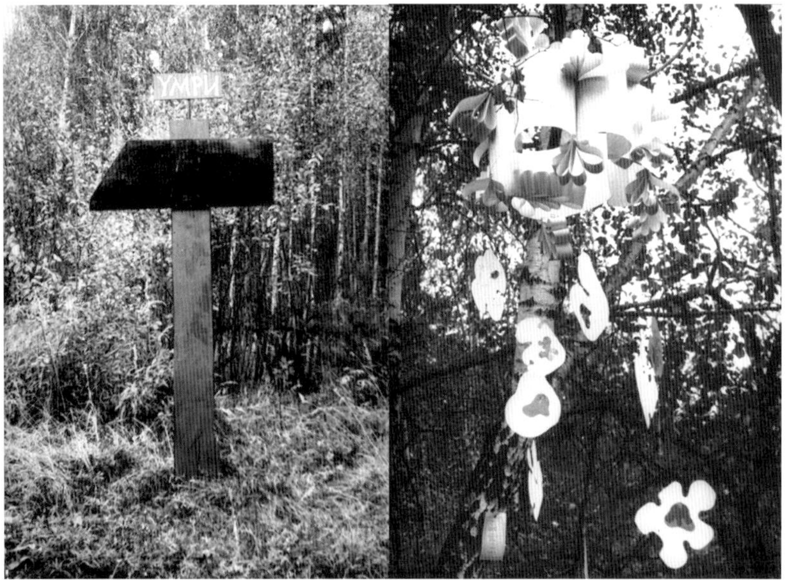

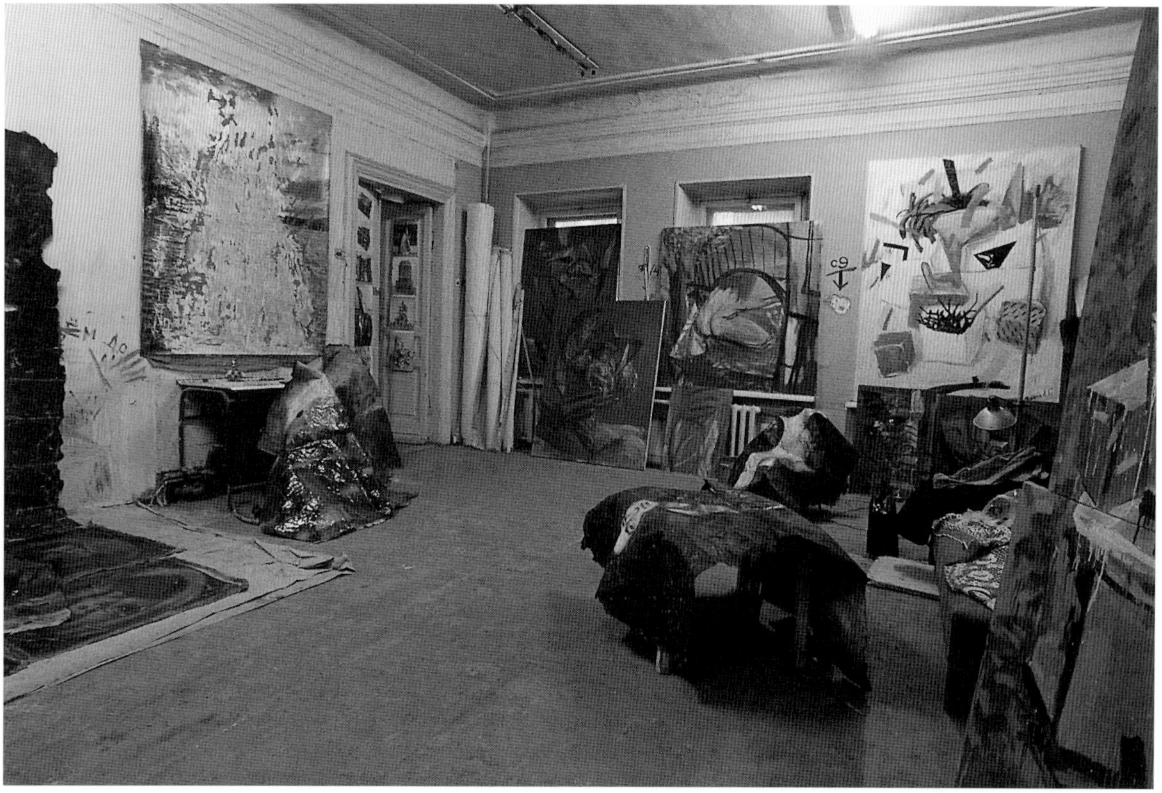

2.34
Installation view, exhibition of the Kindergarten group, Moscow, 1987.

and 1970s.[61] Alongside these exterior forms of reflection, there existed another, internal form of the apocryphal description of Soviet cultural ecology. This language was developed in the late 1970s and mid-1980s by Kabakov and Monastyrsky, who were joined at the end of the 1980s by Pepperstein, Anufriev, Leiderman, and Mikhail Ryklin. In Leningrad, the same role was played by the critics Olesia Turkina and Viktor Mazin.

I should say a few words about an event which took place in the heat of perestroika and which, to a significant degree, drew the Odyssey of the underground visual culture to a close. I am referring to the 1988 Sotheby's auction in Moscow, which brought to realization a successful sale of the works of Soviet alternative artists on their own territory. The triumph of hard (Western) currency over local ideology heralded not only an end to the "two-world" condition between the (neo)communal body of Moscow bohemia and the Soviet establishment, but also the beginning of the disintegration of both.

5. THE 1990S

The list of exhibitions organized in the 1990s both inside and outside Russia is overwhelming.[62] However, the "artistic image of history" was formed in those years on the basis of different expository principles, from the material of different events. Chief among them was the abolition of the USSR in 1991.

The year after, Anatolii Osmolovskii organized an "animalistic project" titled *Leopards Overrun the Temple* at the Regina Gallery in Moscow.[63] Following in Osmolovskii's footsteps, Oleg Kulik—in his 1992 "action" titled *Piglet Makes Gifts*—was the next to enter what Gilles Deleuze calls a "metaphoric relationship with animals."[64] In "Becoming-Animal," Deleuze writes that for "a child that was abandoned or lost . . . and even [for] many adults, . . . there is a reality of becoming-animal, even though one does not in reality become animal."[65] Given the chronic infantilism peculiar to the Soviet population in general and to communal (post)modernists in particular, it is reasonable to assume that in the beginning of the 1990s they were "abandoned and lost" as a result of the disappearance of authoritarian (parental) power, which—de facto—disappeared immediately after the first cue.[66]

On July 15, 1989, a performance by the Collective Actions group, *Tent Number 2*, took place in the Sokol'niki Park in Moscow. As usual, the longest portion of the production turned out to be the one-and-a-half-hour-long stroll in the direction of the place of the action. It was necessary for all of us, both viewers and participants, to walk at a considerable distance from one another until such time as we (in a manner similar to that

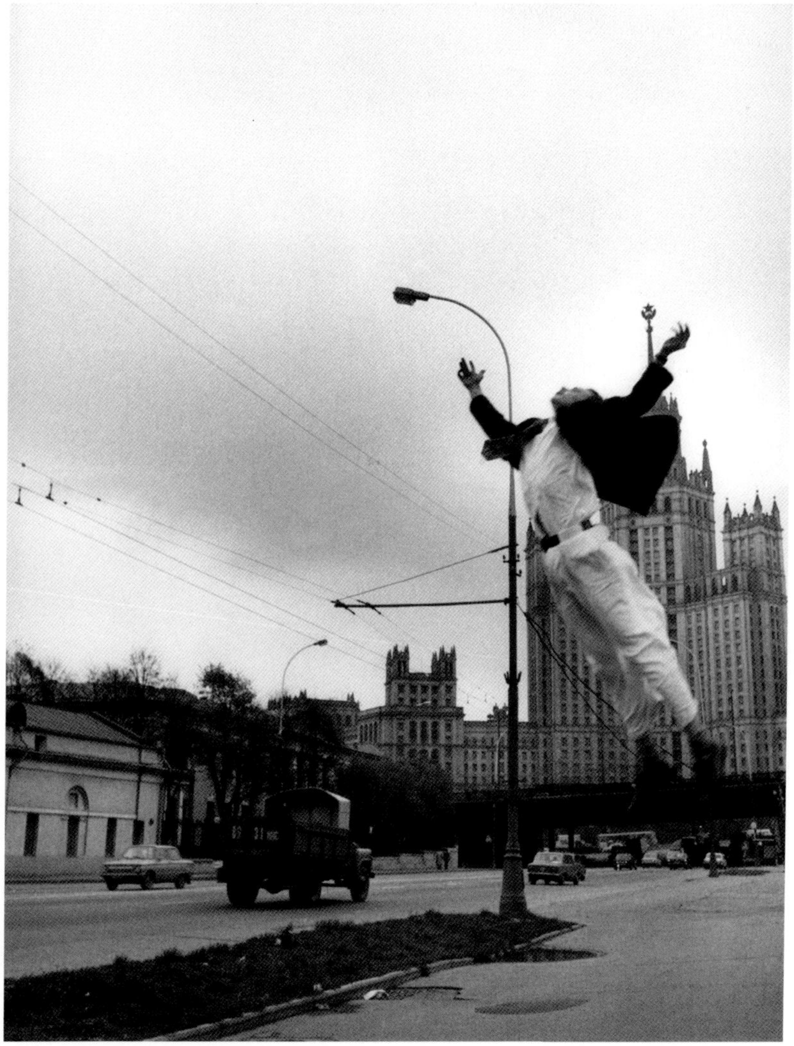

2.35
Champions of the World,
Miscalculations of an Immature Idea,
performance, September 26, 1988.
Photo Sergei Borisov.

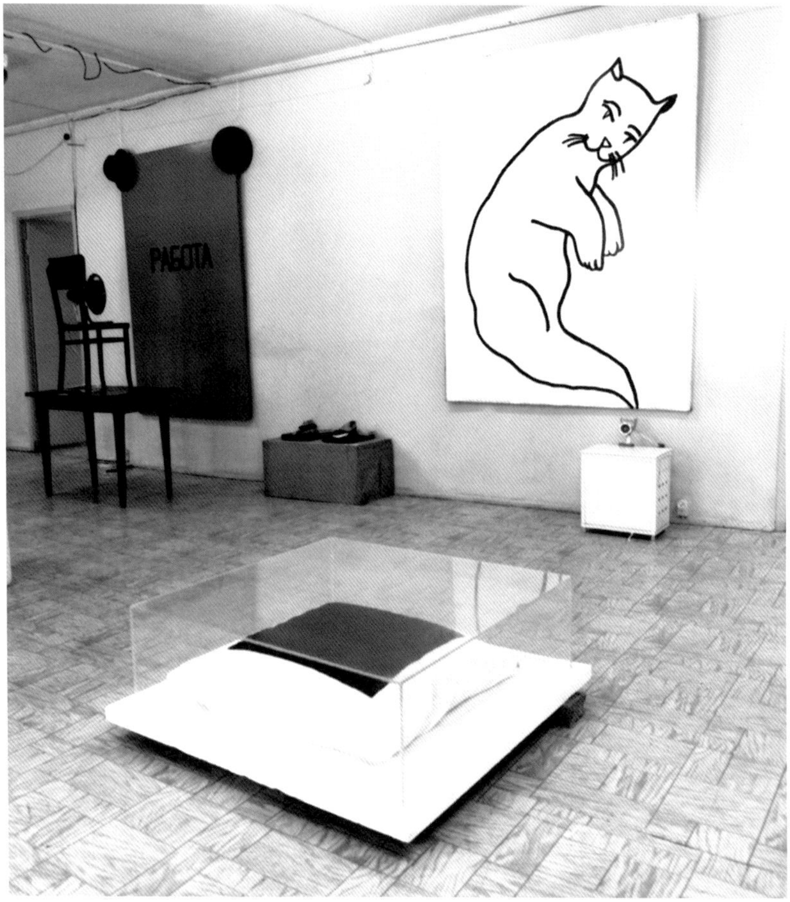

2.36
Installation view, "Perspectives of Conceptualism," Moscow, 1989. Against the wall: works by Medical Hermeneutics; foreground: Mariia Konstantinova's *MKKM (Black Square)*.

of Dante at the very beginning of the *Divine Comedy*) "found ourselves in the dark forest." While waiting there for futher instructions, one was able to witness a certain mysterious twinkling—in all probability about three hundred meters away. A half hour later, having received permission to move forward, we at long last approached the epicenter of the events, and discovered there a polyethylene tent, inside which a lantern burned, shedding light on the round space below it. In this arena, blinking with fires, two toy jeeps drove around, incessantly bumping into one another and giving off indistinct sounds. In American stores like Toys "R" Us or FAO Schwarz, the hallucinatory mise-en-scène described here would be perceived as an advertisement trick, aimed at imposing consumer fantasies and desires on an immature customer. In Sokol'niki Park, these children's fantasies and desires were transplanted into a principally different environment, filled with indifference and alienation. It was hard to believe that around this tent from who knows where and this arena in the round there extended the familiar, entirely ordinary darkness and these rather inconspicuous trees. Something that might be defined as the incompatibility between *hereness* and *thereness* was felt with an incredible sharpness.

It seemed as if the border between the East and the West lay directly before us. The miniature arena identified itself with the gap between fiction and reality, and the Westernized Muscovite counterculture—with two blind jeeps, selflessly transmitting (in an unfamiliar language) a message addressed to no one. "The ecstasy of miscommunication," as Jean Baudrillard might have said. "In a zone of nondifferentiation,"[67] Monastyrsky would add. It is no accident that the direct sum of these two statements has a chance of becoming the best definition of "communal (post)modernism."

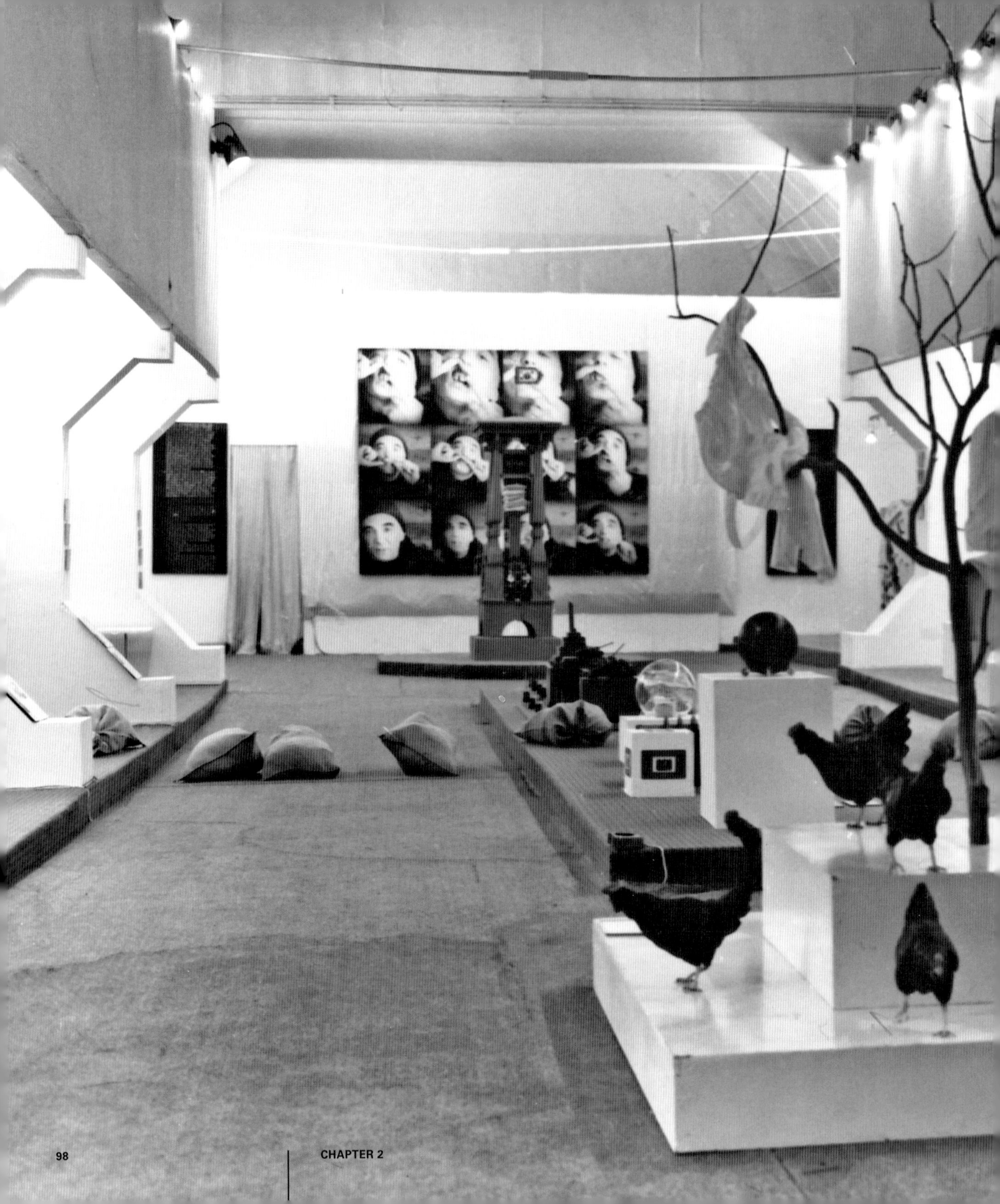

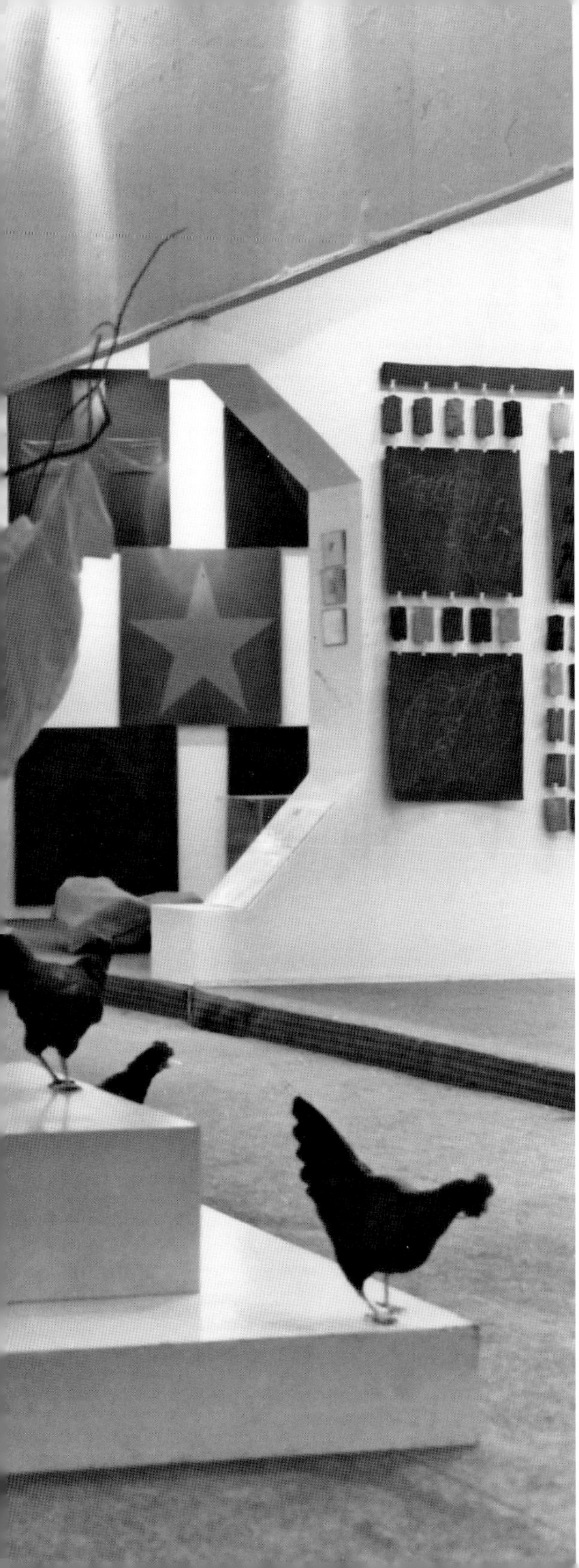

2.37
Installation view, "Schizo-China: Hallucination in Power," Moscow, 1990. Foreground: installation by Nikolai Panitkov.

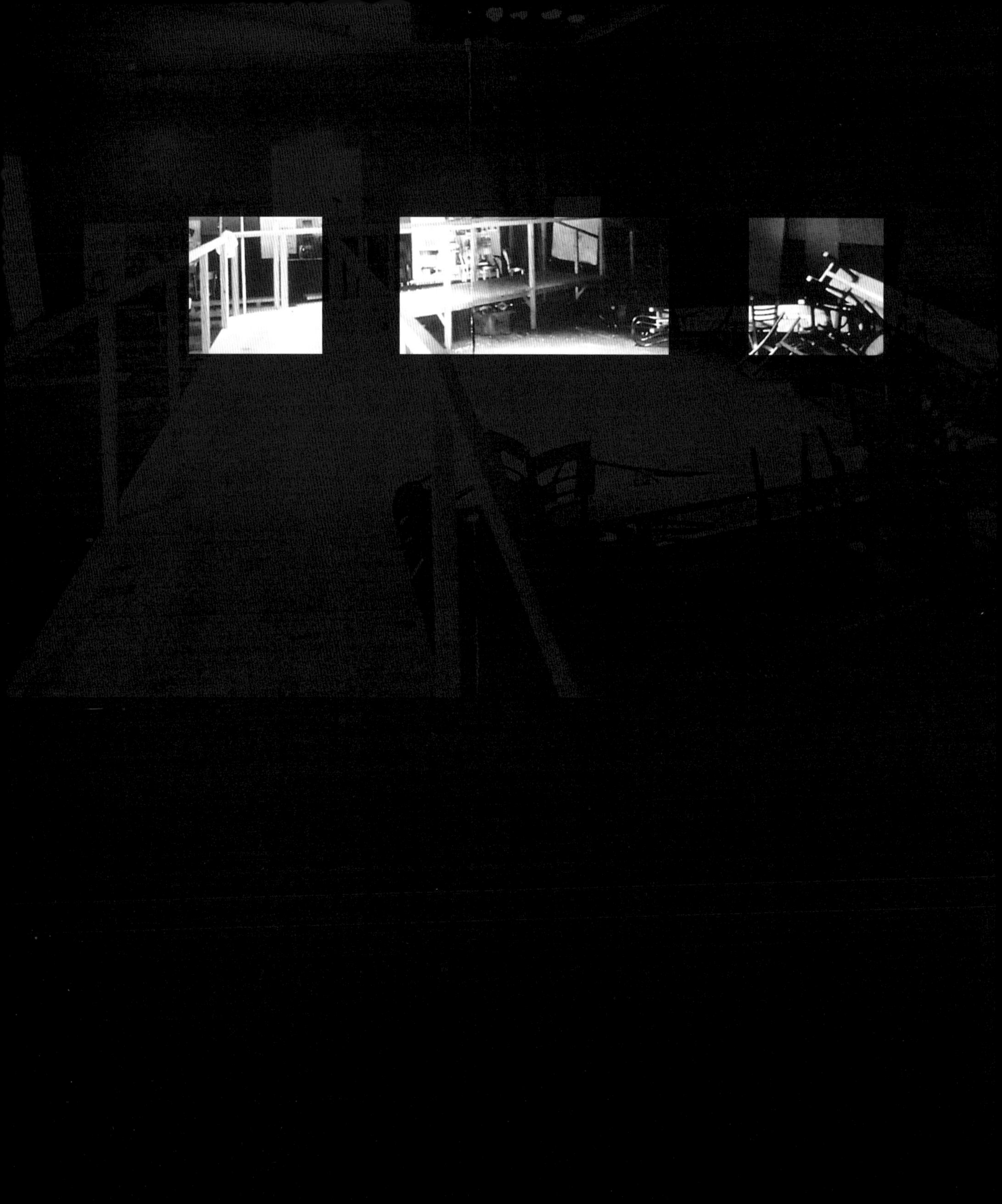

CHAPTER 3

Moscow Communal Conceptualism

Where are we going?
The road is narrow. Deep in the forest
the moss is slippery . . .
Below the mountain below the mountain
wind blows our red banners like a painting.[1]
Mao Zedong

"Time," said Emmanuel Levinas, "is the breath of the Spirit" ("Le temps est le souffle de l'esprit"). Breath consists of inhalation and exhalation, which hints at the existence of two modes of temporality, "positive" and "negative": time to breathe in, and time to breathe out (fig. 3.1). In 1975, I overheard a dispute between two professors from SUNY at Stony Brook. One was a literary scholar from India, the other a mathematician and an orthodox Jew. The first disputant argued that temples in India had turned into ruins long before the "beginning of time" designated in the Jewish calendar; the second responded that those temples had never been destined for completion, because the Jewish God designed or, rather, created them as ruins. The Tower of Babel seems to acutely fit this conceptual framework, a "historical" a priori as an installation, and a past as a deserted amusement park. On the level of signifier, the creation of "symbolic ruins" can be viewed as "proto-postmodernist," for it resembles what Federico Fellini once called "the hallucination of a drunken pastry chef." Clearly, "symbolic ruins" are not necessarily stone or concrete constructions; they can be mental constructs as well.

Bordering these ruins, as if it were "written" between them,[2] the evidence of transitory time is as ubiquitous as the evidence of petrified temporality. Both are traces of what Levinas attributed to a pneumatic nature of *l'esprit*. *Webster's* defines "breath" as not only "time to breathe" but also "delay; intermission; respite" (read: transitory moment). Taken simply, conceptual art is largely similar to a variety of artistic manifestations in which textuality acts as or substitutes for temporality. Taken seriously, it can be discussed in terms of "respiting visuality," given that conceptualism thrives on transitory thinking and writing. In this respect, one may both agree and disagree with Benjamin Buchloh, who in the

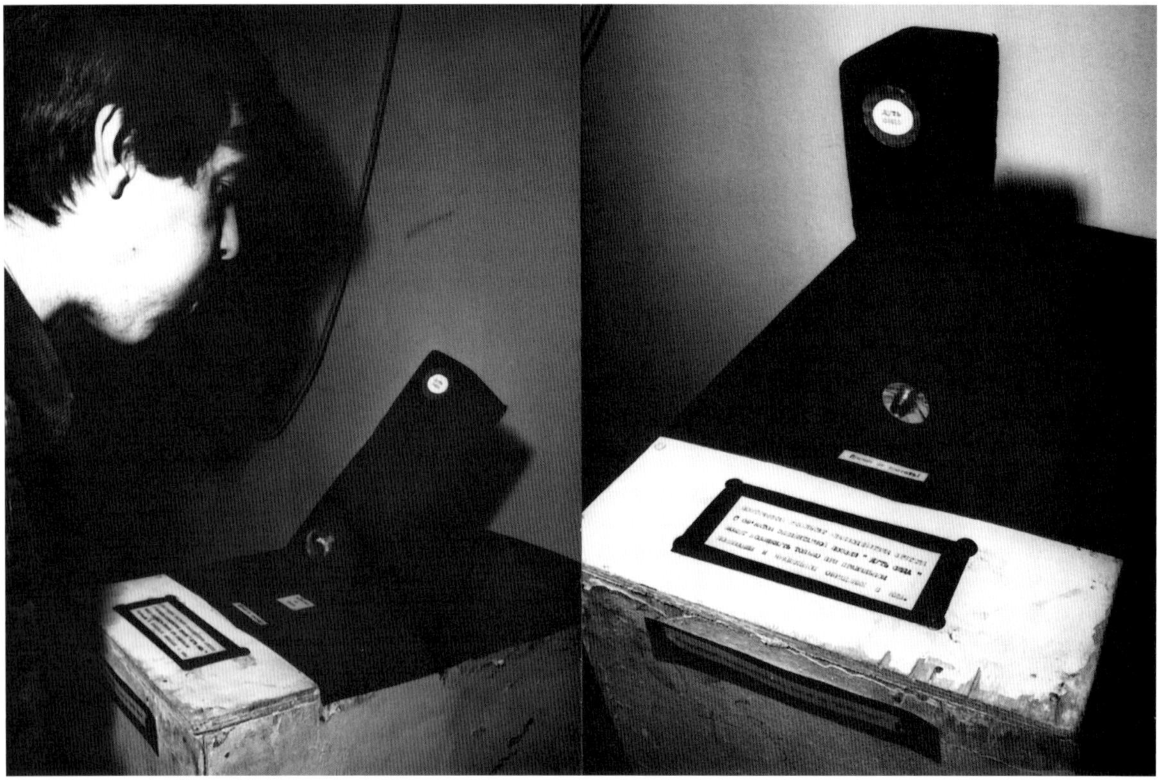

3.1
Andrei Monastyrsky,
Breathe Out Here!, 1983.

1980s enraged Joseph Kosuth by putting the term "post-minimalism" in place of "conceptualism." In truth, the latter, due to its transitory stance, is simultaneously post- and pre-.

As a conceptual artist, Ilya Kabakov welcomes the notion of conceptual art as caesural and at the same time transitional text insofar as this text is visually realized, "written" amid the ruins associated with the installation. However, Kabakov's installation by itself is not an authorial communication, and it would be a mistake to search it for one. The installations are ruins that structure his writing, akin to the way that symbolic language (the language of ruins, the language of the "father") structures the unconscious. The discourse of the Other that emerges as a result is nothing other than the "work of art" itself, the reading of which is assisted by installationary optics.

Like Kabakov, Andrei Monastyrsky belongs to the ranks of the most influential figures in alternative Russian culture. Along with Komar and Melamid, they should be regarded as the founders of Russian conceptualism. If the Kabakovian paradigm of "art as idea"[3] is based upon a metastasizing narrativity, then Monastyrsky hypostatizes conceptualism as discourse, as a theoretical enterprise. In the 1970s and 1980s Kabakov and Monastyrsky were chiefly responsible for the initiation into the alternative Muscovite art world of a new generation of conceptual artists who called themselves the Moscow Archive of New Art circle (MANA, or in a later transcription, NOMA). To designate the place of these artists in the history of Soviet conceptualism, as well as that of the Collective Actions (CA) group led by Monastyrsky,[4] we must take an excursion into the past.

In chapter 1, when discussing the origins of communal speech, I used the term "Law of the Commune." Although this term was coined in the nineteenth century, it aptly reveals the atmosphere of urban life in Soviet Russia. One should not forget that communal speech was an invader transplanted to an urban milieu from agrarian regions. As was already mentioned, in the 1920s migration into cities and industrial regions enabled a segment of Russian peasantry to avoid being drafted into collective farms. This migration engendered a housing problem of enormous proportions, thereby creating a new phenomenon—the Soviet ghetto, where alongside the communal speech the voice of power blared from the radio. On the level of artistic practices, this voice reified itself in the form of the metalinguistic structure known as socialist realism. Interrelations between socialist realism and communal speech were a variety of Bakhtin's "two-world condition." The gap that divided these "two worlds" provided a niche for a third language—the visual lexicon of "Moscow communal conceptualism."

As a term, "Moscow communal conceptualism" stresses not only the acute "speech receptivity" of Kabakov, Komar and Melamid, or Monastyrsky, but also the fact that each of them was the product of communal upbringing and of the circumstances that accompany "institutional" (i.e., obligatory) communality. Unlike them, second-generation conceptualists—or, to be more precise, neoconceptualists—can be linked to "contractual" (i.e., elective, voluntary) communality. This generation includes members of groups that have partially or completely collapsed: Mukhomor, SZ, Champions of the World, and Medical Hermeneutics (figs. 2.35, 2.36).[5] (All the neocommunal bodies listed here deserve separate consideration and, perhaps, a separate conceptual niche, such as, for example, "Moscow neocommunal conceptualism.")

▪▪

Few of Kabakov's Western admirers realize that almost all segments of this artist's oeuvre are essentially representations of the "corporeality" of Soviet communal speech. His "rooms," Masonite panels, and albums are linguistic minefields that explode as soon as the viewer comes into contact with them or enters the site of the installation—limitless as far as the audibility of "spoken kitsch" is concerned (fig. 3.2). The communal ghetto—a *kommunalka*—is Kabakov's central subject, just as the flophouse was Maxim Gorky's in *The Lower Depths.* Kabakov explains: "The flophouse is an extraordinary successful metaphor—a glimpse, as it were, into a pit where myriads of souls swarm. There is no action in Gorky's play, only talk. I call it 'logogyration.' Our Russian life seems exactly the same to me: it gravitates toward zones of speech. Thus the communal apartment turns into [a] Soviet version of *The Lower Depths.*"[6] Beyond the communal walls, Kabakov says, "out there, healthy young creatures are off to display their athletic prowess in the May Day parade through the Red Square, while in here, you, sucker, live like a dog."[7] In Kabakov words, "The degree of the helplessness of communal life before the outside world is horrifying. No one in a communal apartment will fix a loose board or a broken faucet, because all these functions from eviction to repairs are performed by *it*" (fig. 3.3).[8]

When, following its debut at Ronald Feldman Fine Arts in New York in 1988 Kabakov's exhibition "Ten Characters" was reconstructed at the Hirshhorn Museum in Washington, D.C., something unexpected happened. The museum's African-American guards took an active interest in the installation. According to the artist, they enthusiastically promoted his installation and explained it to visitors "for the reason that they found it easy to identify with a representation of a communal world, a world in which they, too, were raised."[9] Their reaction attests that Kabakov is not

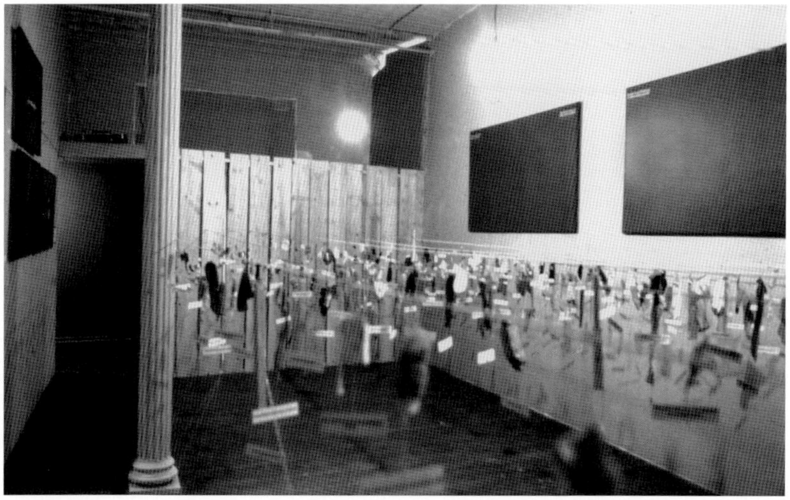

3.2
Ilya Kabakov, *Ten Characters, Kitchen no. 2*, 1981–1988.

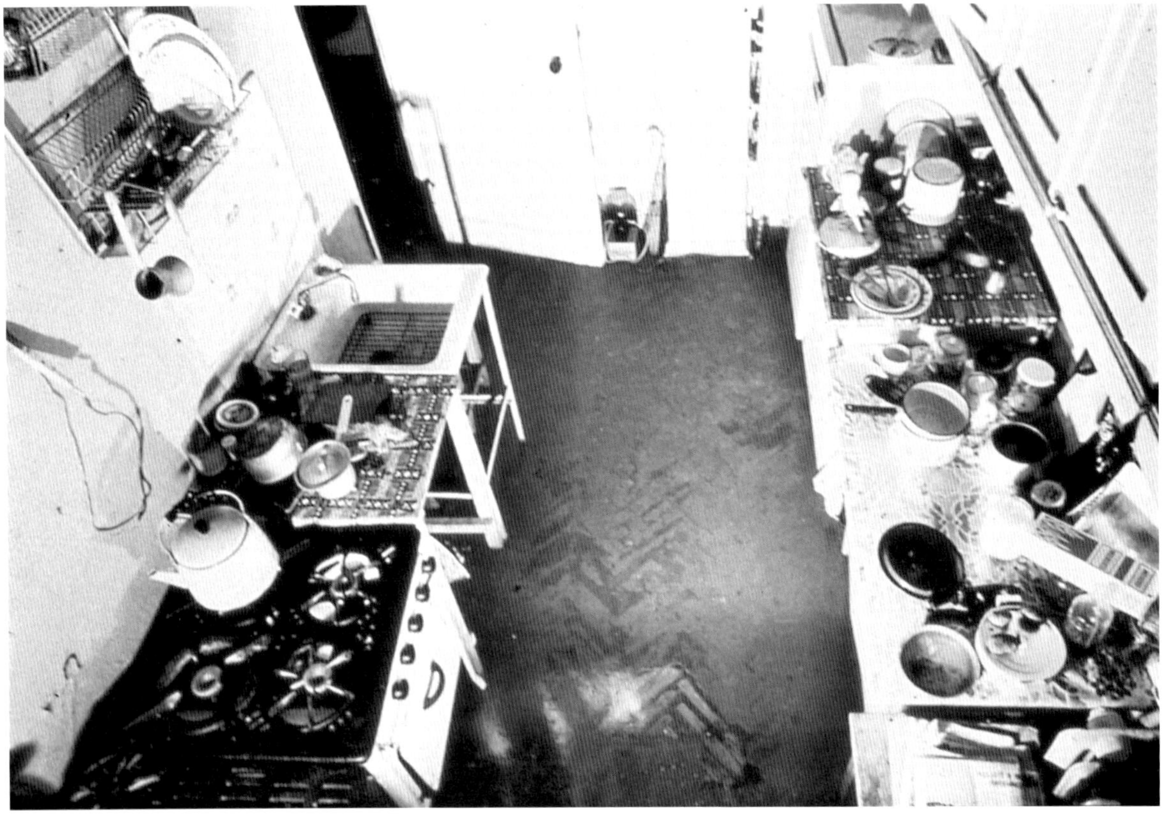

3.3
Georgii Kizeval'ter, from the series *Moscow Communal World*, 1984, used in Ilya Kabakov's albums.

merely the avenging chronicler, but also the bard, the aestheticizer of the fabric of the ghetto-centric utopia that is ruled by a communal speech ritual. Evidently, as Terry Eagleton writes, "for discourse to *refer,* even protestingly, is for it to become instantly complicit with what it criticizes."[10]

Although his *Ten Characters* series became engaged in a deconstructive reading of Soviet communal narratives, Kabakov would always hide his authorial "I" behind legions of characters. It would be ridiculous to fault him for doing that, given the immense (state-imposed) pressure that alternative artists had to bear before perestroika. Besides, fear of identifying oneself had a positive (i.e., "uplifting") effect inasmuch as it contributed to Moscow communal conceptualism, a multimedia practice that embraces the idea of the artist as schizo-producer[11] who operates within the framework of an ephemeral (conspiratorial) authorship. This implies that the schizophrenic division of the authorial "I" can be seen as a prerequisite for the production of a multitude of personages. Thus Kabakov, in *Ten Characters* and in a number of his other installations or albums, seems to fit the definition of "schizo-chameleon": the polyphonic, flexible, and evasive self is, in fact, his ultimate production.

The notion of a schizo-chameleon comes to mind when one recalls Kabakov's 1989 exhibition "He Lost His Mind, Undressed, Ran Away Naked" at Ronald Feldman Fine Arts in New York. The explanatory wall text told the story of a man who failed to keep up with the schedule for the "Universal Order, Rules and Regulations" of the ZhEK (housing committee) that he himself had drawn up. Finally, as attested to by "witnesses," he ran naked from his "red corner" (the "altar" spot of the ZhEK). This narrative can be traced to the artist's past. In an interview I did with Kabakov right after the opening, he recalled: "As a child I had been beaten first by my father and then by my schoolmates so severely that one day I felt like a character from one of the Baron Munchausen stories: a fox who jumped out of its skin and ran away."[12] The subsequent journey of a "naked" man could be viewed as the artist's never-ending struggle to repossess his "original" skin. Hundreds of appearances and disguises have been "tried on" and "peeled off": their "retreat and return" is the main intrigue of Kabakov's oeuvre.

To elaborate on the "uplifting effect" as the byproduct of fear, one can recall Kabakov's insistence that "repression and fear are positioned in the center of the structure, where everything is rotating around panic that if I do not do something—terrible things will happen."[13] The artist's confession echoes both Søren Kierkegaard's *The Concept of Fear* and Harold Bloom's theory of poetic influence as defensive mechanism. In his book *Poetry and Repression,* Bloom argues that "as trope, poetic repression tends

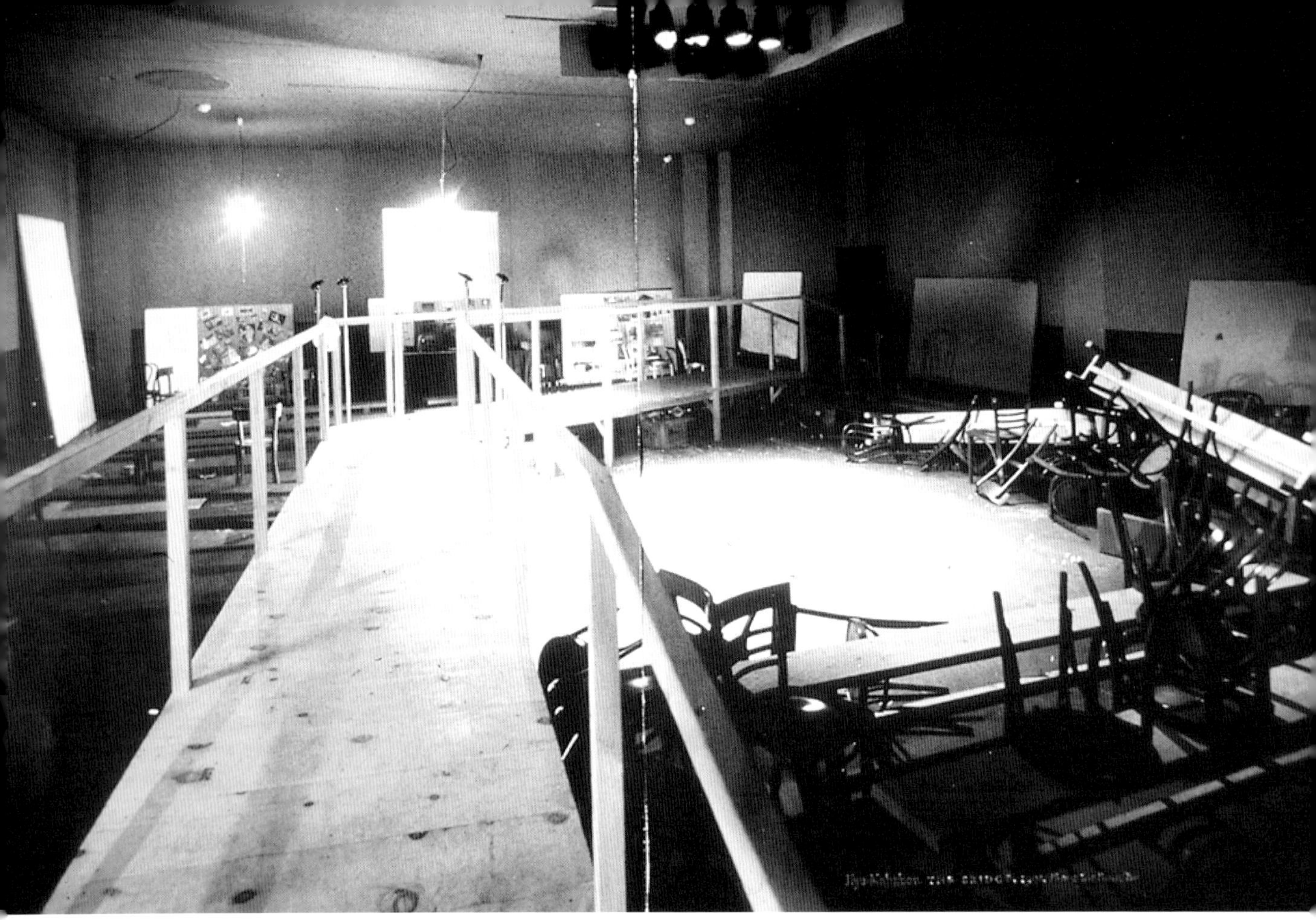

3.4
Ilya Kabakov, *The Bridge*, 1991.

to appear as an exaggerated representation, the overthrow called hyperbole."[14] What it attempts to overthrow is its set of referents: it is a trope's revenge against an earlier trope, the quarrel of any belated creator (read: Kabakov) with his precursor (read: communal speech). In Bloom's opinion, "art is necessarily an *aftering*, and so at best [an artist] strives for a selection, through repression, out of the traces of the language [of art]; that is, he represses some traces, and remembers others. This remembering is a *misprision*, or creative misreading,"[15] which gives way to a selective, preferential vision of the world—vision synopsized by an abbreviational optics (i.e., a view of the visual phenomena as a text made up of abbreviations).[16]

Kabakov's installations are abbreviations of retrospective vision, mediated by the presence of unconscious abbreviatory structures in the recesses of language and memory. A description of these structures (albeit in different terms) can be found in the works of Vygotsky devoted to the study of internal speech.[17] His observations, in conjunction with Lacan's later revelations, confirm that the unconscious is structured like an abbreviation ("total abbreviation").

For Kabakov repression is comparable with "clothing thrown over the skeleton of words"[18]—an allegorized image of *misprision*, conditioned by *aftering*. Both italicized terms are primarily applicable to those artworks which Kabakov has been producing in the West. He would probably agree with Bloom's statement that art "is always at work imagining its own origin, or telling a persuasive lie about itself, to itself."[19] Repression is also detectable in Kabakov's vigorous promotion of an "identity frame," called *musor* (trash). Refusing "to grant speech ontological status," he does "not attribute other, higher meaning to any of the voices. From the utterances of the linguist to the muttering of Mariia Ivanovna (a communal dweller)—who took out the garbage—the texts are annihilated. Noise results. Everything is a communal text, and I can treat it exactly as I do garbage."[20] Kabakov imagines the latter as the opposite of the Kantian sublime, since *musor* is the countersublime.

Kabakov's choice of psychic defense falls upon visual metaphors known as installations. Working in the West, he aims to reinstall the past that he has subjected to an act of "revisionary misinterpretation" or nostalgic "misprision." This was detectable in such installations as *The Bridge* (MOMA, New York, 1991) (fig. 3.4), *Water Music* (Ronald Feldman Fine Arts, 1992), *In the Apartment of Nikolai Viktorovich* (Jablonka Gallery, Cologne, 1994), and "*C'est ici nous vivons*" (Centre Georges Pompidou, 1995).

To a greater degree, creative misreading took place at the Documenta IX (1992), where Kabakov's partiality toward "total abbreviation" prompted him to cross a public toilet with a communal living space. His recollections

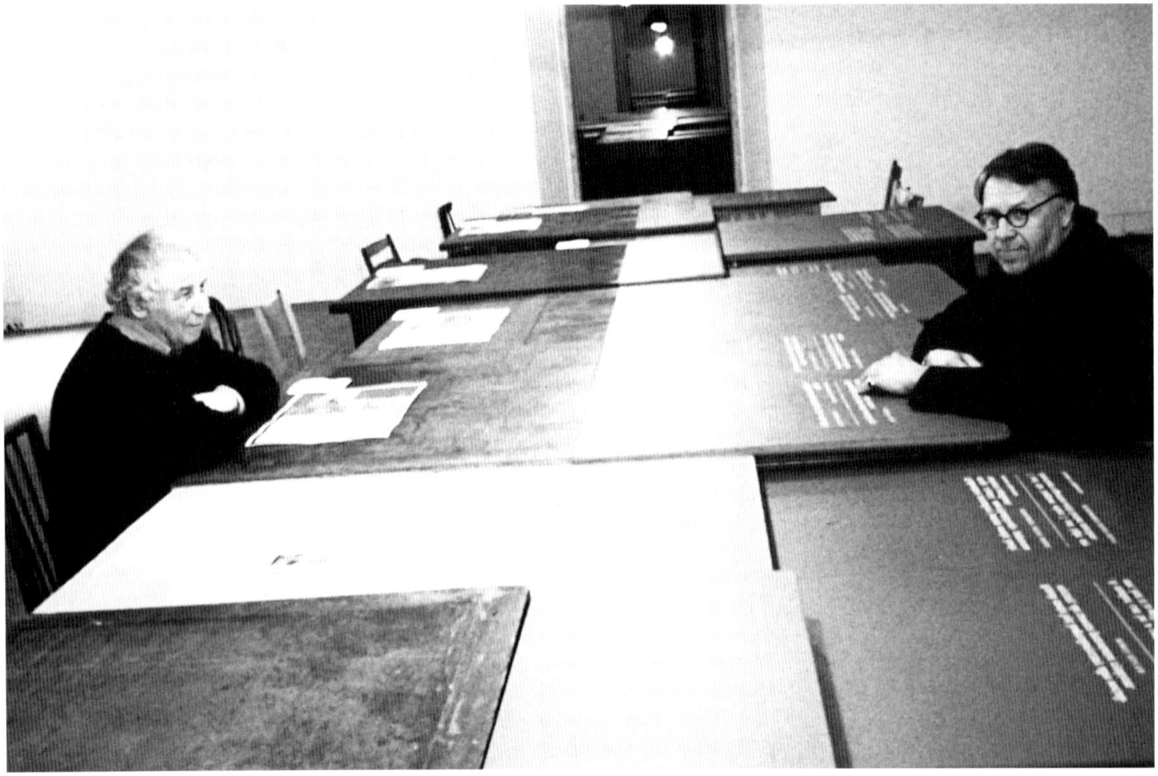

3.5
Ilya Kabakov and Joseph Kosuth, "The Corridor of Two Banalities," Center for Contemporary Art, Ujazdowski Castle, 1994.

had turned surreal, psychedelic, phantasmic; the psychic defense mechanism seemed to run out of everything that fed it. This can be viewed as the consequence of the artist's (by then) six-year-long stay in the West. Evidently, the shortage of "fresh past" resulted in an urge to inflate the "origin" beyond recognition. This not only perfectly fits Bloom's definition of poetic repression as exaggerated representation, but also contributes to the surplus of anguish and fear, thereby inviting another cycle of psychic defense.

Kabakov's installation at Jablonka Gallery serves as an example of what Bloom calls "daemonization," a term based upon the idea that the daemonic is the intervening stage between the human and the divine. The artist contrasts the darkness of the communal environment (read: the human) with a brightly lit Cézannesque landscape, endowed with extracommunal lucency (read: the divine) that suggests the possibility (for one's "mental eye") of transcending the representation. But this suggestion leads to a dead end where the modern sublime is tenants with the countersublime "of belated *daemonization*." Here, if we read both Bloom and Kabakov closely—"the enigma of [artistic] authority can be resolved only in the context of [fear and] repression."[21]

An act of daemonization was staged in Ujazdowski Castle near Warsaw, Poland, where a joint exhibition of Kabakov and Joseph Kosuth took place in 1994 (fig. 3.5). The show, titled "The Corridor of Two Banalities," dealt with the play of differences and/or similarities between communal and extracommunal narratives. The installation consisted of two rows of tables stuck together. On the "Eastern" side, shabby and crooked tables represented Russia; on the other side were the sleek and well-kept tables of the West. Texts were written on their tops: on one row were fragments of communal speech; on the other, authoritarian words (the maxims of famous individuals).

Kabakov's use of word "logogyration" in relation to communal speech practices suggests an association with the Wolf Man's "magic word" *tieret'* (to rub),[22] which brings to mind Vladimir Nabokov's *Lolita,* charged with the mixture of cryptic *jouissance* and alienation. The confessional intensity that characterizes this novel links Humbert's narrative with Kabakov's abbreviational optic in the sense that the latter—like Nabokov's scramble of poetic images, rhymes, parodic and playful stunts—has a high "coefficient of friction." Thus, the *tieret'* of Humbert's confession seems equivalent to the *tieret'* of the installation medium, inseparable (in Kabakov's case) with the rubbing of words against words.

In Nabokov's *The Gift* is the following observation: "What, then, compels me to compose poems . . . if in spite of everything, my words go wide of the mark, or else slay both the pard and the hart with the exploding

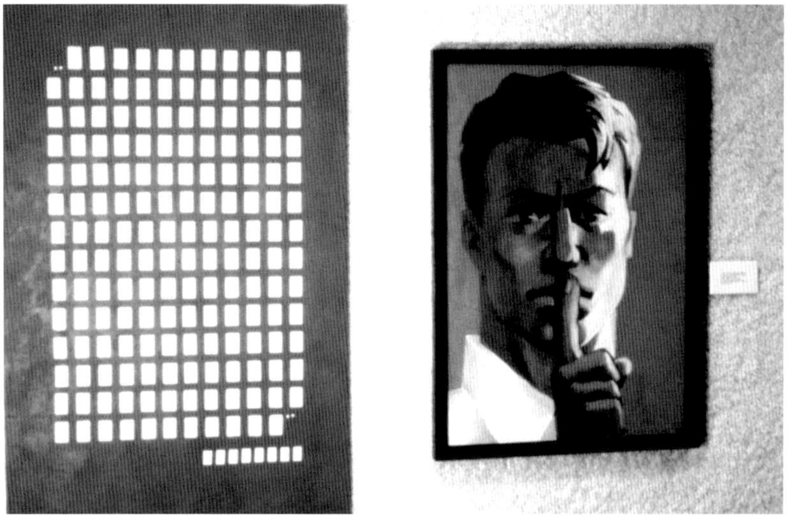

3.6
Vitaly Komar and Aleksandr Melamid, left: *Quotation*, 1972; right: *Do Not Babble*, 1974.

bullet of an 'accurate' epithet?"[23] In this remark the character's creative "I" matches that of Shiva, for whom—according to the myth—one arrow is more than enough to destroy three celestial cities. The art of the "total installation," or total abbreviation, which preoccupies Kabakov, creates a similar effect. The difference, however, is that such an installation appears to be penetrated not by one but by a great many "arrows." As a result, in the installation as well as in the above quoted fragment, the shrapnel of the excessive imagery compensates for the lack of trust in the success of a single shot.

▪▪

However audioclastic,[24] Kabakov's handling of communal speech has always been rather intimate. "It is like caressing"—in this form Levinas's phrase about seeing can be adapted here. Komar and Melamid are artists who also have an audioclastic orientation. In contradistinction to Kabakov, however, they subject not communal but authoritarian discourse to a deconstructive reading. The target of their hunt is the "mythical [extracommunal] speech"[25] that functioned either explicitly or implicitly in the visual clichés of the socialist realist tradition. In the early 1970s, their conceptual projects addressed the problem of logocentrism as manifested in the Soviet painterly canon. Examples of this are *Do Not Babble* (1974) (fig. 3.6), an easel painting in the style of a poster, and the "anonymous" slogans of mass propaganda (painted on red fabric and signed by Komar and Melamid), *Our Aim Is Communism* and *We Are Born to Turn Dreams into Reality* (1972). For all its parodic quality, the gesture of this signing was a phenomenon unique to alternative art. For the first time the communal had encroached on the authorial rights reserved for the extracommunal "it." In the work known as *Quotation* (1972) (fig. 3.6), we see even rows of white quadrangles sketched on a red background and placed within quotation marks. In all, these empty spaces, suitable for the insertion of pearls of authoritarian speech, form the semblance of a minimalist painting. Nonetheless, its eidetic (speech) structure, even without a specific concretized message, is perceived as an incarnation of the will to power and control.

Among the issues most frequently discussed in relation to Moscow communal conceptualism, the approach to the idea of "character" occupies a special place. In the works of Monastyrsky and of the CA group, the "character" is de-psychologized; he or she is an agent of speech bisected into its image and likeness. During the performance, the character's will to speak is repressed while the "verbal time" is filled with action. Speech has its turn after action—at the moment of "compensatory" verbal acts, such as interpretation, description, and recollection. As a result of this time delay, the "character" becomes the subject of speech, in the process

3.7
Collective Actions group, *Ten Appearances*, Kievy Gorki, February 1, 1981.

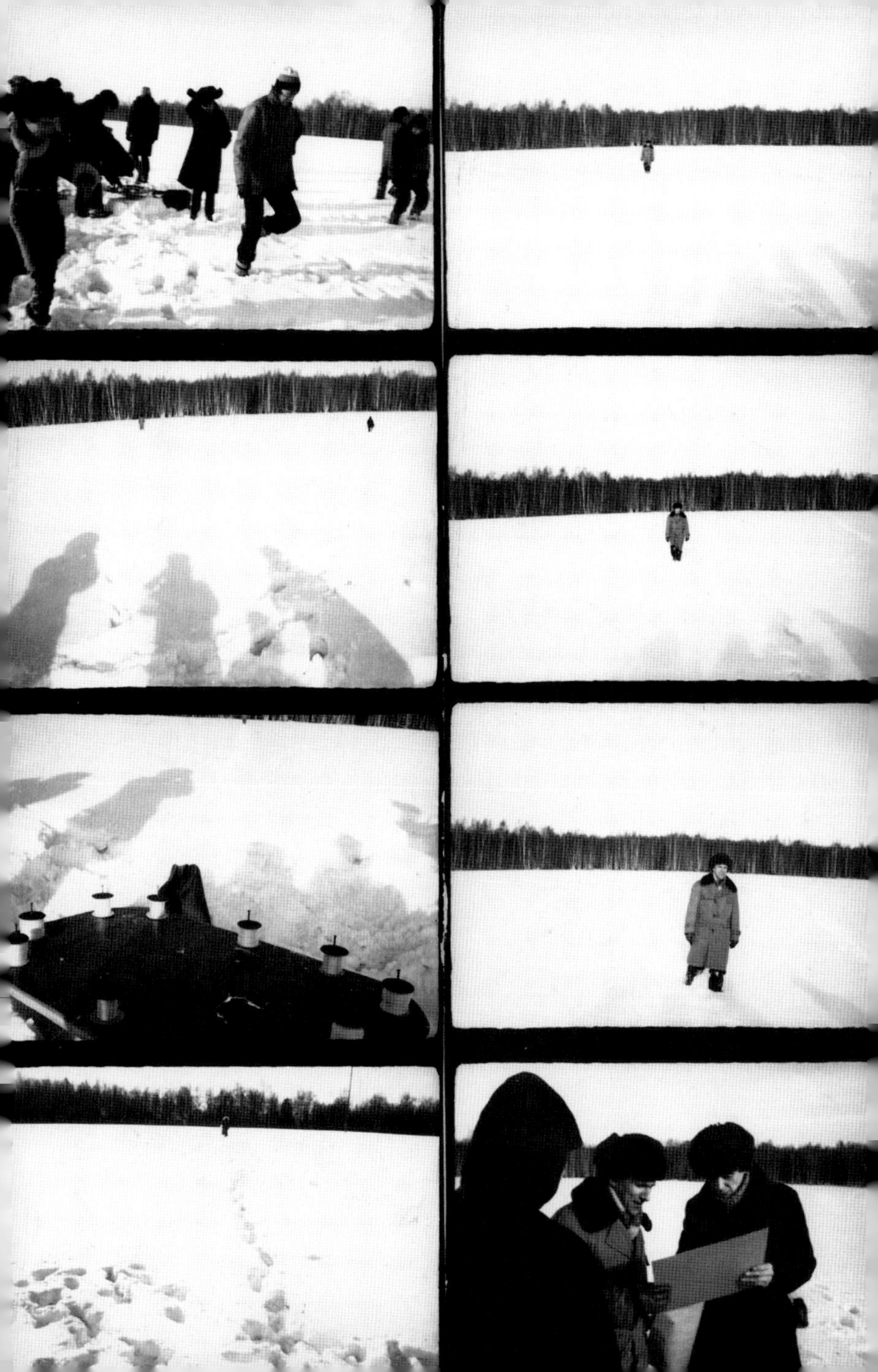

of realizing a posteriori that he or she is its object. In the performance *Ten Appearances* on February 1, 1981, at Kievy Gorki (fig. 3.7), Monastyrsky and his colleagues in the group asked ten viewers to pull ropes from the center of a snowbound field toward the surrounding wood. When these ten people had moved a considerable distance from each other and from the CA members who were observing them, they were photographed. When they returned, they were offered a chance to look at the photographs. Although the photographs were taken with a regular camera and not a Polaroid Instamatic, no one questioned their authenticity. In fact, the photographs were of the CA members themselves, who had visited the field previously and had taken pictures of each other. The distance that made the figures practically indistinguishable contributed to the success of this falsification.[26] The truth was exposed much later, which was the planned culmination of *Ten Appearances*. The truth, which triumphed ex post facto, turned out to be nothing more than a signifier that made explicit the phenomenon of losing tempo and/or *différance* between verbal vacuum and verbal compensation.

For Komar and Melamid, the character is the incarnation of the extracommunal text, either the canonical (Lenin and Stalin) or the apocryphal (Apelles Ziablov and Nikolai Buchumov).[27] For these artists, identification with such Apollonic figures is a form of individuation, an attempt to separate themselves from the faceless, anonymous mass. Unlike them, however, Kabakov has no interest in a carnivalesque rivalry with symbolic "fathers." He usually hides behind the character, breaking up his authorial "I" into a multitude of communal voices, which Nietzsche, in *The Birth of Tragedy out of the Spirit of Music*, identified with the chorus of satyrs. In ancient Greek tragedy, Dionysus, wearing the mask of Apollo, takes a step forward, in the understanding that to achieve self-realization he must invest his ambitions into the Other (into the god of illusion and simulation). And that is precisely where Komar and Melamid are leaning when they abolish the dichotomy between the authorial and the authoritarian. The alternative to this reading of character's nature is Kabakov's version of *The Birth of Tragedy*. His Dionysus takes a step back, leaving the heroes of his narratives, the "satyrs," who appear to us wearing the mask of Apollo, in the foreground. One reason for this retreat is fear of retribution: one need only remember Midas and his donkey ears, or the terrible fate of the satyr Marsyas, skinned alive by Apollo because he dared compete against him in the musical arts.

As cultural texts, socialist realism and communality constitute the USSR's weightiest deposit in what can be defined as *abbreviarium*—a compendium of speech-visions synopsized by an abbreviational optics.[28] It follows, of course, that this should be supplemented with the visual heritage of the revolutionary art of the 1920s that was eradicated in the 1930s by the two aforementioned linguistic dominants. One way or another, having stepped onto a path of self-identification and self-legitimation, post-Stalinist art culture could not avoid a period of overcoming Soviet-style phonocentrism. In this sense the Muscovite alternative artistic milieu of the 1970s and 1980s seems hypostasized by two audioclastic enterprises and one that is audiotherapeutic:

1. Sots art, which identifies itself with an oppositional language and with the travestied deconstruction of state-bureaucratic logos on the stage of individual speech (Komar and Melamid, Erik Bulatov, Aleksandr Kosolapov, Leonid Sokov, Dmitrii Prigov, and others).
2. Idioms of representation of the communal speech-vision aimed at unfolding its noncorrespondence or—in Adorno's terms—"nonidentitiy with itself" (Kabakov).
3. A refusal to take part in the orgy of voices plus a schizoid reaction to the hegemony of dominant speech practices. *Trips outside the City*[29] in search of a common alternative to the language of communality and the language of power (the group CA).

Thus, if sots artists and Kabakov proved to be "deconstructionists" of the basic "dialects" of the Soviet linguistic *oikumenë*, socialist realism and communality, then Monastyrsky and the group CA, having rejected iconoclastic gestures and strategies, undertook the reconstruction of the language of art. They revisited the primordially agrarian space from which the expansion of the "Law of the Commune" toward the cities had begun.

It is remarkable that the discourse of CA oscillates not so much in the interspeech of the basic "dialects" (contraries) discussed here as in the gap between their audioclastic alternatives (subcontraries).[30] The position occupied by CA appears to correspond to the "neutral term" of the Greimasian semantic rectangle below, which serves as an illustration of what has been said:

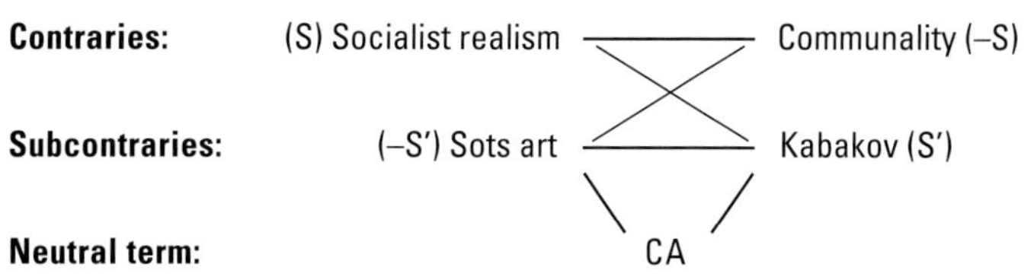

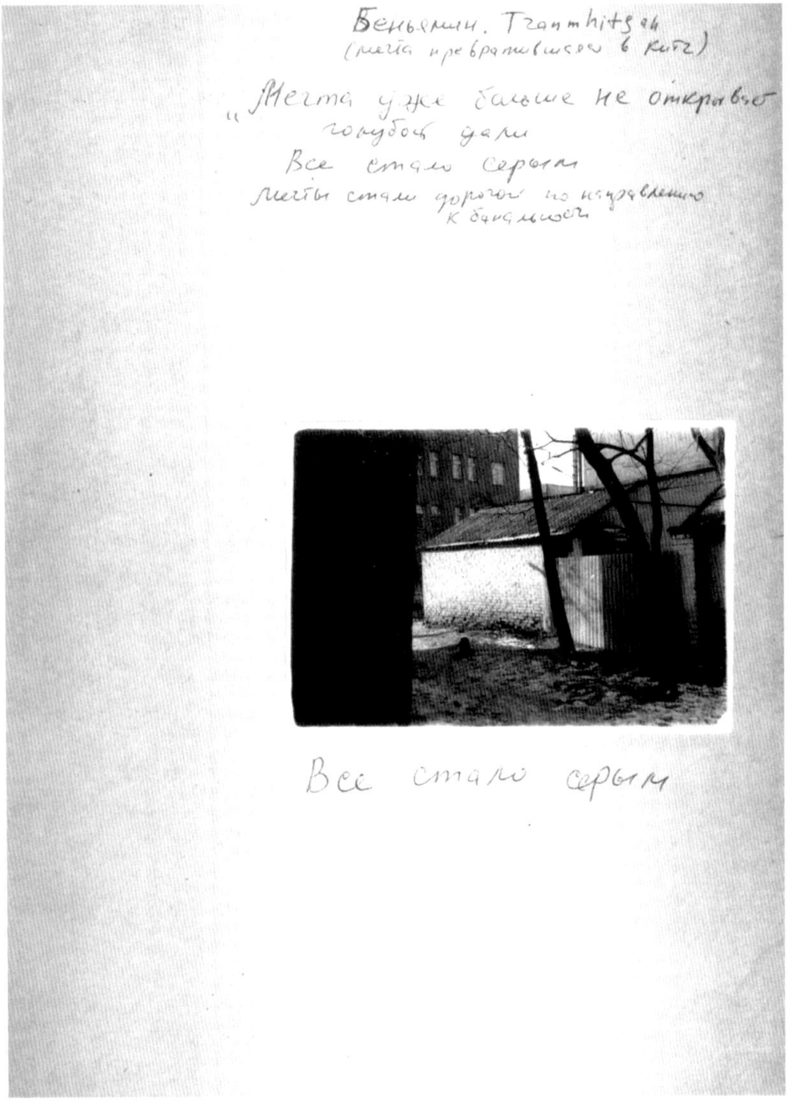

3.8
Boris Mikhailov, page from the album *Unfinished Dissertation*, 1980s.

In a certain sense, the discourse of CA is reminiscent of the strategies of the Art-Language group, whose essential discovery was that a literary sequence exhibited in a gallery context on par with (or instead of) a painting automatically loses the property of legibility while obtaining a visual dimension. This similarity dovetails nicely with Monastyrsky's assertion that "in the actions of CA language manifests itself [is formed] in an utterly unexpected [for the viewers] place,"[31] thereby weakening their "will" to read.

Kabakov has made an installation called *The Man Who Flew into Space from His Apartment.* Monastyrsky would seem to be precisely this Kabakovian character, as he has driven a hole in the ceiling of two types of speech.[32] Thus, in Monastyrsky's case, the pleasure of being in*text*icated is radically altered by switching gears from text-as-an-overdose to text-as-a-remedy. Whereas Komar and Melamid are convinced that visuality is *already always* infected with authoritarian speech, Kabakov refuses to believe in the existence of "communal-free" narratives, for "they all belong to one common trash can."[33]

▪▪

If Western conceptualism positioned itself as a "text," then in the Soviet case, it was repeatedly identified with a communal text (or communal speech). This identification, albeit in different manifestations, is directly related to both Kabakov and his protégé, the photographer Boris Mikhailov, who regards photographic representation "as a part of the text" not in order to exempt it from comparison with other photographs, but "to impart it with yet another meaning."[34] For both of them, mimetic reciprocation between the visual and the verbal is always a possibility, provided that they represent diverse (perhaps mutually deferred), but not entirely different "regimes of phrases" (communal speech acts, communal *faktura,* etc.). In Kabakov's albums, for example, characters are featured as textual allegories, whereas in Mikhailov's photographs, the same personages are introduced as "real" people, whose visual status is secured by the alleged immediacy of the medium. While Kabakov combines photographic imagery with highly impersonal (clichéd) narratives, Mikhailov's authorial inscriptions near the photograph (such as on its margins) tend to be personal and idiomatic (fig. 3.8).[35]

Concerning the textual levels of photography, one may agree that the most elementary (eidetic) level is when the text is photographed, so that it exists "inside" the photograph in the form of an announcement, slogan, heading, poster, advertisement, notice, etc., which—because of its repetitive and clichéd appearance—exerts a certain hypnotic influence over the viewer. The second level concerns the desire to make the verbal coextensive to the visual: in such cases the photographer (or artist borrowing photographic imagery) writes a commentary on the photograph, on its margins (however extended), etc. The third level could be called "staged": having been conceived of by the photographer prior to the moment of taking a picture, the photograph a priori appeals to a certain score or plan that can be expressed in the form of an utterance, even if post facto. Obviously, we are talking about gaze and voice in terms of their mutual predisposition toward convertibility. An example of the fourth level is the socialist realist photograph read as a didactic narrative, a guide to action, a rhetorical figure, etc. The attachment of the word to the image resembles that in a schoolbook, where a specific visual stereotype is consolidated behind each elementary (eidetic) concept. At the fifth level, the photographs and texts are arranged on a wall or in a showcase—whether an album or a series—so that the selection of the links, and their order in the composition, influences the phenomenology of reading. If the photograph is placed in an album, then the very leafing through the pages becomes an exercise that forms the text in the sense that the story unfolds via the transition from one episode to another, from one depiction or photo image to the next. An example of the sixth level is the "indexical" photograph. Some of these perform a service role, which doesn't void their involvement with a text. The sixth level envisages not so much the presence of gaps between the word and the image, as much as the mutual intentionality of the text and the photograph—their *being-toward-each-other.* However, the seventh level has to do with the concept of "communicating vessels" capable of relocating the brunt of the signifying operation from text to image, and—coextensively—from voice to gaze.

▪▪

One hundred and seventy years ago, in an attempt to grasp the essence of Russia, Prince Viazemskii remarked, "from thought to thought [in his country] one must gallop hundreds of miles." This idea confirms that the perception of space in Russia has always gravitated to the extremes, with total disregard toward what lies in between. After the revolution this polarity acquired a hysterogenic dimension, caused on the one hand by the suffocating closeness in the relationships between the tenants of overcrowded communal apartments and on the other by the overwhelming presence of the vast caesural territories. In the former USSR, notions relating to a sense of space (such as migration and travel) would frequently be substituted for or confused with those connected to temporality (be it futuristic sentiment or searching for *temps perdu*). Reflecting upon this phenomenon, Monastyrsky places Kabakov's model of "art as idea" within what he calls the ontology of surface (space). He contrasts this with

Western conceptualism, which for him evolves within the framework of ontology of action (time). Now that it is no longer unthinkable for Russian artists to travel abroad, the dichotomy between Western and Eastern European paradigms of conceptualism seems to be losing its rigidity and sharpness. The withering of this dichotomy is revealed in Kabakov's "communalizing" treatment of both aforementioned ontologics as he unites them under the canopy of what Bakhtin defines as "chronotope."[36] The artist's aim is to create an impression that "from thought to thought one must" *not* "gallop hundreds of miles," because these thoughts can be drawn nearer by welding their visual representations into a (neo)Wagnerian *Gesamtkunstwerk* set out as "total installation."[37]

In conclusion, a few words about "conceptualism in general." Apparently, it has long been impossible to "separate" out a pure form of conceptualism. As a component of multimedia artistic practices, conceptualism has overcome the initial antitextural thrust that was its reaction to the commodity fetishism of the 1960s pop culture. In the 1970s and 1980s, the theoretical text became a commodity. The expansion of commodity fetishism into the sphere of text production, into the realm of knowledge, ideas, and documentation, has reached such a point that the dichotomy of object versus text now seems outdated. As for conceptualism in Russia, its eclecticism and omnivorousness, its ability to live peacefully with other genres and styles—easel painting, photography, etc.—make it a communal phenomenon. It would be a mistake to treat it as something separate, something divided from everything else: conceptualism is a tenant living in the communal ghetto of art.

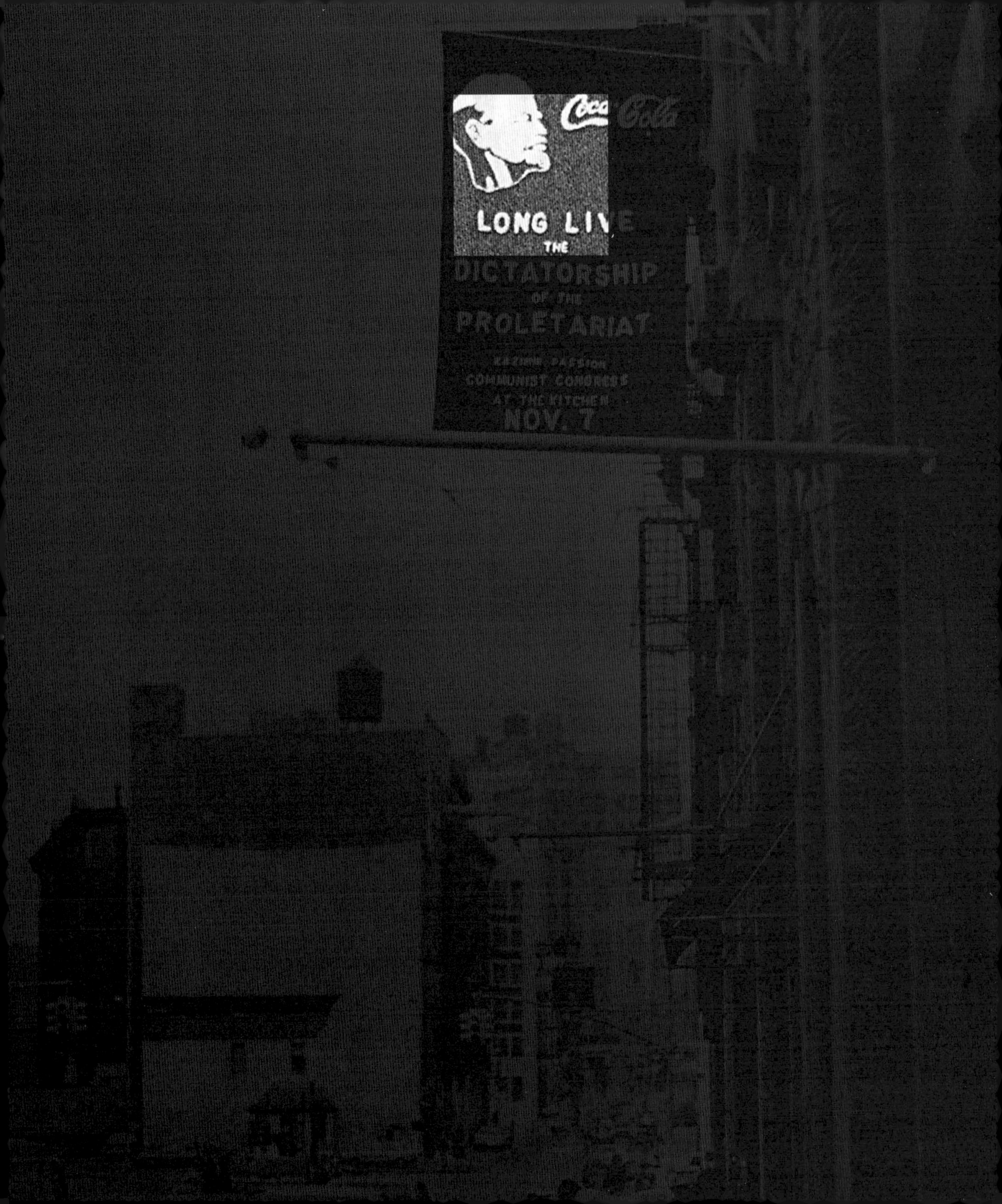
Coca-Cola
LONG LIVE
THE
DICTATORSHIP
OF THE
PROLETARIAT
COMMUNIST CONGRESS
AT THE KITCHEN
NOV. 7

CHAPTER 4

Icons of Iconoclasm

In the mind there is a blind spot that recalls the structure of the eye.... But, whereas the eye's blind spot is unimportant, the nature of the mind means the blind spot will, in itself, make more sense than the mind itself.
Georges Bataille

As I argued in chapter 1, socialist realism was more than just an art movement or a shared sensibility; it was the representation of Soviet identity, and a representation addressing a national audience that was extremely receptive. Under Stalin, due to the excessive proximity of the wakeful eye of the state, manifestations of the "optical unconscious"[1] in official Soviet painting were marked by an elevated transparency ratio. Until recently, the initiative in such manifestations belonged to the Cartesian vision (transparent, cerebral, nonsensual).[2] However, one should not conclude that the Cartesian visual paradigm applies exclusively to official art. The insatiability of the mental eye (nonabstention from the expansionism of vision) is a quality the counterculture sometimes shares with the powers that be. Sots art is the best illustration of this.[3] Having laid the foundations of postmodernism in Russia (in the early 1970s), sots art accomplished everything it sought and everything it feared: after the abolition of the USSR, it became a sort of frozen time in a constantly changing space.

Considering that affirmative depictions are among the most corrupting of constructs, the portrait genre of the Soviet era is in a class by itself. Even though visual image and identity have never existed apart from each other, it was in the USSR that the mass circulation of authoritarian icons, which controlled social identification, reached an unprecedented level. The role of official iconography was to channel this identification in the "appropriate" direction.[4] In other words, it was both a goal and a mediator.

An adequate understanding of the language of the authoritarian icon requires a definition of its functional dimensions: the identificatory, the utopian, and the transreferential.[5] To avoid conflicting interpretations, I will say that in analyzing all three dimensions (especially the first one), I

4.1
Gustav Klutsis, design for the poster *Let's Fulfill the Plan of the Great Projects*, 1930.

will construct the discussion with a view to the "optical unconscious." To describe the first dimension, one can paraphrase Lacan's thesis and say that the psyche of a Soviet man was the epicenter of conflict between the authoritarian *je* and the communal *moi*, with both concepts understood in terms of identification: figurative (*je*) or specular (*moi*). The difference between these means of identification allows a distinction between Lacan's Symbolic order and Imaginary order (the mirror stage).[6]

The mirror stage lasts between the ages of six and eighteen months. The term "Imaginary order" refers to the fact that, in the mirror stage, the child deals with an imaginary wholeness and an imaginary totality. In early childhood, *moi* (the ego) is constituted through optical identification. In everything that enters the infant's field of vision, he recognizes his own self. The "self" here is not some external distinguishing characteristic but a certain totality of image. As for his own body—feeble and with limited mobility—he manages to see it only in part, in fragments, incompletely. According to Lacan, the mirror stage is divided into two substages. The first is characterized by ecstatic identification with the visual image, which contains within it the promise (or anticipation) of totality. Lacan refers to this "promised" totality as orthopedic (*orthos* = correct, *pais* = child). In the second phase, the joyous affirmation of bodily wholeness in a visual image gives way to alienation, arising from the tension between the imagined fullness of the iconic sign and the insurmountable partiality of corporeal experience.

Examples of historic mass identification enable us to speak of a multiple (symbiotic) *moi*, whose identification with the illusory universality of idols, leaders, and celebrities allow the communal unconscious to be treated as a baby glued to a societal mirror. Each of these images is larger than life and contrasts with the fragmentary nature of the collective body. The features of multiple subjectivity are also manifested on the level of the individual: the subject of social identification who calls himself "I" frequently acts on behalf of a "we." Besides, the most intimate of fantasies and desires can be primordially clichéd (the same as everyone else's).

It is one thing when an individual perceives himself as a composite ("the composite image of the masses," etc.); it is another when the masses see themselves embodied in a single individual's image. There is, of course, nothing new about this: suffice it to recall Aleksei Khomiakov's notion of *sobornost'* (ecclesiastical communality), Vladimir Solov'ev's idea of "Godmanhood," and Lev Karsavin's "all-embracing subjectivity."[7] What is of interest here is not the verbal but the visual inventory of the identification of the particular with the whole and of the whole with the particular. As an example, it is worth mentioning El Lissitzky's photomontage of Lenin

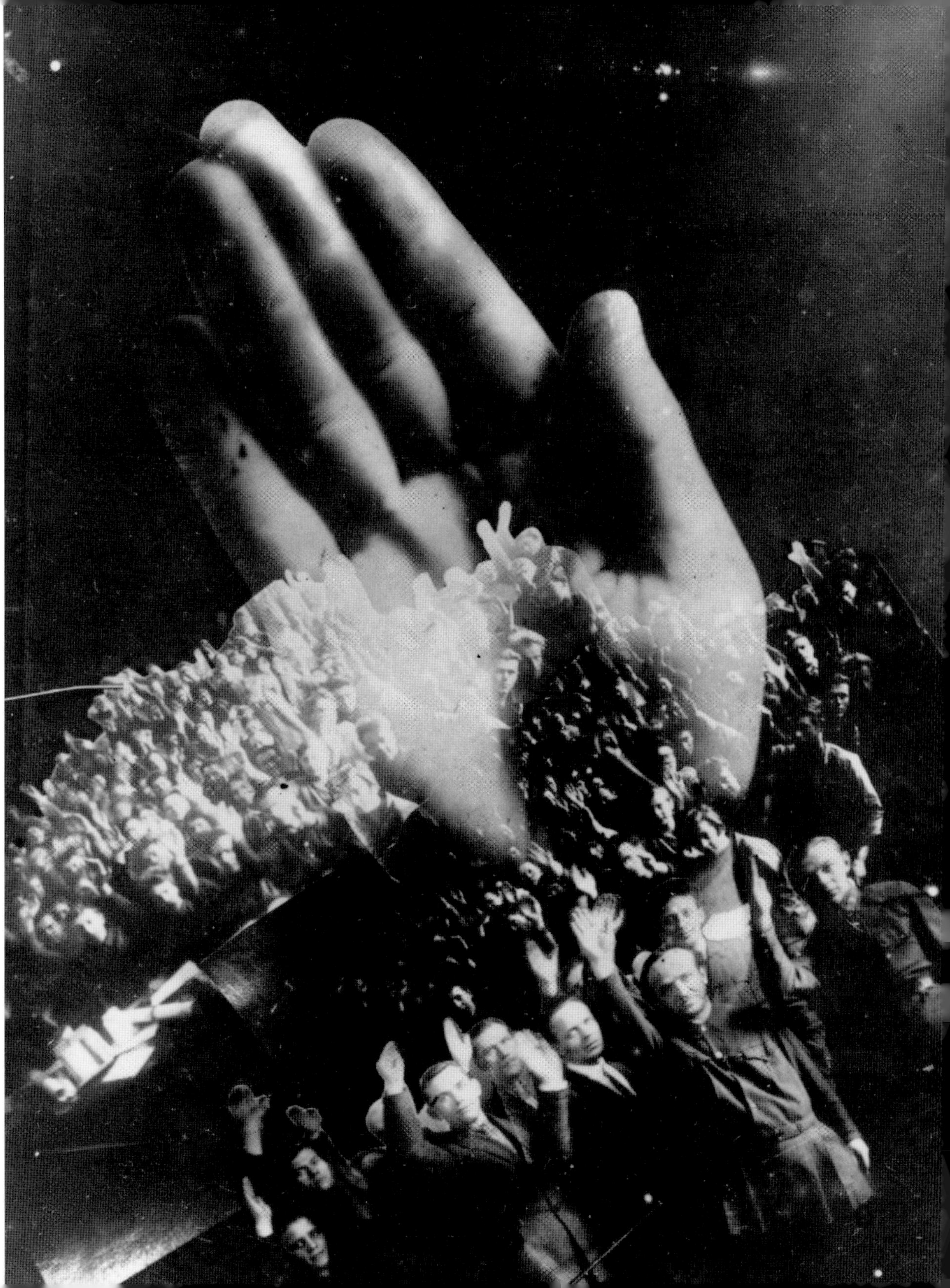

(ca. 1930), in which the head of the leader is stuffed with little human figures. The same idea is used by Gustav Klutsis in his poster *Let's Fulfill the Plan of the Great Projects* (1930) (fig. 4.1) and by John Heartfield in *Every Fist Becomes One Clenched Fist* (1934). In each of these pictures, *the political* is quaintly combined with *the corporeal:* the "masses" are either written onto the body of the sovereign or restrained into the form imposed upon them: a hand raised to vote (Klutsis) or a clenched fist (Heartfield). An example of the opposite is Sergei Sen'kin's design for the magazine *Herald of Labor* (1925) (fig. 4.2). In this photomontage, the worker's figure is constructed out of the leaders' portraits, which enables us to observe not only the king's celestial body (as did Ernst Kantorowicz in 1957)[8] but also the "body" of the proletariat.

Getting back to the visual arts in Russian culture, it is important to emphasize that the tasks of the socialist realists and the Soviet media included the steady delivery to the public of iconic imagery with which the masses were encouraged to identify. Thanks to these efforts, people had nowhere to hide from images of fellow citizens whose conduct they were supposed to emulate and whose feelings they were supposed to reexperience. One must consider, too, that communal vision is equipped with a cathartic optic necessary to reduce the distance between viewer and character, as well as to overcome the alienation that arises from the impossibility of sharing in the hero's condition immediately, on the spot.[9] This applies primarily to cases in which the hero is shown as having obtained his *objet petit a* (object of desire).[10] Ideally, the cathartic optic is in essence the vision of St. Francis of Assisi, that is, a magical vision.

Here we must draw a line between Freud and Lacan—between identification with the father (the "phallic signifier") and identification in the name of the father. Like "real" gods, Soviet leaders rarely encouraged people to look or behave like themselves. Instead, they sanctioned the identification of the communal subject with the appropriate experiences or characters depicted in film, photographs, sculptural compositions, posters, paintings, and periodicals. The portraits of leaders that filled the streets and the media functioned as mirrors (or antennae) that directed the waves of the identificatory efforts of *moi* so that they would bypass the Symbolic register and "return" to the Imaginary. As reflectors rather than targets of identification, the icons of leaders were "in charge" of redirecting these waves from some images to others; that is, they functioned de facto as instruments of synchronicity (the synchronic system of the signifier).

The structure of identification described in the preceding paragraph represents a three-pointed geometric figure. The first point is *moi:* from here, the stream of identification goes toward the authoritarian icon (the

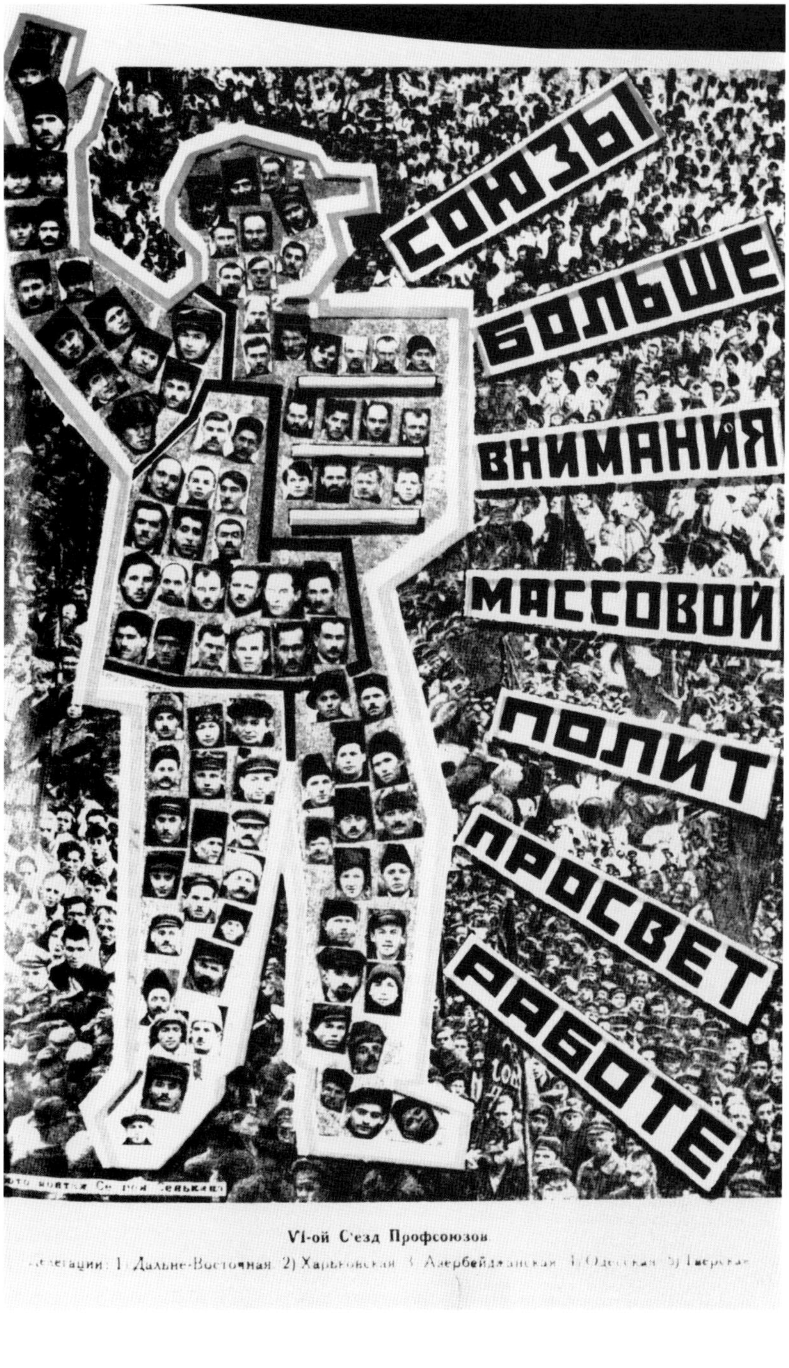

4.2
Sergei Sen'kin, *Sixth Congress of Trade Unions*, page from the magazine *Herald of Labor*, no. 1, 1925.

second point), which sends it to the proper address—point number 3. The appropriation of the image is followed by the return to the mirror stage, or, more precisely, to one of its substages. Hence, there are two roads back, two prospects of repatriation, the first of which promises unpunished possession of the totality, while the second is darkened by alienation.[11] The former is associated with the cathartic paradigm of the Soviet model, characteristic of communal identification with visual images; the latter, with the bourgeois model of relationship to the image (the glorification of the signifier, commodity fetishism, etc.).

The other two dimensions of authoritarian imagery (the utopian and the transreferential) are related directly to the Symbolic order[12] and indirectly to the Imaginary order. The only connection to the mirror stage is the attempt to give authenticity to the myth of the completeness and wholeness of the images involved in identification. This is true primarily of the icon of the leader (the "dispatcher") and the icon of the hero, which must possess, besides completeness and wholeness, capaciousness of meaning, extensity in time and space, and continuity. This lineup of properties refers not to the Imaginary order as such, but to the untranscended (residual) forms of its presence in the psyche of the individual who has long outgrown the mirror stage but returns to it in those instances when he is forced to behave like a communal subject. In general, the transreferential and utopian functions ensure the transfer of the image from one context to another, from one visual narrative to the next. They either narrow the boundaries of the narrative or expand them to infinity, in which case the iconic sign is viewed in relation to other signs, giving it a past, a future, a history, and a myth. The aforementioned functions also establish connections between these concepts in their interaction with unconscious representations, or *imagoes*.

The authoritarian portrait is the sphere in which the utopian dimension reveals itself in the most uncompromising (and at the same time the most infantile) manner. Those in power—and they were usually the ones whom artists painted—believed that having their portraits made could extend their life on earth and make them semi-immortal. The portrait is a zombie, a nightmare that pursues the children after the parent dies. In each portrait, the identificatory function is captured at the moment of mortal agony. This eternal agony is the imaginary immortality granted to the signifier on the basis of its resemblance to the referent—the future as a triumph of mimesis. Nothing else can explain the predilection for portraying the dead Father of the Country as a living man. In America, it is George Washington; in China, it is Mao Zedong; in Russia, it is Lenin, whose mummy can be seen as the place where the identificatory and utopian dimensions meet. The context of this meeting—in its most basic form, reduced to the state of *eidos*—is the mausoleum (the transreferential dimension). Its construction, along with the act of mummification, "was intended to overcome the thought of death, to de-eschatologize the consciousness of Soviet people."[13]

In the mausoleum, the second dimension is united with the third. However, it's at the level of the interaction of different temporal and spatial contexts that the third (transreferential) function fully manifests itself. In socialist realist works created in Stalin's lifetime, the transreferential dimension was required to accommodate the tyrant's desire to project himself into a "historical" context and to correlate his life with the lives of his worshippers. In short, the transreferential function dominates where Lenin, Stalin, and Brezhnev (or lesser gods) are shown addressing ecstatic audiences, kissing children, inspecting construction sites, or directing military action.

The early seventeenth century in Russia was the era of the False Dimitrii (the Impostor). Sots art emerged 370 years later, in the early 1970s, as a bastard child of socialist realism, its self-styled heir or, in Adorno's terminology, the "secret telos" of its visual identity. Sots art is a hole in this identity, a gap that makes possible contact with *le réel*—the third region (register) of psychic experience. Unlike the communal *moi*, whose perception of authoritarian imagery never goes beyond identification and cathartic bonding, sots art declares its right to separation. Sots artworks do not attract but repel the waves of the identificatory efforts of the *moi*. At the same time, sots art is not at all the Impostor of identification. It is only a "shifter"—a road sign of transition from one register to another, from the Imaginary to the Symbolic order, where figurative rather than specular identification dominates. To the question, "What is the relationship between sots art and socialist realism?" one may reply that they diverge as much as the optic of *je* differs from the optic of *moi*. Moreover, sots art is a way of reading a text addressed to *moi* through the eyes of *je*. If socialist realism appealed to the communal perception of images, sots art decommunalized perception (i.e., made it more individualized). The loss of cathartic vision, or "decatharsization," characteristic of sots art is due to the fact that these artists thrive on alienation. And since overcoming alienation is one of the principal forms of socialist realism, we see that yet another insurmountable precipice divides it from sots art.

When foreign guests saw Leonid Brezhnev's portrait, *Soviet Cosmos* (1977) (fig. 4.3), in Eric Bulatov's Moscow studio, they could not understand why an unofficial artist would recreate in his own home a poster from a public place. But Bulatov displaced the work from the sphere of

4.3
Erik Bulatov, *Soviet Cosmos*, 1977.

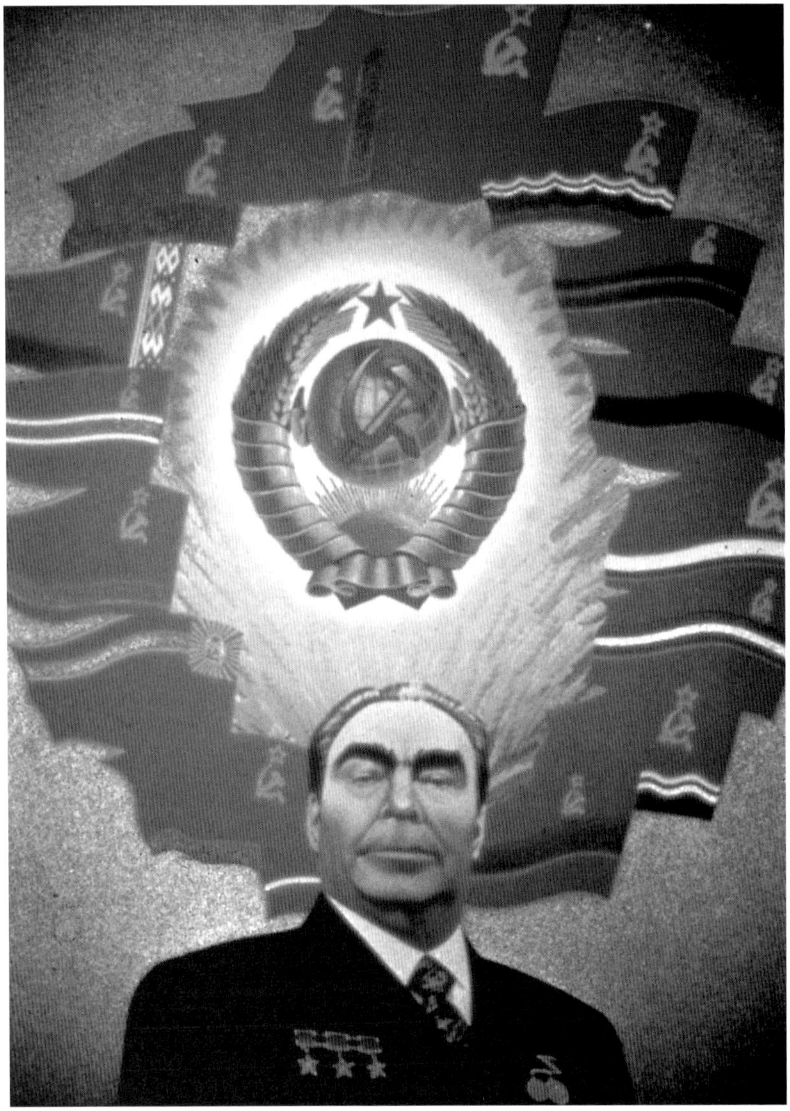

affirmative perception to that of alienated optics: having wound up in the studio of an "alienated" artist, Brezhnev's portrait became a work of alienated art; and, in a sense, Brezhnev was alienated from himself. As a result, a positively anxious image turned into a negatively anxious picture.[14] In the end, anxiety—regardless of its role reversal—remained intact, as if reaffirming itself as an inalienable part of the Russian cultural tradition, visual or literary.

In official art, the identificatory dimension was, of course, dominant. The same is true of sots art, simultaneously despite and due to its rivalry with socialist realism. Socialist realism and sots art cannot be regarded as mutually exclusive concepts: their relationship is one of dialogue, not antagonism. That is why one can say that the mutual presence of the autoritarian icons and of their doubles, the icons of iconoclasm, in the works of sots art has a carnival motivation. In 1994, Komar and Melamid noted: "Sots art could never have been invented by one artist. Only two drinking buddies such as Komar and Melamid could, over many days of talking while decorating a Young Pioneer summer camp, have decided to paint their parents in the style of a poster, and themselves as Lenin and Stalin (fig. 4.4). Sots art emerged only because it was a communal kitchen, a conversation between two people."[15]

The hunting instincts of Komar and Melamid are focused on the visual clichés of the socialist realist canon. Their "omnivorousness" spreads to all three functional dimensions of authoritarian iconography. When, for instance, they show Lenin cutting his nails or carrying a skeleton on his back, one can see an attempt to carnivalize the utopian dimension, a desire to shorten infinity. By "reconciling" the incorporeal icon of the leader with his corporeality, with his worldly cares, and therefore with the concepts of life and death, the artists expose the seamy side of utopian rhetoric. Also noticeable here is the influence of the transreferential function, thanks to which the godlike image is placed into an unbiased context. As a result of this debasement, the icon of the leader becomes an icon of iconoclasm. However, events can also develop in the opposite direction: there have been instances in which the debasement of the leader's image has led to its elevation, immediate or delayed. As Claude Lefort has written, "it is the natural body [of the leader] which, because it is combined with the supernatural body, exercises the charm that delights the people."[16] This corporeal image of power can properly be called "the daemonic body," in the sense that the daemonic—an intermediate stage between the human and the divine—turns out to be a means of unconscious mediation between the two.

Unlike socialist realism, sots art breaks the taboo against identification with the leaders. In sots art, leaders turned from gods into heroes, and

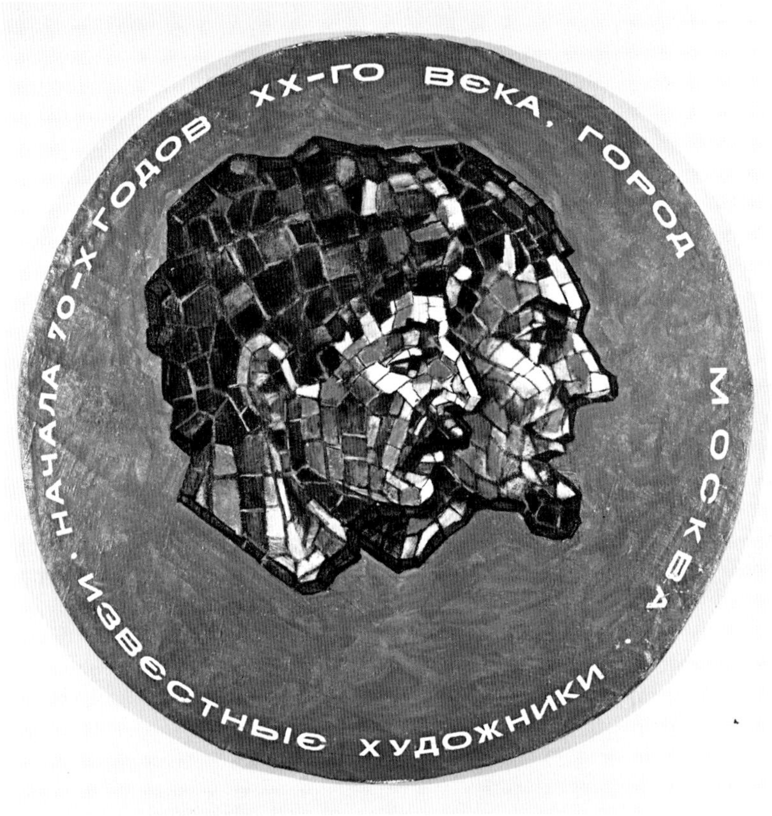

4.4
Vitaly Komar and Aleksandr Melamid, *Double Self-Portrait*, 1973.

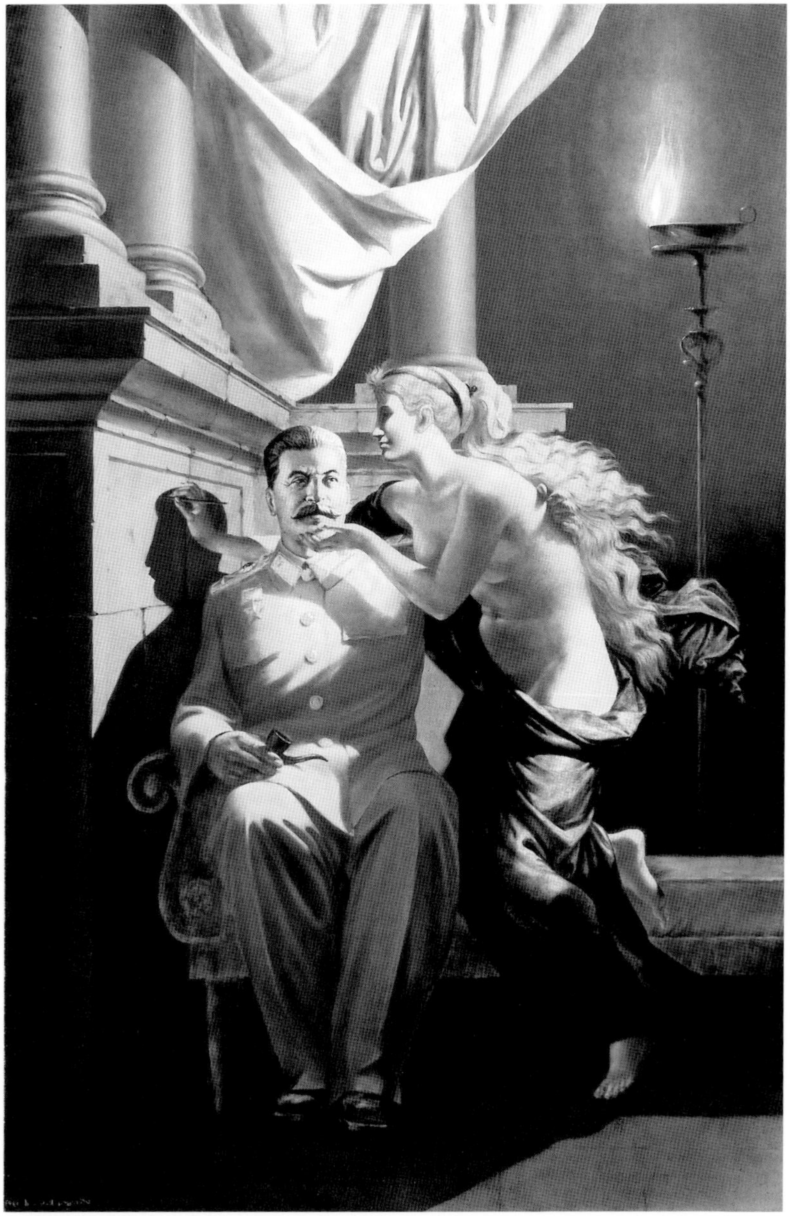

4.5
Vitaly Komar and Aleksandr Melamid, *The Origin of Socialist Realism*, 1982–1983.

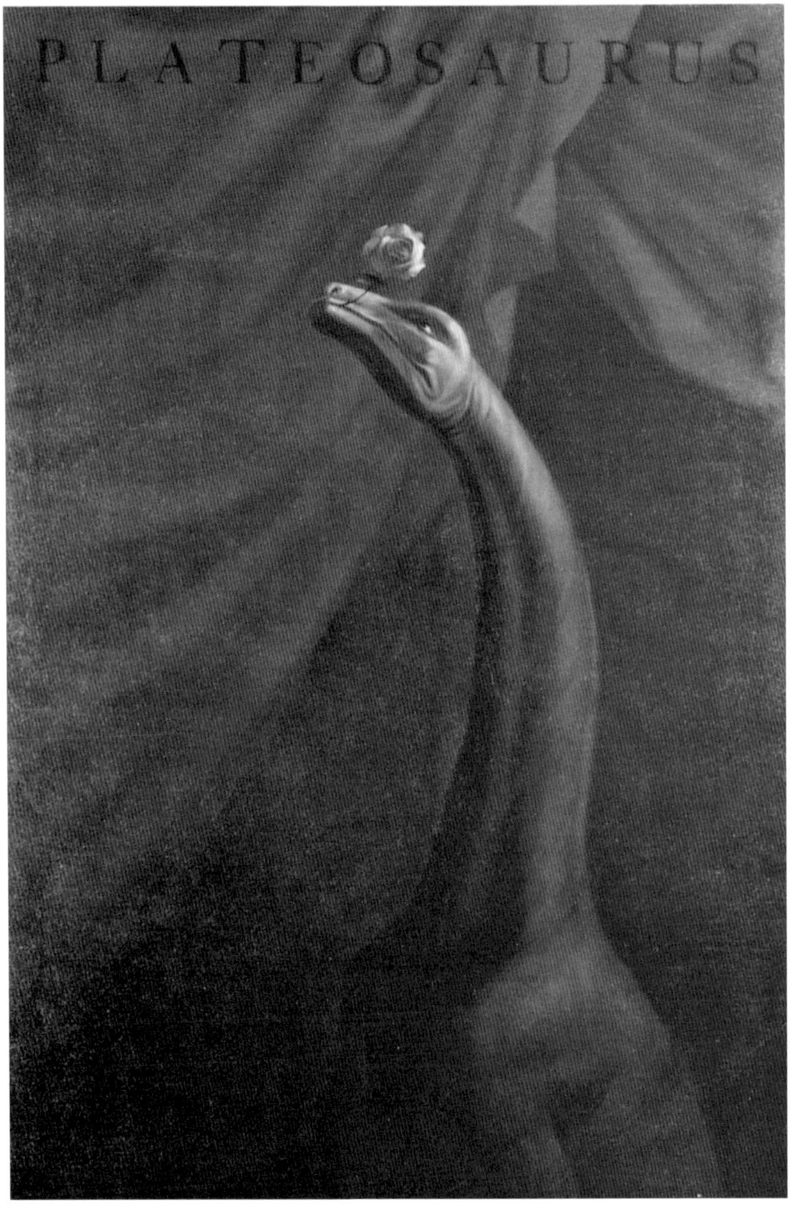

4.6
Vitaly Komar and Aleksandr Melamid, *Ancestral Portraits: Plateosaurus,* 1980. Photo eeva-inkeri.

therefore became accessible for direct identification. *Double Self-Portrait* (1973) (fig. 4.4) is one proof of the modification of the identificatory function. In this piece, Komar and Melamid depicted themselves in the manner of stereotyped mosaic representations of Lenin and Stalin. These authoritarian icons were essentially impersonal, vacant, "eidetic." The most important thing about them was the exhortation to identify regardless of any specific identificatory project. The same is true of *The Origin of Socialist Realism* (1982–1983) (fig. 4.5). In this painting, Stalin is depicted alongside a Muse who is sketching his profile on the wall. The association with the tyrant turns the identificatory function into an imperative: the interest taken by immortals in the leader's image obliges the mortals to imitate their heroes. On the other hand, Stalin's transposition into the context of Greek mythology is an obvious travesty of the transreferential function.

In the fall of 1982, Komar and Melamid's series of paintings done in a deliberately traditional, academic manner were exhibited at Ronald Feldman Fine Arts in New York. The moniker "nostalgic socialist realism" fully reflects the artists' state of mind at the time. The ways in which sots art has changed in emigration are most vividly illustrated by their painting *Thirty Years Ago 1953* (1982–1983). The painting captures a moment of intimate contact between two lovers, transposed—by means of the transreferential function—into a genre scene. All this unfolds against the background of a portrait of Stalin hanging on the wall and by its very presence, as it were, sanctioning the viewer's identification with the event. This portrait on the wall can be regarded as a rudiment or remnant of the identificatory function.[17] Thus, the identificatory icon undergoes a sort of retreat (a displacement to the background), becoming a painting within a painting.

Lacan's notion that "the father [or the ancestor] is an embodiment of the function of symbolic identification"[18] is visually paraphrased by Komar and Melamid in their series *Ancestral Portraits: Plateosaurus* (1980) (fig. 4.6), where dinosaurs are represented as ancestors. In these "portraits," the transfer metaphor is reduced to the level of the absurd: the transreferential function plunges us into the deep recesses of the identificatory dimension. The phallic appearance of the ancestors ("I'm Adonis, here's my penis," wrote the poet Genrikh Sapgir)[19] is in accord with the Lacanian definition of the phallus as the "repressed signifier," which nonetheless "spurs on" all of our identificatory efforts.

As soon as the *moi* → *je* shifter works, the identificatory dimension turns into a palimpsest of identifications. Thus, in one of Eduard Gorokhovskii's 1989 paintings, six images of Lenin can be discerned through the image of Stalin, as if surfacing from the "bottom" of representation (fig. 4.7). Thanks to this technique, the interworking of identificatory mechanisms becomes visible.

The painted sculptures of Leonid Sokov (fig. 4.8) and Boris Orlov can also be "read" in light of the issues discussed here. In a number of Orlov's works, the narcissism of the identificatory function reaches supreme expressiveness. Everything about them, including the excessive decorations on the front of the sculpture, attests to self-satisfaction and self-sufficiency (fig. 4.9). For Lacan, it is *i*(*a*) or *moi idéal*, i.e., the result of the imaginary doubling of the ego in the mirror stage.[20] Other examples of the representation of the narcissistic *moi* are found in the staged photographs of Aleksander Kosolapov (*Untitled,* 1981) (fig. 4.10) and in Komar and Melamid's *Double Self-Portrait.*

Bulatov's *Brezhnev in Crimea* (1981–1985) is an uncompromising embodiment of the identificatory function. The same can be said of his painting *Krasikov Street* (1976), in which we see Muscovites walking toward a billboard that displays a figure of Lenin who seems to be walking toward them. In terms of the earlier discussion, the billboard is a giant reflector, a regulator of identificatory streams that are received and reflected in the direction of appropriate images, appropriate deeds, appropriate values.

If the iconoclastic explosion staged by Oleg Vasil'ev in the painting *Ogonek* (1980) (see fig. 2.8) is seen as a refusal to obey the imperative of identification, in his *Perspective* (1983) a similar effect is achieved without the interference of emotion. In this work, the portrait of the leader is partially hidden by a similar portrait of smaller size, in front of which is yet another smaller portrait, in front of which is an even smaller one—and so on, until the row of pictures is reduced to a dot. The search for resemblance to an actual person turns out to be fruitless. In part, the "recognition" doesn't happen because what the painting depicts is not a specific person with whom the viewer is meant to identify multiple times, but the process of multiple identification itself.

Before concluding, I will point out that the contact between authoritarian portraiture and the communal subject is not limited to unconscious impulses only. This chapter focuses on such impulses, rather than on mechanisms of conscious identification, for two reasons. The first has to do with the fact that an adequate reaction to the authoritarian icon (Soviet-style) is possible only under the conditions of communal interaction with it. Therefore, to make a responsible theoretical diagnosis of the cultural legacy of socialist realism, it is necessary to reconstruct its perceptions. The second reason involves my reluctance to deal with iden-

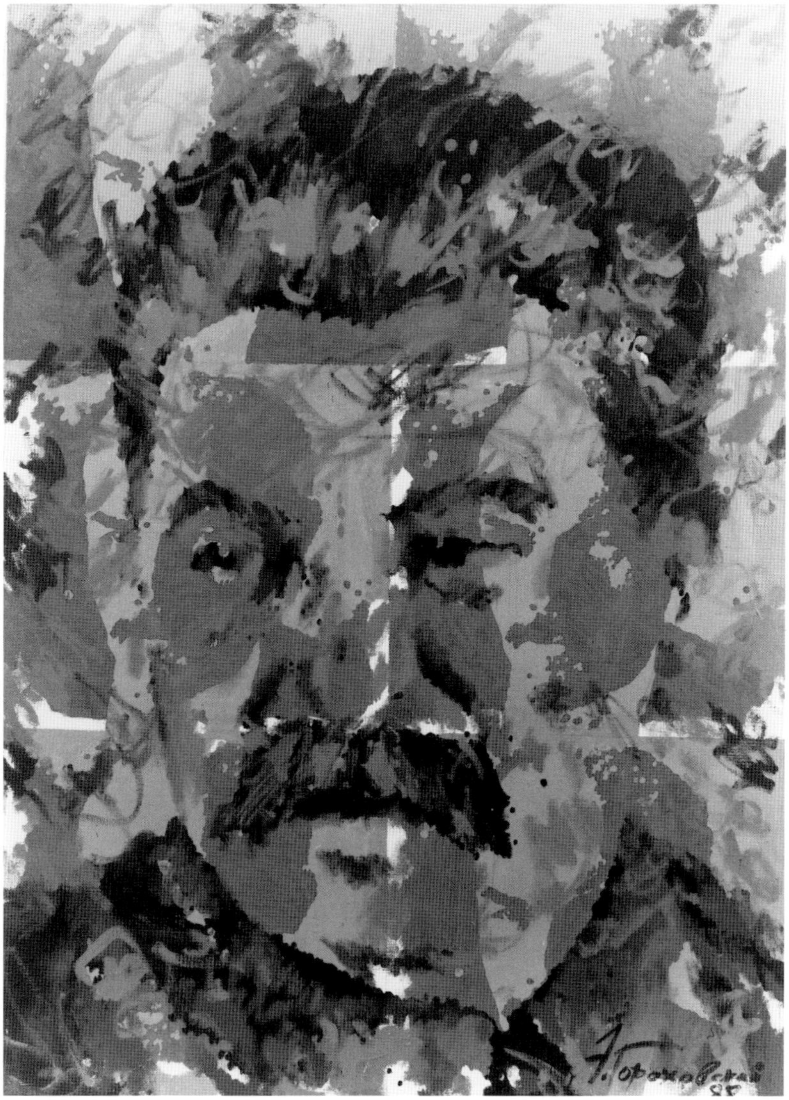

4.7
Eduard Gorokhovskii, *Stalin with Six Lenins,* 1988.

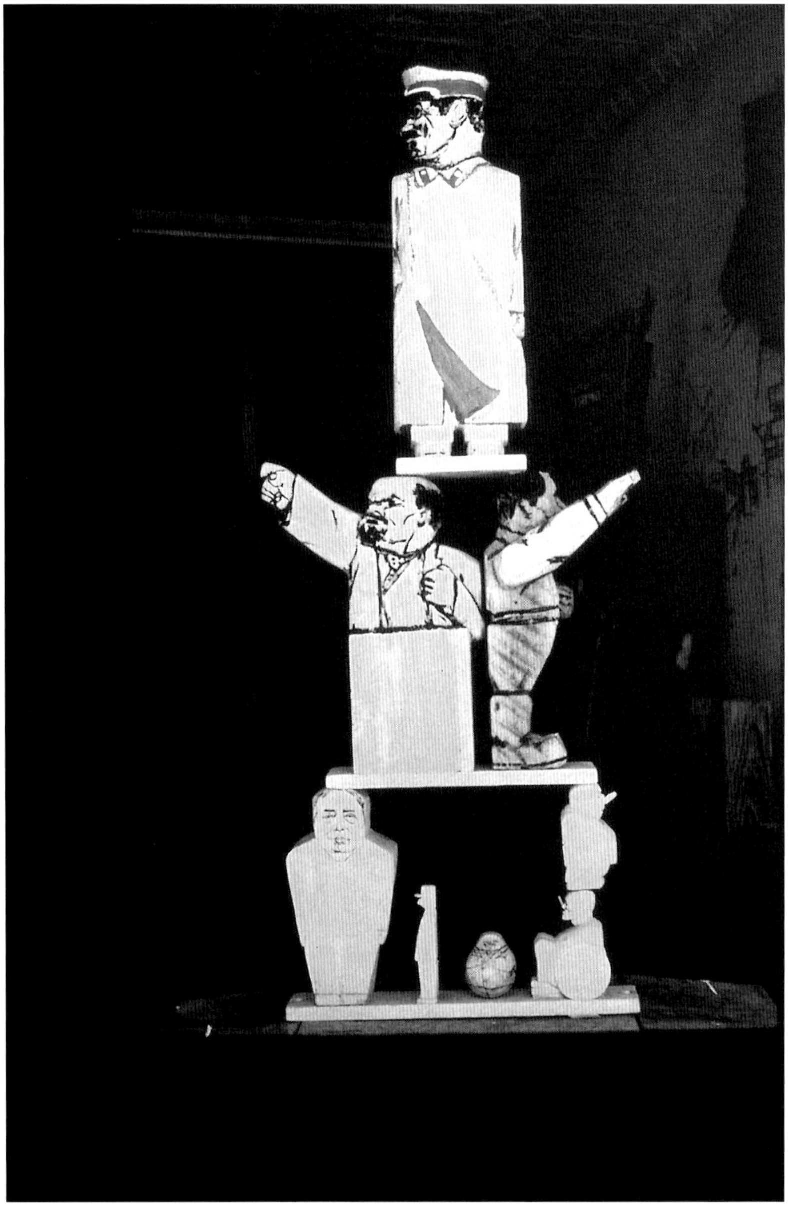

4.8
Leonid Sokov, *Twentieth-Century Leaders*, 1985.

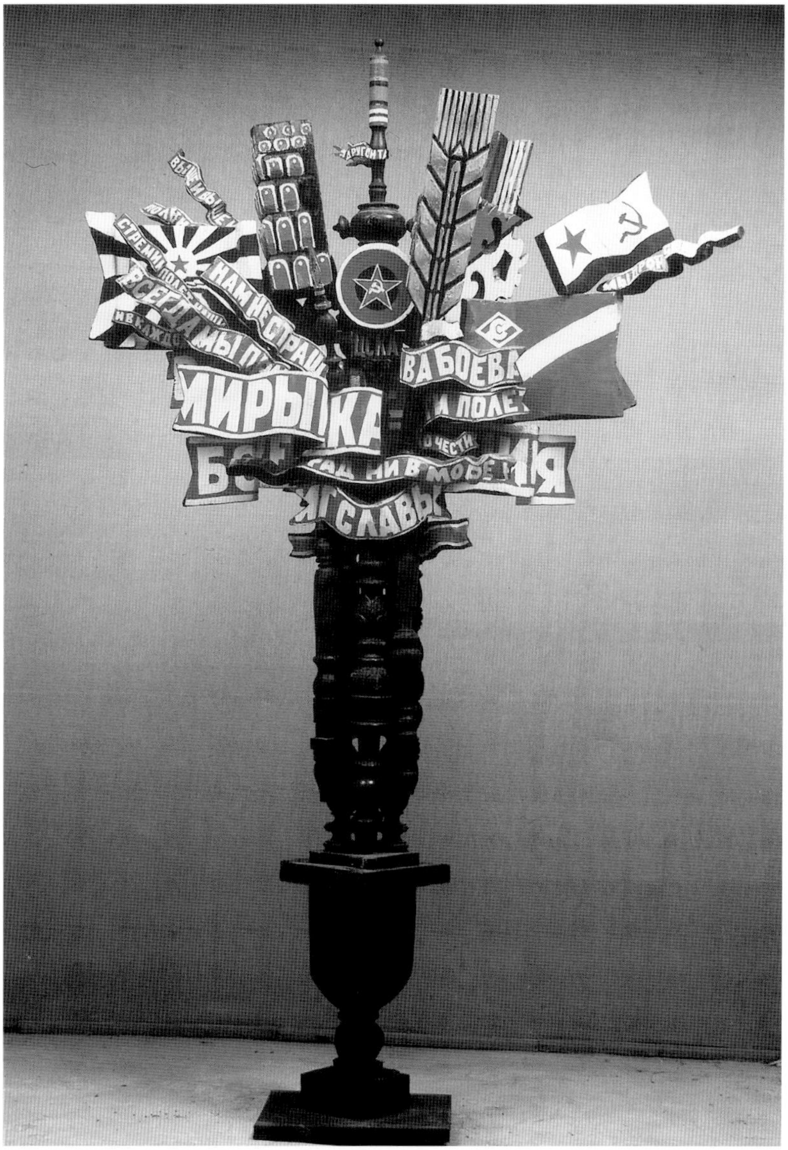

4.9
Boris Orlov, *Bouquet in Triumphal Style*, 1988.

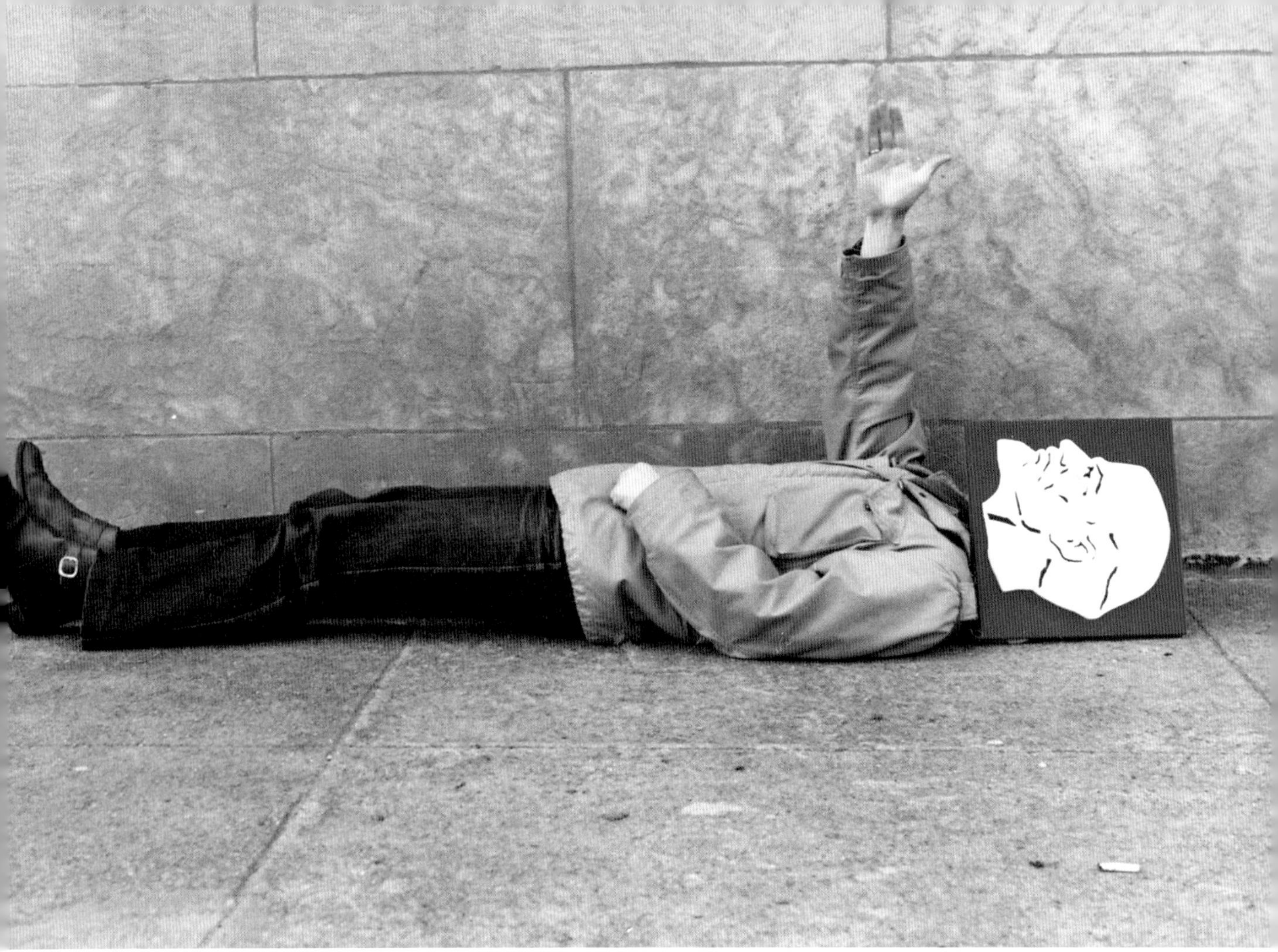

4.10
Aleksandr Kosolapov, *Untitled*,
1981.

tity as a purely mental construct: this issue has already been sufficiently appreciated in the philosophical and sociological texts of many authors.

Most often, we are dealing either with the elemental yearning for identification (identification at any cost) or with the exploitation of this yearning by the "power structures," by market forces, and by other mechanisms that give this unconscious process its conscious shape. The conscious shape, which appears before us fully armed with categories and definitions, internal and external characteristics, criteria and limitations, is what constitutes *identity* (as understood by Adorno and others of the Frankfurt School).[21] Its objectification by those identitarian thinkers and power brokers who might be called the switchmen of identification is far from being the only source of evil.[22] The will to identification that we all have plays a fairly significant part, and until that desire has run dry, identity will remain a "universal mechanism of coercion."[23] This applies, above all, to visual images, which are vacant for identification and which, starting with the mirror stage, possess an unlimited power over our psyche. If an anachronism like visual art is to survive for long, it can do so thanks only to another anachronism: unconscious nostalgia for the mirror stage (fig. 4.11).

4.11

Kazimir Passion banner displayed outside The Kitchen during the performance of *The 28th Party Congress of the Union of Soviet Socialist Republics,* November 7, 1982.

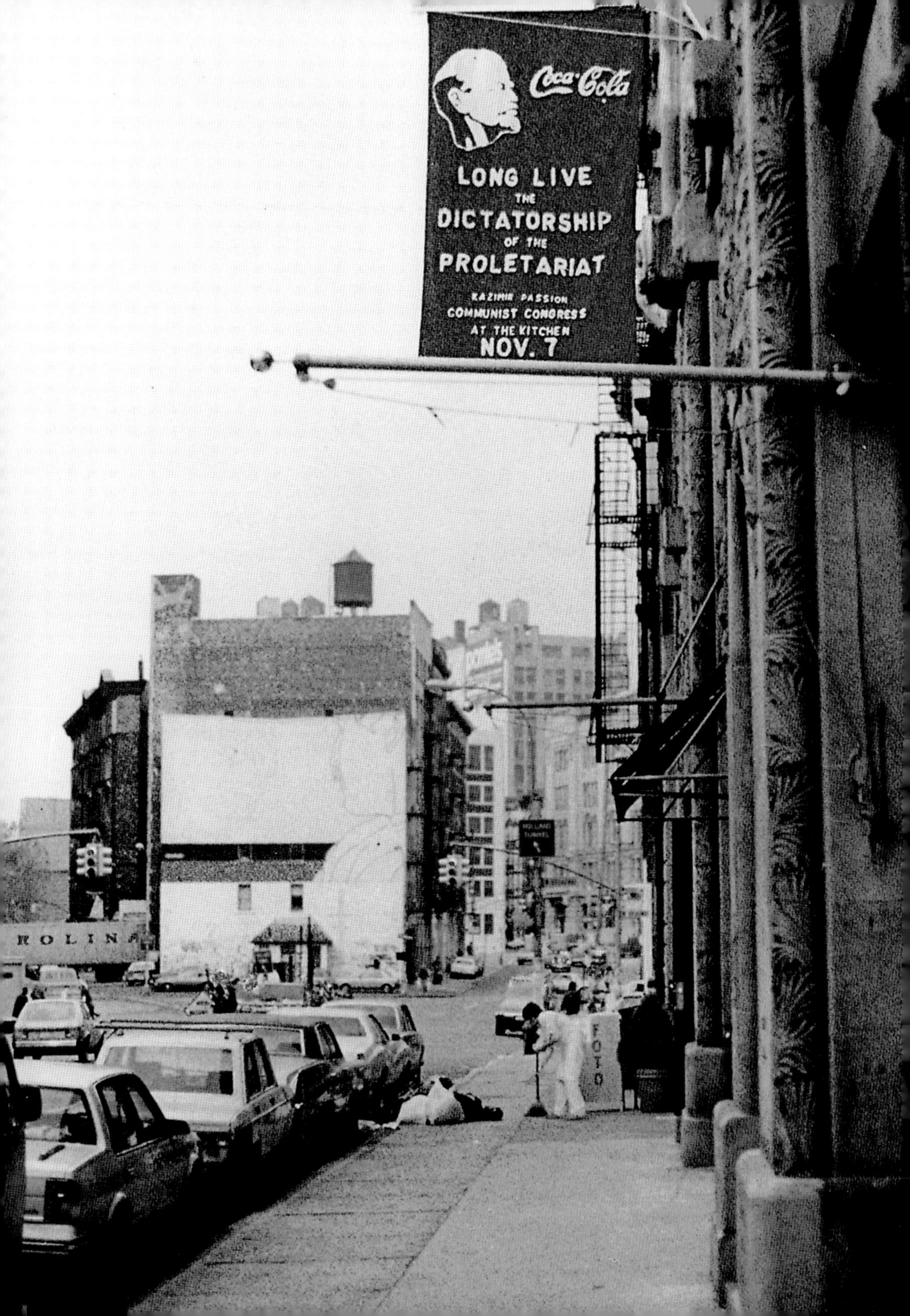
Coca-Cola
LONG LIVE
THE
DICTATORSHIP
OF THE
PROLETARIAT
KAZIMIR PASSION
COMMUNIST CONGRESS
AT THE KITCHEN
NOV. 7
FOTO

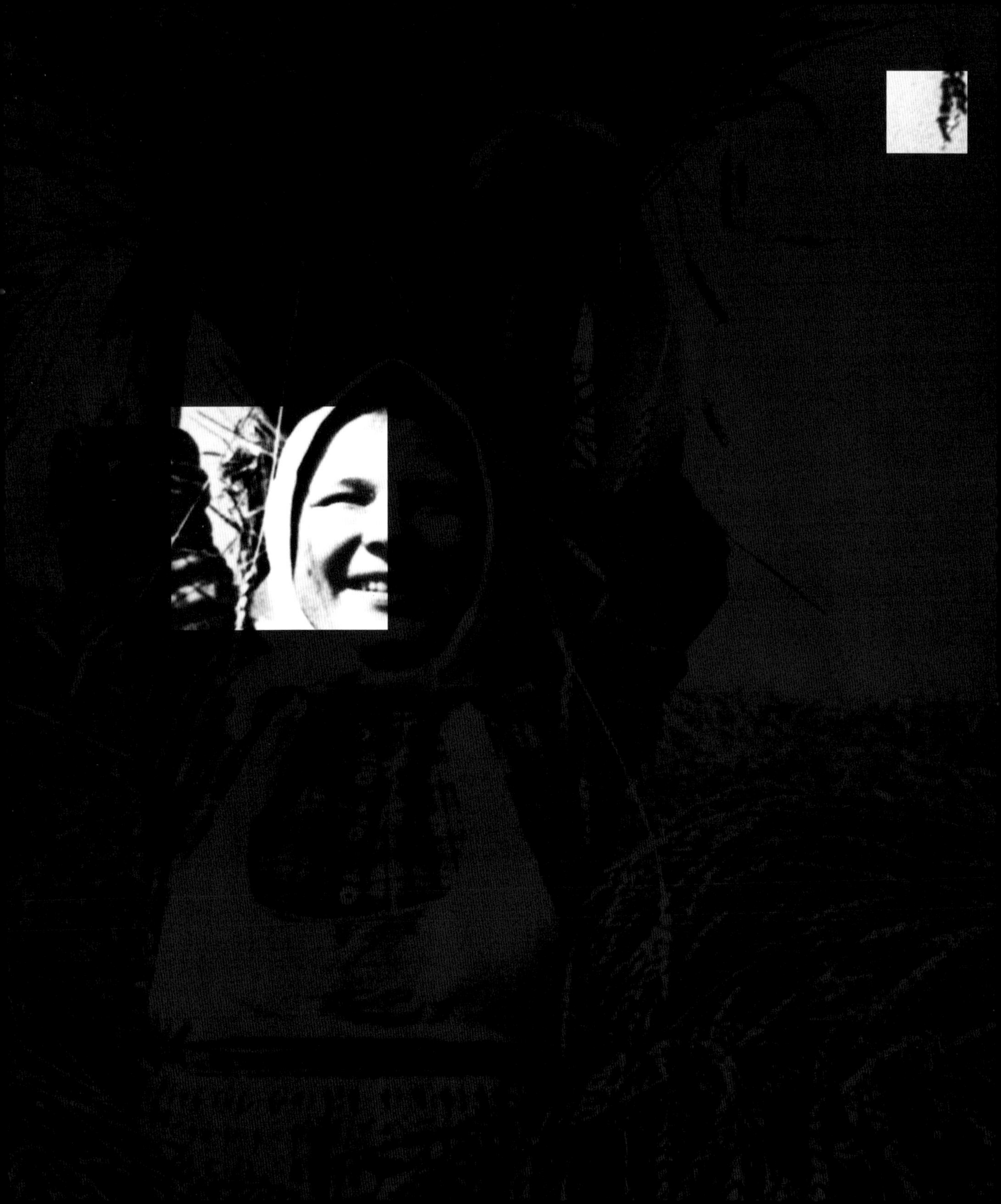

CHAPTER 5

The Sun without a Muzzle

In essence cinema is a question of the sun.
Pier Paolo Pasolini

During the 1920s the collective efforts of leftist Soviet critics and photographers, affiliated with the *New Lef* magazine or the October Association, helped mass-oriented production of images assume the protagonist's position. However, it would be wrong to suppose that the throne of easel painting was usurped by photography. Until the early 1930s this seat of power had been abandoned owing to the "Jacobin terror" of postrevolutionary photography, whose functions included, *inter alia,* guarding the "empty center" from the restoration of artistic absolutism. Nature, however, abhors a vacuum, and the role of legislator of artistic fashion was annexed by the state bureaucracy responsible for implementation of Stalin's cultural revolution.[1] In the process, many paradigms of authorship—except those attributed to authoritarian power—became increasingly nominal. The media (including photojournalism and documentary film) were transmogrified from factographic into mythographic and, in Lyotard's words, joined in the task of "stabilization of the referent, according to a point of view which endows it with a recognizable meaning enabling the addressee to decipher images and sequences quickly ... since such structures of images and sequences constitute a communication code among all of them."[2]

"Photography-as-art" reclaimed its prerevolutionary role, specifically the supplementary status to which it was relegated, Cinderella-like, by its stepsisters painting, sculpture, and architecture, which rule the pantheon of the fine arts. In all likelihood, from the point of view of the Soviet mythologizing machine, photography appeared an insufficiently mythogenic form of representation. The causes of this "innate" insufficiency were photography's lack of an aura of uniqueness, its unreliability as a means of eternalizing, erecting monuments, and gilding pedestals, or—what amounts to the same thing—the problematic nature of "photo-immortality."[3]

The very use of the term "photography-as-art" when applied to the Soviet context of the 1920s and 1930s is problematic. This is because of the ambivalent function of the photographic image, which could be seen both as a communication code ("stabilizing the referent") and as an idiomatic narrative to be read in an aesthetic context. Thus, the photo stills of Aleksandr Rodchenko, Boris Ignatovich, or Elizar Langman, which were intended for the mass media, also possessed unquestionable artistic value as individual photographic prints (fig. 5.1). Yet for these photographers, neither the prints nor the negatives were the final product. For them, quality was to a large extent that into which (in accordance with the laws of dialectics) quantity was transformed, as measured in tens of thousands of newspaper and magazine reproductions. With the rise of socialist realism, the aforementioned idiomatic narratives had gradually dissolved into the swamp of a metanarrative. As a result, photographic language degenerated into what Kabakov defines as the lyrical speech of ideology, albeit in a somewhat different context—that of mythological service, where the primary role was again reserved for the fine arts. All of these, especially painting, were granted the honor of being put to work not only in the sphere of "the stabilization of the referent" but also on the path of its incarnation. Under Stalinism, easel art repossessed its pre-Petrovian role, the role of sacred icon. Accordingly, museums became cathedrals, and albums of Soviet painting took the place of illustrated editions of the Gospels. Monumentalism was the most appropriate form for the total artistic project (Soviet-style), inasmuch as the "parasitic dependence on ritual,"[4] for which Walter Benjamin indicted traditional means of representation, became a modus operandi of socialist realism's symbolic economy. As for the latter, there is something sublimely priapic about it: even a cursory acquaintance with the monuments of the 1930s through 1950s suggests that the erection of a monument is a monument to erection. Kant's sublime and Freud's sublimated, which Jean-François Lyotard faults Jürgen Habermas for failing to differentiate, merged into one under the canopy of "high" socialist realism.

In "Civitas Solis: Ghetto as Paradise" (an allusion to Tommaso Campanella's utopian work *City of the Sun*), the principles of *nalozhenie* (analogous to double exposure in photography) were used to "expose" the similarity between the "solar myth" and official Soviet mythology. There was hardly any intention on my part to endow Soviet mythology with a legitimate "historical a priori"—legitimate in the sense that various modifications of heliotrope and its rhetorics have always been an

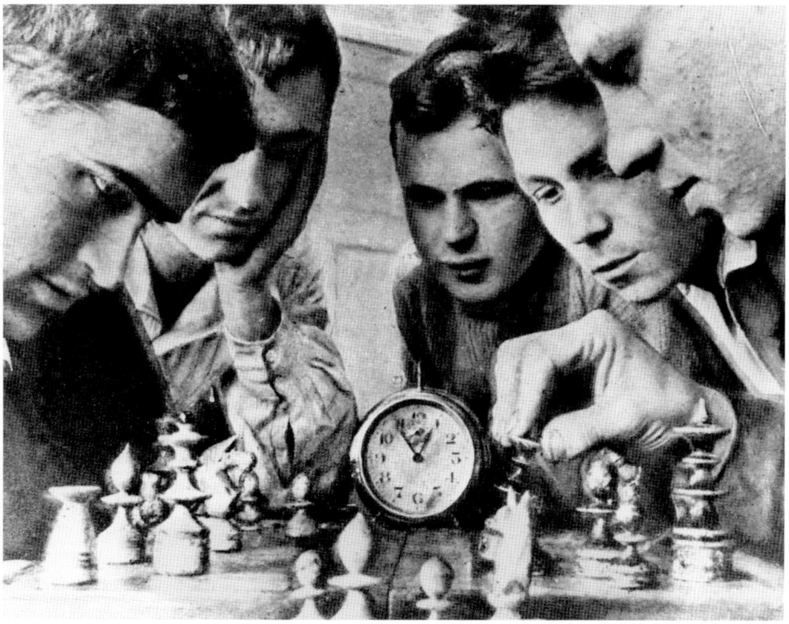

5.1
Elizar Langman, *Commune "Dynamo,"* 1930.

integral part of both religious and secular traditions. My objective was to figure out how the use of these rhetorics has led to what Habermas called "refeudalization of the public sphere."[5]

As was mentioned in chapter 1, for many Russian thinkers, artists, and poets heliotrope was a sense-of-life metaphor, a means for understanding the image of history within the framework of some unifying (albeit radial) principle. If one looks at the photograph from that perspective, it becomes disappointingly obvious that it relegates the sun to the humble role of natural signifier, of concrete (rather than metaphorical) luminescence, shedding light on fragments as well as on the whole (totality). It is the source of light energy and radial shining, which affects (without the mediation of mythological lenses and mirrors) the sensitive surface of film or the mix of gelatin and silver salts laid on paper or glass.

This "immediate" contact with the real sun (the sun without muzzle) rather than with its allegory was quite acceptable to the postrevolutionary photographers of the 1920s. With the ascendancy of socialist realism, the situation changed drastically: reality was annulled. Both the *Polis* and its Leporello—art—began to draw on an inventory of metaphorical clichés subject to the jurisdiction of the solar myth. Direct reference to the sun, technologically intrinsic to the photo genre, became politically incorrect, not to mention the fact that in the Soviet model of Civitas Solis, the status of solar icon was most often attributed to Stalin. Consequently, the utopian paradigm associated with postrevolutionary culture underwent a number of modifications in the 1930s. The presumption of the proximity of *utopos* became a "moral imperative"; therefore, the symptoms of preparadisal anxiety became an inalienable part of any artistic project. Here we should remember that when a ship approaches a pier, it slows down to avoid a wreck. That is why the "speed of time" in the situation perceived as "five minutes to paradise" is far lower than it was in the first two Five Year Plans (1928–1937): the instantaneousness related to the desire to "capture" a rapidly changing reality had ceased to be an urgent necessity. Moreover, since utopianism, paradisalism, and other varieties of apocalyptic discourse are hysterical phenomena, the incarnations of their corresponding referents no longer "look good" in black and white; they demand polychromatic, festive, psychedelic representation. It is possible that the color hallucinations produced by the communal unconscious in the years of terror and purges (which escalated as the desired goal drew nearer) motivated the "engineers of human souls"—as Stalin called artists—to abide religiously by the painterly principles appropriate to the nature of these hallucinations. The colors of the hysterical became the colors of the historical. Because of this—and also because, in those years, color photography was not yet technologically feasible[6]—the victory of the fine arts over photo discourse can be seen as determined by both economic and symbolic factors (the "symbolic" economy).

From the late 1930s, the paradisal and the colorful could not be imagined separately. However, in those rare cases where there would arise a need for nonaffirmative iconography, for capturing the painfully instantaneous state of things or for the use of a factographic approach, socialist realist painting (particularly in scenes of the unmasking or condemnation of enemies of the people) reverted (suddenly!) to black and white.[7] Through such "nonaffirmative" manifestations, painting yet again underscored everything that was characteristic of its usual (affirmative) state: its uncritical and paradisal quality and its appetite for totalization.

On one hand, the deficit of reality, characteristic of that era, stemmed from the corruption of the factual by the mythic. Photojournalism was ideally supposed to "shed light" on such a course of events, but—as Henri Cartier-Bresson pointed out—"documentary photography" is the wrong term; the right one is documentary-style photography. On the other hand, the preference for the optical over the metaphorical was not free of phenomenologial bias. This bias was the result of the reductionist attitude toward the referents (i.e., economic facts). The referents were believed to be capable of entering the realm of representation "devoid of all theory" and "any judgment."[8] The *mythical speech* of industrial photography, documentary film, newspaper, or radio reporting rested on the assumption that the sum of all possible representations constituted (like Leibnizian monads) the total panorama of context. This illusion was skillfully used by apologists of socialist realism, who believed that the "victory" over reality belonged to those who controlled its representation and neutralized suspicions of the existence of its Other (i.e., the Other of representation). Such suspicions were "cured," and are still being "cured," by hypnotizing us with the magic of repetition inherent in mass printing. Our inferiority complex in the face of huge numbers, large scales, and long distances manifests itself in the inability to distinguish between "much" and "all." Consequently, the accumulation of "quantity turning into quality" became so all-encompassing that it seemed as if things could no longer hide from the light of representation.

▪▪

In the 1970s and 1980s, some Moscow artists, particularly members of the Collective Actions group (CA), became involved in the creation of an extensive photographic dossier by documenting the events of alternative art life for the Moscow Archive of New Art (MANA). Among these artists were Igor' Makarevich, Andrei Abramov, Georgii Kizeval'ter, and Andrei Monastyrsky, who were later joined by Sergei Volkov, Andrei Roiter, and Mariia Serebriakova.[9] They all shared interests with Kabakov, who served as a connecting link between them and his long-time friend Boris Mikhailov. But whereas the members of the MANA circle were largely amateur photographers, Mikhailov represented the group of professionals who, like him, dwelled on the margins of Soviet photographic practice. This latter group consisted of Vladimir Kupriianov, Igor' Mukhin (fig. 5.2), Igor' Savchenko, Sergei Borisov, Valerii Shchekoldin, Galina Moskaleva, Sergei Kozhemiakin, Sergei Leontiev, Nikolai Bakharev, and Vasilii Kravchuk. Their photographic oeuvre could be defined as neofactography. Its distinctive characteristic is that, unlike the productions of the October Association or the Revolutionary Society of Proletarian Photographers (ROPF), which serviced the Soviet mainstream in the 1930s, the neofactographers of the 1970s and 1980s documented manifestations of marginal practices and activities. Moreover, if the fixation of the events of the 1920s and 1930s can be described in terms of "factography as affirmation," then the neofactography under discussion here is "factography as resistance."

The word "factography" has multiple connotations. In 1929, the contributors to *Lef* magazine published a collection of essays, *The Literature of Fact,* that propagandized the idea of "extra-artistic subject matter." The editor of the collection, Nikolai Chuzhak, asserted that "one need not be afraid of uninteresting content. The only thing that is required is the ability to present the uninteresting in an interesting way."[10] Actually, in addition to the "factoviks," the inspiration for factographic discourse can be traced to Mikhail Bakhtin. In his *Toward a Philosophy of the Act,* he revealed filiations between the topics of "answerability," "oughtness," and active "participance in once-occurred being in an emotional-volitional, affirmed manner."[11] In this text, worked on during his stay in Vitebsk (1920–1924), Bakhtin insisted that there was "no alibi in existence," and advocated bridging the difference between experience and representation of experience, between the motif of the "actually performed act" or deed and its product.[12] Bakhtin's *Toward a Philosophy of the Act*—which preceded treatises on the same subject undertaken in the late 1920s by Sergei Tret'iakov, Osip Brik, Chuzhak, and Walter Benjamin—comes closest to the idea of factography.[13] Anticipating the question of which facts are valuable and which are not, Bakhtin argues that there is no contradiction between unique and "affirmed value-context." He writes: "the unique 'I' must assume a particular emotional-volitional attitude toward all historical mankind: I must affirm it as really valuble to me, and when I do

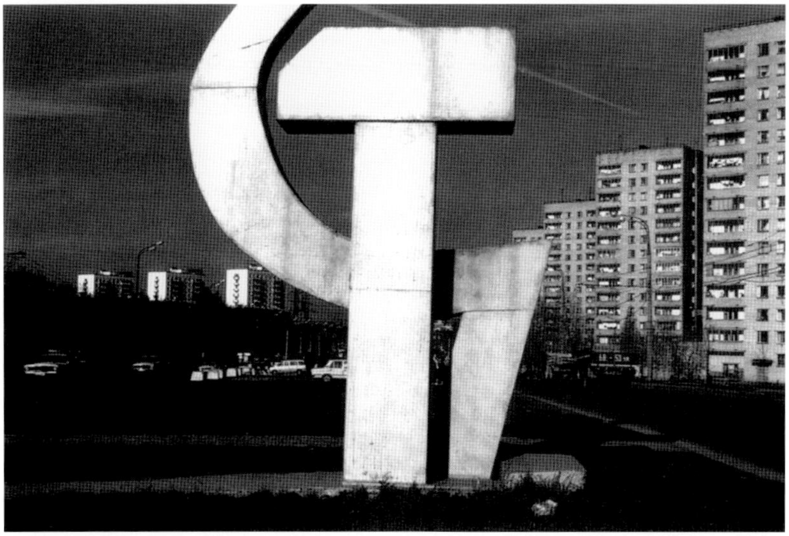

5.2
Igor' Mukhin, *Research Investigation of Soviet Monumental Arts*, 1989.

5.3
Andrei Abramov, *Skyscraper,* 1978.

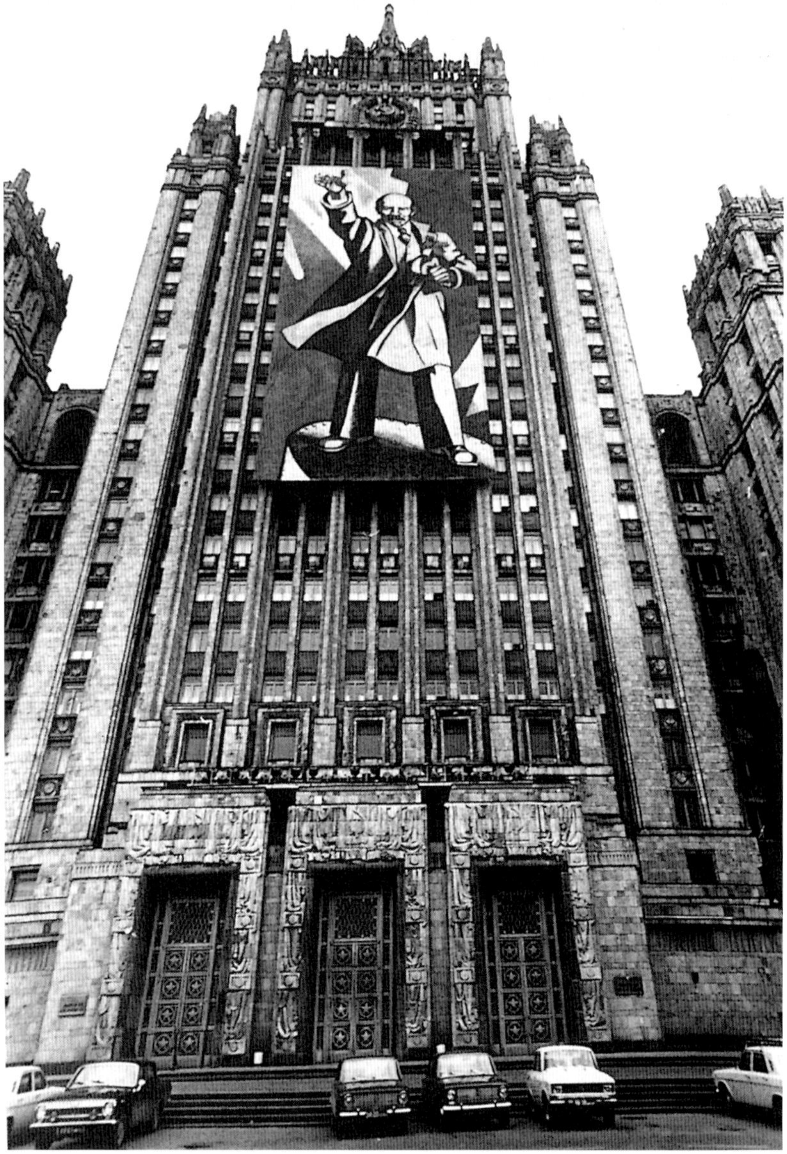

so everything valued by historical mankind will become valuable for me as well."[14] However, the factographers (most notably the members of the October Association) radically altered Bakhtin's "event-ness of Being" and "universality of the ought" as they narrowed the boundaries of "historical mankind" to contemporary, socialist ones, or, more precisely, to the reality of Stalin's Five Year Plans.

In essence, the neofactography of the 1970s and 1980s was an attempt to provide new answers to the questions: What is fact and what is reality? Is it whatever has received the grace of mass representation, or can phenomena pinned down by means of amateur snapshots, typewritten descriptive texts, letters, diary notes, and so forth, be referred to as true factuality? Adopting the latter viewpoint, factography-as-resistance set out to implement the principle that, in becoming facts of linguistic reality and therefore communicable, idiomatic narratives are endowed with a destabilizing potential capable of shaking faith in the invincibility of the affirmative culture of socialist realism and in the totality of its self-representation.

From time to time photographers from the MANA circle acted as deconstructionists unmasking the Soviet utopia. In the mid-1980s Makarevich shot several rolls of film depicting the subterranean friezes of Moscow's metro stations, especially those that included socialist realist iconographic and narrative clichés. At the time, special permission was needed to photograph in the metro,[15] an indication that the authorities regarded this space as sacred. The transgressive nature of Makarevich's action was embodied in the expansion of private factography into public space, which (from the authorities' point of view) meant infringing on the rights reserved for the official media. A similar approach to the same subject matter can be found in Abramov's and Shchekoldin's photographs of Moscow's skyscrapers, one of which is "draped" (Christo-style) in a giant portrait of Lenin, another, in that of Brezhnev; one can only imagine the frustration of civil servants forced to work in such conditions (fig. 5.3).

To be precise, Abramov's photograph depicts Lenin's portrait on a skyscraper, whereas Shchekoldin's Brezhnev was installed on the wall of a tall building. Both taken in 1978, the photographs were framed in the tradition of Rodchenko, at an angle creating a "worm's-eye view." Such an avant-garde representation of kitsch (Stalin's architecture) unambiguously brings Abramov's and Shchekoldin's photography into the neofactographic genre. Generally speaking, the ogling of authoritarian iconography through the lens of individual authorship as manifested by Makarevich with the metro's baroque interior, and by Abramov and Shchekoldin with Soviet skyscrapers, completes the deconstructive odyssey initiated in

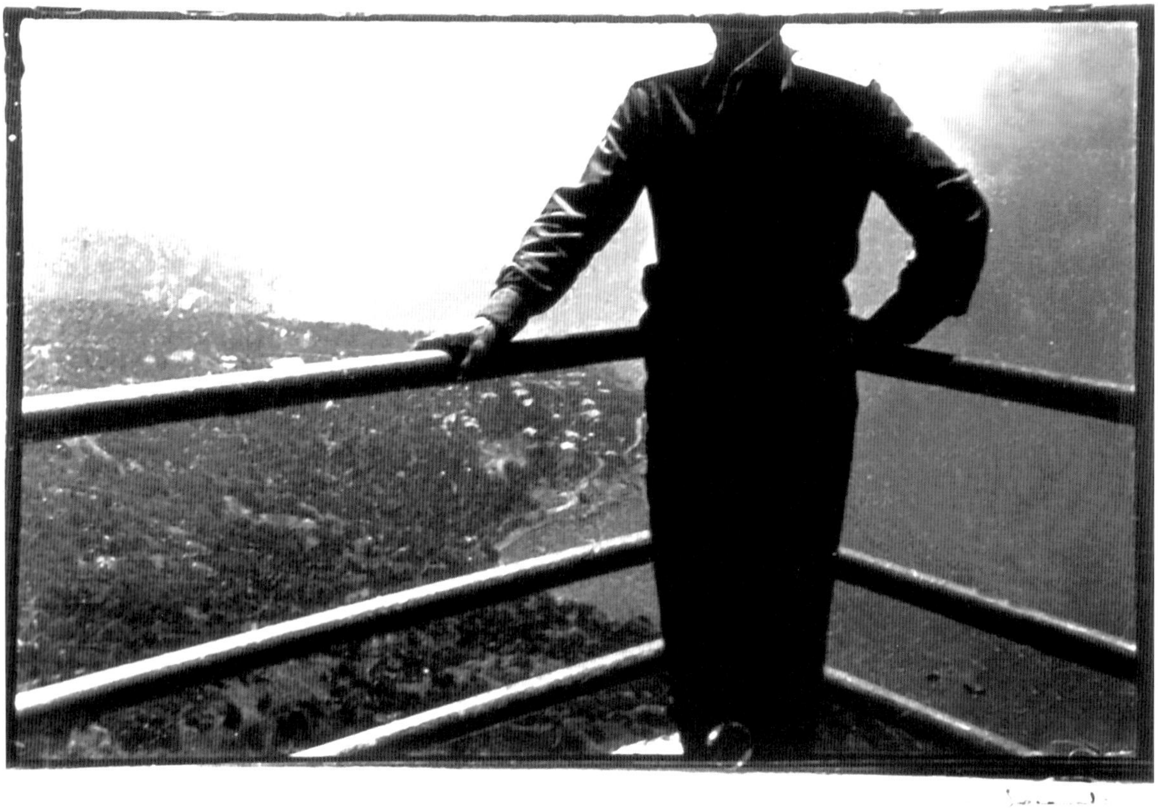

5.4
Sergei Kozhemiakin, from the series *Presence*, 1990.

the early 1970s by Komar and Melamid with regard to easel art, and by Mikhailov with regard to photography.

One cannot bypass the apologists for "backward vision" who attempt to reconstruct the image of the past by revisiting its "lacunae" and "marginalia"—that is, everything that has dropped out of the official media's scope of vision. Such revisitation is not directly nostalgic or retro. Rather, what is at issue here is an epistemological project of the reassessment of values that is related to the revision of the institutional version of the past, and to a heightened interest in apocrypha. It is from this angle that one can interpret the use of somebody else's amature photographs ("archival waste") by Kozhemiakin (fig. 5.4), Kravchuk, Savchenko, and Moskaleva, as well as the use of the photographic readymade in the collages of Serebriakova (fig. 5.5) and Aleksei Shulgin. History as traditionally conceived (with a capital *H*) is an inventory of names, events, and dates "deserving of attention." Knowing that the selection and presentation of this inventory is the prerogative of the powers that be, alternative artists and photographers question the authenticity of the historical heritage imposed on them, and give preference to the *other.* The *other,* in this instance, is the photo archive of accidentally preserved testimonials to an unofficially recorded, anonymous past, whose recording falls to neofactography. Thus, post facto, in the process of an a posteriori repossession of the truth—a truth that was unacceptable to the mythographers of the 1940s or 1950s—the prosaic realities of those years are reclaimed from oblivion: fragments of everyday life; the haggard faces of heavy-drinking war veterans caught unaware in moments of "leisure"; portraits of relatives and friends; unremarkable landscapes; street and backyard scenes; casual, pathos-stripped scenes of a de-heroized yesterday. The generosity with which these artists search for the lost and ordinary time of others leads one to think that *das Sein* cannot lay claim to authenticity without compassion for *Dasein.*

In some instances, this generosity does not stretch to encompass the ethics of representing human misery and degradation. At times, concern for humanity-as-a-whole triumphs over compassion for an individual. This reproach, however, cannot be addressed to Mikhailov, who once admitted to American photographer Diane Neumaier that he would never let his camera take advantage of humiliating moments or aspects of human existence, unless these moments and aspects are engendered by social causes. His *Salt Lakes* series (1985) perfectly illustrates Mikhailov's ethical vision. While showing hundreds of sick and elderly people bathing in a salty and polluted swamp next to a deserted water-freshening plant, he remains

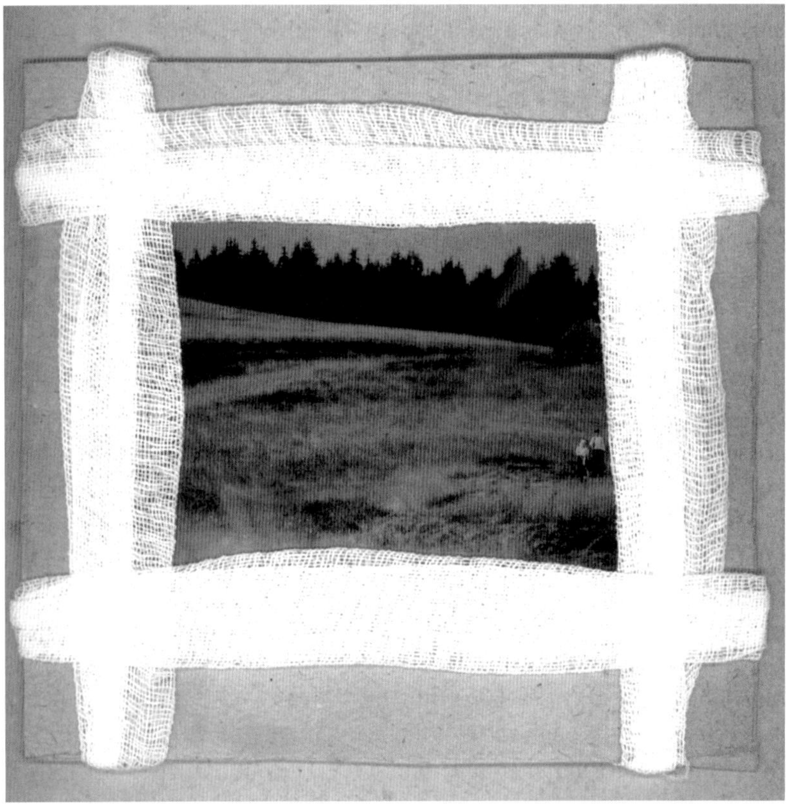

5.5
Mariia Serebriakova, *Untitled*, 1989.

hopelessly unable to capitalize on the "apocalyptic" *plaisir* of witnessing pain and suffering.

In the photographic section of the 1995 exhibition "Damaged Utopia,"[16] Mikhailov's photographs (from *By Land*) (fig. 5.6) were placed next to Anatolii Skurikhin's *Harvest* (1937) (fig. 5.7) and Boris Kudoiarov's *At the Glass Factory* (1950). The objective was to juxtapose the rhetoric of anticipation (peculiar to the Soviet mass media of the 1930s) with the current tendency to present evidence of unfulfilled anticipation. Among the contemporary photographers who participated in the exhibition were Shchekoldin, Volkov, Borisov, and Makarevich. Their contribution to "Damaged Utopia" consisted of *nonaffirmative* images examined vis-à-vis the *affirmative* photography endorsed by the state from the 1930s through the early 1950s. The themes of the nonaffirmative photographs ranged from damaged infrastructure to crowds of exhausted and depressed people, and accentuated the phenomenon of decaying utopia. Mikhailov and his colleagues also attempted to demonstrate the transformations that had occurred in the politics of representation of the human body as it shifted from the heroic, healthy, and youthful to the mundane, sickly, and aged. This approach leads one to pose the question: Can our lost and falsified past be recaptured, or is it just another dream, seen backward?

Although Mikhailov's urban landscapes are entirely inhabitable, one cannot "enter" them: the eye can only glide over the surface of the print. Entrance into the no-exit predicament, to which Mikhailov's photographs attest, is problematic because of the increased psychological, rather than demographic, density of the image. The photographer's desire to give it weight makes it akin to diving into mercury, where immersing oneself is as difficult as surfacing. This observation, however, applies less to the hand-colored prints than it does to the toned photographs from the blue and the brown series—*Murk*[17] (or *At Dusk*), of 1991, and *By Land*, of 1993. While socialist realist art has frequently been discussed in terms of enticement, cathartic merging, and so on, *Murk* evokes the phenomenon of repulsion (the mercury phenomenon). The strategy employed by Mikhailov to identify and record this phenomenon is close to the kind of neofactographic genre that could be described as the factography of decathartization.

The murky mood of *Murk* is also present in the works of Leontiev and Bakharev (fig. 5.8). What distinguishes them from Mikhailov is that in their photographs—regardless of how depressive they are—the center of gravity shifts from the urban landscape to the personage, which is not true of *Murk*, where the hopelessness is impersonal. All these deviations are attained at the price of crashing through Mikhailov's "mercury barrier"

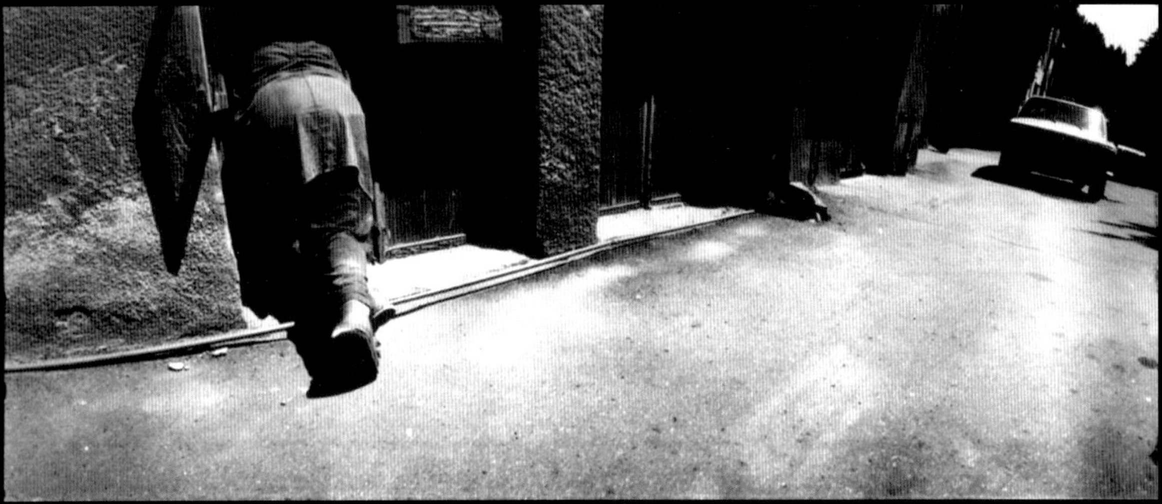

5.6
Boris Mikhailov, *By Land,* 1991.

5.7
Anatolii Skurikhin, *Harvest,* 1937.

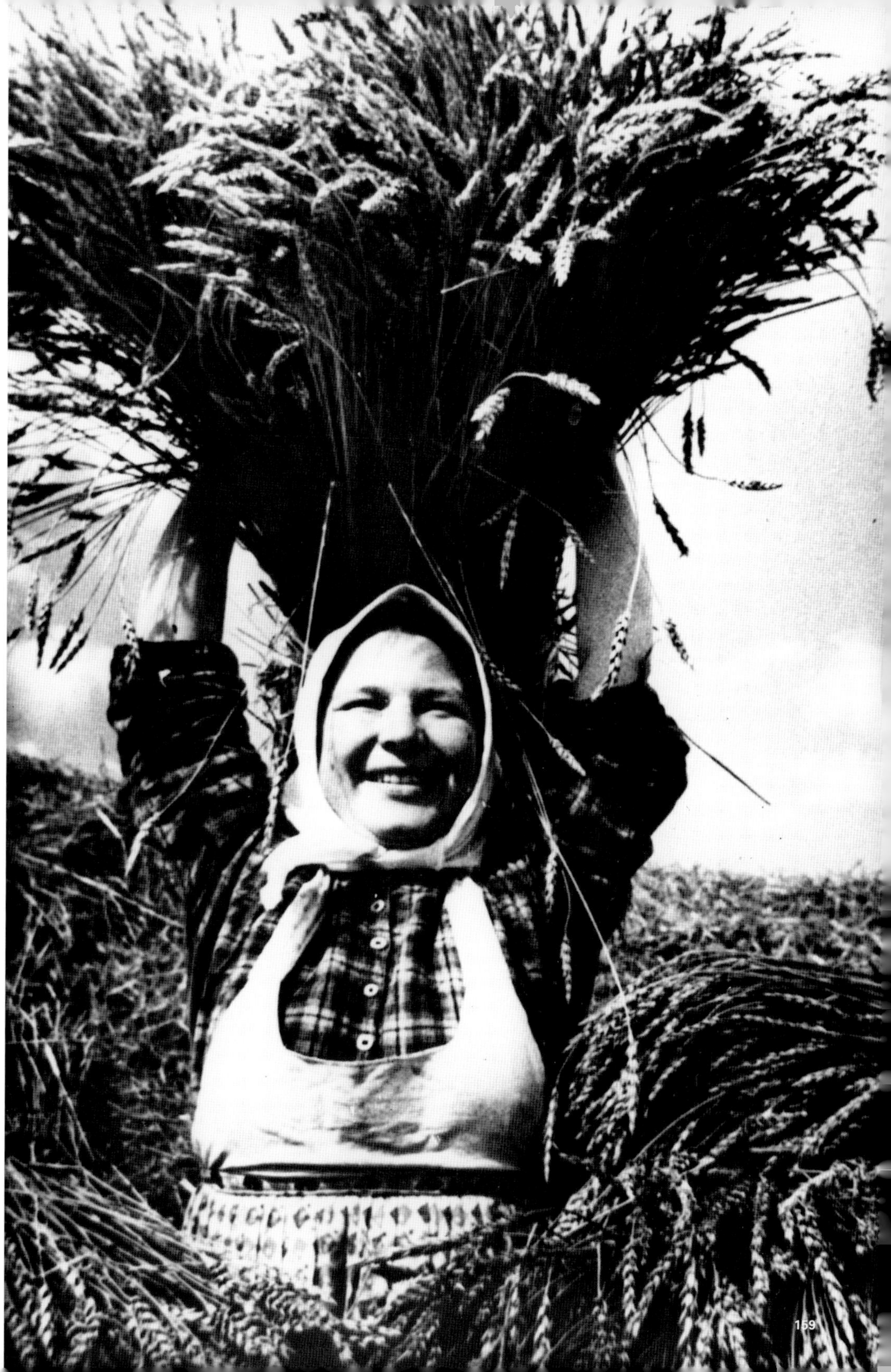

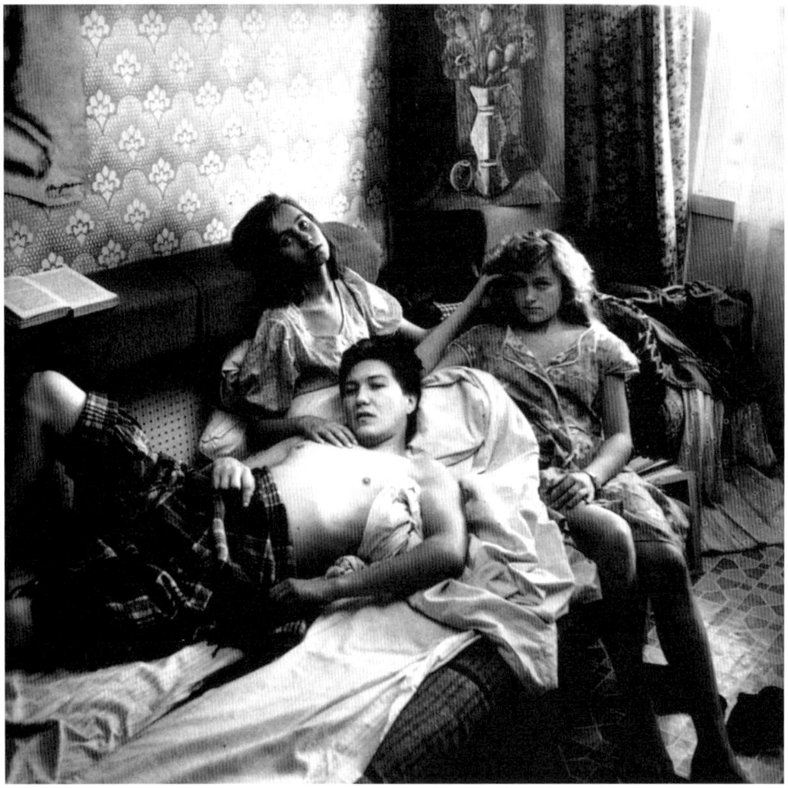

5.8
Nikolai Bakharev, from the series
Our Life Is Not a Castle, 1989.

that protects us not simply from confronting the horrors of reality, but—to some extent—from the discomforts of enjoying them (i.e., from experiencing an "apocalyptic" *plaisir*). With the brutality and naturalism typical of their method, Leontiev and Bakharev put on display the "seamy side" that remains hidden in the background in Mikhailov's photographs. This allows the "respectable public" to see desperate people crushed by the hard ships of day-to-day existence. Among the shortcomings of such excessive empiricism is its tendency to take a voyeuristic stance or to have a didactic attitude toward people's miseries. Here, one can think of Diane Arbus and Garry Winogrand, as well as of Richard Billingham's *Untitled, 27 Tales* (1993–1997) or Donigan Cumming's photographic series *Pretty Ribbons* (1993). Cumming's works, in their nerve-wracking pitch and lack of spontaneity, are comparable to the revelations of Leontiev and Bakharev.

Borisov has a photograph in which Vera Mukhina's cyclops-like sculpture *The Worker and the Female Collective Farmer* literally blocks out the sun, while a plane's Apelles' line (vapor trail) slices the sky. The allegory is transparent: the earth, nature, and the sky belong not to Physis but to Mythos. The abolished reality creates a state of weightlessness, or rather a situation in which metaphors alone possess weight; they cause a monstrous hysterogenic pressure, compensated for by rare moments of equally unbearable happiness. The series of photographs in which Borisov recreates the lightness of the movements, demonstrated by Champions of the World, vividly illustrates the above (see fig. 2.35). The Champions' record-setting jumps, their flight in the air against a background of bulky Stalinist architecture, exacerbate the contrast between the weight of petrified metaphor and the ephemeral quality of existence. In this respect, Borisov's series recalls Kabakov's album entitled *They Fly* (1972–1975).

Another important part of Borisov's oeuvre conveys the texture of daily life (*byt*) in the time of perestroika, with its incestuous relationship between the old and the new unfolding amid the ruins of Civitas Solis. In each of these photographs, the sense of internal ruin is attained with a selection of tourist-poster views of run-down fountains, monuments, the Kremlin towers, or the Moscow River embankments as background. The "underhandedness" of this choice lies in the fact that this entire set of architectural codes, meant to attest to the indestructibility of the solar myth, has long been ruined; moreover, it was not stone or concrete constructions that were destroyed but rather mental constructs, that is, "solarly engaged" metaphors. This debacle, which consisted of the collapse of the heliotrope rooted in the communal psyche, is the main subject of Borisov's photo narratives.

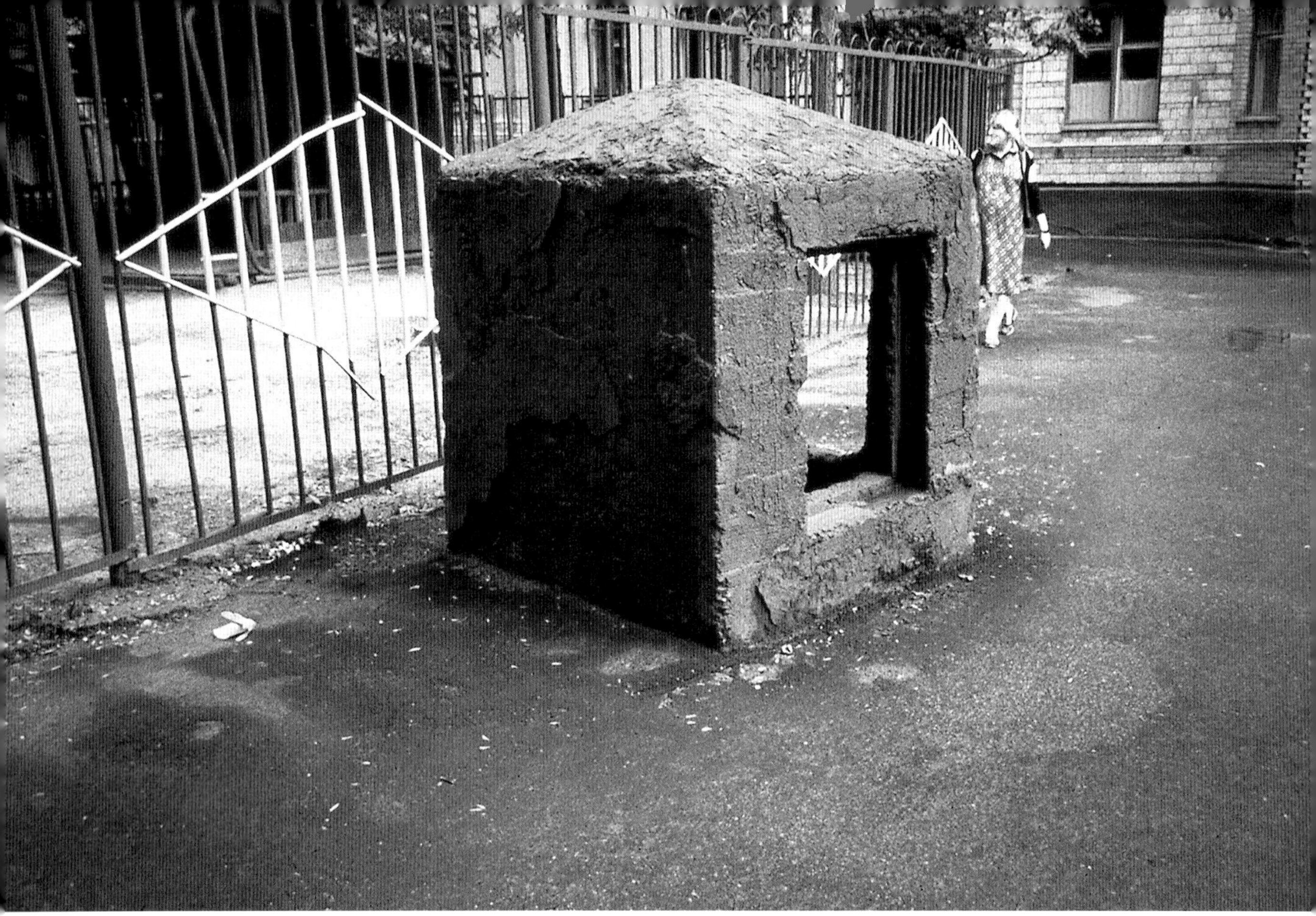

5.9
Andrei Roiter, *Untitled*, 1988.

A similar motif can be traced in the works of Volkov and Roiter, both of whom were involved in the factographing of chaos, withering, and disintegration (fig. 5.9). Later, their thanatalogical palette of neglected garages, fences, and trash heaps became integrated, by them and by others, into paintings, installations, and three-dimensional objects. With Makarevich, the representation of this subject matter takes us back to the concept of "inner speech" proposed by Vygotsky: photography captures the neon letters of the slogan "GLORY" reflected in the window of a slum building—in such a way, moreover, as if it were coming from deep inside the room rather than from across the street. Makarevich's fellow CA member Kizeval'ter paid his own tribute to the documentation of Soviet *byt* in a series of photographs commissioned by Kabakov and representing the environment of the communal apartment (see fig. 3.3). If the evolution of the Russian avant-garde of the 1910s and 1920s can be perceived as movement from *faktura* to factography,[18] the 1980s marked a merging of the two within the framework of the deconstructive paradigm defined as "factographic *faktura,*" that is, factography by means of *faktura.*

Mikhailov's "factographic *faktura*" is saturated with intertextuality: some of the pictures are crowded with his own hand-written remarks about the images or reflecting upon recent conversations with friends. In one of the pieces from his *Sots Art* series (1975–1985), he writes a typically Soviet song on the margins of the photograph: "The armor is stiff, and our tanks are fast." Beside the text is an image of a playground with the "skeleton" of a make-believe tank for children, painted red. The juxtaposed narratives—verbal and visual—are lethal in relation to one another: their rhetorics become deconstructed, which seems to be the author's intention. In *Unfinished Dissertation* (1984), photographs with Mikhailov's writings on their margins are glued to the back of pages of a doctoral thesis by an unknown scholar who had vanished before the dissertation was completed (see fig. 3.8). In this conceptual work Mikhailov reenacts the making of a palimpsest, which serves as an analogy of the ruthless overcoding immanent to our cultural and historical "Being-toward-death."[19]

To follow up on the notion of factography, I will cite Derrida's essay "Back from Moscow, in the USSR," in which he comments on Walter Benjamin's letter to Martin Buber, written a few days after Benjamin's return from the USSR, on February 23, 1927, and rife with what Derrida calls its author's "desire to present his diaries in such a way that it would appear as the referent's self-description, without being—as the phenomenologist would put it—'constituted' by Benjamin."[20] The deconstructionist's target here is Benjamin's promise "to succeed in allowing the creatural to speak for itself" and "to write a description of Moscow at the present moment, . . . which would thereby refrain from any deductive abstraction, from any prognostication and even within certain limits from all judgments—all of which . . . cannot be formulated in this case on the basis of spiritual 'data' but only on the basis of economic facts."[21] In Derrida's view, there is a philosophical claim of enormous proportions in these lines, where "the interpretive content is endowed with pre-interpretive status."[22]

Regardless of who takes responsibility for drawing the line between "truth about lies" and "lies about truth," the criteria governing factographic discourse have never been clear-cut. The mystery of factography is that it can be both the labyrinth and an Ariadne's thread, and when the latter takes turn, it gives hope that despite its phenomenological bias, (neo) factography is still capable of resisting forces that impose on us their vision of past and present.

▪▪

The critique of representation, as articulated in *Anti-Oedipus* and *A Thousand Plateaus* by Gilles Deleuze and Felix Guattari, found new expression in a performance by the CA group called *Ten Appearances,* described in chapter 3 (see fig. 3.7). In this project, ten spectators were invited to participate in the action, and were then given the opportunity to look at what were presented as photographs of themselves taken from a considerable distance and therefore not easily identifiable. No one doubted the authenticity of the pictures, though in fact they had been taken several days prior to the performance.[23] *Ten Appearances* demonstrated the fragility of the border between representation of fact and the fact of representation. Incidentally, rather convincing critiques of both the pictorial and factographic ambitions of photography were offered by Shulgin in his *Rotating Landscapes* (1991) and by Andrei Filippov. Shulgin mounted color photographs on plywood with a small electric motor on the back of the frame; due to rotation, everything was out of focus, which distorted both the aesthetic and factographic dimensions of the representation. Filippov—in order to fill the vacancy of the "historical a priori"[24]—ironically appropriated photographs from CA's *Ten Appearances* in order to "invade" them with his trademark images—double-headed eagles, the symbol of Russian monarchy.

In the West, the tendencies related to the critique of representation are realized in the genre of ironic imitation of the processes immanent to metanarrativity itself. The photogenic nature of these processes is a phenomenon that has not escaped the attention of post-photographers (post-factographers) whose ranks include Kupriianov, along with Barbara Krueger, Richard Prince, Louise Lawler, and Jeff Wall. At the level of the "politics of the signifier," the distinctions between him and his American colleagues are insignificant. Each uses a strategy that condones the expansion of the textual (verbal) into the territory of the visual. In Kupriianov's 1982 photo album *A Work after Pushkin* (fig. 5.10), two kinds of public property—cultural heritage and mass propaganda—are brought together with riveting persuasiveness. Here, lines from Pushkin's poetry are juxtaposed with portraits of the Soviet heroines of the labor front, photographs made from street displays or "boards of honor." As a result, the present parachutes into the past, while the past receives the right to reside in the present. In the process, an act of deconstruction takes place that unmasks the extratemporal ambitions of Soviet cultural thinking, full of the "metaphysics of presence."

In 1984, Kizeval'ter made his *Umbrella Album,* consisting of photographs of Moscow's alternative artists. Each of those who posed—whether indoors or out—was photographed with an umbrella, whose presence (if one forgets about rain) could be interpreted as a preventive measure against two evils: the searing rays of the physical sun, and the light pressure of *heliocracy.*[25] Umbrellas, especially open ones, resemble parentheses, suggesting an association with the phenomenological bracketing (*epoché*) of that variety, which centers on the so-called ontico-ontological difference and, in this instance, the difference between sun-as-such and sun-as-metaphor.

The mystery of the "true purpose" of the umbrella was, in all likelihood, revealed to Nietzsche. Otherwise, his note in the *Nachlass,* "I have forgotten my umbrella,"[26] would not have generated such an abundance of interpretations in philosophical literature. One of the numerous solutions to this puzzle is that the umbrella, in accordance with the tradition of Nietzschean poetics, can be easily interpreted as a fragment of the veil of Maya, which camouflages the "unattractive" factual state of things. Therefore, to forget one's umbrella is a choice equivalent (particularly for the author of *The Birth of Tragedy*) to a preference for the Dionysian over the Apollonian. A fundamentally different solution to the same problem is framed by James Joyce in *Finnegans Wake:* the injunction "Love me, love my umbrella" hints at the possibility of reading it as "love my Dionysian hypostasis, love the Apollonian one"—and in particular, the latter is that individualized version of the veil of Maya for which the umbrella serves as a metaphor.

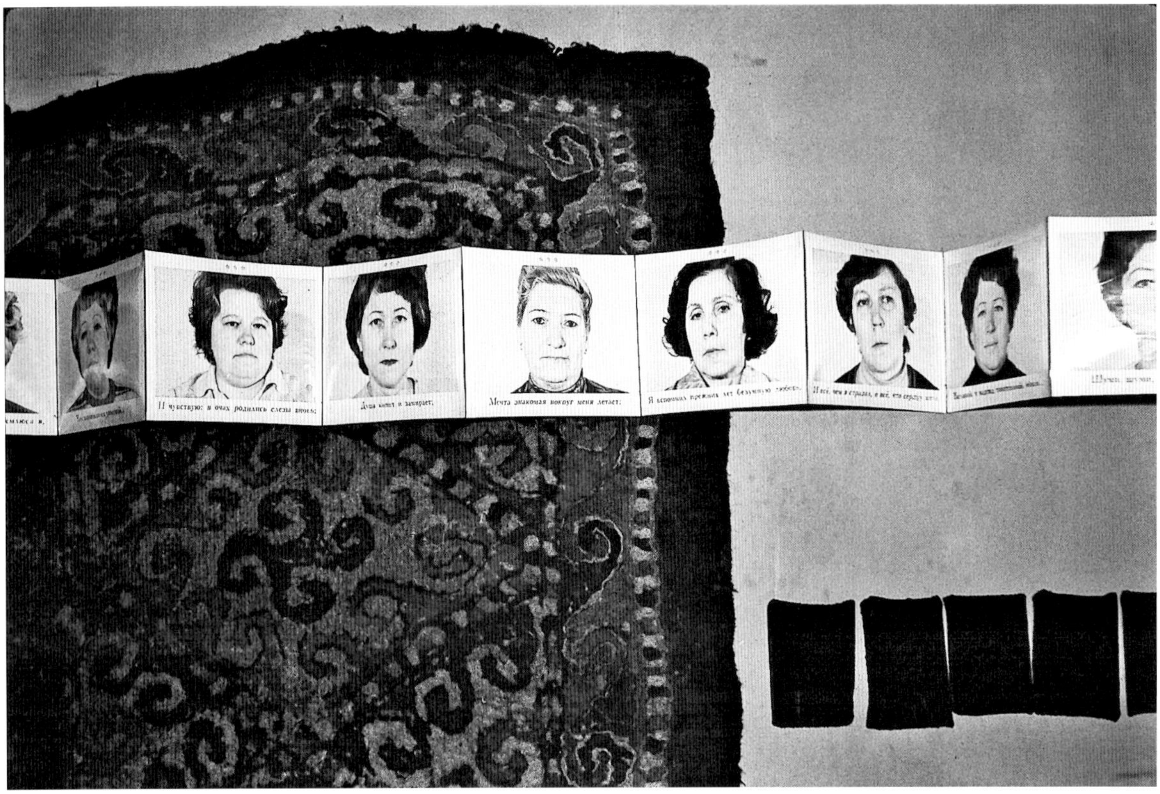

5.10
Vladimir Kupriianov, *A Work after Pushkin*, 1982.

"Rats are the doves of the cellars," the Leningrad poet Vladimir Burich wrote in the late 1950s. For him—as for his peers—reality was associated with something frightening, corporate, toxic, possessing ratlike qualities and habits. "Fate prowls in dovelike steps," said Nietzsche, for whom the contrast between the Apollonian and the Dionysian boiled down to the distinction between anesthetizing stability guaranteed by myth and the absence of all guarantees on the part of that which "prowls in dovelike steps"—of circumstance, identified with fate. Hence, the sense of horror we experience when encountering reality—expressed in the fear of rats, which was exploited by O'Brien in George Orwell's *1984* to break down Winston's resistance. In essence, the latter feared rats (i.e., *la réalité*) more than he feared his adversary.

In Lyotard's opinion, the abjectness of reality is explained by the shortage of it ("peu de réalité")[27] caused by the overabundance of metaphor. This conclusion is correct with regard to the half-century of Soviet history dating from the early 1930s to the late 1980s. In the 1990s, the situation was turned inside out in the sense that the shortage of reality gave way to its metastases. The post-perestroika *byt* spread out before the camera lens has become more Dionysian than before. The fragmentation of the Apollonian, whose veil of Maya once gave the illusion of a communal (total) umbrella, has led to the emergence of a multitude of individual small umbrellas, attesting to the fact that an *authoritarian* ideology has disintegrated into a myriad of *authorial* ideologies. Their legitimation requires new structures and institutions, including artistic ones. While these are at an embryonic stage, the features of the new metanarrative are as yet unformed. Therefore, the question of the status of factography in the post-perestroika era remains open.

CHAPTER 6

If I Were a Woman

During the late nineteenth and the early twentieth centuries, the image of woman was used in ways similar to the representations of nature: both were praised and simplified, idealized and exploited, admired and derided. To substantiate this point, one may focus attention on Mikhail Vrubel.[1] This "Russian Cézanne" (as Moscow art historians call him) died in 1910 after spending ten years in a psychiatric institution. At the the end of the 1890s Vrubel created a series of drawings and canvases plotted around Mikhail Lermontov's poem "The Demon," the love story between an innocent young beauty, Tamara, and the Evil Spirit. If Vrubel is comparable with Cézanne, then it is only in the context of the "supplementarity principle" laid bare by Derrida in his analysis of Rousseau's texts. Where in Cézanne's landscapes "that dangerous [read: demonic] supplement" can be seen as the fragmented nature of modernist vision (or the fragmented character of modernist optics), in Vrubel's art the "supplementarity principle" acquires an anthropomorphic guise as it manifests itself iconically through the image of the Demon. The Demon's love, Tamara, is endowed by Vrubel with a role similar to that of Mont Sainte-Victoire in Cézanne's paintings: both represent Rousseau's ideal of Nature. However unwillingly, both Vrubel and Cézanne slay the ideal, the former with the Demon's kisses and the latter with his brush strokes.

After the October Revolution, Russian women were liberated to the degree that they were required to serve not only their husbands, but also the government. Their actual participation in the decision-making process was exaggerated by Soviet propaganda. In the former USSR the representatives of the "weaker sex" dealt with a double patriarchy, first with their spouses and then with the masculine authority of the state. The representation of women in the Soviet mass culture of the 1930s became

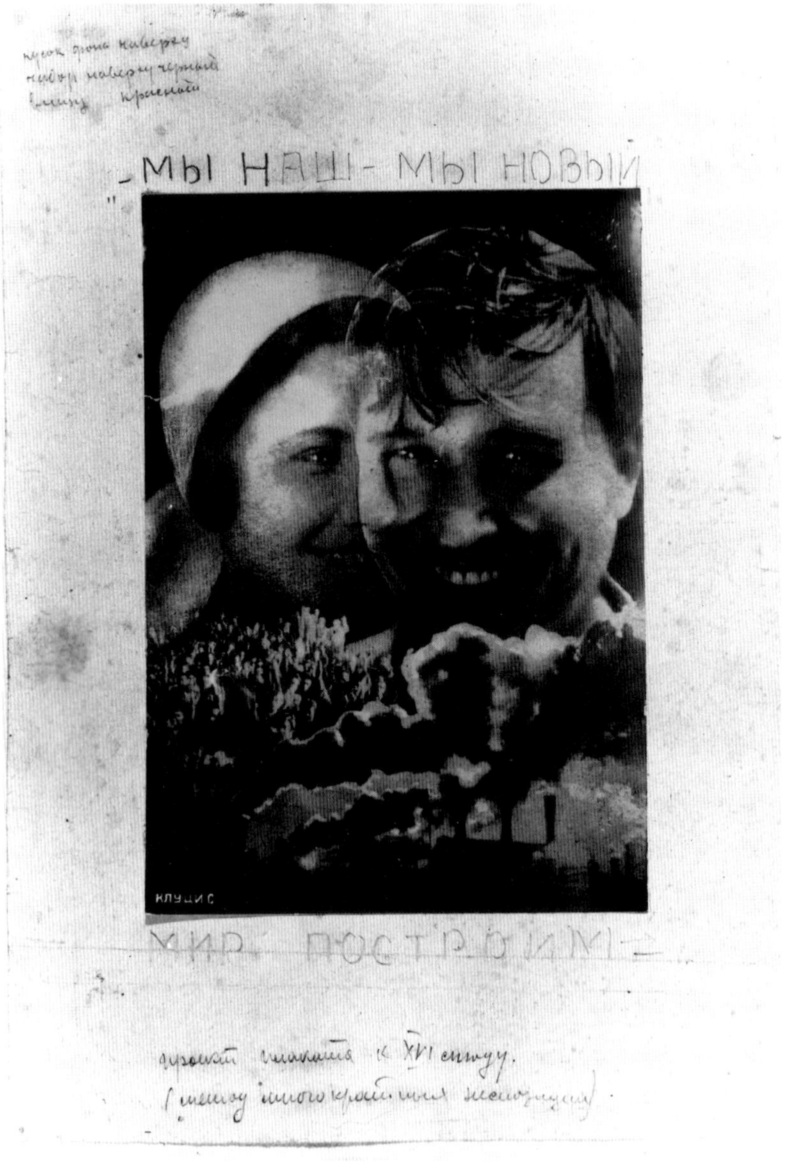

6.1
Gustav Klutsis, design for the poster *We Will Build Our Own New World*, ca. 1929.

gradually androgynized. Femininity was ejected from the "Society of the Spectacle" (Soviet-style) as a result of the official media's efforts to depict women as genderless utopian machines. This can be seen in El Lissitzky's design for the 1929 "Russian Exhibition" in Zurich, in Gustav Klutsis's ca. 1929 poster *We Will Build Our Own New World* (fig. 6.1), and in Vera Mukhina's 1937 sculpture *The Worker and the Female Collective Farmer.*

Perhaps it is never too late, especially for those involved in Soviet and Russian studies, to begin scrutinizing issues that the Russians either ignore or view as Western imports. Among these are issues of gender, homosexuality, and feminism. Curiously, the most severe responses to feminism are fermenting among women. Thus, a presentation by Swedish critic Maria Lind at a symposium on contemporary photography at the Central House of the Arts in January 1994 was followed by irate comments from a Moscow colleague. The latter stated that unlike Western feminists who fight for equality with men, "the Russian woman enslaves them with her body." In her opinion, the West has far less social experience than Russia. The first of these statements is inadequate because a side effect of male dominance in society is to involve women in a competitive, win-lose situation, the masculine nature of which is beyond doubt. Therefore, for a woman to "enslave [man] through her body" means that she must become him—or, in other words, become a phallic woman. As for the second statement, one cannot help recalling both Baudrillard, for whom "socialism [Kremlin-style] is the death of the social," and the fact that until the early 1990s, the experience of Soviet citizens was communal, not social.

Incidentally, everyone at the symposium was struck by the excessively long skirt, sleeves, and collar height of the person who urged women to "enslave through the body." At a later date, she was photographed naked with two equally naked males, the Moscow critics Vladimir Sal'nikov and Andrei Kovalev. The photograph appeared in the catalogue of Oleg Kulik's exhibition at the Marat Gelman Gallery in May 1994 (fig. 6.2). Although the woman's name was not mentioned, it turned out she was Ludmila Lunina, an art critic. All the individuals in the picture are fairly well fed, so the problem of "bodily aggression" can be read (in this visual context) as something entirely real. Moreover, a closer look reveals that "enslavement through the body" is the prerogative of the masculine, not the feminine "principle." Lunina is crouching and supporting, caryatid-like, the genitals of the atlantes towering over her—thus demonstrating the inadequacy of her thesis.

Until the mid-1990s, feminist intellectual praxis was not welcomed by Moscow's alternative artists. In 1987, Natalia Nesterova and several other Muscovite women artists ardently denied any attempt by critics, colleagues, or the public to view their artistic oeuvre within the framework

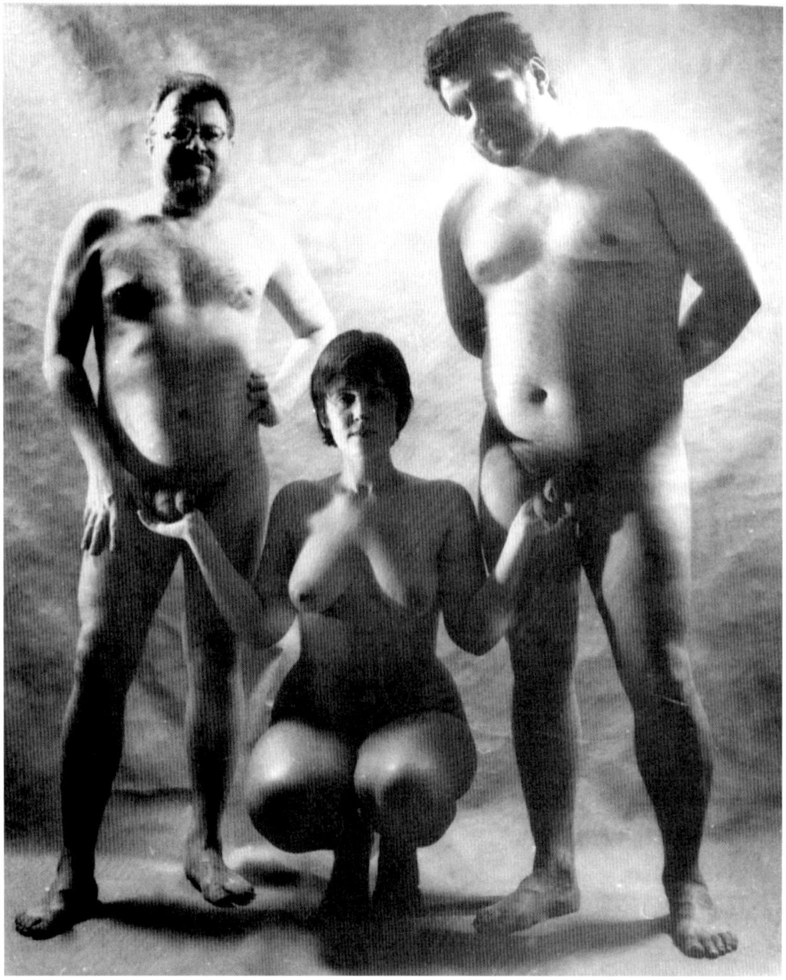

6.2
Anonymous, *Untitled*, 1994.

of a feminist agenda. One can perhaps relate this resistance to their lack of awareness of the importance of gender, body politics, male dominance, and sexism, and the artist's responsibility to critically reflect upon these issues. This sort of attitude is gradually changing thanks to a steady stream of Western literature that flows into Moscow. A specific example of such a change was the organization of the first feminist art exhibition in Moscow at the Oktiabrskaia Exhibition Hall in September 1990. The show's participants were Anna Al'chuk, Elena Elagina, Mariia Konstantinova, Vera Miturich-Khlebnikova, Irina Nakhova, Sabina Haensgen, and Elena Shakhovskaia (figs. 6.3, 2.36).[2] In this exhibition, titled "Female Worker [Rabotnitsa]" the artists engaged in a subversive reexamination of the ways women are represented officially and privately in codes, signs, and visual stereotypes throughout the culture.[3] One should also mention two other exhibitions of women's art: "Visitation," of March 1991, and "Hearts of the Four [Serdtsa cheterekh]," which took place in the summer of 1992. Rather than attempting to analyze gender politics, these events were more playful in nature. For example, the male curator and some male artists decided to participate in "Visitation" under female surnames, thus confusing and diminishing the issues of feminism.[4]

Earlier, I cited examples of utopian androgynes in the art of the 1920s and 1930s. But even today, the specter of androgyny continues to captivate the imagination of artists seeking a way out of the blind alley of identification. In this respect, one of Nesterova's 1991 works, which depicts an angel with many eyes on his wings, is most revealing. Anyone familiar with the idea of the Annunciation, or who has seen paintings with that title in museums, knows that the immaculate conception was the result of verbal intervention: the wordless vision was fertilized by the invisible word filled with divine revelation. Any interpretation of the Annunciation in the context of the dichotomy of male and female leads to the feminization of a number of concepts, including that of "nonverbal vision."[5] As a result, visuality becomes a surrogate for virginity (a.k.a., verbal "innocence," the condition of the feminine consciousness before its marriage to the masculine word). The subordination of seeing to speaking is precisely what Nesterova decisively repudiates in this work. Her wing-eyed divinity is a symbiosis of speech and vision, of the masculine and feminine principles united in one being: an angel or an androgyne.

Of all the female artists who began to work in the 1950s (the "feminist precursors"), Lidiia Masterkova occupies the most significant place. The mention of her name brings to mind paintings with circles ("planets") and ciphers, subordinated to musical rhythms. For the most part, these ciphers are either zeros and ones or nines. These numeric spacings bear witness

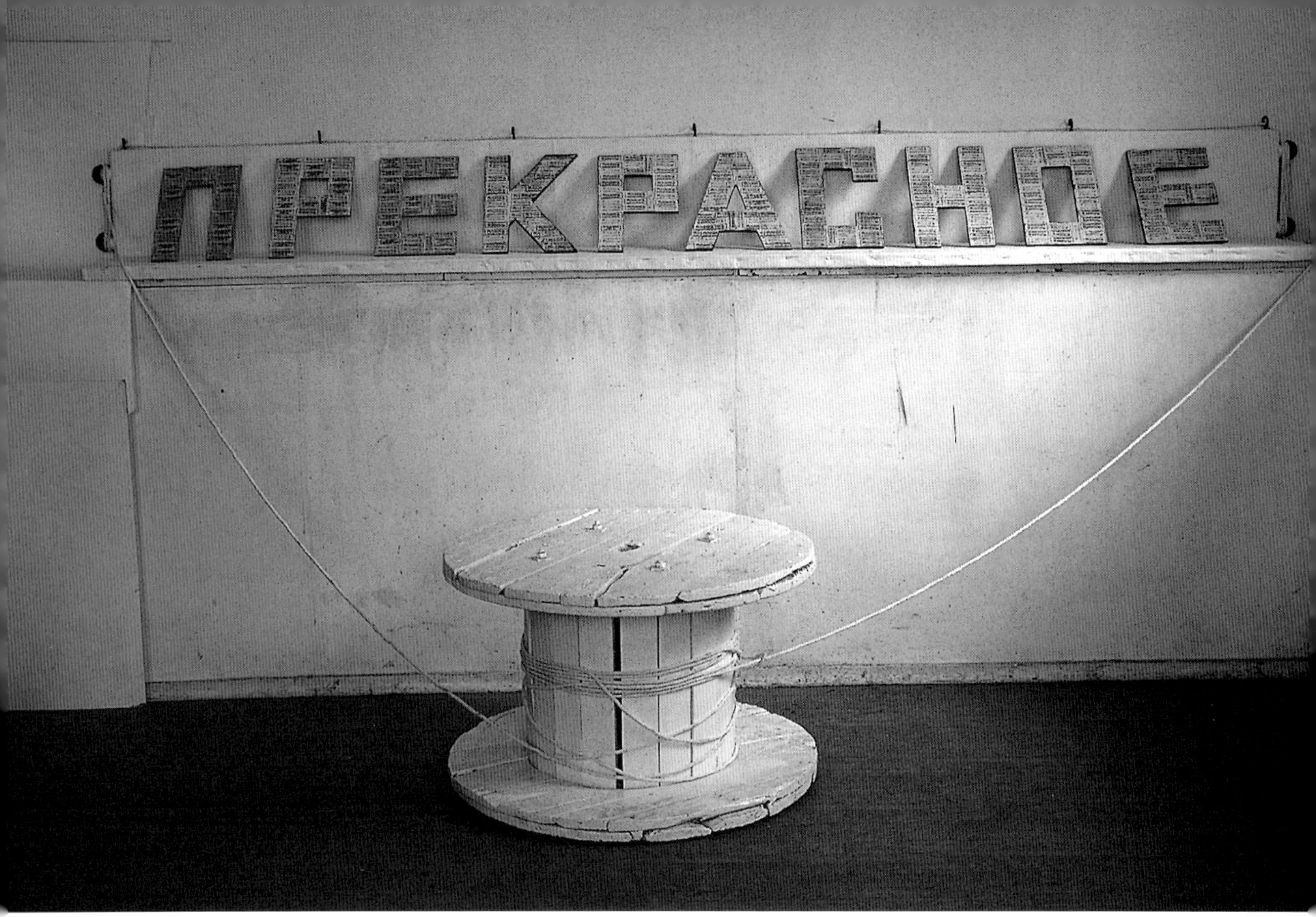

6.3
Elena Elagina, *Beautiful*, 1989.

to maximalism and an uncompromising quality that excludes any reconciliation with the idea of an "arithmetic mean"(fig. 6.4). Masterkova's first abstractions were distinguished by the passion of their organic forms and their colorful colliding surfaces. Later, she began to glue old bits of lace and fragments of ecclesiastical attire (chasubles and the like) to the surfaces of her canvases (see fig. 2.2). The purpose of these brocade fabrics, reminiscent of the vestments of orthodox priests, was to identify socially nonengaged creation with religious asceticism. This use of lace and brocades (which in the context of those years may be considered the antithesis of the "masculine" relation to *faktura* [texture] and to the "politics" of material selection) placed the artist in an isolated position in the patriarchal world of Muscovite alternative art.

Generally speaking, however, the notions of being one of the "chosen" and of having a spiritual mission (ideas that were common in Masterkova's texts of this period) were not alien to other representatives of "dissident modernism" (i.e., unofficial art of the 1960s and early 1970s). But with a younger generation of female artists, this kind of heroic individualism (inspired by supernatural forces or associated with Zarathustrian—read male—attitudes to cultural production) was destined to meet its Waterloo.

Among those who represent the "younger generation" of female artists are Elagina, Konstantinova, Kopystianskaia, and Nakhova. Elagina aims to reveal the presence of masculinity in what is institutionally defined as the successful woman, thereby demythologizing the Soviet version of a "phallic mother." Among such figures is the writer E. Novikova-Vashentseva, a sixty-year-old peasant woman, whose consciousness was transformed after her husband hit her on the head with a log. Elagina's reading of this story is the premise of her 1994 installation in the exhibition "Damaged Utopia."[6] A portrait of Novikova-Vashentseva was placed in a massive wooden frame—a hybrid between a part of an iconostasis and the window molding of a Russian cabin. Inside the frame a birch log rested on an altar. In a 1995 interview, Elagina pointed out, "as a whole, the installation represents a Temple of the Great Utopia, decorated with a number of appropriations. The dominant material is wood, reflecting the fact that images are perceived through an old peasant woman's consciousness fertilized by the blow of the log; it is also a symbol of the element of fire, a hypostasis of sunlight."[7]

Elagina often collaborates (in the tradition of the Russian avant-garde couples) with her husband, Igor' Makarevich, who is equally interested in juxtaposing "creationist" myths with their "doublets," such as—for example—the story of Pinocchio. In this sense, Makarevich and Elagina's

6.4
Lidiia Masterkova, *Afghanistan*, 1982.

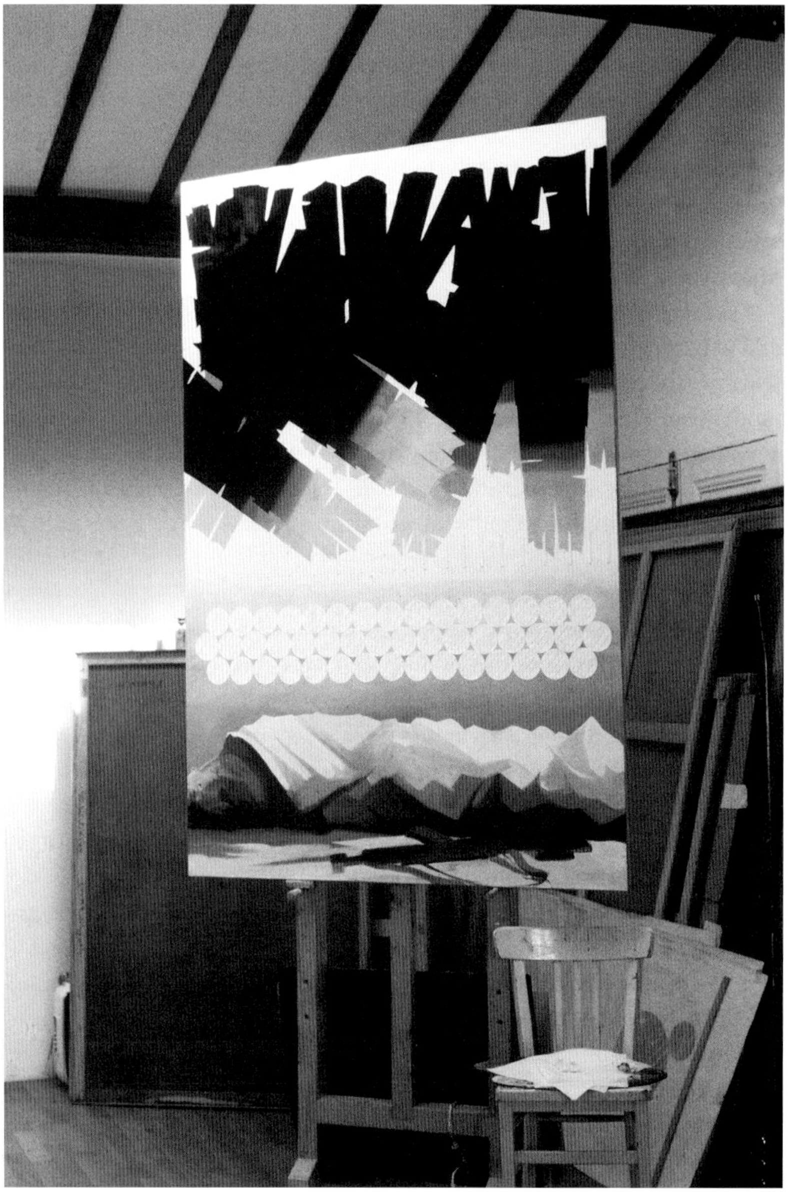

method in art is the method of Gepetto, who picks up a log—an *eidos,* as it were—and uses it to create a wooden puppet, endowed with a striking vitality and a taste for adventure. Gepetto deserves mention also because he is a folklore double of Professor Henry Higgins in George Bernard Shaw's play *Pygmalion.* The difference is that Gepetto breathes a soul into an object (the log) by giving it freedom of choice, while Higgins, who deals with a "living thing" (notably a woman), tries to objectify her and bring her into an eidetic state. If Gepetto appears to us the way God could have been, Higgins (i.e., Pygmalion) is above all an artist. Artist as God. And "the creator." That is how male artists are commonly designated in Russian publications that have no relation to religion or eschatological discourse.[8]

Kopystianskaia's method is to "lay on" texts from classical literature, domestic and foreign, in various configurations, on canvases primed with oil (fig. 6.5). Given that all the texts she chooses have been written by men, Kopystianskaia's paintings and installations suggest an exemplary submissiveness, even an admiration, which some (if not all) men of letters expect from their readers and/or students. But the subversive nature of this submissiveness reveals itself in the distortion of the primary text. "I write and then crumple up," says the artist. And yet when asked if the ways in which she crumples her canvases had anything to do with the libidinal, she ardently denied it. According to Kopystianskaia, "all our Russian art has a literary basis. With many painters an illustrative type of artistic thinking dominates. Therefore, when I make a landscape out of words or letters, I want to unite, or, conversely, separate the figurative language from the literary, that is, create the illusion that we are reading a book figuratively depicted, create the illusion of combination."[9] Although Kopystianskaia agrees that "in Russia women artists face problems," she thinks that "it is not within [her] power to resolve it."[10]

In 1983, Nakhova began to combine the architectural background of residential space (that is, her Moscow apartment) with painterly, graphic, and sculptural elements (fig. 6.6). This installation genre, known by the name "room as a medium," is associated in the West with Günter Förg, Gerhard Merz, and Reinhard Mucha. At the same time, Nakhova became interested in reflecting in her paintings the features of a post-catastrophic consciousness: ruins, fragments of bygone cultures, and uninhabited spaces. Unsuitable for ecologists, these works are nonetheless endowed with a sense of peace and harmony.

In 1992, at Phyllis Kind Gallery in New York, the artist showed her sculptural reliefs made from a kind of petrified foam in an exhibition titled "Momentum Mortis." While working on the project, Nakhova had to wear a gas mask and protective clothes, as the technique uses chemicals

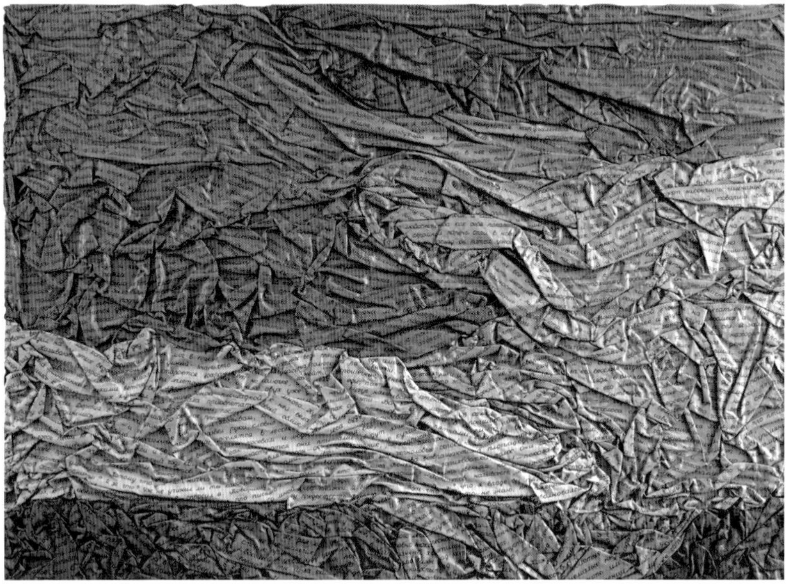

6.5
Svetlana Kopystianskaia,
Landscape, 1988.

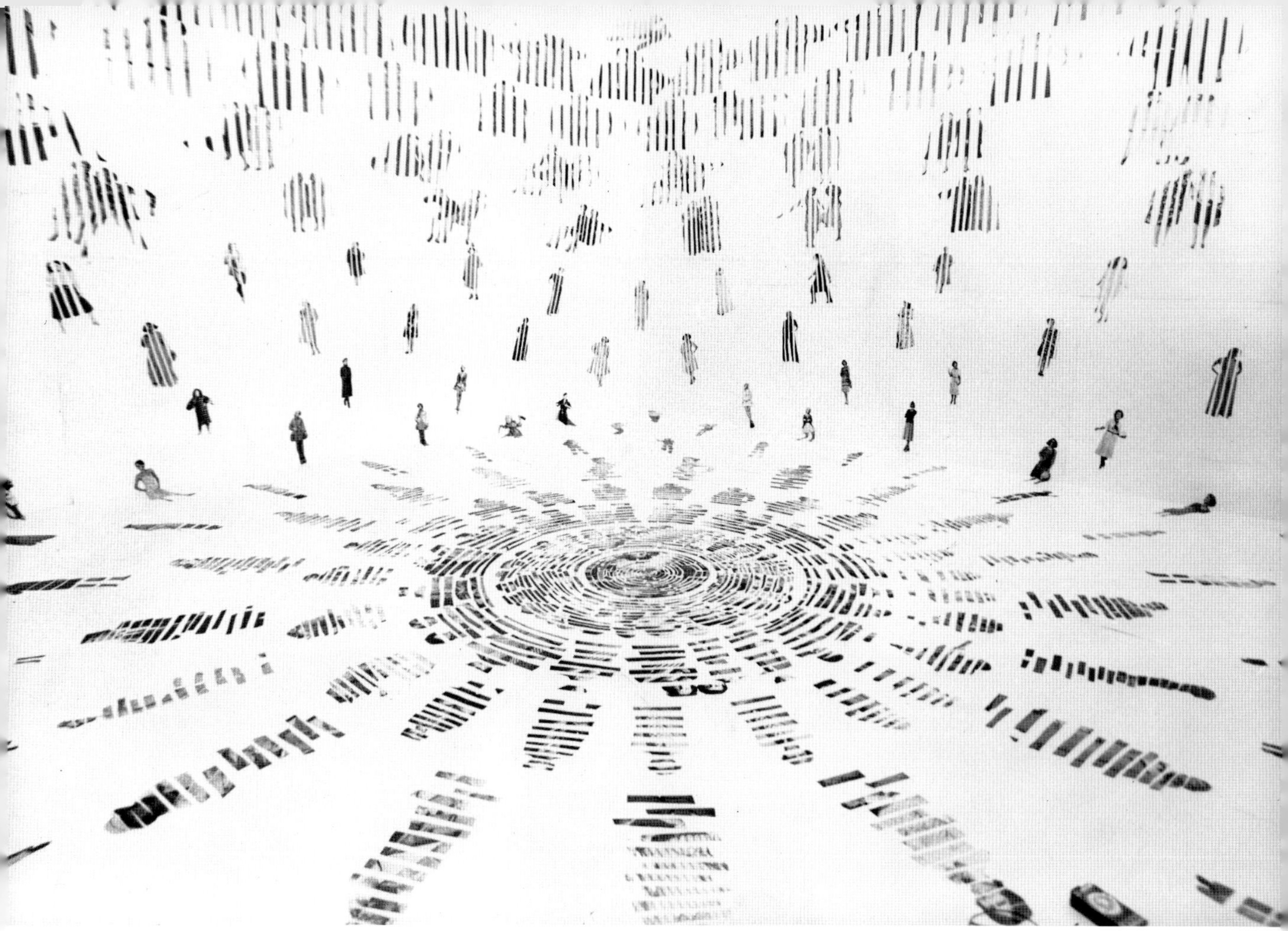

6.6
Irina Nakhova, *Room no. 1*, 1983,
artist's apartment, Moscow.

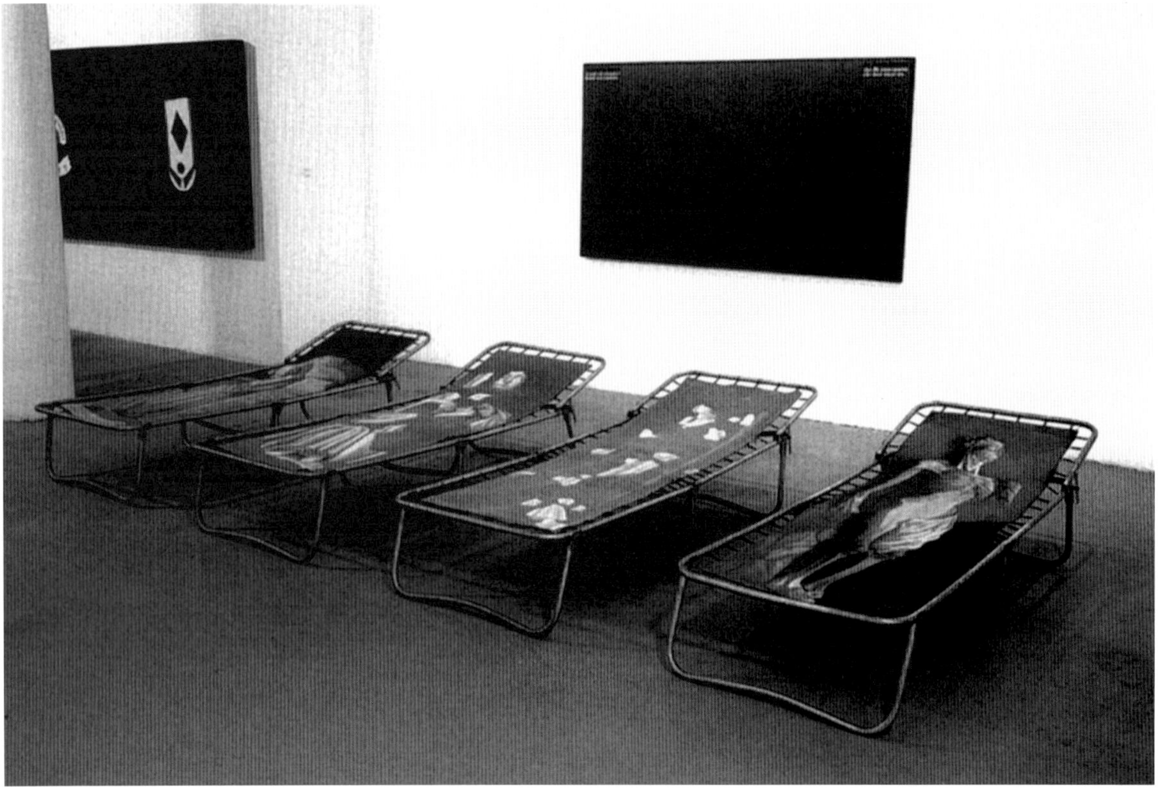

6.7
Installation view, "After Perestroika: Kitchenmaids or Stateswomen," Centre International d'Art Contemporain de Montréal, Montreal, Canada, 1993.

with carcinogenic components. The installation site was reminiscent of a volcanic eruption that captured people at the moment of death along with their household objects and artifacts. Apparently, the viewer was expected to become not only a witness to but a fellow sufferer of a sudden, catastrophic event. A "funeral" procession of large photographs depicting dust, withered grass, burnt remains, and ashes led to the downstairs gallery where the images of a dozen mythological dignitaries were stamped on the stretched canvases of cots (fig. 6.7). A videotape of the gallery's previous opening (incidentally, of a show by a male artist) played on the monitors and suggested that the viewers of the preceding show could have been among those subjected to Momentum Mortis.

The apocalyptic theatricality of Nakhova's project, combined with its pseudophallic ambitions, served, in a way, as a paradigm of false identity, an anasemic rule capable of both simulating and undermining the sense of compliance with the codes of patriarchal creativity.[11] The word "apocalypse" suggests the possibility of an archaeological dig with the aim of exhuming the nymph Calypso from the depths of her crypt. Due to this possibility, apocalyptic metaphors (or, rather "cryptaphors"), especially when employed by women, acquire a new transgressive meaning. But if "Calypso" is chiefly a "pleasure word," her allosemic double, Circe, represents a hysterogenic agency of the same crypt.[12] For, as one can imagine, finding oneself turned into, or rather exposed as, a pig (most likely, a male chauvinist one) was truly apocalyptic for each of Ulysses' companions, whereas for Circe it could have been just a figure of deconstruction.

Unlike other artistic communities in urban Russia, St. Petersburg's is characterized by a progressive attitude and openness to issues that Muscovites usually dismiss as being "too vulgar" and/or "overtly politicized." Among these are the concerns of gender and feminism, which I have already touched upon. Another such factor is the visibly homosexual milieu of St. Petersburg's art world (associated with Timur Novikov, Denis Egel'skii, Georgii Gur'ianov, and Vladislav Mamyshev-Monroe).[13] The heterosexual Muscovite art world has criticized art on the banks of Neva as not as "intellectually charged" as that of the Moscow neoconceptualists. If this were the case, it would definitely be a paradox, as in the West feminism and homosexuality are attended by high levels of discourse and theoretical study. Apparently, to be an alternative artist and at the same time a homosexual in Soviet or even post-Soviet Russia, to experience double otherness, is twice as difficult.

Besides being a product of upbringing and tradition, the way we identify with creativity, with creative inspiration, and its realizations also relates to the history of how the female image has been perceived. For example, one of the curious characteristics of classical art is its flirtation with the allegory by the name of Muse. The Muse is not simply a mythical creature of the female gender, but is a position, a role, a vacancy to be filled. To a large degree, this association has to do with a shifting of lexical and behavioral stereotypes from the sphere of love affairs into the realm of artistic creativity. Even when it deals with nonfigurative subject matter, patriarchal literary or painterly thinking tends to relate to its *objet petit a* as though it were a woman, once again fitting this sublimated object of artistic desire into the framework of *Pygmalion*. For, until the hand of the master touches something "rooted in nature" or lacking in ability to express itself, this "something" (read: Eliza Doolittle) has no chance to overcome her stifling limitations.

Eliza's new personality, a construct created by Professor Higgins, embodies his mentorial, erotic, and above all aesthetic aspirations; the transformed Eliza is a work of art upon which the grace of his authorship descends. Likewise, many contemporary artists would still Higgins-ize their fantasies and desires in relation to artistic production, including work in which the imagery used is neither anthropomorphic nor fetishistic. Unlike art, which, following Claude Lévi-Strauss, can be referred to as "cooked," creativity is "raw." Moreover, creativity exists under the condition of a permanent incompleteness identified with femininity. One should not forget that, when speculating about the "feminine nature" of creativity, we refer not to a "real" female identity but rather to its metaphor, which is constituted by (or at the request of) men. The scope of such metaphors is rather broad and includes Shakespeare's Juliet as well as Sade's Juliette.

Pushkin's insistence that poetry has to be "slightly stupid" could be simultaneously interpreted as though it is being addressed to a woman. In this respect, it would be interesting to confront the sensibility held by the admirers of pure visuality with the beliefs of those who attempt to "measure harmony with algebra" (as Pushkin wrote in "Mozart and Salieri"). To a degree, the reason for the growing dissatisfaction with art theory, or with politically charged art, can be explained by the inner working of our aesthetic unconscious, which is capable of shifting our zealous and protective attitude from a "beautiful" gender to the beautiful in general. Thus, the hostility of the patrons of "beautiful women" toward those who put her under intellectual scrutiny (i.e., take her more seriously then one "should") is, at closer look, analogous to the confrontation between art theorists and the "empirical" critics (as I choose to call them). The empiricists argue that the theorists overcomplicate, contaminate, deride, and even prostitute the very nature of artistic creation. They announce themselves to be the (body) guards of "true" art, which "resists rationalization." In doing so, they claim the ownership of the referent, not on the level of discourse (as in the case of their opponents), but by means of discrediting the texts of their rivals, the theorists. "Do not complicate a woman, do not sacrifice her for your discourse"—such is the essence of their message.[14] This sexist orthodoxy, to which the position of the empiricists seems to attest, is still quite popular among the "art lovers."

In April 1997 I received a call from a female editor of the Moscow magazine *Pushkin.* Asked whether I had any texts for publication, I offered her an article about feminism. She replied: "No, thank you. We are not yet interested in this topic." From Moscow artists and critics who visited the United States, I have heard overtly sarcastic tales about political correctness and feminists. The latter, they complained, go so far as to attack renowned specialists of antiquity in whose lectures male names prevail over female ones. From these stories, which I group in the genre of "male folklore about feminism," one can form a general image of a hysterical female who does not know her place and who spoils everyone's mood. But this is precisely how patriarchal consciousness presents those whose actions do not fit into the frames of defined (by this consciousness) behavioral or gender norms and stereotypes. Any attempt to explain that there are a variety of feminisms, which are often mutually exclusive, is received with distrust. "I wish I had your problems," is a common answer to the question "What do you think about feminism?"[15]

Art historian Margarita Tupitsyn told me about a toast made by the director of the Soviet Bureau of Art Export, Mr. Rivkind, at the dinner for the opening of "The Great Utopia," for which she was one of the curators. Raising his glass Rivkind said: "Here is how it all started. The men got together and conceived an idea. Then the girls came and fulfilled it." A similar scenario is connected with a famous work by Vladimir Tatlin, "Letatlin." This flying machine had been stored at the Museum of the Armed Forces and was delivered to the Guggenheim Museum, for exhibiting in "The Great Utopia," by a general. When he arrived in his hotel in New York, the general discovered that the linen on his bed was pink as was the towel in the bathroom. On a side table near a minibar he found a bouquet of pink flowers. All this reduced the Soviet visitor to an unaccountable rage. He most likely thought that girls are supposed to sleep on pink linen and boys on blue. The military man's masculine feelings were offended. As a result, one of the Guggenheim's staff members was awakened by the angry

Russian in the middle of the night. "This is feminist sabotage," the general screamed into the phone.

In the former USSR, women perceived of themselves as an integral part of what Antonin Artaud defined as a "body-without-organs." This genderless blob is hardly receptive to social issues, and Stalin, who had forcibly communalized urban life in Russia, took full advantage of this fact. Any attempt on the part of women to examine their situation through the lens of feminism would have been regarded as a schism, or as anticommunal behavior. Now, with the retreat of institutional communality, Russian women finally seem to have an opportunity to openly express themselves. But, in fact, their day-to-day reality is far more stressful now than it was before. Television commercials, for example, are saturated with sexual stereotypes and with "norms" of femininity considered suitable for the new political and financial patriarchy.[16] These place incredible pressure on impoverished Russian women, forcing them to share spaces of desire with the excessively dressed-up oligarchs' wives or American supermodels whom they frequently see on the screen.

In chapter 9 I discuss two states of cultural consciousness: the "adult" and the "infantile." Since both of these concepts are applied to individuals who have reached the age of maturity, it would be appropriate to speak of infantilism—particularly in the context of Russia's recent past—in terms of the narcissistic ego, and of adulthood in terms of the superego. There are also two additional entities: the "ideal ego" and the "oral mother," who represents communal speech.[17] An analogue of the latter is a certain "composite of the woman" that shows motherly feeling and tolerance toward male childishness and self-absorption. In Deleuze's view, "the narcissistic ego . . . contemplates its image in the *ideal ego* through the agency of the oral mother. . . . The ego undertakes a mythical operation of *idealization*, in which the mother-image serves as a mirror to reflect and even produce the *ideal ego* as a narcissistic ideal of omnipotence."[18]

To conclude the theme of "enslavement through the body," I would like to return to Kulik's photograph. In his catalogue essay, philosopher Mikhail Ryklin argues that "the woman in the photograph personifies Justice weighing the two heroes' testicles to find out who is the greater sinner." But as an allegory of fallen Justice, naked Themis is more likely to identify ("through the body") with the Patriarchal than to alienate it by subjecting it to a feminist critique. In fact, Themis's nakedness suggests that we are all equally naked before the fatherly eyes of the creator, and her kneeling position, readable as Eve's confession that she is guiltier than

Adam, refers to the notion of ultimate identity, more archetypal than gender or than the hegemony of patriarchy. Such an orthodoxy, rife with stretching contextual frames to embrace apocalyptic discourse, makes it impossible to discuss social issues in secular terms. Perhaps one should never forget that there is a secret passage from apo-calypse to Calypso, and through her to Circe. These two faces of femininity are what the "new Russians" need time to adjust to.

CHAPTER 7

Pushmi-pullyu: St. Petersburg-and-Moscow

Men get most of their animals by sneaking up behind them while they are not looking. But you could not do this with the pushmi-pullyu—because no matter which way you come toward him, he was always facing you. And besides, only one half of him slept at a time.[1]
Hugh Lofting, *The Story of Doctor Dolittle*

1.

A comprehensive examination of St. Petersburg art has been long overdue. The capital of Russia before the October Revolution, St. Petersburg (formerly Leningrad) had been famous since Petrovian times for its pro-Western (read: secular) sociocultural attitudes and sensibilities. In 1918 the government of Soviet Russia moved to Moscow, and soon after Lenin's death in 1924 the name of the "Northern Venice" was changed to Leningrad. The country governed by one-party rule and a single ideology could not sustain the prospect of two (competing) cultural centers; thus, Leningrad's art gradually acquired a supplementary status and remained for many years in the shadow of Moscow. Even with perestroika, alternative Soviet artists who started exhibiting in the West were in most cases from Moscow rather than from Leningrad. To compensate, the Stedelijk Museum in Amsterdam, in cooperation with art historians and critics involved in the production of the magazine *Kabinet,* organized an exhibition in which St. Petersburg artists of various orientations participated: from visionary psychology and pop linguistics (the "charades" of Sergei Bugaev [known as Afrika]) to playful decadence and "beauty-centrism" (the members of Timur Novikov's "Academy") (fig. 7.1). This 1997 exhibition was conceived as an opportunity to look at oneself from the outside, and also as a way of becoming acquainted with what had been brought over in the ark of communal "salvation."[2] Since the ark is (generally) an unimaginable concept, the description of its form and content can be evaded by focusing on the fragments, rather than the totality, of the "communal vessel." One may even compare the fragments that characterize visual thinking in St. Petersburg with their counterparts in Moscow, especially when representatives of these two cities are paired—for example, Bugaev (Afrika) and Sergei Anufriev in the late 1980s to early 1990s. Since both artists participated in

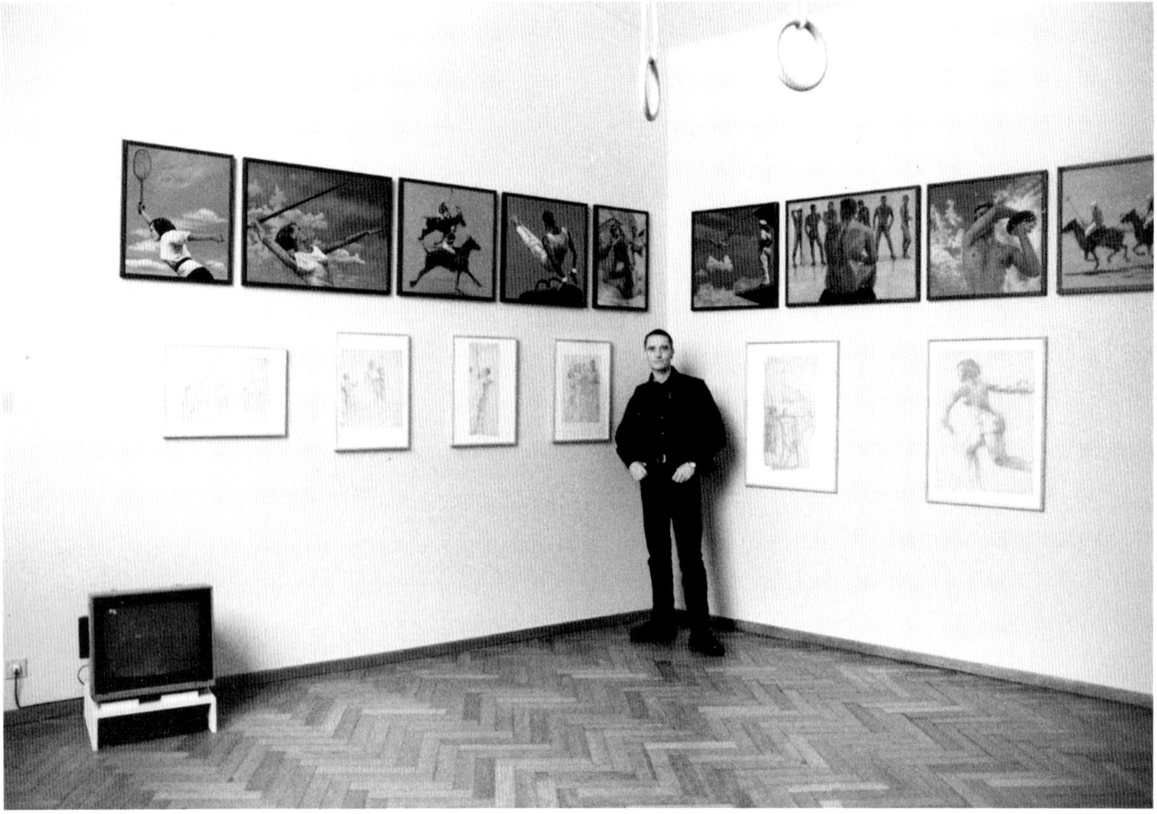

7.1
Installation View, "Kabinet" (Georgii Gur'ianov near his works), Stedelijk Museum, Amsterdam, 1997.

the *Kabinet* exhibition, it is worth saying a few words about their earlier collaborations.

The centerpiece of Afrika's exhibition at the Queens Museum (New York, 1991) was the "intrigue" surrounding the desacralization of the holy object of socialist realism: Vera Mukhina's sculpture *The Worker and the Female Collective Farmer* (1937). The act of desacralization went as follows: armed with a stepladder, Afrika, accompanied by Anufriev and photographer Sergei Borisov, made his way to the pedestal of this mastodon of a sculpture (fig. 7.2). Having pried open the metal door (read: hymen) leading into the collective farmer's vaginal passage, the deflowerers took turns climbing inside and then, after having their photographs taken, retreated, carrying away the door, which they had wrested off its hinges.[3] A reader of Derrida will most likely hasten to characterize this priapic feat as phallogocentric. Besides, it is hard to sidestep (at a purely theoretical level, too) the question of why, in an act of copulation with a sacred object of both sexes, the collective farmer's vagina was chosen over the worker's anus. Was it simply because the latter had no door? Or because, as we know, there was not a single male among the sculptors who assisted Mukhina? Mukhina herself, incidentally, fully meets the definition of the "phallic woman" who enters an incestuous union with the "father," in this case the sadistic superego of Stalinism. The offspring of such "artistic incest" are androgynes,[4] a priori indifferent to "the politics of (their) defloration." Thus, because of the androgynist unity of *The Worker and the Female Collective Farmer,* copulation with one of them equally affects the other.

At the Queens Museum exhibition, the ill-fated "door," now a part of Foucault's pendulum, was swinging back and forth against the backdrop of an altar space, typical of Afrika's installations, which comprised photographs of the postrevolutionary era, a diagram of a caesarean section, and other images. Placed at the center was a monumental canvas depicting a Gaussian curve. *The Worker and the Female Collective Farmer,* I would like to remind the reader, was produced for the Paris World's Fair of 1937. The fragments, made of rustproof steel, were transported from the USSR to the French capital, where assembly was completed. The Soviet Pavilion was designed by Boris Iofan, that of Germany by Albert Speer. The two buildings stood facing each other as if foreshadowing events of the coming war.

At the end of Paris World's Fair, Mukhina's sculpture (which had been awarded the Grand Prix) was dismantled and returned home, where, unlike Humpty Dumpty, it was put together again and placed at the entrance to the All-Union Agricultural Exhibition (VSKhV, later VDNKh).[5] Since the dismantling in Paris also affected the above-mentioned "vaginal door" (the rustproof hymen), the act of Afrika and Anufriev should not be

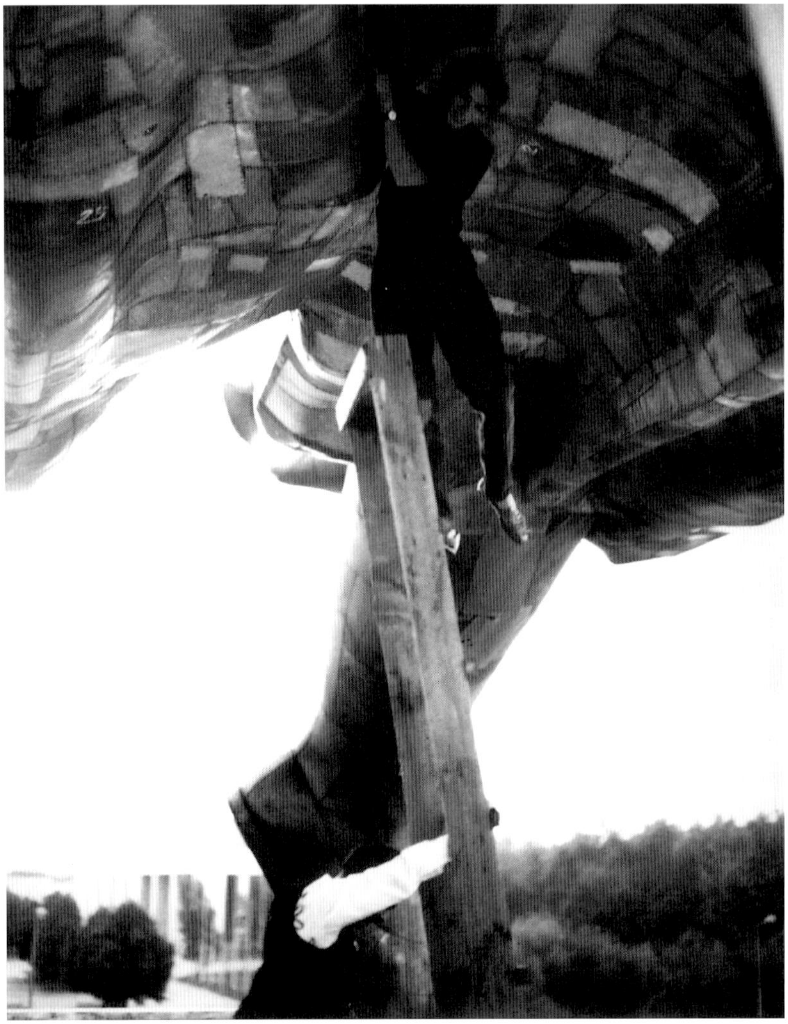

7.2
Afrika (Sergei Bugaev) and Sergei Anufriev entering Vera Mukhina's sculpture *The Worker and the Female Collective Farmer,* Moscow, July 1990. Photo: Sergei Borisov.

regarded as an "original" penetration, attributable to the priapism of modernists, but as yet another paradigm of postmodernist mimesis, of going around in circles, of repetition. This interpretation should also apply to Afrika's abduction of Mukhina's "vaginal door" beyond the Soviet borders (fig. 7.3). The door's epiphany in the West is no more than a mimetic act: it had been there before (in 1937); and it had even received a grand prize . . .

2.

To those familiar with Russian folktales, Leshyi is something like a wood goblin, for his function is "to lead the way and lead astray but never arrive anywhere." Many Russian folk heroes and historical figures fit this definition. An example is Ivan Susanin, a peasant who agreed to become a guide for the Polish army as it advanced toward Moscow in the Time of Troubles (the early seventeenth century). Susanin led the Poles to a dark, snowy forest from which "no way out could be found." Moses possessed the same abilities: under the "pretext" of the Jew's exodus from Egypt to the Promised Land, he "led out" the Pharaoh, his horsemen and chariots to the bottom of the Red Sea. Curiously, Moses continued to be a Leshyi to his own people until his very death. From this vantage point, goblinry is a form of activity directed at the nonrealization of any *idée fixe,* nonattainment of any final frontier, nonreturn from any flight. Goblinry is equally prone to provoke and to delay the moment of culmination. The sort of "culmination" meant here (and the one suggested by this entire book) would be a "final" balance between communality and individuation. In this sense, goblinry constitutes a seismological set of devices capturing the symptoms that promise either the future hegemony of communality or a boom of individuation. Meanwhile, the goblinesque sensibility thrives on deferral and anticipation.

In Soviet children's literature there were two familiar characters—*Znaika* (Knows-It-All) and *Neznaika* (Know-Nothing).[6] Before perestroika, the mission of *Znaika* was taken on by the party-state ideocracy, while the label of *Neznaika* was pinned on the adversarial artistic intelligentsia. Let (S) denote *Znaika*'s claims of "knowing what to know." It follows that all those uninitiated into "truth" are those (–S) "not knowing what to know," ($\underline{S}$) "not knowing what not to know," or (–$\underline{S}$) "knowing what not to know." The last type, naturally, falls into the category of goblinry, while the ($\underline{S}$) model of knowledge turns out to be embodied in the character of *Neznaika.* Meanwhile, the communal subject can be associated with (–S), those "not knowing what to know."

In contemporary Muscovite art, the notion of goblinry usually comes to mind in relation to Ilya Kabakov and Andrei Monastyrsky, whereas in

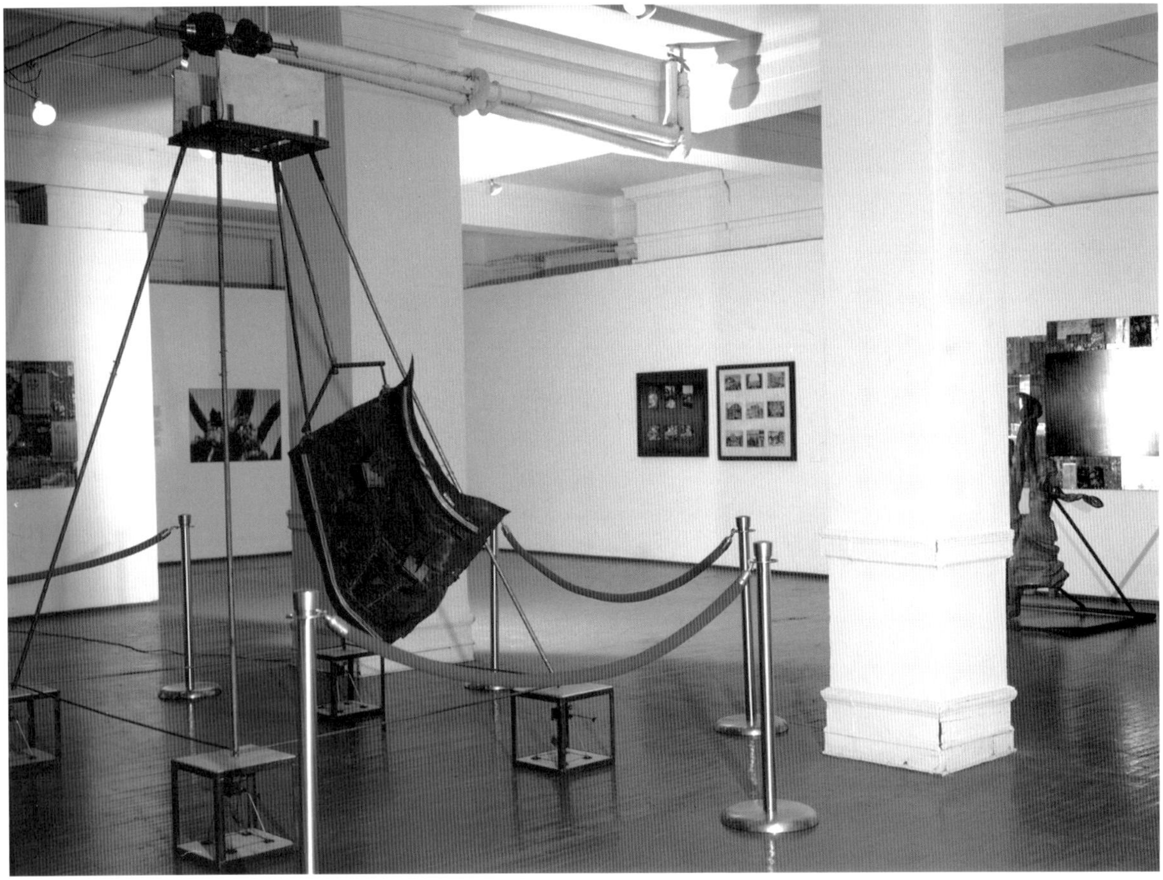

7.3
Afrika, *Donalddestruction*, installation view (the door of Vera Mukhina's sculpture *The Worker and the Female Collective Farmer* used as a pendulum).

St. Petersburg it has always brought to mind Afrika (and still does).[7] All of them, because they "know what not to know," are mediating figures in the interaction between *Neznaika* and *Znaika.* At times, these artists act as double agents, simultaneously representing those who seem "not to know what to know"—that is, the communal body—as well as the forces engaged in its decommunalization. Moreover, decommunalization, in this case, is performed by injecting the negative "not,"[8] which transforms one "*not* knowing what to know" in the sense that he or she becomes one "*not* not knowing what *not* to know," or (since double not = 0), one "knowing what not to know" (the wood goblin). With regard to item (S), the uncompromising "not" transforms one "knowing what to know" into one "*not* knowing what *not* to know," that is, into "Know-Nothing." On the other hand, the double negative (not not = 0) brings it all back to square one.

Pushmi-pullyu: St. Petersburg-and-Moscow

As for both dramatis personae, the secret of the mutual harmony between *Neznaika* (Know-Nothing) and the wood goblin is that they are not reduced to one another on the paths of pure negation alone, in other words by means of injecting the "not" into ($\underline{S}$) or (–$\underline{S}$). The "epistemogram" presented below illustrates the interrelations between "contraries" (S and –S) and "subcontraries" (–$\underline{S}$ and $\underline{S}$), constituting the semantic rectangle:

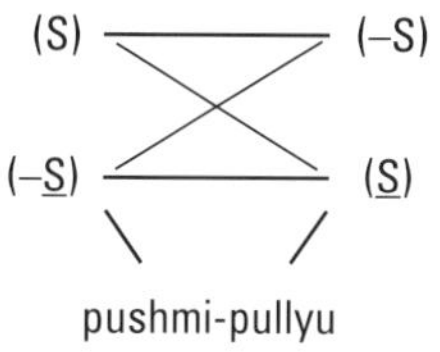

Contraries: (S) = "knowing what to know," (–S) = "not knowing what to know,"
Subcontraries: ($\underline{S}$) = "not knowing what not to know," (–$\underline{S}$) = "knowing what not to know."

In one way or another, the union of *Neznaika* with the wood goblin (–$\underline{S}$ combined with $\underline{S}$) is the Moscow–St. Petersburg version of Hugh Lofting's pushmi-pullyu (played by Afrika and Anufriev). This, in the context of our epistemogram, serves as a "neutral term," whereas the "complex term" (S combined with –S) may be recognized as Mukhina's *The Worker and the Female Collective Farmer.*[9]

3.

Remember how Orpheus finally lost Eurydice: he looked at her shadow despite the warning he had received from Persephone. However, bearing this lesson in mind does not always help. For example, it is rare to find contemporary Russian art examined without mentioning the 1930s. Accepting this cliché (this pattern of reference) and simultaneously aiming at its deconstruction, one may recall a telephone conversation between Stalin and Pasternak regarding whether Osip Mandel'shtam was "our man or not our man," as Stalin put it. Pasternak responded by pointing out that "Mandel'shtam represents St. Petersburg literary tradition, whereas I belong to the Moscow School." This answer did not—at least in a direct way—give preference to either of the two schools, nor did it attempt to label them as "our men" or not. But indirectly, especially in the context of the Great Terror, this nominalist play of identities ("a" belongs to A, "b" belongs to B) so innocently performed by Pasternak could be interpreted as an affirmative gesture in regard to Stalin's politics of identity, fraught with repressive measures against those who are "not our men." One can even suggest that the negativity of the symbolic function intrinsic to metaphor in general and to poetry in particular is what a tyrant shares with a man of letters engaged in "violence" in relation to linguistic material.

And yet numerous human factors and phenomena of nonlinguistic reality unfold themselves amid abstraction: identitarian thinking fails to say what they come under. Its inability to take stock of Being hints at the fact that "the supposition of identity is indeed the ideological element of pure thought"[10] and that hidden in the "lower depths" of identification is the seed of its own death: nonidentity. The inadequacy of the concept of identity—professional, national, sexual, religious, political, linguistic, aesthetic, or any other—is an irritation for those who, in the rush to absolutize the phenomenon of negativity (repression as a means of producing not only literary, but social metaphors), endorse the notion of a single identity frame shared by an artist and by a power broker. As Mikhail Ryklin noted correctly in his book *Iskusstvo kak prepiatstvie,* Vladimir Mayakovsky's versified confession, "I am delighted watching children die," is no reason to equate the young poet's affectations with the "art of will" to sign death warrants or carry out the executions.[11] Moreover, the "nondifferentiation of differences" between idiomatic narratives and political "speech acts" is one of the manifestations of the identity principle.

This observation bring us back to an old controversy over our belief or disbelief in the existence of the so-called blind spots reserved for a creative "I" within overtly political environments. On the one hand, a "blind spot" may inflict blindness upon our critical insight; on the other, the denial of such an option contributes—as in George Orwell's *1984*—to the triumph of total transparency. The notion that the authorial and the authoritarian are related or interchangeable is precisely what Stalin tried to force on Pasternak. Especially in this day and age, the insistence on such a position (without aiming at deconstruction or subversion) is a manifestation of "enlightened" cynicism.

When Mayakovsky wrote that "he [was] delighted watching children die," he most likely meant the literary watching of literary children who die just as literary a death. But what is literature? "Everything," replies Philippe Lacoue-Labarthe.[12] And the body? "The body, too." The only difference is that the body can feel nonliterary pain and suffering. "The subject has to make up for what it has done to non[literary]identity," writes Adorno.[13] In this sense, my own bodily "I" is the bulwark of resistance to literary objectification. Hence, the heightened interest in "bodiliness" on the part of contemporary artists. Quite in contrast to the physical body, the literary body is in the state experienced by the pushmi-pullyu. The component parts of such lines by T. S. Eliot as "Morning stirs the feet and hands / (Nausicaa and Polypheme)"[14] push and pull in different directions, with no chance of a rendezvous—except for a purely literary one. But when the flesh of a literary body is torn apart, it fascinates; lacerations of the physical body, on the other hand, cause torment comparable in intensity only to physical pleasures. Nor is there any reason to believe that a breeze of transcendental truth comes from the gashes and the gaping caesural holes that rend apart the literary pushmi-pullyu. The inability of flesh to coexist with alien forms of identity (cancerous cells and so forth) makes it nonidentical to text, whose health is not threatened by any tumor (including itself). That is why attention shifts either to the sphere of bodily experience or to the unconscious. However, the unconscious "compromises" itself by living the life of (or being structured like) language, and thus resembling literature. In this way, all roads lead to the body.[15]

The problem of artists' reaction to social disjunctions and discontinuities is interesting in itself. Before perestroika and glasnost, the attention of the alternative milieu in Moscow and Leningrad was focused not on bridging the gap between culture and life but rather on preventing their interpenetration. The desire to accentuate such an escapist gap stemmed from the necessity of preventing a cathartic fusion with representation imposed by the powers that be. In the 1970s, such prophylactic measures (toward the alternative milieu) were proposed by the artists Kabakov, Viktor Pivovarov, Monastyrsky, Erik Bulatov, Ivan Chuikov, and Vitaly Komar and Aleksandr Melamid. They became adepts of the dichotomy, zealots of ruptures and clearances, which they regarded as the only possible manifestation of the real (*le réel*) in reality (*la réalité*). Having created the language for describing fragmented public and private narratives, they realized a project that under normal circumstances would have required armies of historians, sociologists,

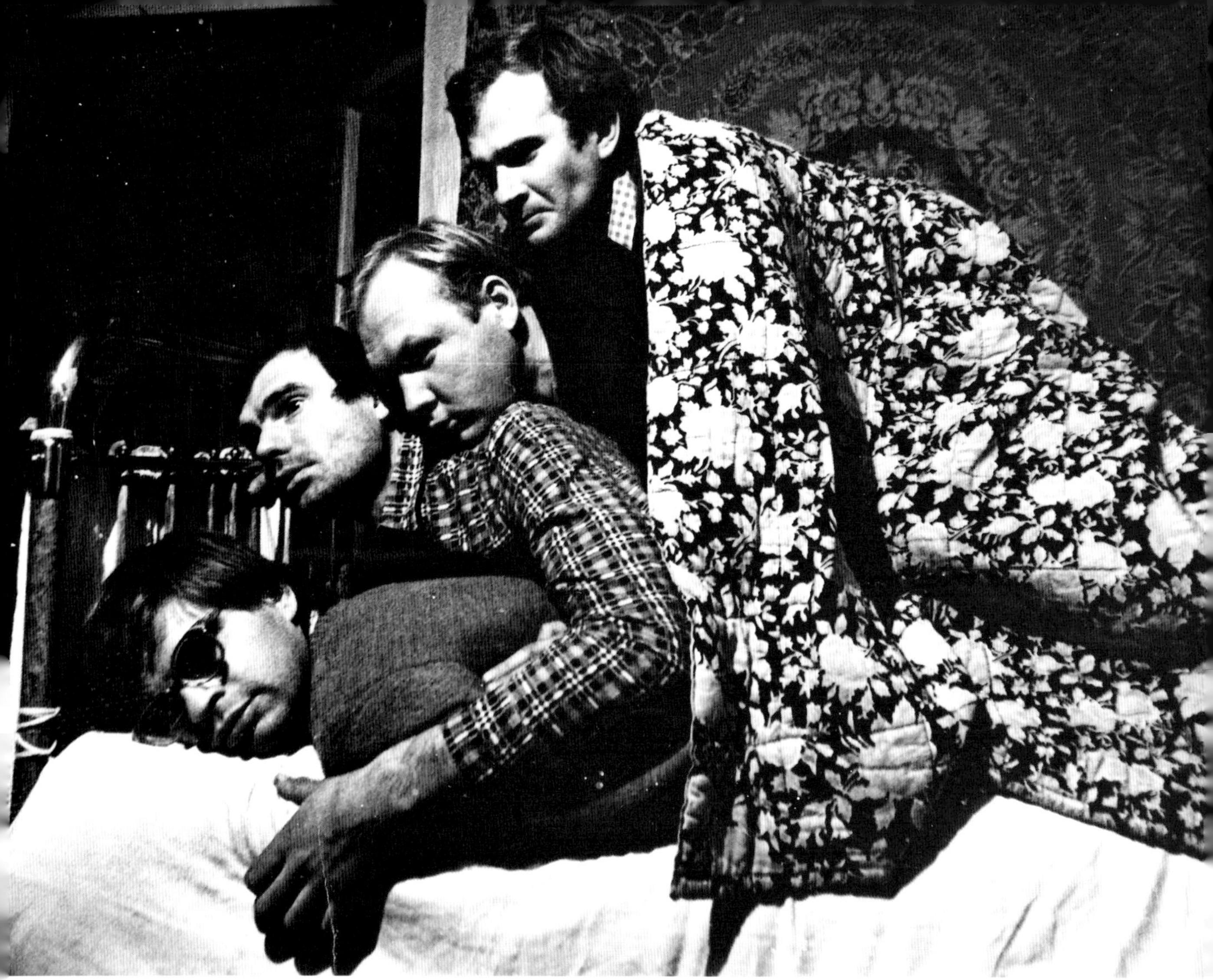

7.4
A scene from Evgenii Iufit's necrorealist film, late 1980s.

and therapists. Simultaneously, the exculpatory motivations that justified the prolonged stay in the zone of the "blind spot" were exhausted.

4.

Pushmi-pullyu: St. Petersburg-and-Moscow

Artists and critics living in both St. Petersburg and Moscow constantly change identity, while like Oedipus they try to guess the answer to the sphinx's riddle: "Who are our men and who are not?" The difference, however, lies in the fact that today the capital A and capital B happen to be the Moscow and St. Petersburg art schools along with their respective paradigms of artistic mentality and sensibility. Since both groups of artists consist of the members of alternative milieus, they are still eligible for conferral as "nonidentity within identity." And yet accentuation of the cultural dichotomies between the cities is needed, especially at this point in time, to undermine the existing tendency to perceive the post-Soviet vanguard as a unicellular totality.

Given that the distance between the two cities exceeds 700 kilometers, it is appropriate to describe Leningrad art as being somewhat peripheral vis-à-vis its Moscow counterpart. Compared to that of other urban centers, Moscow's cultural life has always been characterized by a higher level of "transparency" due to the closeness of the state leadership's watchful eye. This partially explains why manifestations of the "optical unconscious" are generally more opaque, corporeal, and sensual on the banks of the Neva than they are in Moscow, where the initiative—until fairly recently—belonged to conceptual art (read: transparent, sterile, intellectualized). Thus, Moscow's visual paradigm can be characterized in terms of an "aesthetics of transparency" as opposed to the "aesthetics of a blind spot" (in St. Petersburg's case). These polarities reveal themselves as we compare *Parallel'noe kino* (Parallel cinema) of Igor' and Gleb Aleinikov to Evgenii Iufit's necrorealist films (fig. 7.4). Likewise, Kabakov and Collective Actions share no aesthetic programs with Afrika, Novikov, Bella Matveeva, Oleg Maslov and Victor Kuznetsov, Andrei Khlobystin, or Vladislav Mamyshev-Monroe (figs. 7.5, 7.6).

In chapter 3, I described Kabakov's installation in Jablonka Gallery in Cologne (1994), where the artist contrasted the darkness of the communal environment with a brightly lit painting endowed with extracommunal lucency, a Cézannesque landscape. This dichotomy is reversed by a number of St. Petersburg artists in that the attention in their works is shifted back from the "aesthetics of transparency" to the "aesthetics of blind spots," from anesthetized and distilled vision to "bodily" optics. Thus, for Khlobystin, artistic representation is the "apotheosis of dark, dumpy corners," which are interesting not because they can be used for

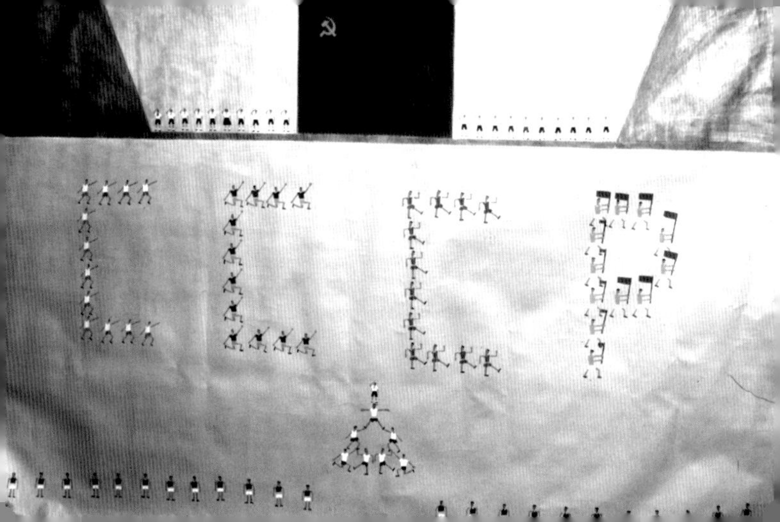

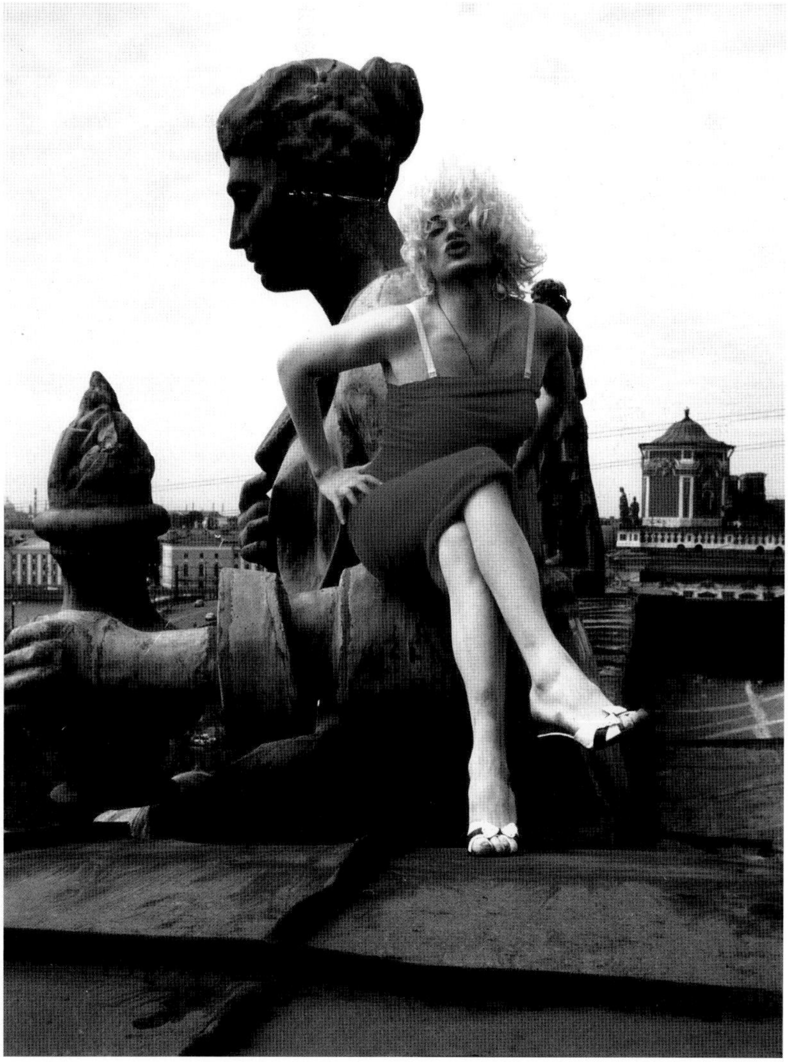

7.6
Anonymous, Vladislav Mamyshev-Monroe on the roof of the Hermitage, St. Petersburg, 1992.

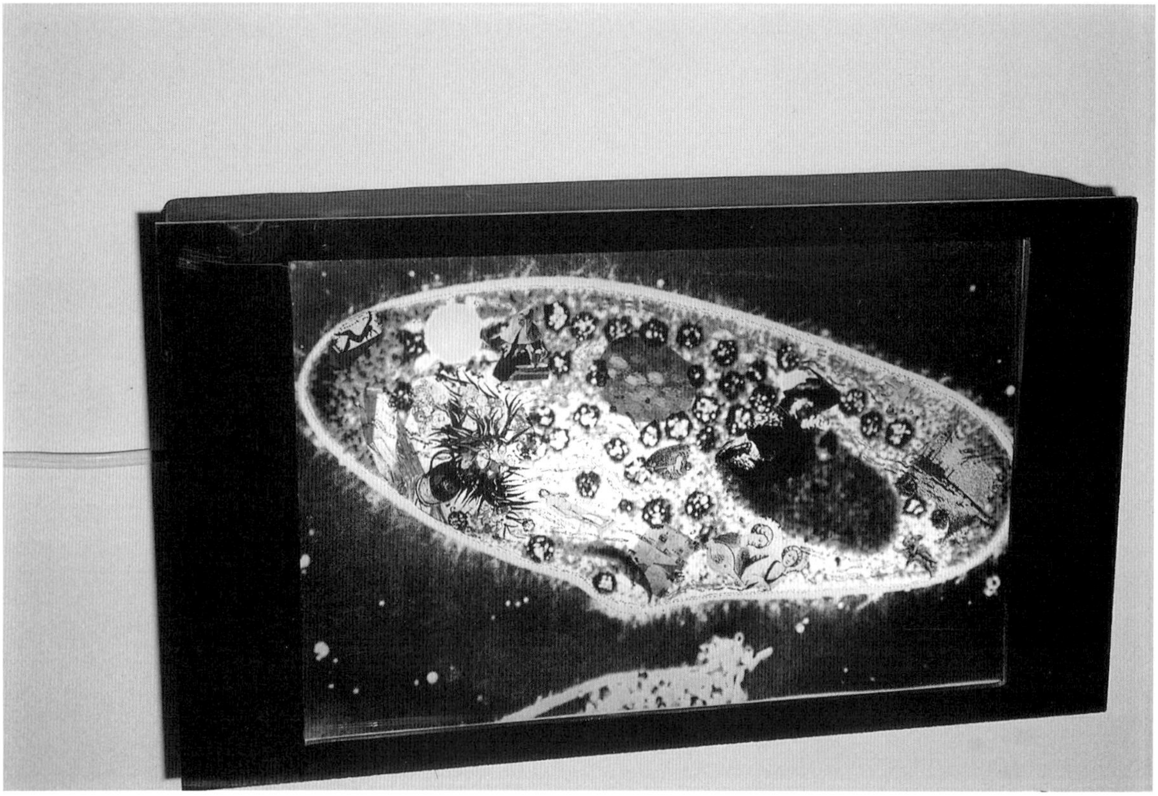

7.7
Andrei Khlobystin, *Art-Causing Agent*, 1991.

meditation, but because of the intriguing nature of their life structure (fig. 7.7). Khlobystin's latest works are precisely such "corners," installed not at the center but on the periphery of cultural facilities. The images etched onto the surface of blurry film and functioning as indexical signs point to nondiscursive zones, filled with what Paul de Man described as "blindness inseparable from the moments of greatest insight."[16] While Kabakov's *Man Who Flew into Space from His Apartment* (first realized in the artist's Moscow studio in 1985) penetrates the roof of the communal "chaosmos," which the artist identifies with trash, Khlobystin relegates "penetrating" vision to the same fate. For him, as for necrorealists (who were also exhibited in the Stedelijk), the value context is governed not by Kant's sublime but by Freud's sublimated.

Absolute transparency is a condition that the egocrat requires to distinguish those who are "with us" from those who are "against us." In *Farbenlehre,* Goethe wrote that the abundance of light "allows the eye to differentiate—to contrast object to object and one part of an object to another." In his words, excessive "transparency is fraught with loss of sight, blinding those whose eyes are open too wide to the shining of light."[17] Any photographer knows that excessive transparency causes film to become exposed or overexposed. Likewise, aspiration toward unlimited transparency borders on self-blinding (the castration of vision). One may also realize that a Cézannesque "shrine" implanted by Kabakov in Cologne assumes the role of identitarian agency, separating the viewers into "our men" and "not our men." Given that among the things darkened in the Cologne installation is its author's own position, our rage for siding with the right cause seems even more delirious than that faced by Pasternak during his chat with Stalin. Apparently, the inseparability of "blindness and insight" is not so clear-cut.

In some communications, the most important idea is that which the speaker (author, addresser, etc.) cannot, will not, dares not (or does not know how to) say. "The spoken thought" is thus a form of repression toward other thoughts, linked to the "desire" to extend (their) state of unspokenness, an unconscious attempt to block or defer the moment of utterance. Those who study contemporary Russian culture know that in the three preceding decades, the emphasis in this field has been placed on decoding, comprehending, and interpreting the messages communicated to us by artists, writers, and philosophers. The time has come to become sensitive to unspoken as well as spoken thoughts, to become interested in allegories of silencing—in unspokenness as a signifier.

CHAPTER 8

Batman and the Joker: The Thermidor of the Bodily

In Russia, where the bodily (the corporocentric) has become synonymous with orthodoxy, artistic acts like public masturbation or bestiality performed by the so-called *telesniks* are affirmative in nature.[1] At a time when the brutal stage of victorious capitalism is exacerbated by widespread physical violence, the autochthonic gesture is read as one of identification, that is, as the desire not to be different from those who call the shots. Although a number of contemporary thinkers find appeals to "the body" endearing, their scholarly meditations remain at a considerable distance from the direct apologetics for bodiliness. In their texts, the search for the "lost body" is conducted in roundabout ways, without advertising the reductionist subtext of this quest.[2] The irresistible desire to "press against the body," characteristic of late postmodernism, allows an analogy with Darwinian doctrine, in which—despite a joyful declaration of humanity, the complete and final separation from the animal kingdom—one still senses, as well, a sentimental longing for the ape.[3]

The most consistent of all the *telesniks* grown on Russian soil are Oleg Kulik, Aleksandr Brener, and (to some extent) Anatolii Osmolovskii (fig. 8.1).[4] Kulik has become famous by simulating sexual intercourse with domestic and wild animals, by slaughtering a pig in a gallery space, and by outdoor performances in which the artist posed naked, acting the part of a mad dog intent on biting passersby and the audience. Considering the mores of the Russian nouveau riche, as well as the fact that the people making mad money in Russia are mostly those who are involved in criminal or semicriminal organizations (the shadow economy) and for whom violence is a way of life, Kulik's performances are a rather accurate reflection of the present. The problem is that they do not examine it in a critical way. Trying to become even more bestial than the world around him,

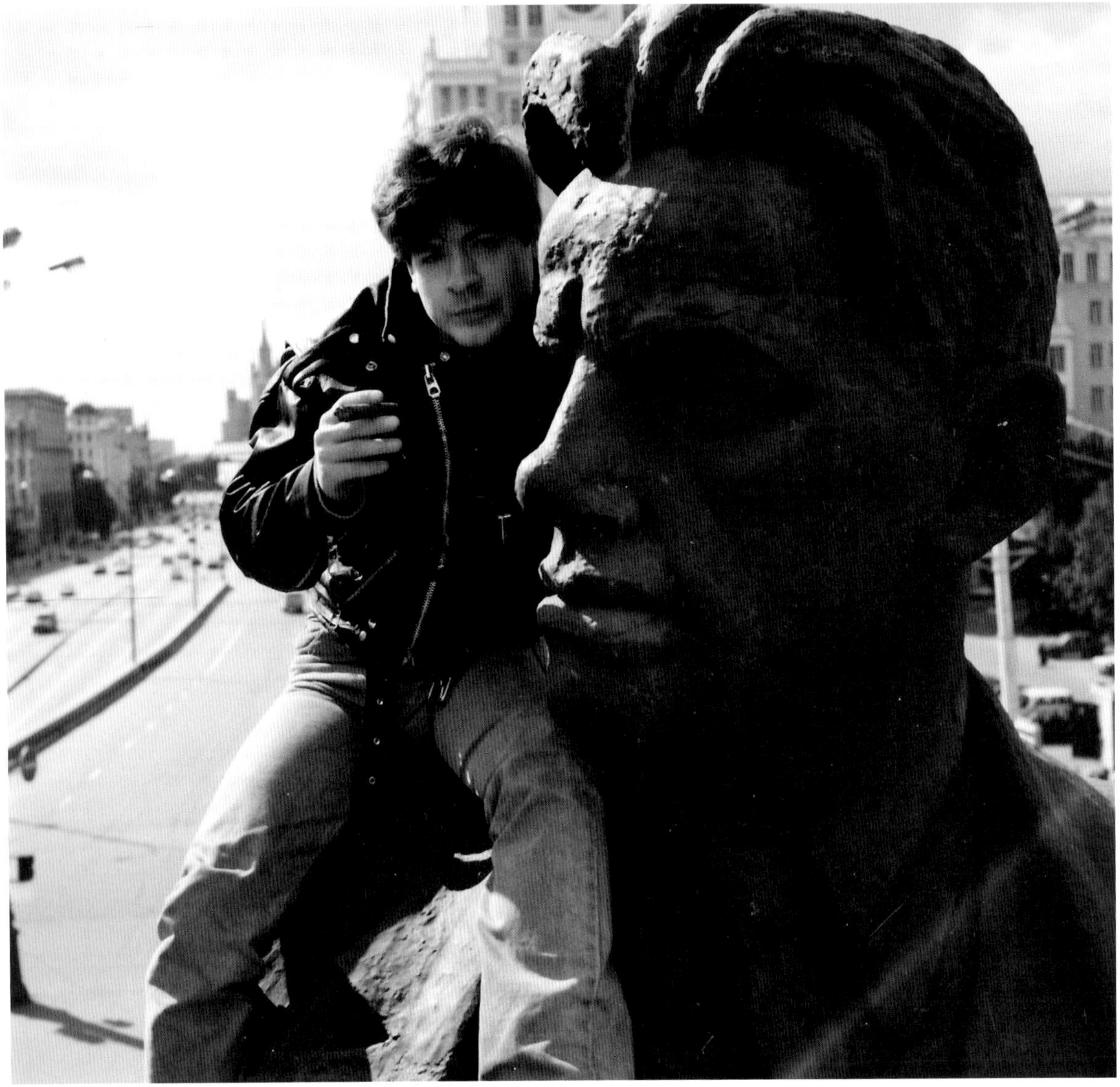

8.1
Anatolii Osmolovskii, *Untitled*, performance, 1994.

Kulik, at best, lays it bare for deconstruction. However, the deconstructive connotations are not picked up by the "new Russians," who are, more than likely, entertained by these acts. Also, the nouveau riche view the uncritical adoption of their behavior, style, and manners by members of the artistic community as a sign of approval and as proof of their own power, influence, and importance.

On April 16, 1997, by going through customs at the airport in New York in his canine disguise (dog collar and muzzle) and under the supervision of "dog trainer," Kulik performed a reversal of the process described by Mikhail Bulgakov in *Heart of a Dog:* that is, he transformed himself into a dog (fig. 8.2). To give the West a full measure of the delights of a dog's life, the Deitch Projects Gallery on Grand Street in SoHo kindly provided Kulik with a cage specially built for him. *New York Times* critic Roberta Smith wrote that Kulik "looks very efficient as a dog." According to her, the "dog" is a frightening, unpredictable, and territorial animal. The name of the piece—*I Bite America and America Bites Me*—is a paraphrase of Joseph Beuys's 1974 performance piece titled *I Love America and America Loves Me,* involving a coyote at the Rene Block Gallery in New York. The difference is that for Beuys, man and animal remained separate, while Kulik makes them one. In a fax message dated April 18, 1997, the senior editor of *Art in America* magazine, Christopher Phillips, wrote to me that the principal visitors to Kulik's cage were "dog trainer" and Jeffrey Deitch. Phillips attributed the lack of outcry (or excitement) over the piece to the fact that SoHo's streets are filled with crazy people who are no less doglike than Kulik.[5]

With Brener, it would be enough to mention his masturbation in the Moskva public swimming pool, the pile of shit he wanted to leave in front of the Van Gogh painting at the Pushkin Museum of Fine Arts,[6] and his attempt to challenge President Boris Yeltsin to a fistfight (Arthur Cravan-style) (fig. 8.3). One could leave it at that, were it not for Brener's last "action" in the Stedelijk Museum in Amsterdam, and the trial stemming from it. In late fall of 1996, Brener painted a green dollar sign on a Kazimir Malevich canvas, for which he was arrested and sentenced to five months' jail time.[7] Brener chose the Stedelijk because of the mildness of Dutch laws: at first, he had planned to carry out this action at the Metropolitan Museum in New York, but a lawyer advised him to select another, more "suitable" place: "In the United States, you can get ten years for it." Afterward, at his trial, the defendant made a statement: "There is a crisis of culture comparable to the greater disaster of the twentieth century, World War II. We distinguish only the voices of people who make machines and the voices of those who have

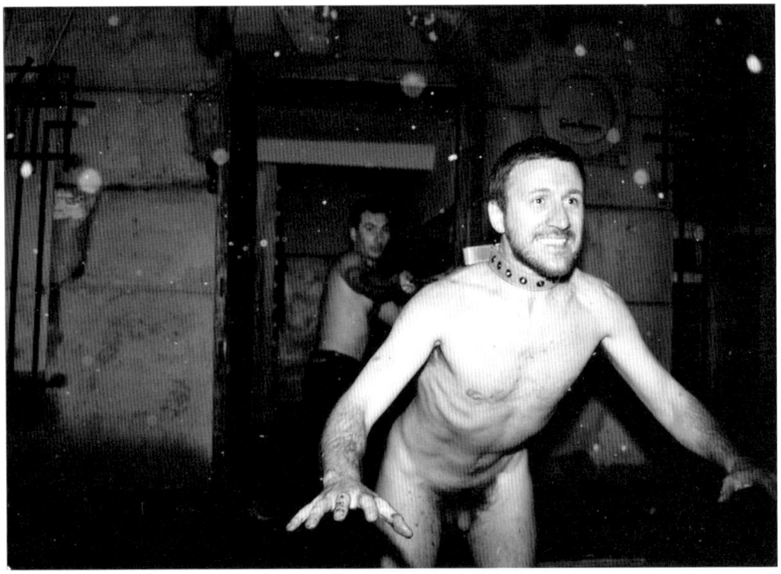

8.2
Oleg Kulik, *The Last Taboo,*
Gelman Gallery, Moscow, 1994.

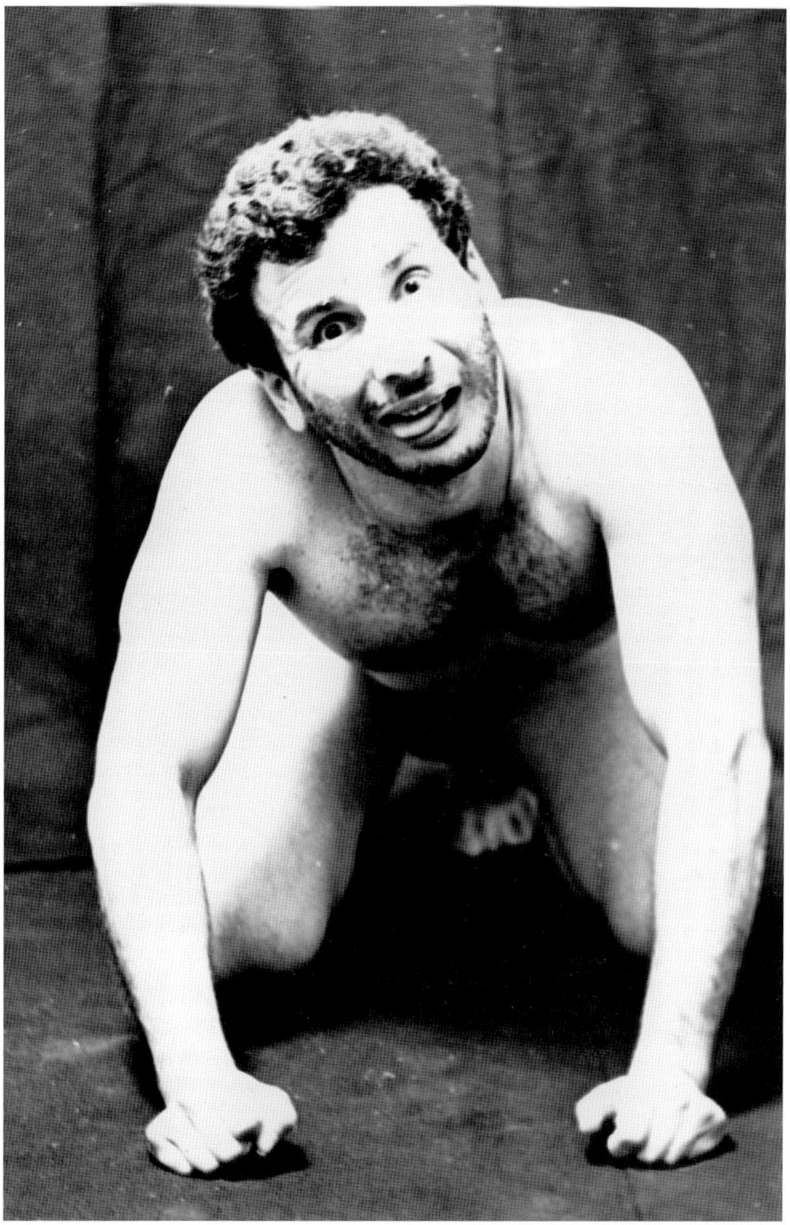

8.3
Aleksandr Brener, *Chimeras, Join Me!*, Gelman Gallery, Moscow, 1995.

power. I am speaking in the name of culture which has retained a human voice."[8]

According to Brener, the modern artistic elite has slammed the doors on the new worlds that Malevich opened for us. Though his action at the Stedelijk was an expression of "well-tempered" right-wing fanaticism using the cover of rhetoric about the democratization of culture, Brener's "initiative" deserves commentary.

The value of works of modern art is a fairly relative concept linked to the modernist "myth of originality" and, in particular, to the way this "myth" is converted into fiscal denominations. In such situations—that is, when it comes to the relationship between value and price—Marcel Mauss and Jean-Joseph Goux might have used the term "potlatch," defined as the modus operandi of symbolic exchange.[9] But my interest is in something else. It is clear that, as an art object passes from owner to owner and becomes the property of an individual or of secular institutions, it loses its symbolic value. And there are two possible attitudes we can adopt toward the museum: either we recognize it as a religious institution and, accordingly, believe in retaining the symbolic ingredient of art within its walls; or we regard it as a secular institution and, to some extent, as an instrument of the abolition of the Symbolic. This abolition or, as Brener would put it, usurpation of the Symbolic is what troubles him most. In order to prevent it, he acts in the name of tribal, totemic traditions, in the spirit of what some of his like-minded allies describe as "the sacral path." But Brener's "sacral path" is the course of an individual (a singular transgression), whereas the symbolic exchange is mediated by the psychosomatics of the collective body. Therefore, anyone who opposes the convertibility of symbolic values into semiological ones (for instance, monetary signs) has to determine the measure of transgression in agreement with others like himself, in accordance with a tribal consensus. Brener's actions were not sanctioned by a collective body; therefore, they must be classified as individualistic, and hence in contradiction of the symbolic law's creed. The only "bodies" that could have shown solidarity with his action in Amsterdam are the "bodies of violence" spawned on the ruins of totalitarianism, which prefer economic to political terror. It is clear to many of us that a museum is a well-lit safe, whose functions include not only the preservation of culture but also its suppression. The museum is precisely where, despite "free" access to works of art, we feel the bottomless depth of our alienation from them. The question is, Would we be unable to recognize the gravity and urgency of all these problems without Brener and his ilk?

In Tim Burton's 1989 film *Batman,* the Joker and his goons break into a museum and spray-paint works of art. In doing so, they become the co-creators of these paintings, or, as Brener's attorney put it at the trail, they "raise the price of the artwork." This implies a symbolic injection in the form of, or in the disguise of, defilement. What happens is a rupture that raises the plank higher: the archaic raises the bottom of discourse, and its surface is clouded over with an ecstatic foam. Freud, arguing with Jung, called this "black mud." Should we limit ourselves to a disinterested analysis of the events, identifying the conditions conducive to the manifestation of this or that phenomenon, or does the critic's role presume something more than that? The danger is that, in becoming the Joker's opponent, the critic risks becoming an apologist for Batman (which is no less problematic, considering the authoritarian tendencies and the conservatism of the zealous defenders of good and beauty). The solution is to refrain from giving preference to either "actant" in the binary opposition by classifying their actions as affirmative.[10] The exception is when the actants do it themselves, that is, prove capable of a critical analysis of their role functions.

The kind of apocalyptic rhetoric found in the speech acts and performances of the Russian *telesniks* betrays their kinship with the pro-life movement in the United States. As a rule, the anti-abortion activists are men who question—sometimes violently—a woman's right to be in charge of her own body and destiny. The core of the movement consists of Protestants from rural areas. Surprisingly, in Italy, where the Catholic church and abortion are incompatible, there is hardly any terrorism against "certified killers" of embryos. For an ordinary Catholic in Europe, the responsibility for this matter is—to a large extent—yielded to the institutions (both religious and secular), whereas the way of thinking peculiar to Protestants in North Carolina or Nevada is not institutional by nature. Their congregations are fairly autonomous: each of them has their own line of communication with the Lord, whose will is mediated through various charismatic leaders. Due to their efforts, the provincial sectarian teleology with its appetite for moral judgment and worldwide imposition of (American) good and justice is kept alive not only inside the country, but also in geopolitics. This maximalism is what America shares with Russia.

The opponents of the Moscow *telesniks* accuse them of lacking the artistry of their predecessors, both in the West (Beuys and the Viennese actionists) and in Russia (Vladimir Sorokin and, to a certain extent, Kabakov). When viewing their videotapes, one begins to suspect that Kulik and Brener are zombies, so artificial and lifeless do their actions appear. But there may be another way of looking at it: clumsiness may be an attribute of artless authenticity, whereas grace is the carnival costume of death. This feeble and fairly stale argument is the only thing I can find to say in defense of the *telesniks*.

In April 1997, on the way back from Naples, I decided to spend a night in Venice. In the morning, taking a stroll through the half-empty city, I stopped by a magazine kiosk. The cover of the Italian edition of *Flash Art* caught my eye. It was graced by a depiction of Brener standing in a romantic pose next to the Malevich painting. The artist who did the cover didn't know, of course, what his hero looked like, and made him resemble the young Tony Shafrazi, who gained notoriety many years ago by defacing Picasso's *Guernica*. At the Frankfurt train station, I was met by the artist Eduard Gorokhovskii. He was waving a fresh issue of the English-language *Flash Art* in which the publisher, Giancarlo Politi, declared his love and respect for Brener. According to Politi, Brener is "far more alive than the static Malevich" and must therefore be released from prison. In Brener, Politi has finally found an ideal that reminds him of himself. Before Brener, his ideal was usually his opposite, for example Tony Negri, Félix Guattari, or me.[11] However, this flirtation with intellectuals never turned out well, as Politi's enthusiastic interest in them inevitably gave way to antipathy, antipathy to hostility, and so on. In all likelihood, in identifying with the physical (bodily) act of "creative violence" performed by Brener, Politi applauds the Thermidor of the bodily in Russia, hailing the "masters of life" of whom he is one.

For Kulik and Brener, the bodily is linked, first, to the choice of form—the texture of the gesture, the system of mediation and filiation—and second, to the fact that significations are inspired and controlled by the peristalsis of the referential body. The signifier is corrupted by flexions to such an extent that there is no possibility of reflection. The similarity between these "politics of the signifier" and the behavioral norms of the new bourgeoisie is so great that "finer" motifs and modulations, if they exist at all, are indistinguishable. They are like the buzzing of a mosquito trying to compete with a choir. One such "finer" motif (apparently) is the entirely justified discontent of Russian artists with the way they are treated abroad. But isn't the unkindness of the other something to provoke efforts to revive culture at home? In the West, we often disparage modern art museums, and they certainly deserve it. But when one doesn't have them, the deficit of the energy needed for the reproduction of culture is keenly felt. The fact that the alternative Russian art of the three previous decades is not on permanent display in museums primarily hurts the artists of the 1990s. As Margarita Tupitsyn points out, "it's like a house with several stories missing."[12]

I remember how bewildered I was by the philosopher Mikhail Ryklin's question about Kulik's chances of repeating the success Kabakov had had in the West. Strangely, our reaction left Ryklin equally bewildered, which, in a way, impelled me to break the "rules" (until recently, I had staunchly refused to make any public comments about Kulik and Brener). I recall, too, the trip to the Ligurian coast we made with Politi and Helena Kontova in 1989. Politi bought a huge bottle of olive oil in one of the seaside towns. On the way to back to Milan, the bottle burst, and the four of us spent over an hour cleaning up the interior of the publisher's favorite Mercedes with tissues. "Well, that's all right," he finally said. "It's not a Malevich, after all."

CHAPTER 9

The Body-without-a-Name

The only thing I was sure of was my name.
Luigi Pirandello, *The Late Mattia Pascal*

1.

From the early 1960s to the late 1980s, Western perceptions of Russian culture were based on a rather crude model, reduced to the opposition between Soviet orthodoxy and dissent. The triviality of this model was balanced by the fact that the dissidents' perceptions of the West were based, in turn, on a presumption of identity—which was imagined as something beyond dichotomy, devoid of the differences and contradictions that generate ideological discourses. In alternative Soviet circles, the division of the inhabitants of foreign (bourgeois) countries into liberals and conservatives, left-wing and right-wing radicals, and so on, was received skeptically and, as a rule, attributed to official propaganda.

Familiarity with Western art of the postwar era was made possible by several exhibitions of American and European painting in Moscow, and also by an influx of coffee-table books and catalogues published abroad. As was mentioned in chapter 2, the heritage of Kandinsky, Larionov, Goncharova, Malevich, Tatlin, Rodchenko, and Lissitzky had far less influence on the Soviet artists of the 1960s than did the works of Western modernists, who sheltered the specter of the Russian avant-garde unwelcome at home. Knowledge of this "ghost of Hamlet's father" was displaced from individual and institutional memory; this was equally true of cultural consciousness and of the cultural unconscious. In psychoanalysis, this kind of radical displacement is known as *foreclosure (forclusion, Verwerfung)*. Foreclosure results in paranoid ruptures in the fabric of memory and language, which generally occur in patients who, as young children, were witnesses to, participants in, or victims of a crime. Such memories evoke discomfort (horror, shame, etc.) and must be effaced, leaving irreplaceable gaps, clearances, "empty centers." Further, even though the eradication of memory is usually analyzed in terms of individual rather than collective psychic defense, the analogy with foreclosure also works for mass, or societal, catalepsy.

The consequences of foreclosure can be traced in the example of the socialist modernists who have been repossessed from "procrastinated time" only partially, if at all. The socialist modernism of the late 1920s and 1930s, which pleased neither the pure avant-garde zealots nor the Stalinist art mavens, coexisted with the Association of Artists of the Revolution (AKhR)[1] and early socialist realism but, unlike both, was able to establish a style of its own. The architecture of Moscow's first metro stations, book and magazine design, posters, photography and photomontage, the decoration of workers' clubs—this is only a partial list of the areas in which the socialist modernists (Klutsis, Lissitzky, Rodchenko, and Stepanova in their late periods, as well as Sen'kin, Valentina Kulagina, Solomon Telengator, and many others) worked. The protopostmodernist course of their position, compared to the historical avant-garde, is in the dialectical transcendence (removal) of negation, that is, in the transition from negation to affirmation. Giving this fact due credit, socialist modernism may be viewed as an affirmative avant-garde.

Louis Althusser's reading of Marx's *Capital,* undertaken in the 1960s, makes the persuasive argument that society's economic "I" is organized according to the same principle as the psychic subject in Freud or Lacan. Althusser makes an analogy between the developmental stages of productive capacity and the developmental stages of the libido. He describes the transition from one stage to another in terms of displacement *(Verschiebung)*[2]—which does not mean that the libido is determined (or even informed) by economics. The economy only supplies a portion of referential "raw material," projected onto the inner world of the subject in the form of unconscious representations (*imagoes*). Thus, it is not a question of conversion but of (repeatedly mediated) correlation. What is also at play here is the "dangerous liaison" between the mode of production and modes of exchange—such as, for example, psychomimetic reciprocation. While Lacan regards the unconscious as the discourse of the Other, Althusserian Marxism reveals a similar subtext in the relationship between the base and the superstructure. During Khrushchev's thaw, the base and the superstructure of alternative art production were separated. Due to this "outsourcing," superstructural signifiers were imported from the West, while the infrastructure (art materials, studios, etc.) retained its local address. The gap between them—or, as Althusser would argue, between somatic and psychic dimensions of culture, between flexions and reflections—contributed to the emergence of additional blank spaces in the artistic psyche, prone to be filled with incarnations of "procrastinated referents." Because of these gaps, non–socialist realist art differed from socialist realism not only in its creative premises but also in its diagnosis.

2.

In the wake of the successful 1988 Sotheby's auction in Moscow, Russian artists began to travel regularly to the West, where they had exhibitions and sold their works to well-known and nameless collectors alike (fig. 9.1). In museums and exhibition spaces of varying caliber and importance, they hung their taciturn paintings and erected installations that attested to the impenetrability of their context. As for Western connoisseurs and sympathizers, their (fleeting) alliance with Russian art deserves special attention. In the years of perestroika, this relationship was an expression of the center's curiosity about the periphery. Russian protégés (including intellectuals capable of vocalizing their fellow artists' visual messages) were given the preassigned part of those who couldn't be denied patronage and solicitude. Their revelations were worthy of understanding only if they followed the rules of the game and did not generalize or theorize. "Man Friday" turned out to be a supplier of the raw material—of events whose discursive processing was licensed by "Robinson Crusoe." But the real paradox here is the absence (or, once again, the procrastination) of reciprocal interest in the context of art on the part of the visitors, from West to East or from East to West. When viewing foreign exhibitions, even those who can hardly be suspected of being fascinated with "pure" form invariably limited themselves to the strictly formal, aesthetic plane of artistic representation. And this is despite the fact that, for many of them, "visuality is skin stretched over the skeleton of words."[3]

When traveling abroad, a work of art from the former Soviet bloc countries is often viewed as a "part-object," an organ available for donation (with or without consent). Taken as an exotic commodity, this kind of artwork loses its critical charge and thus becomes more commercially "oriented" (in a blunt, derogatory sense) than its Western analogue. A Western artwork faces a very similar problem in Moscow, Warsaw, or Budapest. This crude aesthetic objectification is due to the critical function's procrastination, which follows migration from one context to another. Paradoxically, cultural (or multicultural)[4] exchange and the artistic colonization of the Other tend to result in the diffusion of our critical vision. However useful (e.g., as an anti-alienation pill or a medicine against stagnation), this carnivalesque diffusion seems unfit as a long-term project, for it proves to be remedy and poison at the same time. Such was the case for American and French exhibitions in Moscow at the end of the

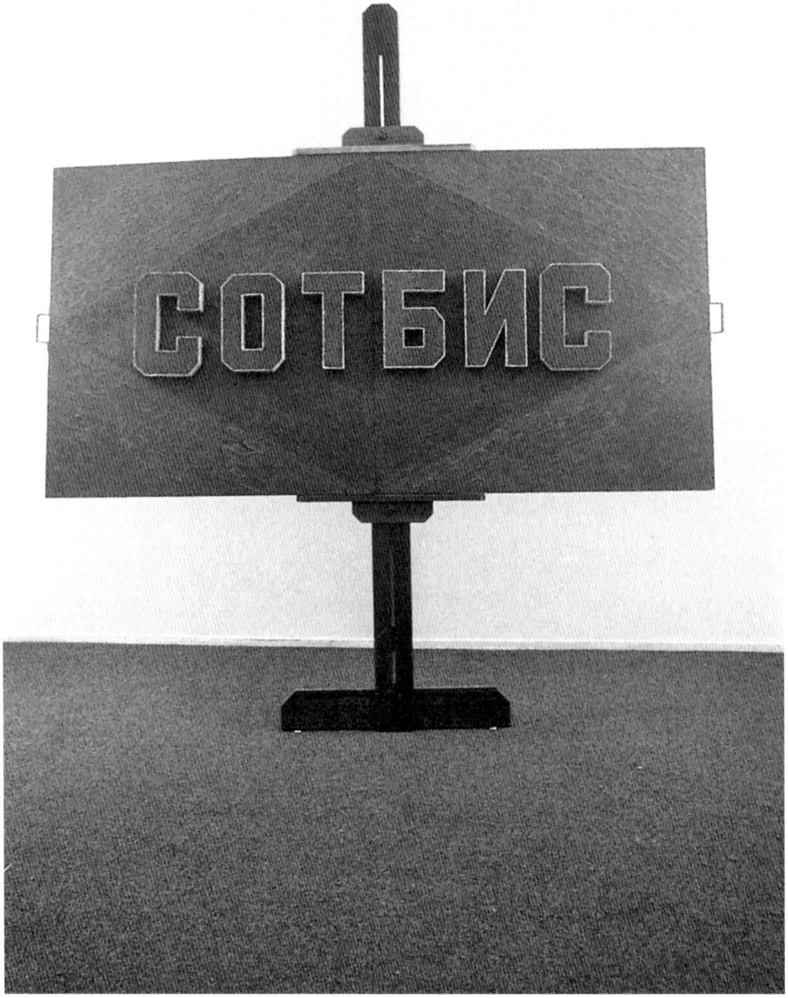

9.1
Igor' Makarevich, *Sotheby's*, 1989.

1950s: on the one hand, both events carnivalized the rigid and stale art life of the Soviet capital; on the other hand, they manifested the triumph of the signifier at the expense of the referent.

In Russia, as in many other countries, the masses still strive to recognize themselves in the icon of the leader. Suffice it to recall Boris Yeltsin, who was elected to office twice, not for being uniquely qualified, but because he fit the stereotype—the "collective image" of people in their deplorable state. Although this stereotype is not fully reflective of what the Russian population is really like, it nonetheless betrays some notorious qualities—such as, for example, drunkenness, bodily ruination, and arrogance. It seems that in casting their votes for Yeltsin people displayed a variety of odd emotions, ranging from self-pity to self-hatred. In fact, although his opponents tried to emphasize the president's severe health problems in order to invalidate his candidacy, these problems only helped Yeltsin get reelected in 1996. Thus, in a desperate attempt to hold on to its vanishing *entirety*, the *entire* nation painfully, if not masochistically, revealed its sickness by identifying with their *entirely* sick leader. If Yeltsin were sober and healthy, he would probably have had to fake inebriation, a heart condition, and his consequent surgery in order to succeed.

The same was true, in part, of Bill Clinton. Regardless of (and simultaneously due to) numerous sex scandals involving him, the public's desire to identify with him was never lost: his troubles reminded people of their own. For, as long as the president's personal life is a mess, it makes him no different from most of his contemporaries all over the world, thereby erasing the gap between the powerful and the powerless. Therefore, a mess turns out to be the unifying factor. This comes as no surprise, considering that unlike other (regional) means of unification—languages, traditions, national borders, and so on—a mess is easier to globalize. Perhaps this is the only universal identity we will be left with.

Today the "body-intellect" dichotomy appears to be worn out. But there were times, to be sure, when it seemed intriguing, especially when the minds of a handful of individuals were occupied with the needs and concerns of the collective body (the masses). For an intellectual who dedicates himself or herself to thinking, the Other is the one who either lacks the same ability or is deprived of it due to social (class, racial, sexual, etc.) injustice. This is true of those historical figures whose lives were chiefly cerebral, but who nonetheless encouraged the workers and the rest of the needy to gain access to material welfare and bodily comfort. Regardless of how this comfort was envisioned by Marx, Lenin, or Mao, it subsequently turned out to be not comfort per se, but the idea of it: its replacement in the form of a "comforting" mental construct. Perhaps the failure to enjoy bodily wholeness and totality in a visual image, which we all experience in early childhood (the mirror stage), prompts some of us to compensate. Sometimes the compensatory effort takes a disastrous form, as history bears witness.

The bodily is far from being a harmless figure of identity. In light of the perturbations (called the "Thermidor" in chapter 8) to which Russian life was subjected in the 1990s, those in the art world who defend the right of art to be autochthonic can be compared to the pillars of affirmation: the caryatids and atlantes who uphold the status quo. Even though "the bodily" is now interpreted as "national in form," it was almost completely absent from socialist realism, which, in turn, had nothing to do with socially engaged art. This assertion also applies to the *telesniks*[5] (Oleg Kulik, Vladimir Dubossarskii and Aleksandr Vinogradov, etc.) who have been mislabeled as social artists despite being cheered on by the nouveau riche in a country swept by corruption and mercantilism (fig. 9.2).

To the extent that a utopia which gravitates toward the creation of artificial superbodies is subordinated to the Cartesian (i.e., mental) eye, dystopia is governed by corporal (dis)charges. This includes impulses whose de-procrastination can occur only when utopian time has elapsed. Under the impact of these impulses, utopian superbodies begin to disintegrate in order to come together again—on the basis of a different, autochthonic logic, in accordance with which the "Thermidor" of the bodily, in the countries of the former Soviet bloc, is accompanied by an increasingly vicious partiality. The body of Eastern Europe has been dispersing nomadically. In some cases (Bosnia, Kosovo, Chechnya), the separation of republics and regions can be compared to a surgical intervention. And in this sense, the former Russian president's surgery (the severing of arteries, the grafting of new veins, etc.) suits these events perfectly, as if attesting to the fact that in Russia the process of immersion in autochthony parallels the contortions and agonies of territorial secession. Thus, establishing its position in the culture, the bodily becomes a protagonist in the geopolitical arena.

3.

As conveyed in chapter 6, the feeling of resentment toward feminism on the part of both male and female artists in Russia can also be analyzed in terms of procrastination. Feminism is suspected of a desire to expand beyond the boundaries of the communal "body-without-organs."[6] The latter is tolerant only toward the "bodily optic," which I previously called the "caressing" vision. In such bodies, critical responsibility is procrastinated: it gives way to an affirmative responsibility and abstention from

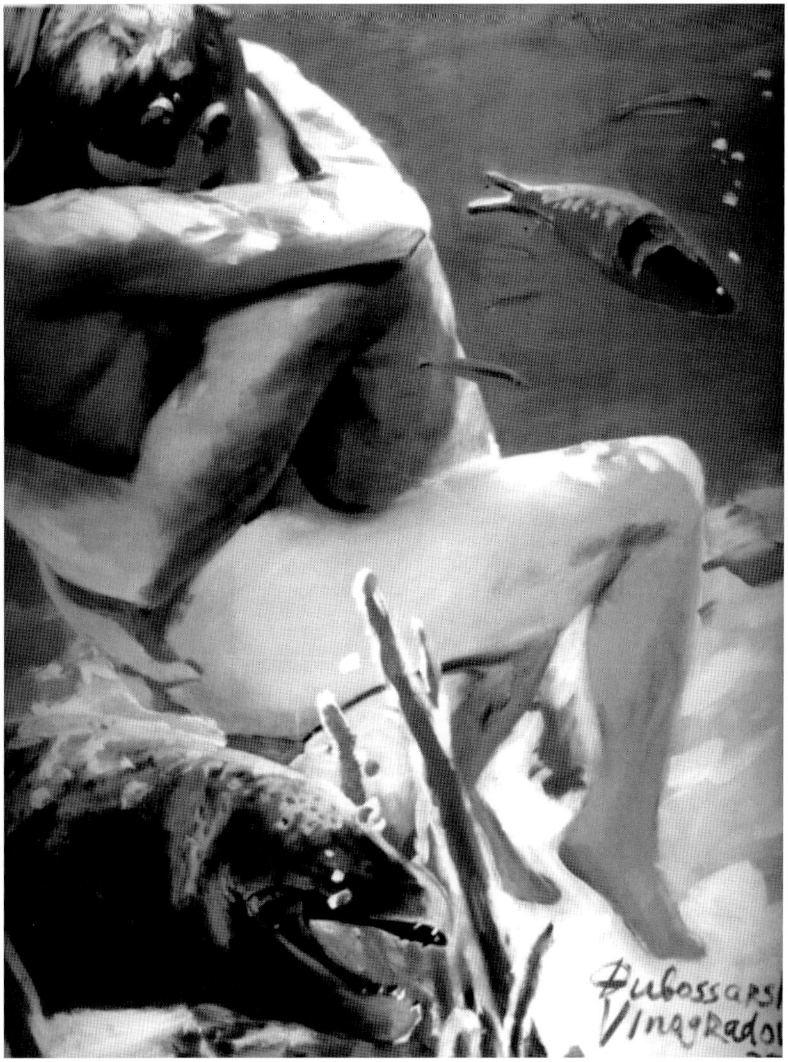

9.2
Vladimir Dubossarskii and Aleksandr Vinogradov, *Underwater,* 2002.

judgments, which lie outside communal identity. This, in turn, does not preclude internal conflicts: on the path of confession, everything is permitted—from the repentance of one's own sins to accusations against one's neighbor—in order to avoid a critical distance from the principle of confessionality itself. (A similar position, related to the "modern black Diaspora problematic of invisibility and namelessness," is characterized by Cornel West as "moralistic in content and communal in character.")[7] In other words, we are talking about responsibility from within, which does not allow either *ostranenie* or *Verfremdungs-effekt* (alienation effect).[8] If the "alienation effect," for example, is rife with the potential of apology for averted vision, in the world of communal traditions such vision is viewed as irresponsible. This world is bodily and homogeneous; it does not allow clearances for critical maneuvers whose purpose is to divert attention from interpersonal evaluation to the extrapersonal critique of institutions.

In the communal world, speech is constantly in motion: one has to leap into it as one would jump onto a moving streetcar. Considering the instantaneous nature of speech acts, the communal "I" aspires not toward maximum ethical adequacy (which would be impossible) but toward a behavioral strategy that minimizes responsibility for irresponsible moral judgments—from labels to personality cults. The combination of the immediacy of ethical intervention with its inevitable procrastination (delay, loss of tempo) challenges the effectiveness of spontaneous moral decisions formulated in terms of *maxima moralia*.

The subject of communal speech is speech itself. It is also the object of speech acts. That is why there is something hermaphroditic in the relationship between the subject and object of "logogyration," or "texturbation." This is confirmed by the permanent use of impersonal and indefinite forms ("it," "as if"), and also by the figures of blocking the referent, or silencing, through which one can see the silhouettes of displaced traumas and unfulfilled or procrastinated desires. The sphere of the conspiratorial, coded "it" (*ono* in Russian) also includes the unknown, a category exploited exclusively by Moscow's communal conceptualism—the apotheosis of impersonality, nonbindingness, diffuse sexuality, of "hermaphrodism." This last term should not be confused with "androgyny": androgynes are adepts of the sadistic superego, while hermaphrodites are representatives of masochistic discourse.[9]

Whereas the concept of androgyny is offered here as a utopian construct, as the triumph of unity over contradictions—extending to the possibility of symbolic copulation with "oneself," necessary to the reproduction of the totality—the hermaphroditic libido suffers defeat in the attempt to invest itself in itself, since it is unable to overcome the crisis of identification. Unlike socialist modernism, which managed to retain some links with the international modernist project until the mid-1930s and from which Moscow conceptualism inherited its hermaphroditic incompleteness, androgyny is akin to the Stalinist cultural heritage.[10]

4.

The "Thermidor" of the bodily, which I discussed in chapter 8, is accompanied by attacks on intellectualism. This is true not only in Russia: the same is happening in Western Europe and North America, albeit in different forms and on a somewhat different scale. Critical theory and critically engaged cultural practices are being expelled from the art scene and from the pages of the art press. Apparently, an affirmation of the body and affirmation through the body is what characterizes the present situation in Russia and beyond. Accordingly, the texts written about Russian art at home are not criticism but affirmation. The diagnosis leaves much to be desired: the procrastination of critical responsibility continues, and the revival of interest in the critical function is yet to occur. So far, references to Brecht, Adorno, or Benjamin do not resonate in the "collective soul" of critics in Moscow or St. Petersburg. "Responsibility for what? Art is a completely useless thing," one Moscow artist declared in a conversation with me. Another opined that the important thing about any ("true") work of art is that "it cannot be used in any other way." The infantilism of such declarations is explained by the extreme childishness of the male half of the Russian population, including the artistic intelligentsia. This phenomenon can be described as a procrastination of adulthood. In the words of Kabakov:

> A person who feels like a child is able to escape the canons and boundaries of being in which he or she is, as it were, assigned a place. You develop an entirely different attitude toward reality. It is perceived as a theft, even though it is, in fact, not limited by anyone and therefore belongs to you in unlimited quantities. This is space without dimensions: it can be shortened but can also be expanded. What starts from such attitudes (or criteria) is the prospect of complete happiness and eternal childhood.[11]

"Be ye therefore as children," Christ urged his followers, "for theirs is the Kingdom of Heaven. Verily I say unto you: whosoever does not accept the Kingdom of God as a child will not enter the Kingdom of God." Self-perception as an eternal child (a phenomenon that demonstrates the similarity of Soviet traditions not only to Christianity, but to Zen Buddhism) harks back to a time when the burden of adulthood was placed on government bureaucracy. Everyone else was inculcated with the idea that "the only privileged class in the USSR is children." Therefore, the prospect of the loss of such (class) privileges, anticipated by the "communal unconscious," caused the tempo of maturation to slow down.[12] Something similar is happening in today's art world, the difference being that the role of MOSKh's art councils and purchasing committees has been taken over by curators, critics, and art dealers. It would seem that if the creative personality is an *enfant terrible,* to enter a professional relationship with such a person is to engage in the exploitation of child labor, and therefore to violate both moral and legal norms. That is why relations between the child (*enfant*) and the adult do not usually go beyond the "symbolic economy": the child is expected to be diligent and well behaved in exchange for gifts and praise from adults. Such, in general terms, is the "compulsory assortment" of sociocultural infantilism. Nonetheless, the inconveniences that burden permanent childhood are more than adequately compensated by the conveniences acquired as a result of abdicating social responsibility.

An infantile vision of reality is conservative and, in a sense, reactionary, especially when held by adults. Paraphrasing Ryklin's term "terrorologic," one can introduce the idea of a "terroro-optic."[13] The child, after all, is simultaneously a prince and a pauper, a sovereign and a vassal, persecutor and persecuted. The infantile model of communal subjectivity rests on the presumption of the wholeness of the world, on belief in the totality and continuity of being, while representing, at the same time, an example of aggressive egocentrism. Following Lacan, one can maintain that "the characteristic modes of the agency of the [communal] *moi* in dialogue are the aggressive reactions,"[14] and that "aggressivity is the correlative tendency of a mode of identification that we call narcissistic."[15] From this aggressive egocentrism arises the notion of a "worldwide" cultural context as a quasi-syntagmatic chain of events, combined with a naive longing for accidents—accidents equated with de-procrastination of *le réel*—as normative events.[16] Among the paradigms of childishness is the carnival-like (festive) perception of acts of violence, best illustrated by the conviction that "even dying is good if the world is watching." Translated into the language of urban problems, immaturity is the ghetto, whose contribution to culture is nothing other than kitsch (contrary to Clement Greenberg's belief, it is not avant-garde). Those who came out of the ghetto often turned out to be the most zealous guard dogs of convention and orthodoxy, the angelic host entrusted with sentineling the authoritarian power. As a psychodrome of forcible territorialization regulated from the outside, childhood is a machine of retribution, a compressed spring of de-procrastination. Among the side effects is the criminalization of the

Russian infrastructure; from this standpoint, the post-Soviet mafia, despite its lawlessness, is the lawful heir to communal tradition.[17]

Despite their chronological proximity, childhood and youth are not metonymically close: unlike childhood, youth does not feel comfortable in the position of onlooker fascinated by the conflict and the unity of opposites. Rather, youth is characterized by social altruism, rebellion, and an intolerance toward everything invested with "paternal" prerogatives. On the other hand, the iconoclastic gesture does not befit childhood (eternal, stagnant childhood), for which inertia and a taste for an apocalyptic vision of the world are "appropriate"—whereas youth is aflame with a desire to alter the existing order of things. In other words, both youth and the youthful are missing from present-day Russia, where childhood and adulthood remain the principal psychosocial niches.

Sometimes in the course of a conversation, one surprises oneself by saying or agreeing with something that contradicts one's convictions. The compartmentalization of viewpoints and principles characteristic of verbal interaction does not apply to the written word, which, as we know, once written, cannot be erased. This happens, primarily, because oral contact reserves for itself the privileges and exemptions granted to "the only privileged class," the residents of "neverland," and secondly, because of the communal engagement of the audile signifier. In contrast to the nonbinding and immediate nature of the latter, the written and printed word cry out for responsibility, political correctness, and the necessity to connect infantile speech acts with a mature textuality. One example of this can be found in the census taken to measure the passenger load on the Moscow metro in the early 1970s. At the entrance, everyone was handed a printed form explaining the census, which had to be presented upon exiting. One passenger, in a state of extreme inebriation, staggered, balancing miraculously on the edge of the platform. Nonetheless, he did not suffer the fate of Anna Karenina and the train did not become the hero of this tale. At the end of the line, the drunken passenger had to be assisted out of the car by others. However, on ascending the escalator and seeing the representatives of the registration service, he was instantly sobered up and produced the document in question, thereby successfully performing a "socially responsible act." The return from childhood to adulthood transpired in seconds (the "de-procrastination effect"). The printed word of the form was a sobering (maturing) factor.

For many representatives of alternative art, from Kabakov to Viktor Pivovarov, illustrating children's literature was not just a matter of earning a living. The force lines that ensure the metabolism of the "body-without-organs" go through this genre. One can discuss the experience of working in *Detgiz* (Children's State Publishing) or the *Malysh* (Little One) publishing house in terms of schizotherapy; without this experience, contemporary Russian art would look very different. The infantilization of iconography which also characterizes these artists' "grown-up" drawings is in fact a symptom of the dulling of the will to representation. The same can be said of the textual heritage of "Moscow communal conceptualism" with its characteristic borrowing of names and terms from children's books or Russian folktales (*kolobkovost'*, *Neznaika*, etc.). In other words, infantilism is not an ornament or a carnival suit, but the defining aspect (*point de capiton*) of communal subjectivity.

In the space of communal speech, one feels like Gulliver among the Lilliputians. This effect is due in part to the infantile babble of adults, filled with words like *smertushka* (little death), *mogilka* (little grave), *bozehn'ka* (little God), *tvorozhok so smetankoi* (little cheese with little sour cream), and the like. On the lips of grown-ups, babyish lexicon manifests itself in diminutive suffixes as well as borrowings, imitations, and repetitions. "Repetition is the mother of learning," states the well-known truism imported from the scholastic practice of memorizing the sayings of great men, slogans, and literary texts. Part of the same tradition is our ability to merge with our *objet petit a* (be it a real or fictional object of love, envy, fear, or fascination), to "move in" with him or her, "move him or her in" with us, and so forth—right up to "moving in" with one's own self as a literary character. Continuing on the subject of borrowing, imitation, and repetition as attributes of schoolboy manners and infantilism, one has to mention postmodernism, for which these are key concepts. Regardless of the borders, any "spectacle order" that presently exists in the West (including Russia) can be contemplated as the play of similarities and differences between postmodern infantilism and its transcendence (the youth paradigm).

5.

If we agree that in the 1990s, following the euphoria of perestroika, "all things Russian" were out of fashion or going out of fashion in the West, we must recognize another and no less obvious fact: the dwindling of interest in the Russian social and cultural experiment outside its territorial boundaries is the sad culmination of the drawn-out love affair between the Soviet regime and its fans in Europe and the United States. It's enough to look at the reminiscences of intellectuals intoxicated with Russia (from René Etiemble and André Gide to Benjamin and Althusser)[18] to understand to what extent the pre- and postwar Western intelligentsia was mesmerized, not only by the chronicles, but by the artistic representation of Soviet life; and by each triumph of socialist construction, by each unmasking of the "enemies of the people," by each nuance of the ideological struggle. In the 1990s it became clear to everyone that Russia was a sunken *Titanic* (the *Titanic* of Utopia), and the intellectual elite began shrinking from it the way a vampire shrinks from the cross. This coldness and haughtiness were payback for seventy years of bottomless spiritual and mental investment in the Soviet utopian project, which had collapsed. Once, those who looked to the future also looked to Moscow; now that life in Moscow increasingly reminds Americans and Europeans of their own past, it is mainly the would-be guardians of time gone by—that is, essentially, retrogrades—who are interested in it.

In Europe and in America, "art for art's sake," as well as its corollary myths, are, to a large extent, depreciated. However, all who professed such beliefs in the USSR were drawn into resistance to the giant machine of depersonalization by the very fact of their existence, and often against their will. And even though, compared to the legions of devotees of "socially disengaged" art in the West, their numbers in the Soviet Union were minuscule, the idiom of the artistic language they cultivated was a stumbling block on the road to the total stereotyping of culture, to "monolexism." In other words, the denizens of the "ivory tower" were paradoxically healing a world that was trying to corrupt them.

The history of oppositional modernism echoes the myth of Ulysses, who was able to blind his imprisoner, the Cyclops Polyphemus, not only literally but figuratively: to Polyphemus's question, "Who are you?" Ulysses had responded with his usual foresight, replying that his name was "Nobody." After being blinded, Polyphemus turned to his seeing brethren for help; but when they asked the name of his offender and he replied, "Nobody,"[19] the collective sanctions did not follow. Commenting on this subject, Peter Sloterdijk—in his book *Kritik der zynischen Vernunft* (1983)—credits the positive aspect of physical survival, which, in the case of Ulysses, was made possible by a "negative" aspect, that is, at the price of repudiating the definition (naming) of one's identity.[20]

For Ulysses, convincing Polyphemus of his namelessness was a "minimum goal," while the "maximum goal" was to exit the cave. To discover "Being-as-Nobody" in the context of the Cyclops's optic does not equal liberation, since the cave itself serves as a metaphor for form, for definition, for naming, and, ultimately, for identification. Insofar as naming imitates what is proper to it, Ulysses' "nobody" becomes "nobody from the cave of Polyphemus," essentially acquiring a name and address defined by a place, by circumstance, and by limitations. Thus, in the context of extracavital (beyond-the-cave) vision, uncontested by Soviet or post-Soviet homegrown myths, "nobody" is read as "nobody from the USSR," "nobody from Russia," "nobody from the Moscow art underground," etc. The fact that these names are provisional makes them eligible for future corrections, which brings to mind Socrates, for whom the act of (re)naming makes no sense unless it is permanent.[21] The first thing to note is that the Cyclops wouldn't let his "nameless" captive out of the cave, as if knowing that the locus of meaning is the name/thing relation. Is this what Polyphemus was supposed to watch over and shield from daylight? It is possible that "rumors" of the physical blinding of Polyphemus by Ulysses are the result of mythological banalization. The defect of mental vision is another matter: here, it is useful to refer to the Cartesian allegory of blindness and, accordingly, of the cave. Criticizing the new science antagonists, Descartes compared them to the militant blind man who lures his opponents into the darkness of the cave and thus deprives them of their sole advantage—vision. The repudiation of (self-) naming is remarkable in that, under the influence of such denominalization, the "body-without-organs" becomes a "body-without-a-name." This is precisely what happened to the Polyphemus of totalitarian power, discouraged by the Ulyssean cunning of three generations of Russian unofficial artists, who, until the early 1990s, avoided social identification. The procrastination of the moment of self-naming enabled them to dodge contact with society and with authorities. Ironically, in the year 2000, "*nobody* for president" was the winning strategy for Vladimir Putin. This strategy—given the Russian population's annoyance with all the usual faces—enabled Putin to take charge of the Kremlin cave. Apparently, "nobodiness" is a two-way ticket—to get out (Ulysses) and to get in (Putin).

In the post-perestroika years, the situation changed radically. The apologetic motivations that reconcile us to the "politics of nonpoliticality," attributable (in Russia) to the alternative art of the 1960s through 1980s, do not extend to the present generation of creatively engaged people. The overabundance of metaphor has given way to an overabundance of reality. And yet the death of ideologies announced by Lyotard seems to be an exaggeration, especially in the midst of stabilization of capitalism and all its corollary structures and institutions. It is precisely in these extremely complex conditions that the "body-without-a-name" loses the "buffer zone," or "isolation belt," that protects both the avant-garde and its Other from mutual aggression. In the Khrushchev and Brezhnev years, this "isolation belt" was formed by members of the Moscow or St. Petersburg scientific and literary milieu, who comprised a significant portion of the alternative art audience. Their present-day impoverishment has deprived these artists of a supportive environment. For these and other reasons, the world of reflections has found itself pressed up against the world of flexions, face to face with the destitute population and the nouveau riche.[22] Given that "nobodiness" has ceased to be a viable niche for the post-Soviet art milieu, one is left wondering who (or what) will be its new name-maker.

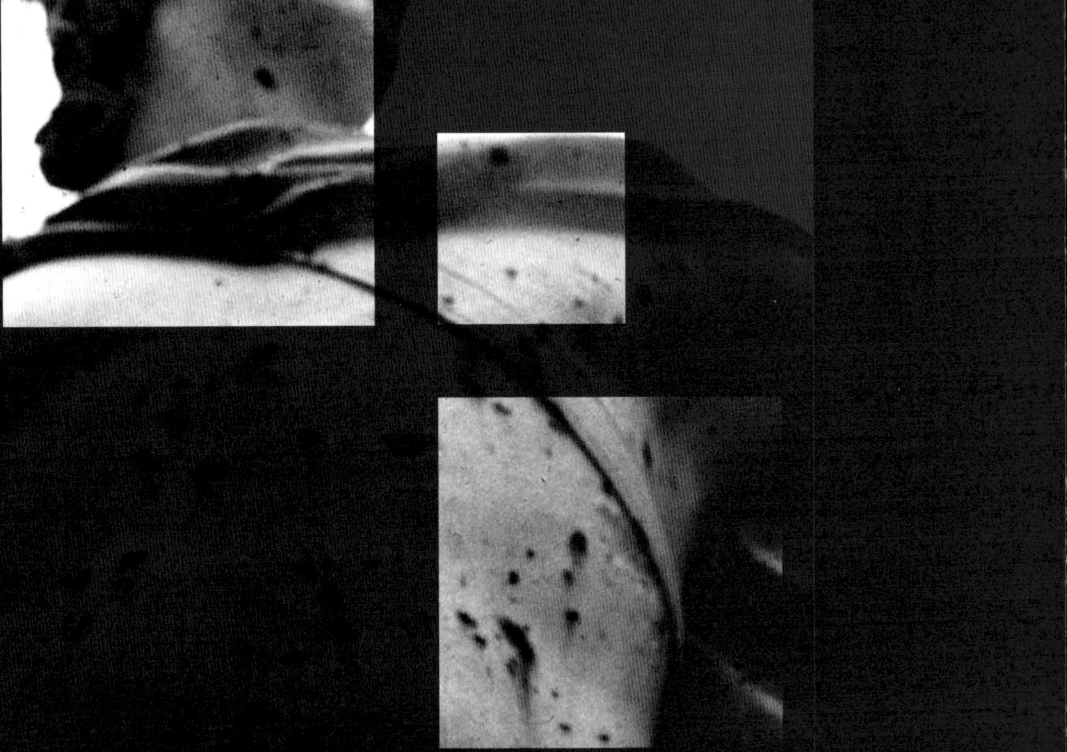

CHAPTER 10

Notes on the Museological Unconscious

1. MUSEOLOGICAL FUNCTION

To begin, I will refer to Karl Jaspers's museological dream revealed in the introduction to his *The Great Philosophers*.[1] This text can be described as a museification project—the museification of a historico-philosophical space. Whereas Lacan's vision of the Unconscious is bound to the three registers, the residents of Jaspers's philosophical museum[2] are partitioned into several (fraternal) groups and subgroups. Their members are present there only in the sense that they represent the symbolic function. Jaspers projected his philosophical "hall of fame" as the place suitable for a successful combination of the dead and the living. One may argue that similar combinations take place in the Symbolic register (due to the transfer of "the name of the Father"). In a way, Jaspers's museum resembles both Dante's *Inferno* and Raphael's *School of Athens*. The similarity lies in what Foucault attributes to heterotopia,[3] and Bakhtin to verticality (the "chronotope of vertical time"). When time is vertical, all events occur simultaneously; deferred histories become synchronized; thoughts and visions attain the state of timelessness. Hence, "vertical" is synonymous with "ahistorical," which partially explains why our eagerness to *verticalize* history culminates in erecting museums. This is particularly true of Jaspers, whose *Die massgebenden Menschen* seems inconsistent with his own *horizontalist* agenda, with what he called "the all-embracing historicity." It also reveals how comfortably the ahistorical "hides its ass" beyond the looking glass of historicity: their longing for one another should be viewed as a tradition rather than a chancy outcome.

▪▪

Yet another tradition has been revived; artists are cosponsoring publications about themselves, in which they control both the selection of material and its interpretation. Examples of these include Kabakov's memoir *The '60s and '70s,* as well as his notebooks (texts, designs, and projects which, for one reason or another, were not featured in his exhibition catalogues); Vladimir Nemukhin's *Monologues,* dedicated to the lifestyles of Moscow unofficial artists; Igor and Svetlana Kopystiansky's archives (annotated by themselves); Leonid Sokov's self-compiled monograph aimed at publicizing his sculptural oeuvre; and the Collective Actions group's five-volume chronicle *Poezdki za gorod,* which looks as if it were authored by the referent (subject matter) itself.[4]

The eternal Russian question, which apparently has no answer, is "What is to be done?" In this case the question is, What is to be done with art that has not realized its "museological function" in time, even if this is through no fault of its own?[5] The museological function has a communicative dimension; it generates the illusion (comparable with children's reliance on the power and accessibility of a spoken word) that every creative act is common property. This falls under the definition of egocentric speech[6] or, more specifically, the egocentric speech of the signified, with all its external and internal articulations—for example, articulation of the Imaginary through the mouthpiece of the Symbolic. Thus, the principal purpose of the publications listed above confirms their egocentricity: they are attempts to reproduce the museological function (and even to replicate its institutional format) at the artists' own expense and on their own terms.[7] Understandably, the embryonic state of the museological function creates unbearable psychic discomfort, whether we admit this or not. Many feel a desire to compensate for this yawning gap and attempt to do so in a variety of ways, including the publication of self-made books and catalogues or the belated realization of old art projects. In all such projects, the artists lay out their creative biographies (and their oeuvre) in a direction deviant from signification.[8] What takes place in these antisignification plots is the return of the author, hitherto "buried" by Barthes and Derrida.[9] This return is expressed, above all, in the attempt by the art practitioners to redefine their function: to become psalmodists of their own "scripture," their own visual *texts.* To *read* them in a direction deviant from signification means to engage in an egocentric reading regarded as an alternative to an institutional one. Rather than resisting institutional control over the formation of meanings, egocentric readings can compensate for the absence of institutions. The important point for the majority of noninstitutional artists today is not the subversion of the mechanisms of signification nor the disassembly of the museological function, but their renewal, upgrading, and re-creation.

A passion for an egocentric reading of one's own text—whether this is an artwork, critical inquiry, or theoretical investigation—can be matched only by some authors' ability to constitute the unity of what they think and how they look. In "Marcel Duchamp in America: A Self Ready-Made," Moira Roth argued that "Duchamp's choice of America in 1915 was the right one for a man obsessed with the making of his own image, the perpetuation of that image, and total control over its reading."[10] However obsessive, Duchamp's desire to control and to "museify" his image pales in comparison with Clement Greenberg's eagerness to control the image of American abstract painting.[11] In a desperate attempt to run ahead of signification, Greenberg—in his 1948 article "The Situation at the Moment"—wrote that "the future of Western art . . . depends on what is done in this country [the United States]."[12] Ironically, Greenberg's statement fits his own vision of "deceiving hopes," which egocentric speech "is able to install in places of power," amid the Symbolic.[13]

Speaking of "places of power," there are very few secular institutions capable of turning the clock hands counterclockwise as successfully as museums. But the truth is that the mnemonic functions performed there are utterly reflective of the things these institutions present or hold on to. As a result, all "free range" signifiers—especially those that partake in our identificatory efforts—are fastened up and pinned to certain items, whether artworks or cultural memorabilia. In such places, everything (including our reflections on the past) can be instantly objectified (museological objectification). However compulsive, this mnemonic activity is yet another industry (coextensive with the culture industry) that produces memory.[14]

What needs to be reassessed here is our model of *temps perdu,* which we mentally pitch into one or another historical range in order to convince ourselves and others that "that's exactly how it was." Apparently, the "authentic past"—if it is appropriate to even speak of such a thing—has always been subjected to repression. In this sense, the past is a psychoanalytic concept. What has always reigned and still reigns in place of the past is a representation based on one or another set of facts and acceptable to those who have a stake in constructing a linear model of cultural identity. They use this construct as an ideological alibi, as well as for didactic purposes—a warning, a lesson, a moral, and so on. Nothing is as prostituted as the past (fig. 10.1). But to rescue it from the present (especially, in "one piece") is an enormous task, a utopian project of immense proportions. At the same time, the health of culture can be improved by awareness not only of connections to the past, but also of those breaks from it

10.1
Boris Mikhailov, from the series *Susi and Others*, early 1970s.

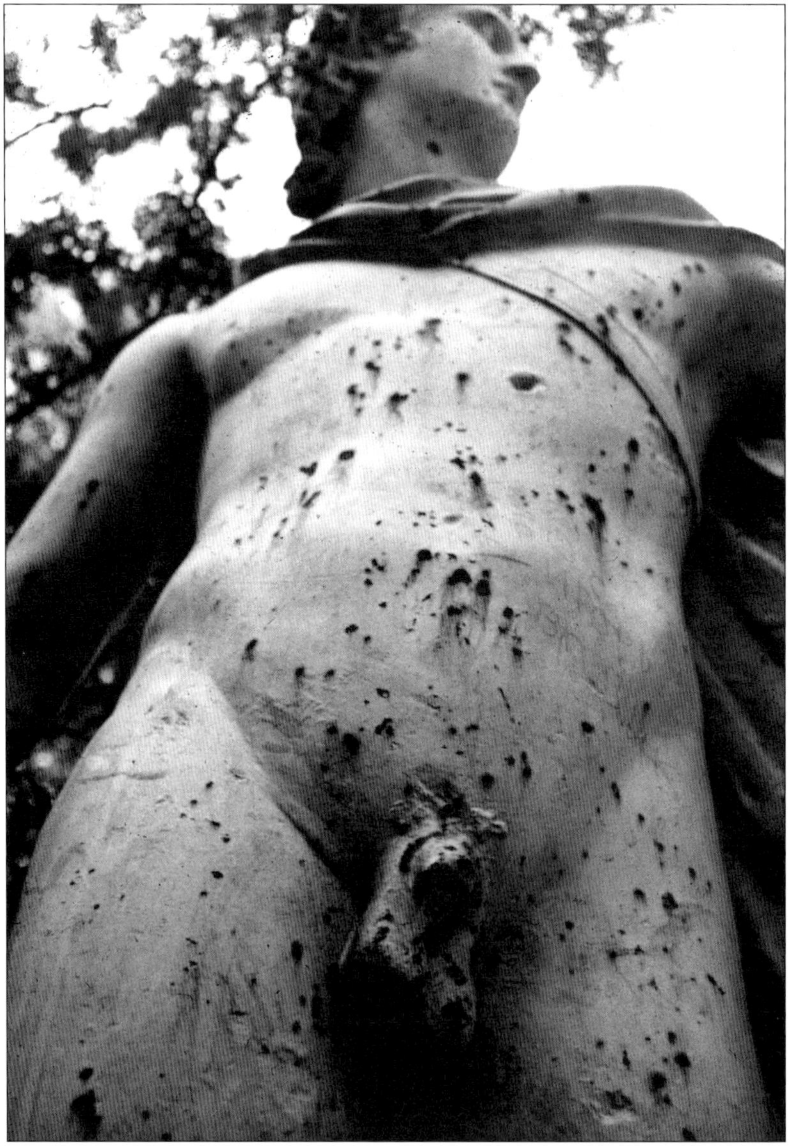

which contribute to our contact with *le réel*. This is why I completely understand Kabakov, Sokov, or the Collective Actions group when they make a break with the institutional historical function that, in the case of most Russian artists, does not work.

It makes sense to compare the publications under discussion (I am referring to the book-as-diary, book-as-museum, book-as-ark) to Gerhard Richter's *Atlas* (1962–1996).[15] In *Atlas*, almost all the fragments are asignificative, and lack autonomous artistic merit or self-sufficiency. The museological emphasis in this work is placed on its mesmerizing comparability to life; its temporal, spatial, and bodily aspects; its duration and finality. And that's what underlies our vote of confidence. We forgive Richter the tediousness, the pedantry, and the excessive length of his boring enterprise only because we recognize ourselves in all of it. The point, however, is that to recognize ourselves in *all of it* is not, in this case, an ordinary or routine act of reciprocation. Rather, it is an opportunity for Richter and his audience to rejoice in a cliché, and—above all—to rejoice in it under the museum roof. For, once inside the museum, we reexperience sameness in a different way, different in the sense that in a temple of art—unlike in a shopping mall or in a subway—our reflections are mediated by the aesthetics of the Sublime. Thus, with *Atlas* (as an exemplary work of art in the age of museological reproduction), our craving for all kinds of unifying clichés—and, more, for their presentation in an affirmative way—becomes legitimized on the highest secular level, that is, through the museum.

On the theme of rejoicing in a cliché, Kabakov believes that "we all have a mysterious capability to merge with the inner vision of writers, poets, and artists. Such a merging is possible because somehow and for some reason, the vision of the *other* turns out to be absolutely contagious, infectious."[16] And yet to determine what borrows from what—a picture from life, or life from a picture—is hardly clear-cut. Ultimately, visual culture has affected us in such a way that we have started to see the world, and ourselves in it, through the lens of representation. Thanks to the mass media, this phenomenon has become universal. Jeff Wall's photographs *Mimic* (1982) and *The Sudden Gust of Wind* (1993) share compositional similarities with *Paris Street, Rainy Day* (1877), a painting by Gustave Caillebotte, and Hokusai's *Travelers Caught in Sudden Breeze at Fuji* (1832), respectively. This similarity suggests the possibility that the photographer is merely explicating the impact of the museological function, which a priori, even before the moment of contemplation, impels us to perceive reality as the product of a mimetic act, as a replica of art.

2. CLUES AND SYMPTOMS

Both inside ex-Soviet territory and outside its borders, Russians utter the phrase "Museum of Contemporary Art" in a special, dreamy, breathless way. There have been, and continue to be, attempts to create a contemporary art museum based on private collections.[17] A lot of their material is trash; but trash, as we know, is the best material for creating a world (think of primordial dust). With each attempt we are witnesses to a cosmogonic act. The birth of a museum is like the beginning of time; time is counted from that moment on (fig. 10.2). The museum's founders, curators, and artists whose works are in its permanent collection behave accordingly. One gets the impression that the museum is a sanctuary for some infra-aesthetic ideal that fuels our will to art,[18] particularly since the imprints of its "presence" are in abundance on museum walls or in storage rooms.

It is a well-known fact that museums are a phenomenon that date back to the late eighteenth or early nineteenth century. The museological function, however, is far older, as is the "museological unconscious." No one was present at its birth, and how "it" appeared remains a mystery. The fact that the unconscious is the discourse of the Other does not help unless we identify "it." For artists residing in the former USSR, the image of the institutional Other was (until the turn of this century) firmly fixed on the absent museum of contemporary art. The evidence and signs of this absence have constituted the psychedelic repertory of visual culture in Russia, and they can be regarded as the language that structures the museological unconscious. This caesural language, the language of displacement and anticipation, is far from being the only architectural principle on the basis of which invisible museums, libraries, and archives are created. In addition there are other, compensatory languages that allow the individual to comprehend his or her own thoughts, actions, and psychic impulses as something "already always" depicted (or instantaneously appearing) on the canvas of Being. This gives way to an aesthetic evaluation conditioned by contemplating the events from several standpoints: that of the character, that of the author, that of the viewer, and most importantly that of the connoisseur. When this last standpoint prevails, we can speak of the phenomenon of museification—museification of the individual's inner world and of the collective psyche, for this is how the museological unconscious manifests itself. In essence, our ability to perceive life as a work of art, along with the ability to transfer this perception from ourselves to others, and from others to ourselves, is quite consistent with Lacan's notion of the transition from the mirror stage to the Symbolic order.

The individual's museological "I" is less a museum than a "private collection." In this case, the museological "I" appropriates all roles,

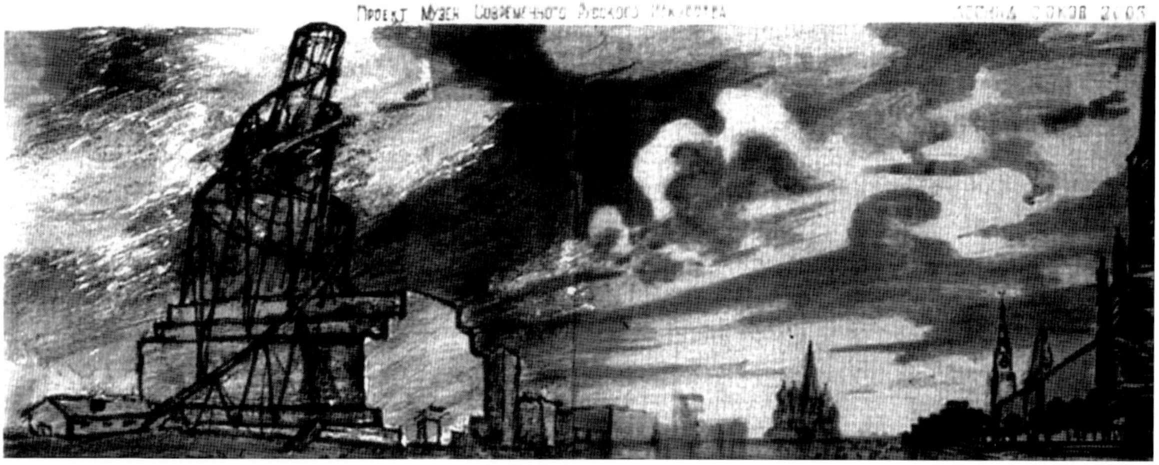

10.2
Leonid Sokov, *Project for a Museum of Contemporary Russian Art*, 2003.

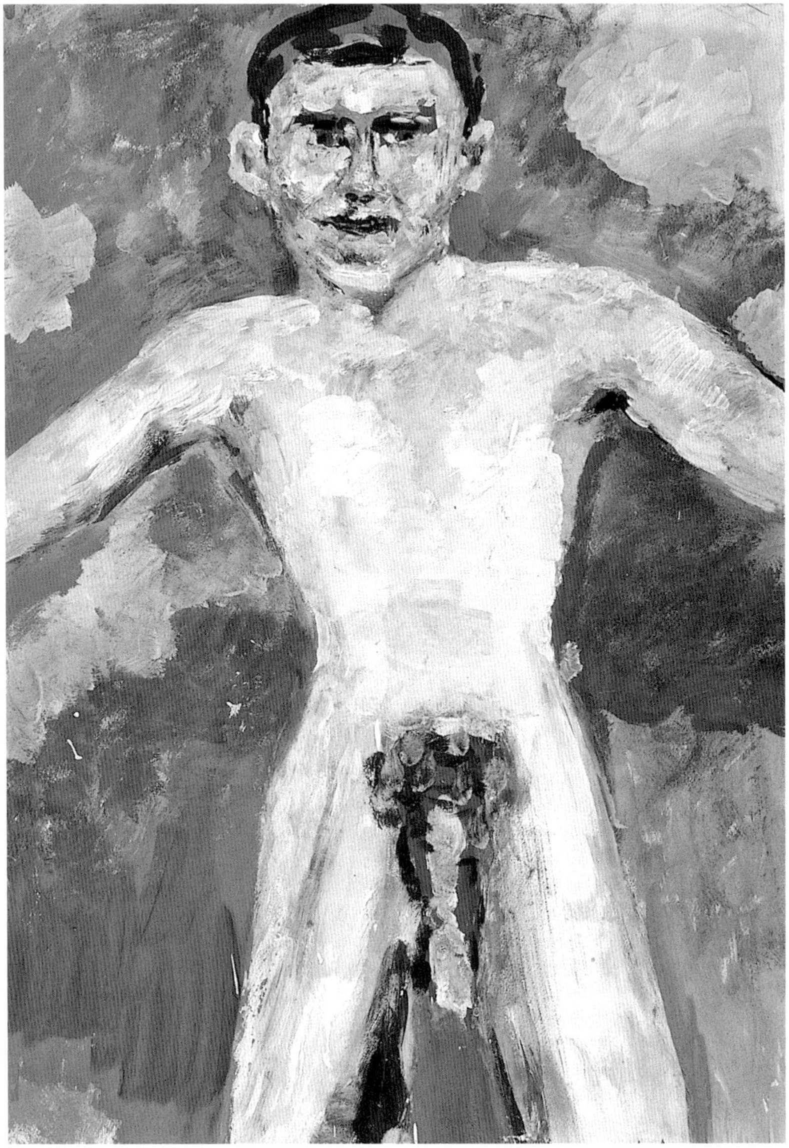

10.3
Vladimir Iakovlev, *Self-Portrait*, 1971.

functions, and prerogatives: it is the author and (simultaneously) the creation, the collector and the collection, the archivist and the archive, the exhibition space and the exhibition, the art connoisseur and the work of art. In the case of a plural "I," we are dealing with a "corporate museum," and thus with a collective author. At any rate, art whose time has gone compensates for the *temps perdu* with "museological time." It is not in anyone's power to hinder or help this process. Be it as it may, the concepts of "museological time" and "museological merit" are the surplus value acquired by a work of art when it has been emptied of its content and its connection to the unique cross-section of circumstances that generated it. To mention such circumstances, if only in passing, the buildup of the socialist culture industry in the 1920s was a decisive factor contributing to the avant-garde's transformation into socialist modernism.[19]

In chapter 1, I argued that the contents of the "communal unconscious" are channeled from one group of individuals to another—either in the form of visual stereotypes[20] or through verbal exchange, including communal speech acts. The same is true of the museological unconscious: regardless of how much it needs rigorous examination, attention should also be paid to the "secondary sources," bordering on frivolous analogies, popular myths, tales, and fantasies of a carnivalesque nature, attributable to the "the will to enclose in one place all times, all epochs, all forms, all tastes."[21] Most of these items open onto what Foucault viewed as heterotopias[22] that are proper to the museum and, retroactively, to the museological unconscious.

The museological unconscious manifests itself in a number of stories and involves "paradigmatic" characters, such as, for example, the Moscow artist Vladimir Iakovlev, featured in Nemukhin's *Monologues* in an episode that took place in 1975, at the sculptor Ernst Neizvestnyi's birthday party.[23] The celebration reached its peak when the wife of filmmaker Sergei Yutkevich informed the guests that she had a *big* Picasso in her possession. "I have a *big* dick," said Iakovlev in response. "I beg your pardon?" she inquired, and then turned to the host for help. "He too has a *big* Picasso," explained Neizvestnyi (fig. 10.3). This carnivalesque nondifferentiation between a sex organ and a masterpiece reveals the libidinal subtext of museification, suggesting that the latter is the phenomenon of phallic origin.

There are two more characters to bring into play here—Jackson Pollock and Yves Klein. As a child, Pollock witnessed his alcoholic father, Roy, come home every night and urinate furiously onto a white wall, illuminated by a hanging lamp swaying in the wind. From his bedroom window, Jackson would watch this Roy-al spray sparkle under the light, making it look like a cosmogonic act. Later, when Pollock reached artistic manhood, the piss-sprayed wall, and the act of spraying itself, transformed into what Harold Rosenberg dubbed "action painting." But Pollock's father continued to haunt him, not only in the realm of sublimation but in his social life as well: he once pissed into Peggy Guggenheim's fireplace in front of all her party guests.

According to his friends and admirers, Klein's "blue" series refers to a period in the artist's life when, while suffering from a bout of childhood bedwetting, Klein repeatedly dreamt that he was a mermaid swimming in the blue waves of the Mediterranean Sea.[24] Klein's dream evokes the death of King Ludwig the II of Bavaria, who drowned in a court pond not far from Richard Wagner's grotto. Upon learning of Ludwig's misfortune, Ivan Turgenev wrote the story "Mumu," in which a serf, Gerasim, obeys his mistress's orders and drowns the little dog Mumu—the only friend he had. This story left an indelible impression on a naval officer who eventually became the captain of the *Titanic.*

Another dimension of the museological unconscious is linked to coprophagy (feeding on shit), which is somewhat related to a more Platonic fascination with feces shared by writers and artists like the marquis de Sade, Pier Paolo Pasolini, Piero Manzoni, and Joseph Beuys. Among the more recent examples is Paul McCarthy and Jason Rhoades's *Shit Plug* (2002): shit collected from critics, visitors, artists, and curators in the public toilets during the opening weekend of Documenta XI and then "pressed in a suitable form"—a sex toy, to which the *Shit Plug* bottles make formal reference. The film *Jurassic Park* has a memorable episode in which Laura Dern finds a grand pile of feces in the woods, and shortly afterward also finds its "author"—the dinosaur, weakened by its "creative" effort. When Dern inserts her hand into this pile, she takes on the fate of King Midas, who was doomed to turn everything he touched (including shit) to gold.[25] Regardless of the outcome, she launches the museological function.

Once, an acquaintance told me a story about her students' refusal to accept the fact that *Les Demoiselles d'Avignon* is kept at MOMA, because, in the film *Titanic,* Picasso's painting went down with the ship. In a way, *Les Demoiselles d'Avignon* descended into the depths of the museological unconscious, stripped bare of its provenance and institutional memory. Its "departure" from the museum did not end the spree of museologizing through a variety of forms and devices, ranging from mass media and the Internet to blockbuster films and exhibitions.

I am reminded of my search for a drugstore in a large, unfamiliar (and unusually deserted) city. After wasting an hour on endless wanderings, quite exhausted, I finally saw a neon sign that said "Pharmacy." Inside, disappointment: it was a stationery store. On my way out, I glanced back at the treacherous sign, which now read "Stationery." My desire to find a pharmacy had been so great that unconscious optics[26] had overcome the usual visual reflexes and produced the wished-for sight. Anticipation proved stronger than reality. Reality, it turned out, can easily be washed off the mirror surface, which then reflects the *idée fixe*—exactly as I imagined it, even though such an anticipatory image is nothing more than an optical illusion. The same applies to a wide range of phenomena and activities. In modern societies, virtualization has risen to such a level that optical illusion has become a "normative" phenomenon. Aside from the fact that a mirror reflection of oneself is frequently substituted for the image of the Other, these reflections are often framed—not in a baroque frame like a work of art, but in a "museological" one. Thus, thanks to the museological unconscious, we have become a part not only of the Spectacular,[27] but of the Specular order.

3. ADORNO *AVEC* LACAN: OBJECT DOUBLE A

In *Aesthetic Theory* (1970), Adorno argues that "through its objectification (*Vergegenstandlichung*) aesthetic expression becomes ... a nonobjective substance."[28] This analogy between nonobjective and abstract brings to mind Robert Smithson's "abstract geology," with its accentuation of the similarity between "one's mind and the earth." Smithson's *Spiral Jetty* (1970) was an attempt to organize a "mess of corrosion into patterns, grids, and subdivisions."[29] The side effect of this attempt, and of many other "liberatory" efforts related to earthworks, is that in the course of such actions the primordial and cosmogonic become museologically objectified. Now, nearly forty years later, objectification and the departure from it can no longer be seen as mutually deferred phenomena. This makes it difficult to justify Adorno's belief that art objects are "afterimages of the empirically living,"[30] but not the other way around (i.e., that *die Empirie* is an afterimage of the artistic).

Since the time when *Aesthetic Theory* was written,[31] the relations between "autonomous art" and "its Other" have entered an entirely new phase—a phase of instant reciprocation. Apparently, the "de-reified activity" (associated with the autonomous and negative aesthetic vision) and "the universal mediation of life through commodities" can no longer be sequentialized in any orderly fashion. The immense speed of reciprocation has finally turned these phenomena into masks or gloves one can rapidly take off or put on. The transfer from one personality to another, from one optical register to the next, takes virtually no time.

Adorno's critique of "being-in-reification" can be updated first by taking these changes into account, and second by demonstrating that the way people relate to art is often mixed with psychedelic repertory, directly or retroactively reflective of their encounters with (a) the culture industry, (b) the museological unconscious, and (c) psychomimetic reciprocation between (a) and (b).

In *The Sublime Object of Ideology*, Slavoj Žižek links Lacan's notion of "surplus-enjoyment" to the notion of "the surplus-object," which Žižek defines as "the leftover of the Real eluding symbolization."[32] The extent of this elusiveness is yet another matter, considering how many unthinkable, uncollectible, and previously undesirable things have already been culturally processed and museologically mediated. The byproducts of this mode of production are all over the place—formless or piled up in the shape of museified structures, as if justifying Chris Burden's attempt to break a museum floor in order to excavate the "source" of art and to lay bare its base.[33] Yet there was another promising excavation site that did not catch Burden's attention—the museological unconscious.

What seems to be at stake here is the prospect of psychomimetic exchange between conscious and unconscious modes of museification, as well as the possibility of exploring this and several other issues—either directly or by adapting Burden's recipe of having access to the right information in the wrong place. Thus, if we define autonomous art ("object double a," in my terminology) as that which escapes reification, then the question arises of whether the "hard-to-get" appearance of double a is reflective of some "presymbolic" defiance of things, susceptible to symbolic embodiment. Clearly, autonomous aesthetic activity cannot be fully in charge of this matter, nor can it be regulated by the culture industry, for there should be some other agency—one that does not necessarily obey the rules of logic or care for safeguarding the values—high or low, with or without "surplus"—and that is how one can arrive at the concept of the museological unconscious. Thus, the museological unconscious is the culture industry's psychic subsidiary, which acts like a double agent—working for and against its customer by adopting different and, at times, mutually exclusive modes of production. Objectness is extracted from this reservoir: it lays the ground for "being-toward-object" (the economy of the mental eye) and—simultaneously—paves the way to de-reification (the "impossibility," embodied in the "object double a").

Hypothetically, there is enough room within the museological unconscious to nestle the would-be reification—its promise, its underlying conditions, as well as those that are affiliated with symbolization—a dichotomy, somewhat analogous to Lacan's model of the mirror stage, divided into two substages.[34] On a map, the dichotomized landscape may have looked like an archipelago—a constellation of overlaps, marked by double identity—imaginary and symbolic. Each of them is the repository of signifiers, pinned to their places (regardless of their cultural significance) in order to acquire a museological identity and museological horizon through which they are connected with all other signifiers—fixed or on loan to various museological niches.

The museological unconscious is amenable to the emergence of an auxiliary identity (in this case, the museological one), which manifests itself not in a single draw from a deck of cards, nor in the accessibility of the whole deck, but apparently in the figure of the croupier who tosses the cards. In Deleuze's "Coldness and Cruelty," this museological croupier assumes the "image of death . . . holding up to the ego the cold mirror of its twofold rejection. But death can only be imagined as a second birth, a parthenogenesis from which the ego reemerges, liberated from the superego. . . . The reflection of the ego in and through death"[35] can be traced by enabling the viewer to realize that the border dividing the artworks displayed in the museum is that very reflecting surface that death installs in the consciousness of the viewer, making him an angel of death and simultaneously a witness to the second birth. As a result, parthenogenesis becomes a visual phenomenon because, in addition to the aforementioned museological identities, there is something else that dies and is reborn again in the process of the viewer's circulation around the museum—art.[36]

The side effect is the "blur," the inability to distinguish between art and life. Such is, in Foucault's view, "the heterotopia of the mirror,"[37] constitutive of a situation in which anyone can be an artist, and anything can be art. Everything has become creative: work and leisure, trust and fear, violence and retribution, exchange and deceit. Our perception—not only of the outside world, but of our own selves—is hopelessly artified, not to mention the fact that the mentality and terminology of art have taken root in every sphere of life, without exception. Art has replaced itself with "creativity," and creativity at present has no Other. If—given the circumstances—one were to imagine a person who, from the moment of birth, was known to be completely devoid of the creative reflex, such a mythical character would have undoubtedly become an important cultural phenomenon. The media would follow every moment of his or her life, attesting that as months and years go by, he or she never does set out to paint a painting, write a poem or a novel. Merely by lying on the couch, this person would be seen as engaged in a struggle for the liberation of humanity from a "bad habit"—creativity—while the couch itself would become a laboratory for achieving the noncreative state. The question then arises: How would such a character be substantively different from all those whose principal pastime is doing nothing? Since "the heterotopia of the mirror" provides no such distinctions, this entire situation should be regarded as purely hypothetical, if not hallucinatory. Nonetheless, if someone among us could attract attention as a bearer (or "creator") of the noncreative condition, both that person's biography and the person him- or herself would become museologically objectified and absorbed into the culture industry.

My reference to an auxiliary identity (e.g., a person who lacks creativity) is hinted at by the questions related to "Moscow communal conceptualism." Among such questions is the notion of "character" posited as the incarnation of communal (or extracommunal) speech. In the present text, however, the emphasis is placed on yet another kind of dramatis persona—the visual. Incidentally, we tend to speak of it in passive terms, forgetting that we not only look but also produce vision. I am referring to the numerous clichés of seeing—the scenes and images that are present in ourselves, and in the image and likeness of which we "see." In Adorno's time, "the consumer [was] allowed to project his . . . mimetic residues on to anything he pleased, including art."[38] Today, "I-presentation" of an exemplary artist can be characterized as either an "afterimage" or a "counterimage" of the culture industry. It may well be seen as a "psychomimetic event"[39] scarcely related to what we naively regard as "direct visual experience."

4. IMPACT OF THE MEDIA

Although the role of the media in the creation of significations is obvious, they simultaneously erode this process, fitting everything that emerges on the horizon of culture into the Procrustean bed of anticipation, that is, of ready-made beliefs, stereotypes, and evaluations. This is especially true of artists who become representatives of an unfamiliar context, and whose works are viewed as its "test samples." By an unfamiliar context, I mean something outside the "authority" that is supposed to register, evaluate, and judge cultural phenomena, and then find them a "proper place" in the inventory of other (already museified) items or entities. This process often culminates in displacement. Currently, something like this is happening everywhere. I am referring to sign formation without enrichment, displacement as a result of the substitution of value content with a devalued and often content-free enumeration of commonplace truisms. These truisms are anticipatory in nature; they are the most easily discernible objects in the act of cognizance. Visual experience is no exception: the answer to the question, "Exactly what do I want reality to be like?" is simple: museified as much as possible and in harmony with its "after-image" in my museological unconscious.

Even though the egalitarian assertion that "everything is text" no longer discriminates between the high and the low, the dichotomy continues to exist, and the only difference is that now the words "high" and "low" are more frequently used in reference to technology, as high-tech or low-tech. Art, for example, falls under the definition of a low-tech mode of production and thus can be seen as the last seat of rebellions against the expansionism of high-tech culture. In this context, one may rephrase Fedor Dostoevsky by declaring that low-tech beauty will save the world.

The impact of "high-tech culture" (electronic media, TV, the Internet) on our perception of "low-tech culture" (creative writing, arts, critical discourse, philosophy, psychoanalysis, cultural and political theory) has altered us in such a way that we react exclusively to fractions of phenomena,[40] events, and experiences—to a diet of shortened thoughts, shortened plots and narratives. In other words, these are not "whole numbers," but "fractional" ones. Fractionality is, to some extent, a sort of pornographic device. Structurally, TV news and commercials aren't all that different from peep shows: they are equally content with fragmented moments or momentous fragments. Museums such as the Guggenheim and Tate Modern try to do roughly the same thing; that is, they adopt this media technique—the technique of manipulating fragments in order to endow them with the false (or exaggerated) sense of universality. There is nothing new about expanding to universality or "constructing" it out of fragments, just as there is nothing new about fractionality. The novelty of the situation is in how extreme it is. As for the viewer's ability to comply, one is allowed to suppose that "only an imaginative intending can attain that ideality."[41]

Once ensconced in a museum, artworks begin to resemble the relics of holy martyrs (stumps and fingers) displayed in order to mobilize our consciousness. To what purpose? Mostly, to make a "Treaty of Versailles" with fractionality, for which we pay dearly with a heightened sense of the whole and with a desire to detect in a part the general picture of what is happening. The fractured nature of this illusory totality is leveled by technology; the seams and the clearings become invisible. Every part-object appears before us in media packaging, in the sense that partiality is presented not as an innate quality of reality, but as a pretext for submitting a claim that has to do with the restoration of the lost or promised wholeness of the image. In other words, the fractional is perceived as an "anticipant" of the whole, as evidence of its "undisputed" presence in medial space.[42] Largely, it has to do with the universal a priori, especially when we focus on overcoming alienation between the fractional and the whole, the partial and the general. The lower the level of medial discourse, the higher the agency it appeals to. Similarly, pornography appeals, however implicitly, to ideal objectness and eidetics of pure experience without admitting its relation to them.

In order to explain how the effect of fractionality manifests itself in the context of the museum, and how it is employed in art exhibitions, I will cite the example of the Tate Modern. On the walls of this museum, before the entrance to one or another exhibition room, one can see a multitude of accompanying sentences that can be read from a distance. The size of the letters befits the cathedral-like dimensions of the building, a former power plant. One is struck by the abundance of snappy titles through which one can see the barely discernible shapes (or fractions) of issues and discourses, the way one can see watermarks on dollar bills. Upon closer inspection, one finds that this is nothing more than a media trick that relies on "an imaginative intending" on the part of the viewer inclined (or made to incline) toward extrapolation. Subject to extrapolation, for instance, are the fractions that determine the level of connection between the discourses announced at the exhibition entrance and the eclectic expositions inside. The same argument can also be applied to other fractional phenomena (part-objects, part-concepts, part-insights), whose ephemeral nature is the best possible pretext for medial extrapolation. On the one hand, the notion of fractionality applies to everything that appeals to both "expanded field" and "extended vision."[43] On the other hand, there are different modes of fractionality: while the media have been dealing in extremely small units for many years now, museums have only recently "succeeded" in attaining this goal. As a result, the exhibition is no longer fulfilled in a museum, but in the gaps between commercials and news reports.[44]

5. DARK MUSEUM

Viewing the paintings of Renaissance artists on the walls of the Uffizi Gallery, one should note that they were created in an era of a fierce struggle between ideologies in art. The Renaissance was an arena of hostilities not only between artists but between their patrons—the Medicis, the Borgias, the d'Estes, the Vatican. Thus, the paintings hanging on museum walls are mimetic residues of these conflicts, and projections of warring ideologies. Yet, when placed together, they amazingly reconcile, "forgetting" all about past wars and about the ideologies that generated them. The museum is thus the model of "paradise," in which each object is at peace with other objects, eternalized in a series of curatorial rituals and therefore consigned to oblivion, or to recontextualization, which essentially amounts to the same thing. The paradox, however, is that in such a "paradise," sedimental ideologies are reactivated by the throngs of visitors from all over the world, and this motley audience is an embodiment of ideological variety. Today, warring ideologies no longer meet *on* a museum wall, but *in front* of it. Thus, the "visitors in paradise" reideologize anew that which was resting in the arms of a museological Morpheus. Like any paradise, the museum space is whole and indivisible, but the viewer who invades it brings in the virus of difference. That is why in the "ideal" museum, the only image to be shared with the public should be the sign "No admission."[45]

This brings to mind the idea of the "dark museum"—a museum without lighting where the viewer can come with a small flashlight and illuminate only fragments of artworks as he or she moves through the halls. In this way, the works are protected from "virus" carriers, and the carriers themselves are protected from ideological inferences, since the fragment makes it impossible to arrive at any conclusion, or even to identify the artwork accurately, in its totality. Thus, the paradigm of the "dark museum" could be a new opportunity for nonideological vision.

The "dark museum" is the appropriate meeting place for intellectuals whose ideas or opinions have already been "museified." As a rule, nothing extraordinary can be heard from them in a conversation or in other forms of one-to-one correspondence. Regardless of one's access to the "champions of mind games," it is unthinkable to engage them in a professional exchange if its context fails to qualify as sufficiently museological; that is, if it is not comparable to a showcase or a museum wall suitable for the display of the masterpieces of their thinking—rhetorical statements, viewpoints, interpretations, etc. But once the museological function is activated, the behavior of "paradigmatic" individuals suddenly changes, as if they had been caught in the auction house. In a split second these people become fully engaged and prepared to put all their lexical artifacts on the counter.[46] This degree of receptiveness with regard to market value—be it monetary or Symbolic—is a "family trait" of the museological unconscious.

The museological unconscious should certainly have a place (at least a filing cabinet) to store repressed information about objects that are "sick" of being symbolically embodied and reified in the way that "animals are sick of surplus value."[47] In this respect, Damien Hirst's tiger shark in his *The Physical Impossibility of Death in the Mind of Someone Living* (1991) deserves a brief comment, for it has settled scores with the artist by

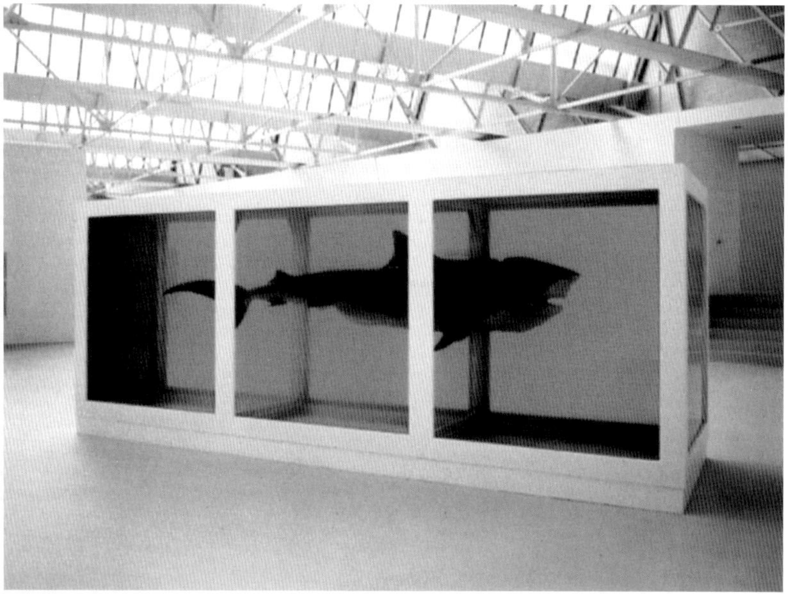

10.4
Damien Hirst, *The Physical Impossibility of Death in the Mind of Someone Living*, 1991.

invalidating the title of his work (fig. 10.4). Years spent in a glass tank of formaldehyde resulted in the shark's wrinkling: the "animal" has ceased to be a slick object, and may eventually be relocated from an art institution to a museum of natural sciences, or a marine biology lab. This traitorous recontextualization is a blow to the culture industry: it shows that the museological unconscious is capable of undoing reification and can cause trouble, including the transition from one phantasm to the next; an object that is meaningless in the context of an art museum can be meaningful in some other museological niche.[48]

Harking back to the notion of surplus enjoyment (which is positively defined), one may wonder if the set of arguments developed by Lacan and his school is sustainable in the case of surplus negativity, or "negative affection" (replaced rather forcefully, albeit routinely, by "pozitiv affektsional" in Anatolii Lunacharskii's 1904 book *Osnovy pozitivnoi estetiki*).[49] The fact that utopia is unattainable does not prevent it from being a source of joy. Sisyphus, who had to push the rock up the mountain and then watch it roll back down again, most likely also enjoyed those "failures." After all, the sight of a rock rolling down was probably far more entertaining than the act of its "capitonnizing" on the peak of the hill. What Albert Camus's 1942 text *Le mythe de Sisyphe* clearly missed is the very essence of utopia's economy that this myth portrays. Whereas negativity is utopia's mode of production, its surplus value is (ideally) utopia itself—utopia proper. For what else qualifies as the symbolic embodiment of negative affection? Given that the latter defies identity, utopia is the only "UFO" that fills this vacancy.

I will conclude with Pavel Pepperstein's essay "Filosofstvuiushchaia gruppa i filosofskii muzei," in which philosophical categories are compared with Fabergé eggs, while philosophy itself is regarded as "Fabergé discourse."[50] "From a political point of view," writes Pepperstein, "these luxurious eggs are reactionary. With all their precious scales, pearls and diamonds, they endlessly multiply reflections of that spark which lights up the very heart of reaction. I am speaking of a categorical need for tranquility, of an exemption from disturbances."[51] Pepperstein also suggests that "instead of philosophy, any philosophizing group of people unavoidably creates a philosophical museum . . . [which] must be incredibly expensive, for one needs all the riches in the world in order to buy some peace of mind."[52]

CHAPTER 11

Negativity Mon Amour

1.

American abstract expressionism made its first appearance in Moscow in 1959. Its "return" to Russia took place forty years later, on the eve of the opening of the exhibition "Motherland and Death" (known as MAD), in which many members of the Moscow conceptual school were represented. The occasion for this "return" was the crisis in Yugoslavia. The walls of the United States embassy served as the canvas, while ink, eggs, and canned vegetables purchased in the store across the street were used for paint. On March 27, 1999, while driving on the Sadovoe Ring (on the way, ironically enough, to the MAD exhibition), I felt a renewed love for art when I saw all those yellow, red, black, and violet splashes of color on the embassy walls. My doubts about the political nature or "social bases" of abstract expressionism (the thesis advanced by Meyer Shapiro) were instantly removed (fig. 11.1).

Since I have brought up the story of the return of abstract art from across the Atlantic to Moscow, I will also mention its chief apologist, Clement Greenberg. His assertion that American modernism was superior in value (and in "freshness of content") to the European kind fits his own definition of vulgarity—that "truly new horror of our times [which] totalitarianism is able to install in places of power."[1] Since this reproach was directed at Russian art, its current interests and aspirations—the castles in the air that it "installs," no longer in places of power, but in places of power loss—must be given their proper due.

During my stay in Moscow, I heard a wide variety of responses to the iconoclastic act of Avdei Ter-Oganian, who invited Manezh visitors to chop a paper copy of a Russian Orthodox icon to pieces with an axe. To some extent, this gesture is a scream of power loss in "places of power."

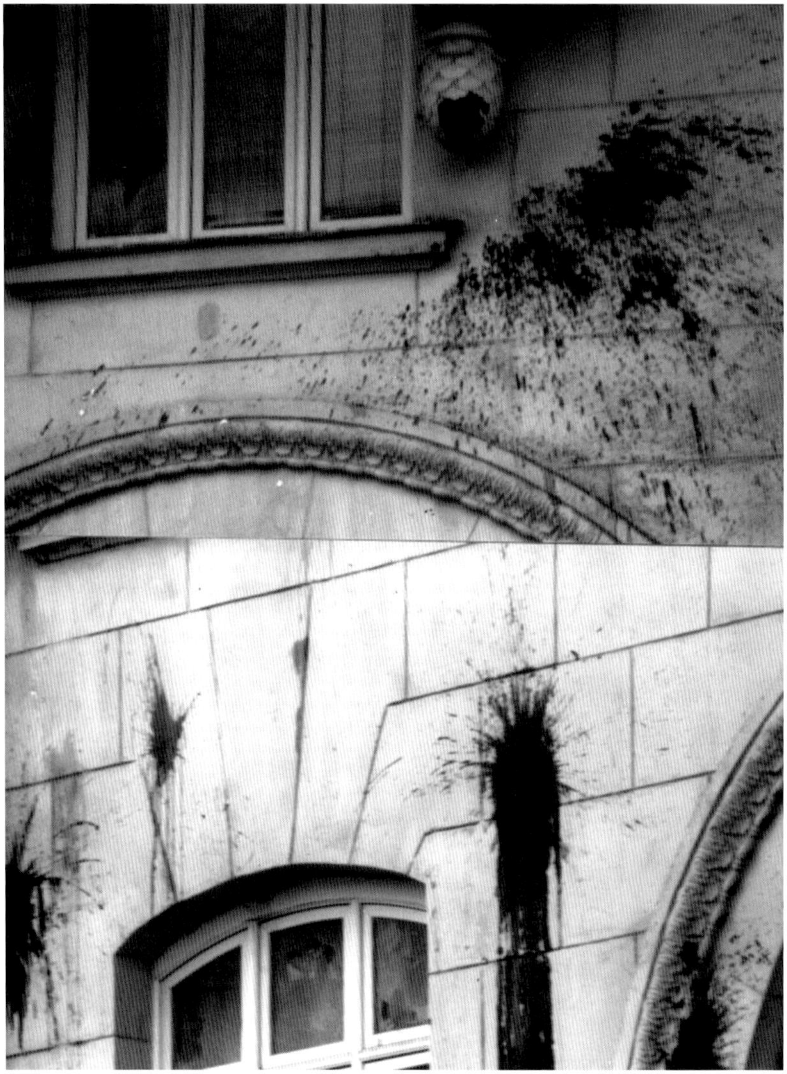

11.1
View of the American Embassy in Moscow during the protest against NATO's bombing of Serbia, Moscow, March 27, 1999. Photo Igor' Makarevich.

However, upon more serious reflection, one can also trace a similarity between the actions of Ter-Oganian and those of Andres Serrano, whose *Piss Christ* greatly enraged the Congress of the United States, leading to cuts in art subsidies. In other words, the attempt to prosecute Ter-Oganian (which is what the clergy and some citizens' groups are demanding) is reminiscent of the sanctions imposed by the U.S. Congress, not only toward Serrano (or Robert Mapplethorpe's *X Portfolio*), but also toward Yugoslavia. At least that's what the Moscow artists with whom I've had a chance to talk about this tend to believe. In their view, the moment art stops testing the boundaries of what is permitted, the boundaries of comfort, it inevitably turns into its own opposite (for instance, into the facade of the American embassy prior to its transformation into an "exhibition" of abstract expressionism).

Since the late 1990s, any efforts to globalize and synchronize aesthetics have been extremely unpopular among Moscow artists. They perceive the project of "globalization" as an American invention,[2] while such notions as primacy or secondariness are declared to be imports from the sphere of sports or commerce into culture. In their view, focusing on the aberrations that arise when artistic models are transferred from one context to another is far more productive than pointing out who came first and who came second. The members of the Moscow art world believe that *la différance* (e.g., contextual deferral) is their principal resource and, moreover, an aesthetic phenomenon. As for the "painting" of the walls of the U.S. embassy, it illustrates once again the inadequacy of NATO's political doctrine,[3] based on the presumption of simultaneous and identical perception of events in every region of the world.

As a cultural enterprise, globalization can be equated with an effort to horizontalize the vertical, to line up the truncated and curtailed metaphors in concordance with the museological world order. Because the unconscious mechanisms partake in it, this process is not an easy target for critical reflection, especially when "visual" and "visionary" are treated as mutually deferred phenomena. As for an effort to "horizontalize the vertical" on a worldwide scale, one should mention Documenta in Kassel and the Venice Biennale, which—along with their commercial counterparts (international art fairs, etc.)—aim at presenting an *overall picture* of contemporary art. Even if such a picture were a displayable concept, it would still require a different means of presentation, different from those presently adopted by the museums and exhibition curators. The installation paradigm would have to become reflective of the non-Euclidean nature of *contemporaneity*, a phenomenon that has been hopelessly flattened and sequentialized by both institutions and individuals.

2.

The new wing of the State Tret'iakov Gallery now houses a collection of alternative art from the 1960s to the 1980s.[4] The curator of the collection, Andrei Erofeev, was given temporary use of the building for two years. The opening took place on March 15, 1999. A third of the exposition was devoted to neomodernism—"the unfinished project of modernism" (to use Jürgen Habermas's terminology), which was renewed in Russia in the late 1950s and early 1960s. Among the institutions that have taken on this function is the Moscow gallery called Obscuri Viri. From the moment the gallery was created in 1994, it has displayed objects of a special kind that—by analogy with the name of the exhibition niche—could be called "obscuritarian." I use this term in order to emphasize their existence apart from their own objectness. They dissuade us, as it were, from acquiring them, from transferring them from the obscuritarian niche into the world of visual consumption where everything is optically processed, itemized, objectified. And that is not because they lack some necessary qualities, but because of their own indifference to the possibility of such a transfer. Each object might as well bear the inscription "Not for sale, admiration, or identification." On the level of day-to-day needs, human passions, and ambitions, the authors of these works, of course, have nothing against fame or money, nothing against leaving the confines of the obscuritarian ghetto. But it is precisely this obscuritarian field that has an incredible ability to create and maintain a sensation of disembodied objectness, or objectness held in suspense.

The objectness discussed here is a fairly unique phenomenon. In the case of Western conceptualists or, for example, of the representatives of Arte Povera, these were Cinderella objects, orphaned objects, foundling objects, secretly or openly yearning to be accepted in "polite" society. By contrast, the obscurity of the objects exhibited in Obscuri Viri is not camouflage; it is the chief distinction between "Moscow communal conceptualism" and other *faktura*-clastic practices.

Discussing this paradigm of objectness, one must remember the 1920s and 1930s in Russia, when the bonds between the communal subject and the communal object were defetishized. I am referring to contact with objects of communal day-to-day life (Soviet-style)—kitchen utensils, clothes, furniture, and similar lowly, faceless things. It is possible that, in some sense, "communal conceptualism" still holds on to these traditions. My own experience of visiting Obscuri Viri has once again attested to the fact that nobody knows what art is, since it presupposes a special, inexplicable consent to "go I know not where and bring [i.e., bring back] I know not what." Attending a show at Obscuri Viri is also reminiscent of a visit to a nursing home to see a senile relative—a relative who has forgotten his own name as well as yours. What does the view of this unfortunate but beloved creature suggest to us? The phenomenon of obscuritarianism? The impossibility of transcending its boundaries? The hidden but inevitable commonality that binds the subject of visitation to its object—a thing or a character that embodies your own inner obscuritarianism and your own (progressive) oblivion of the self within yourself? And how, may one ask, does one assess the value of the obscuritarian object? To answer this question, here is a story that I heard from a friend about his visit to a hospital. He went to see his dying grandfather, who was known for his skill at making money. Seeing a gold watch on the old man's wrist, the grandson offered him a good price for it. After intense bargaining, the grandfather prevailed and died with a smile on his face.

3.

In March 1999, Boris Mikhailov's photographic series *Case History*, which represents homeless people in Kharkov, Ukraine, was printed in a book by Scalo Verlag (fig. 11.2). Unlike romantic negativity—idealistic in nature and subject to the mental eye—Mikhailov's way of seeing the world around him is not simply negative: it is bodily negative. Prior to discussing his book,[5] I would like to remind the reader that the notion of the bodily in its relation to literary practices was prompted by many authors from Bataille and Pierre Klossowski to Barthes and Deleuze. While in Barthes's writings bodily *jouissance* is spelled out as "pleasure of the text," Klossowski takes it one step further, insisting that "there is nothing more verbal than the excesses of the flesh."[6] As for Mikhailov, he knows that affirmative images and identity have never existed apart from each other. After all, he was educated under socialist realism, one of the most affirmative of all cultures. To liberate himself, he embraced negativity. Seen from this perspective, Mikhailov's negative vision appears to be his "ultimate identity." And yet negation negates itself, making the aforementioned "identity" unfit to inhabit. To maintain it, negativity has to be constantly reproduced. If Benjamin's theories apply in Mikhailov's case, then this author is definitely a producer: a producer of negativity. "I think negatively, therefore I am." Expressed in this form, Descartes's *cogito* teams up well with Mikhailov's photographic production.

It has been claimed that photographers like Nan Goldin have truly experienced (with their bodies) things they feed into the viewfinders. But do they really transgress voyeurism or engage the referent into metonymic exchange with the signifier? Whereas Goldin positions herself inside of the *what*, Mikhailov is an insider of the *how*. The latter (for him) is

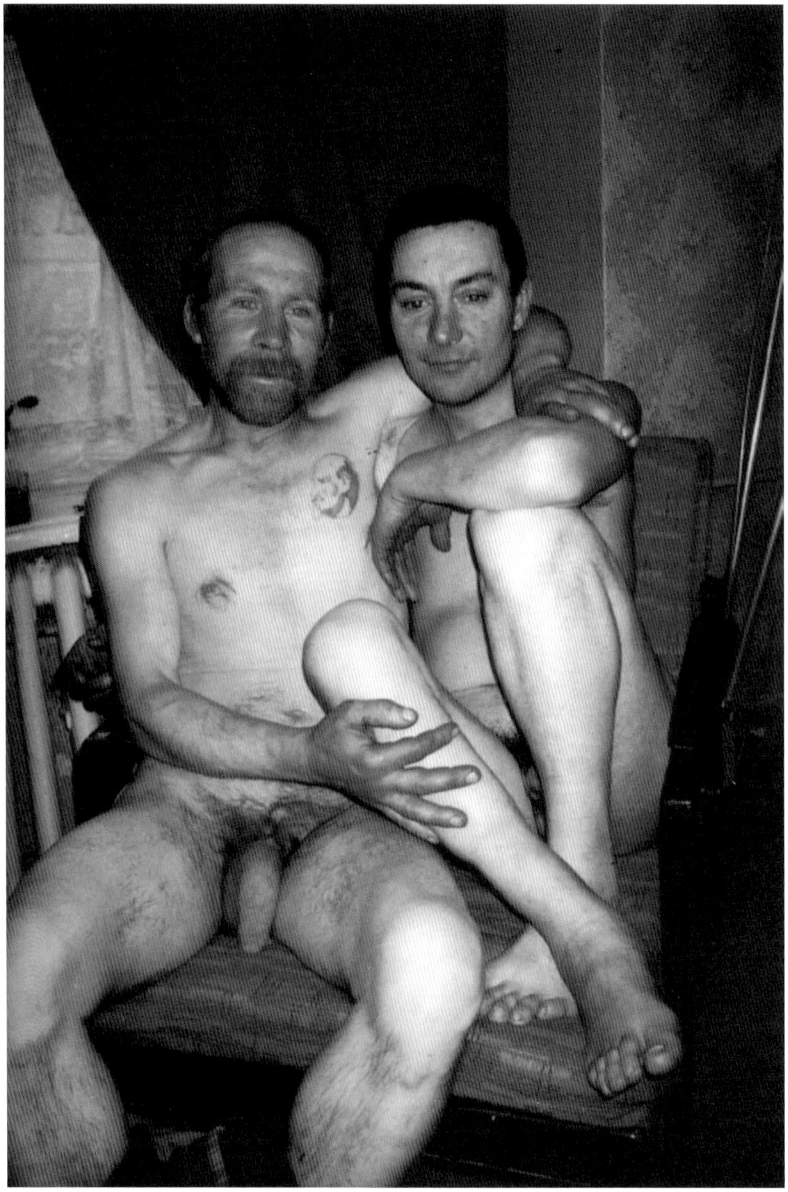

11.2
Boris Mikhailov, from the series
Case History, 1997.

negativity: he is wholly engrossed with it and has no room left for voyeurism. Therefore, it would be a mistake to say that Mikhailov degrades or abuses the people he takes picture of with his vision. On the contrary, he caresses them. Such is the nature of his optic: affectionate, yet simultaneously negative and panicked.[7] But this panic is not caused by something specific, real, or distinct—for instance, the sight of a beast, a train coming straight at you, etc. In Kabakov's opinion, "it's a question of total panic—a perpetual state of panic a person feels in response to everything that surrounds him. Anyone who has spent many years living in Russia is familiar with special safety zones—the bomb shelter, the friend's apartment—rather than special danger zones."[8] And yet the opposition between safety zones and dangerous places is what the language of negativity thrives on. Negativity is thus the taxonomy of panic, and Mikhailov's urban landscapes bear witness to that.

One picture is of a six- or seven-year-old boy and girl in a wasteland, smoking near a utility pipe. These kids are clearly neglected by their parents. In another photograph, a child of privilege wears expensive roller skates with his watchful mother hovering in the background; not far from them a man lies on the ground, either drunk or dead. Once again we witness a play of differences that, regardless of any specific narrative or even contextual frame, highlights the very nature of negativity—its addiction to the language of binary oppositions (dichotomies). Negative optics can also be perceived as a mental grid, imposed on reality a priori, that is, prior to the moment of taking the picture. To dichotomize is to stage; therefore all Mikhailov's photographs—rehearsed or spontaneous—are staged beforehand.

There are several landscapes here. In one of them red flowers are juxtaposed with an industrial fence, as if separating beauty from ugliness. Sexual organs—both male and female—are in large quantity. Women are shown urinating or displaying their vaginas, men their penises. All are highly disinterested in what is happening. No doubt they pose for money. Most of them are people driven to extreme misery and fallen to the lowest steps of the social ladder. They epitomize alienation: it splashes out of them. Mikhailov wants them to pose naked, as if trying to undress the object of his desire—negativity. The abundance of sex organs in *Case History* is related to the photographer's desire to convince viewers that they are looking at human beings, not enigmatic aliens from outer space whose sufferings evoke no pity because we don't know what is and isn't normal for them. The sexual organ is one of the most universal clichés: when exhibiting it, the homeless (sick, persecuted) person evokes a special, incomparable sympathy, not only mentally but physically.[9]

To comment on Mikhailov's treatment of nudity, I will bring into play the concept of the "post-Soviet uncanny," which yields two different readings. With regard to the naked body, the reading of the phrase "uncanny nude" is equivalent to the assertion that no one has yet known it (the body), and therefore the viewer has the opportunity to be "the first." The explanation for this is in the etymology of the word "canny" (originally from the Latin for "to know"). In addition, "canny" means *heimlich* or "homey," which is why "uncanny nude" refers to a nudity not only *unknown* but (also) *homeless*. Its homelessness can be read as lack of connection to the nuptial bed of knowledge.

The notion of "uncanny sex organs" echoes, to some extent, Nobuyoshi Araki's monstrous representation of the vagina in his serious *The Parts of a Love* (1987). Here, the idea of homelessness is associated not with the ejection of a nude body from the house to the street but with what Freud described as "displacement" when, in his essay "The Uncanny" (1919), he wrote about the displaced effects of castration anxiety.

Mikhailov once said that a good photographer is like a street dog, a mutt. He is willing to spend three hours at the train station in anticipation of the moment when the wind lifts the skirt of a woman sitting on the steps. A moment like that (a "punctum," in Barthes's terminology) is captured on a photograph: the cunt is caught off guard. According to Mikhailov, the fact that he suspected the absence of underwear is due to his mutt's intuition. This print is particularly striking because it attains a symbolic level. Negation caresses itself, confusing its origin with the vagina—an aberration that fits the notion of *méconnaissance*. There is, of course, nothing new about this: in 1866, Gustav Courbet painted a vagina and called the work "The Origin of the World." The painting had been lost for years (it was last heard of in 1945), and then resurfaced in the collection of Lacan's former wife, Sylvie.[10]

Mikhailov is an exceptionally gifted artist, but speaking of him in these terms is the same as saying that a shark is an exceptional swimmer: this is self-explanatory because it lives in water. A similar argument applies to Mikhailov's bodily swimming in negativity. For as long as he stays there, his artistic competence is hardly in question. What is at issue here is the itinerary of his journey.

4.

One of the most questionable utopias is the utopia of kinship and mutual support between intellectuals, and in particular, between intellectuals of East and West. The confessional intensity found in texts printed in Moscow, Sofia, Belgrade, Poznań, Zagreb, or Ljubljana—in reference to

East European identity—suggests that these texts appeal to some higher (if not transcendental) criteriological authority—to what one could call (paraphrasing Husserl) the collective "I-presentation" of the intellectual élite. However pointless, such appeals are never out of fashion.[11] It may be that impassioned calls for identification, combined with the visionary projection of identitarian constructs, create the only possible "ecosphere" that identity can dwell in.

The specificity of intellectual identity is the absence (or denial) of this identity, for identification and intellectual reflection are largely incompatible. Their contract is a result of affectation.[12] To equate them would be imprudent, since identity is an affirmative (*positive*) concept while intellectual reflection is a *negative* one.[13] For some intellectuals, identity is a "necessary evil"—a way of resisting oppression with regard to race, ethnicity, sex, gender, religious and human rights, as well as professional or political belief systems. It can also be based on a mutual anticipation of something yet to come—an ultimate identity (communalist, global consumerist, apocalyptic, transcendentalist, etc.). To other intellectuals the identity principle is not sustainable unless it involves emotions and passion.[14] In their opinion, one needs to *feel* identity, not to *think* it. But doesn't that imply an instant conversion into a confessional-cathartic being, which for an intellectual is analogous to the loss of negativity? And isn't it true that to fear such loss (or to passionately and emotionally mourn it) would be the same as to admit that negativity can actually be viewed as intellectual identity? This can be avoided only by adopting a totally different image of the intellectual—as an evasive *de-framer* of identity who is capable of quickly switching gears from distancing to cathartic merging with what he or she criticizes.[15] What makes such intellectuals somewhat *identical* to one another is that their identitarian dreams are libidinally mediated. As an example I will point to the United States, where the image of the intellectual remains unclaimed, in the sense that he or she cannot be seen in movies, newspapers, magazines, or on TV. And yet at the same time, the intellectual ghetto (university professors, scholars, theorists, etc.) reflect on pop culture and the mass media with vigorous passion and craving.

In *Anti-Oedipus,* Deleuze and Guattari identify negativity (regardless of its political inclination) with an oedipized way of thinking and living, that is, with paranoia.[16] Another sobering pronouncement comes from Derrida, for whom the meaning of any text—negative or affirmative—is indefinitely deferred. This gives way to a suspicion that the critique of false consciousness may well be as false as what it criticizes. Insightful as they are, neither schizoanalysis nor deconstruction takes into account that negativity is, at times, inseparable from the pleasure of being negative and that ideology (i.e., false consciousness) can, in fact, be enjoyable. The difference, however, is that for as long as the negative remains less clichéd than its counterpart, our ability to collectively rejoice in negativity by turning it into a pastime is limited. This is especially true in the United States, which is indeed the "society of entertainment." Intellectuals who seek notoriety in such a "society" might as well learn how to promote negativity as an entertaining feature—a source of enjoyment, a leisurely item of mass consumption, and so on. Along this path, an effort should be made to spectacularize negativity, instead of trying to de-spectacularize society.[17] Given the specificity of American cultural tradition, it seems unlikely that the vacancy of an *entertaining* Other will ever be filled by intellectuals. The most effective way for them to be visible is to become (or remain) an eyesore. As for the postmodern cultural environment with its artificial leveling of all differences and dichotomies, intellectuals can only benefit from derailing this process, that is, from radicalizing their negativity, rather than subduing it (fig. 11.3).

Despite the ghettoized status of the adherents of negativity within "positive" (affirmative) culture—be it the culture of France, the United States, Russia, or Yugoslavia—they are not only pressured from the outside by the mainstream, but also divided internally. Alliances between intellectuals are either defensive or expansionist in nature.[18] In the latter case, the alliances can be compared to NATO jets whose purpose is to seek more and more places where they can drop their discursive bombs and subsequently return to their prior (moralizing or melancholically detached) image. And thus, we are back where we started—with the war and the events in Yugoslavia (fig. 11.4).

The war analogy that I have used and the reference to the aggressiveness of discourse are not excuses for sitting out the conflict in a bomb shelter. Intellectual wars are usually bloodless. The spoken (or printed) thought is not identical to the subject of expression or to its addressee. The abolition of the subject and the entry into the sphere of "collective utterances" automatically confers the status of totality (universal identity) upon text. Because of their universality, textual strategies resemble carpet bombing, which in turn becomes a reason to retaliate, to feel guilt, or to demand compensation for injured pride. In other words, these strategies can serve any purpose except the construction of a "new subjectivity."

There have been cases of Moscow intellectuals teaching at Western universities who rejected offers of tenure. And this occurs despite the fact that the situation in Russia remains extremely unstable, both economically and politically. Apparently, stability and protection from the vicissitudes of fate are factors that can be perceived as either pluses or minuses. To

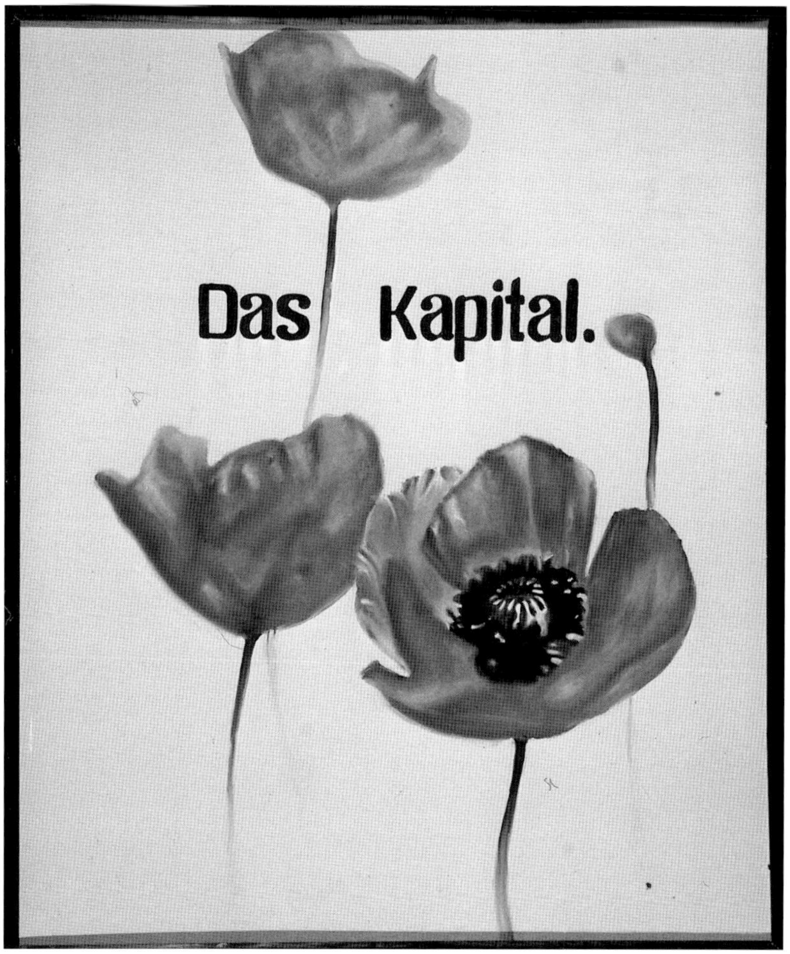

11.3
Andrei Iakhnin, *Das Kapital,* 1989.

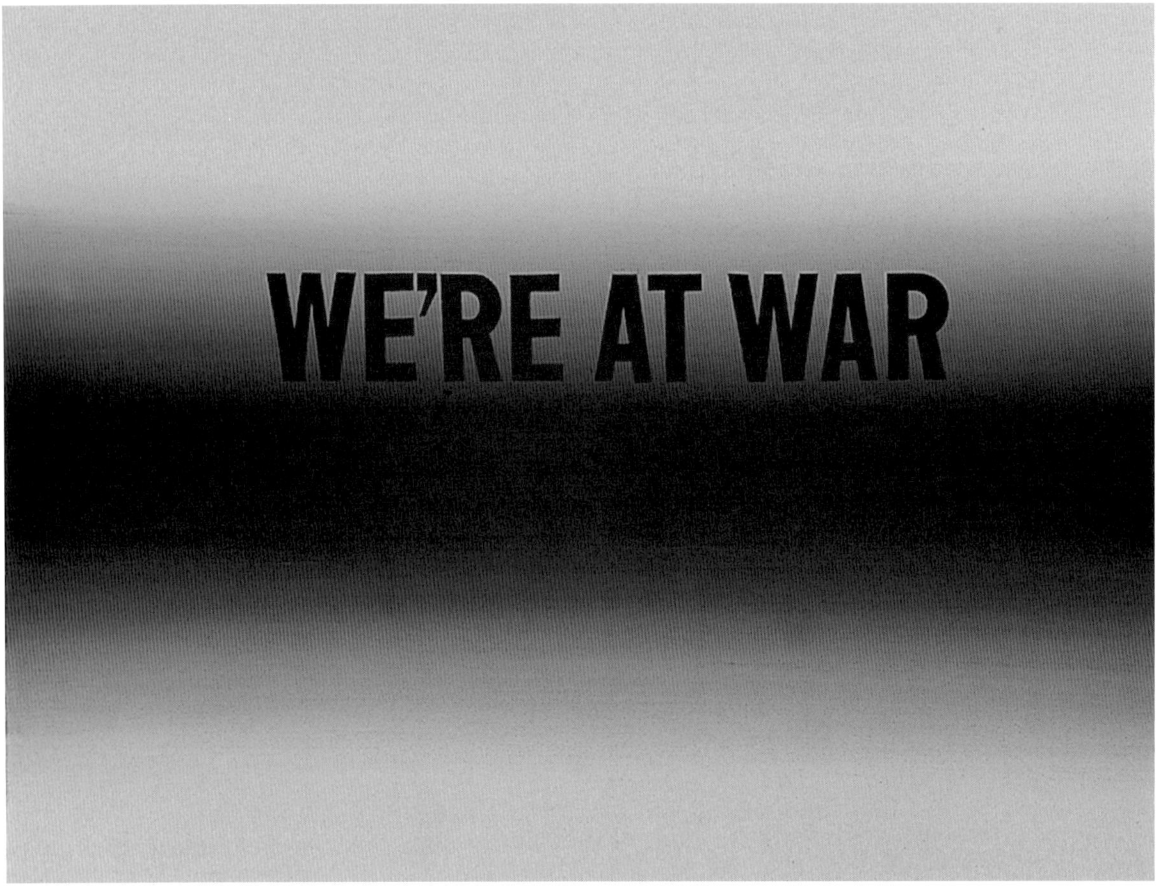

11.4
Oleg Vasil'ev, *We're at War,* 2002.

back up my assertion, I would like to cite the writer Vladimir Sorokin. He says that life in Western Europe seems too anaesthetized: "Being there, one gets the impression that no one dies of cancer, no one fears old age or loneliness, no one feels inner torment."[19] For myself, I will add that the ritual of silence Sorokin talks about also extends to the war in the Balkans and the problem of refugees.

The Russian intellectuals are attracted only to "apocalypse" or, at the very least, to catastrophe.[20] They value moments of disaster because of the opportunity to rejoice in the experience of pain, to suffer and to feel empathy for the suffering of others, to breathe the air of tragedy and dark premonition, and to be on the edge between hopelessness and deliverance. A secure, "well-tempered clavier" of existence is not to their liking. They are apocalyptic creatures who feel *good* only when they feel *bad*. Daily life, as they understand it, is a carnival of contrasts. A good example of this is Kabakov's comment, "Life has to be pretty—like roses around a body in the morgue."[21]

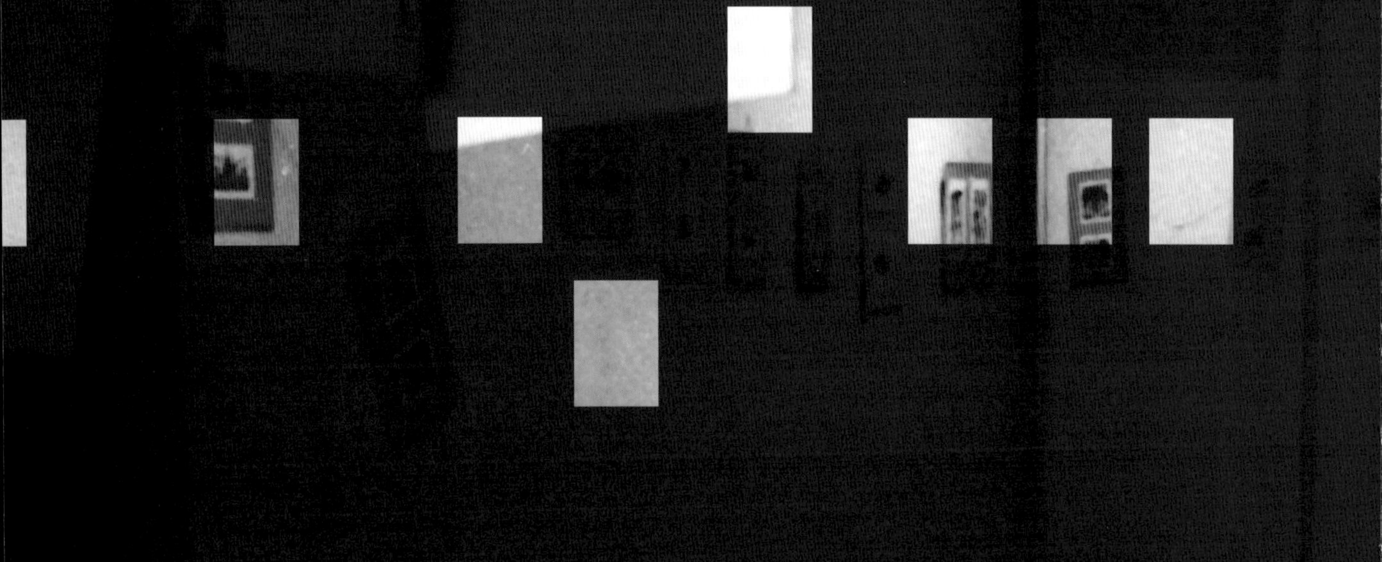

CHAPTER 12

Post-Autonomous Art

It becomes impossible to criticize the culture industry without criticizing art at the same time.
T. W. Adorno, *Aesthetic Theory*

1.

I will begin with some reflections on the theme of the installation medium. To an extent, the installation is an intrusion of orthodoxy onto the territory of a modernist or postmodernist world picture—not only in the realm of visual representation, but in the arena of social life in general. I am referring to Debord's "society of the spectacle," or in a more "arcane" terminology, "the society of the installation." Curiously, the most advanced (or technologically equipped) spaces of mass complicity are based on the same principle as archaic ritual spaces, and that's precisely why I connect this to orthodoxy. Moreover, holy rites, mysteries, liturgies, corporate board meetings, and political actions require props, require reorganization of space—that is, installation metaphors. Ritual has always created itself, constructing not only objects of worship and altars, but the very consciousness of the participants ("parishioners").

Artists crave installation because the center of gravity has been transferred from the relationship between art and life to the relationship between culture and ritual, which in turn heralds the repetition—or, to quote Nietzsche, "the eternal return"—of what was once declared passé. This "return," however, is not a copy of the past but a manifestation of it in new circumstances, on a different level, on a different scale. To the question of what has caused such a leap backward, there is no simple answer. The steep rise in the prices of contemporary art in the 1980s, and their subsequent fall, were among the factors. The artificial price inflation was meant to convince people who didn't know much about art that it was still a profitable business, a sensible investment. One should not forget that corporate wheeler-dealers and wealthy investors suffered from a moral inferiority complex vis-à-vis their opposites—artists, servants of "true art" who "would rather be poor than corrupt," etc. The acquisition of a painting was a way of atoning for one's sins, of communing with the world of authentic being.

In the early 1990s, falling art prices resulted in two developments: (1) corporations that had invested in art forswore any trust in the art market as a means of increasing their capital; (2) the reputation of art, which had been corrupted over the past decade, was hopelessly damaged; investors suddenly realized that they were no different from the inventors, since the artists were just as greedy for fame and money as big businessmen, politicians, Hollywood stars, supermodels, and other mass culture idols. What happened as a result of this crash? The practice of art certainly didn't disappear (as Baudrillard had naively predicted); rather, there was a temporary breakup between art and life, between art and lifestyles of the 1980s which more recent art, alas, cannot afford. Unable to compete with the mass media and societal spectacles, art in the West once again began to aspire toward a hermit-like, reclusive, monastic situation, reminiscent of "nonconformist" art in Moscow under the Soviet regime. Ritual has become far cheaper than culture, in the sense that mystical depths do not require extraordinary expenses—especially since the stage for this ritual is limited to the artist's workshop or the darkened rooms of alternative exhibitions. Hence the attempt to go back to "auraticity," to a ritualized mode of production and representation. The interest in installations merely confirms this. The installation is a doghouse where contemporary art mourns its defeat and licks its wounds after suffering a fiasco in its relationship with life; this is the place to rest before a new offense . . . quite possibly in the same direction as before.

2.

The point of reference for this chapter is Damien Hirst's sensational (due to its scope and ambition) show at the Larry Gagosian gallery (New York) in fall 2000. Titled "Theories, Models, Methods, Approaches, Assumptions, Results, and Findings," it became a topic of a conversation between Kabakov, Margarita Tupitsyn, and myself—a trialogue we recorded in early December 2000. Since the publication of this trialogue in its entirety is a separate project,[1] I will limit myself here to summarizing parts of it, either quoting or paraphrasing in my own words. Simultaneously, I will formulate my own position and my view of the statements made by my interlocutors.

In the first part of the conversation, Kabakov characterized the situation of the art world today as "a blow, like being hit over the head with a bag." In his words, "the peculiarity of this recent blow is that the strategies have changed, since the blows delivered in art today affect spheres that are not described by the art world. In fact, they bypass the art world as such. As a result, the shock experienced today by artists, critics, and other casualties is deeper than ever." Kabakov places the blame for this shock on several artists of the new generation, on museum directors, and on institutions whose actions, in his view, are transforming art culture into a global spectacle for tourists who are permanently moving within a range from Taiwan to South America. To refer to this new phenomenon, Kabakov employs such terms as "carpet bombing" and "carpet Apocalypse."

According to Kabakov, the spectator's route today is controlled and lacks independence, in the sense that "the local zone of the museum visitor has been completely de-intimized [stripped of intimacy]." In his opinion, the people who set the policies at museums are essentially not a part of the art world. That is to say, they are not servants of art but "some sort of unbelievable politicians, illusionists, or medical experimenters—you go in and they'll sew a new arm on you." In other words, "these are people of a more totalistic nature, and if you start squawking about art, they'll tell you: We'll talk later."

Kabakov does not believe that Gagosian is simply a representative of the art world and Hirst is only an artist. For him, they are international businessmen who work in tandem with museums, auctions, price-hiking devices, and with everything that constitutes and contributes to the politics of art today. What Kabakov means by the politics of art is "total penetration of economic spheres, in relation to which the zone of art is either a superficial layer or an insignificant part of a general structure." In his view, anyone within this structure who is "fixated on the zone of art is today doomed to extinction."

Kabakov gives a vivid and caustic description of the (failed) project for the new Guggenheim building in downtown New York, characterizing it as "an enormous lopsided barrel, a giant bubble." He is convinced that nothing will be kept in such a museum, while New Yorkers (like Venetians) are fated to become "the service personnel for millions of Japanese, Chinese, Australian and other visitors who will flow into the Guggenheim bubble for a couple of hours, have a cup of coffee and then flow out through other apertures and disappear into the airport. Thus, the model of this building is a museum in appearance only." Kabakov has said many times and on many occasions that "a museum serves as a church, which until recently held a monopoly on everything high—i.e., oversaw the realm of the metaphysical and the mystical. Today, the place of the church has been completely taken over by the museum. The museum oversees the past, since it is connected to the memory of our human origins." But the truth of the matter is that the mnemonic functions performed in museums or in reference to them are utterly reflective of the things these institutions present or hold on to. As a result, all "free range" signifiers—especially those that partake in our identificatory efforts—become fastened up and pinned to certain items, whether artworks or cultural memorabilia. In such places, everything (including our reflections on the past) can be instantly objectified (museological objectification). In other words, this is not memory but *Kulturindustrie* (culture industry) of memory. As Margarita Tupitsyn noted, the museum is a type of "multicultural church where a person is allowed to enter regardless of aesthetic beliefs."

In Kabakov's words, "the first thing that leaps out at Hirst's exhibition . . . is Sol Le Witt's cubes which he covered with glass and filled with water. It's a clever move, since references to tradition have a calming and disarming effect." "What is a working memory?" Kabakov asks. "It means being connected to one's past, because culture in general is built on continuity, on correlation with a past—a revolutionary one, or any other kind. After all, if there is no past, there is no future, either. Then what is there? There is a very narrow crack between morning and evening. I encounter the world, as it were, upon waking up in the morning. And then I act with the energy required of me in the situation—the spatial situation of today. 'Today' is a spatial concept, not a temporal one. I don't think about what will happen tomorrow, because tomorrow the next blow will be delivered, and yet another character will show up in the art world."

3.

The fragment quoted above deserves a commentary, particularly the phrase "a very narrow crack." A narrow crack is what allows events to be snatched out of context, in accordance with the criteria established by the mass media. The complaints about taking things out of context generally have to do with content, though it seems to me that a great deal depends on form. One example is the dynamic of the transmission of visual images and the time limits imposed on their perception. The real issue is that the flow of information disgorged upon us by television screens is a sea that is an inch deep—a sea made not only spatially but temporally shallow. Everything costs infernal amounts of money, be it a commercial, the latest sports headline, or an attempt to assassinate the president. Because TV time is so expensive, units of information are shortened almost beyond recognition. They end up being amputated, and people get used to a diet of shortened thoughts, shortened plots and narratives. In other words, these are not whole numbers but fractional ones.[2] As was suggested in chapter 10, our perception is already programmed in such a way that we react exclusively to fractions of phenomena, events, and experiences. Therefore, when there is an opportunity to take a deeper look at something or to evaluate the true scope of what is happening, we become confused, having gotten used to surrogates and partiality. We have adjusted to watching the world through a "crack," and when somebody discovers that an entire world can fit into such a crack, it is stunning. It creates an illusion that if you open up the fractions of seconds to which the mass media have gotten us accustomed, the resulting opening will familiarize us with the totality of the scene in which everything is taken into account, put on record, and given a place. This media technique—the technique of manipulating fragments in order to endow them with the false (or exaggerated) sense of universality—is precisely what Hirst's strategy relies on. The viewer's willingness to accept it is made possible because, tired of feeding on the fractional and dissatisfied by partiality, we cry out for compensation. The spectacle at the Gagosian Gallery (that is, "Theories, Models, Methods . . .") turned out to be precisely such compensation.[3]

4.

In contrast to artists who give preference to the aesthetic of deviations and incongruities, what is striking about Hirst's career is its unbelievably precise fit with well-worn psychopathological clichés. Starting with his early conceptual works, he showed an interest in items used during autopsies of dead bodies. His then-unconscious identification with a coroner was later transferred to slicing open cows, pigs, and sharks—a period that can be defined as a recurrence of the childhood experience of partiality (see fig. 10.4). This feeling of partiality, which has to do with the lack of a "completeness of the image," is experienced by children in the mirror stage, while adults such as Hirst continue to go back to the metaphor of partiality but on the level of other problems and other symbolic contexts. In his case, yet another change in symbolic entourage was expressed in the transfer of the stigma of partiality from the industry of Physis to the industry of Poesis, in which Hirst sees his own reflection. In this latest, narcissistic stage, he has enclosed upon himself the trajectory of the transfer tested on cows and sharks. What is important, too, is that Hirst has represented the artist as an inalienable part of the eschatological economy, as inalienable as art itself. In his work, the longing for totality, unattainable in the mirror stage, turns into the totality of death—the death of art, the end of the autonomous. Its autopsy is not only carried out but aestheticized, thereby contributing to what the narcissistic ego contemplates in death—the "completeness of the image" as a compensation for its unattainability by other means. And this is what finally unites Hirst with the Guggenheim's director Thomas Krens and the architect Frank Gehry.

As is well known, the principal pathos of Adorno's *Aesthetic Theory* has to do with its author's desire to prevent the transformation of autonomous art into a culture industry. Such a transformation is undergone by every artistic phenomenon that leaves the zone of de-reified activity. Given the inevitability of reification (*Verdinglichung*), the goal of the critically thinking artist is to delay it. However appealing, Adorno's arguments have for the most part lost their effectiveness. The reason for this is the expansion of the culture industry into the sphere of the optical unconscious, as well as the instantaneous mimetic exchange (mimetic reciprocation) between them that has been inspired by new technologies. That which Adorno regarded as nonidentical to the culture industry turns out to be contaminated by it even before the moment of reification.[4] Due to the mass media and the phenomenon of instantaneous exchange, the temporal gap between art and its Other has ceased to exist. Having reached this state, art (read: autonomous art) has reached its own death, which—like everything else—is no longer its Other. However cynical, this was precisely the message that Hirst's "Theories, Models, Methods, . . ." conveyed to the viewer: art is dead, it no longer exists, but this theme itself is art.

But let us return to Kabakov, for whom "art today is show business."[5] Needless to say, he makes this comment with sarcasm, adding that "no one will pay money unless you propose some system of theatrical or circus tricks." Everything is based on shock-inducing effects, since shock and aggression turn any episode into a spectacle. On the one hand, everything has turned into politics—but then the presidential elections begin, and we see that everything has turned into theater. If this has been "engineered" by someone, it was probably so that we, too, could develop a depoliticized attitude toward reality and learn to see it as theater.

In Kabakov's view, "until very recently, artists believed that the art world must defend itself from other worlds. The sensational news is that the art world no longer exists as a fortified camp or city. Instead of fortified walls, we are now defended by tolerance and calm." On the other hand, "there have been periods when radicalism and transgression were not empty sounds. Without them, even if art history could go somewhere, it would have been strictly in a chronological sense." Margarita Tupitsyn backs up this opinion with a reference to Hans Haacke, whose "exposés of the sordid situations taking place in the wings of the art scene made him a hero to radical critics and curators. At one time, they were called 'grouches' because they got on people's nerves and didn't allow such situations to become routine. Today, they've gotten old and have become professors. But new 'grouches,' alas, have not emerged. Generally speaking, what used to be considered avant-garde now automatically makes you retrograde. Some sort of criteria must be developed."

Criteria, Kabakov argues, "can be developed on the basis of past experience—starting, for instance, with the idea of radicalism, which so greatly disturbs us all because we see it as an absolute and final severing of all connections. But in fact, only the radicals have survived in memory." Reflecting on the difference between the radicals of past eras and those who continue the traditions of political activism in modern culture, Margarita Tupitsyn pointed out that the art Kabakov and like-minded artists produced in the USSR in the 1960s and 1970s was also associated with politics: "The question is, with what kind of politics? There is no greater terminological (and ideological) confusion than the one on this subject in the West.[6] To this, one can add that the [conservative] politics underlying the dynamics of the artistic process [today] has to do, first and foremost, with banks, corporations, and wealthy art patrons who always 'know exactly' what art must and mustn't be. It's precisely because the connection between art and radical politics has been severed that it has become harder for us to invest a work of art with any functions except for aesthetic ones."

In all probability, not only external but internal connections have been severed as well. Politics has ceased to be identical to itself, to its structures and definitions, to its teleology. Just as we don't know whether art remains an artistic phenomenon, we no longer know whether politics remains a political phenomenon. And this is not merely because political reality appears to us in a nonpolitical guise: today, politics is practically everything, to say nothing of the relativity of the concept of political radicalism. The "political *epoché*" has lost its meaning, and we are all the losers for it. Even though the triangulation of politics has become an ambiguous venture, we would like to believe in the existence of something politically visible, something with clear conceptual contours, weight, and span. For the French, for instance, the last time the meaning of "radical politics" was absolutely clear was in May 1968. In Iran, it was in the 1980s; as for Russia, there the radical restoration of capitalism took place in the early 1990s. On the one hand, political acts—institutional or contractual, public or private—cannot be separated from nonpolitical ones. On the other hand, despite the hopelessness of this enterprise, we continue to put the world through the sieve of political reduction.

Clearly, in order for political activity—individual or collective—to manifest itself, we must clearly understand the situation in the world and the situation around us, and also what kind of action must be taken in order to assist the revolutionary struggle or the bloodless implementation of social programs. Achieving this goal is actually a complex and responsible task—especially today, when we are all stuffed full of contradictory information and impressions, visual and otherwise. In this context, the notion of political orientation has become extremely muddled. It bears a resemblance to what J.-F. Lyotard defined as the *différend*—a conflict that does not fit within the framework of existing standards, whether logical, legal, lexical, and so forth.[7] For Lyotard, the *différend* was akin to a snowflake that falls on one's hand, only to melt away immediately. Today, this snowflake has turned into a snowball, which grows as it rolls downhill and turns into a global *différend*. Apparently, the number of existing standards can no longer be counted. Like snow, they envelop social and moral problems and the problems of cultural politics. Such a "snowball effect" makes it difficult to adopt enlightened decisions, and hence engenders cynicism. Thus, the furor surrounding "Theories, Models, Methods, . . ." or the new Guggenheim building project was a cynical display of indifference toward art's integration into the culture industry—an event that I find reminiscent of a funeral banquet. This funeral wake has already become a "new" style, and can go on forever, generating cycles and repetitions, as well as requiring the creation of suitable props and sets. Such is the soil in which the new aesthetic will bloom, the aesthetic of the funeral, the art of mourning art. This era may turn out to be longer and more "fruitful" than all the preceding periods.

Reacting to these ideas, which I expressed during our trialogue, Kabakov noted that this argument "reflects the position of the defeated. The question arises: should the situation be viewed as hopeless? Another possibility is to ignore the question itself and to go on living as if nothing happened. Or a third option: to mount something in opposition, something no less active. These are the three strategies." In response to Kabakov's remark, I clarified my position somewhat, saying that if autonomous art becomes a part of the culture industry before it has even had a chance to be born, then the only justification for it is political activism. It's better to be socially engaged than to saturate the art market with "timeless" artistic treasures while thinking that you are shaking the foundations of the world or fighting for creative freedom. And yet it would be naive to expect all the artists and critics to quit what they do and join a punitive expedition or crusade against the culture industry. The point, however, is that those who easily submit their minds and souls to the culture industry are not automatically rewarded by it. To corrupt an adversary (not an ally) is global capitalism's top priority. As a result, some of its fiercest opponents end up being its most celebrated converts.[8] That is why, given the growing incoherence of many opinions (including my own), I try to clarify for myself what political activism and political orientation can mean in this situation. The choice of the so-called "third way" depends on this. But as long as such a way does not exist (or remains unknown), griping against Krens, Hirst, or Jeff Koons is just as senseless as calling a funeral home to protest the existence of death.

In the meanwhile, the image-making media's invasion of our psychic space can be dealt with in such a way that it would impel this imagery and its visual rhetoric to incriminate itself. This is exactly what Derrida calls "*a* deconstruction"[9] (as opposed to *the* deconstruction, for there are numerous ways of doing it). The point is that the culture industry is reminiscent of Narcissus admiring his own reflection and contemplating suicide. All we can do is to help it kill itself, just as the water surface that reflected Narcissus's image did. And that's precisely why the deconstructionist must remain indifferent.[10] Otherwise, the water will be rippled and the Narcissus of the culture industry will not be able to see its "flawless" face.

As for the possibility of a "third way," it would probably lead to a struggle for the liberation of humanity from a "bad habit"—creativity. This utopian project aimed at "the creation of a noncreative state" (which I discussed in chapter 10) is the ultimate recipe for those who believe that creativity is what the culture industry feeds on. The obstacle, however, is that were there ever to be a person who, from the moment of birth, was known to be completely devoid of the creative reflex, such a mythical "role model" would have undoubtedly become "creatively" processed and absorbed into the culture industry.

In the early 1990s, Kabakov described his installations as total. At the same time, their totality was significantly limited by the boundaries of the art scene. Everything beyond that scene was perceived as the Other of art and regarded as unsuitable for artification. Hirst redefined the concept of the total by abolishing the boundaries between autonomous art and the culture industry. This, rather than the artistic merits (or flaws) of his "Theories, Models, Methods, . . . ," explains the vehement reaction to the show by Kabakov and other artists of his generation, his era. As it turned out, the total crumbles not only when some of its fragments fall out but also when it becomes conscious of itself as a fragment of an even greater totality.

Before I conclude, I will comment on some issues concerning Kabakov's success in the West. His success seems to have been due not only to his talent and intelligence but also to the process of recontextualization itself. During Kabakov's career in the West (i.e., since 1987), his numerous installations have successfully neutralized the problem of the referent and the

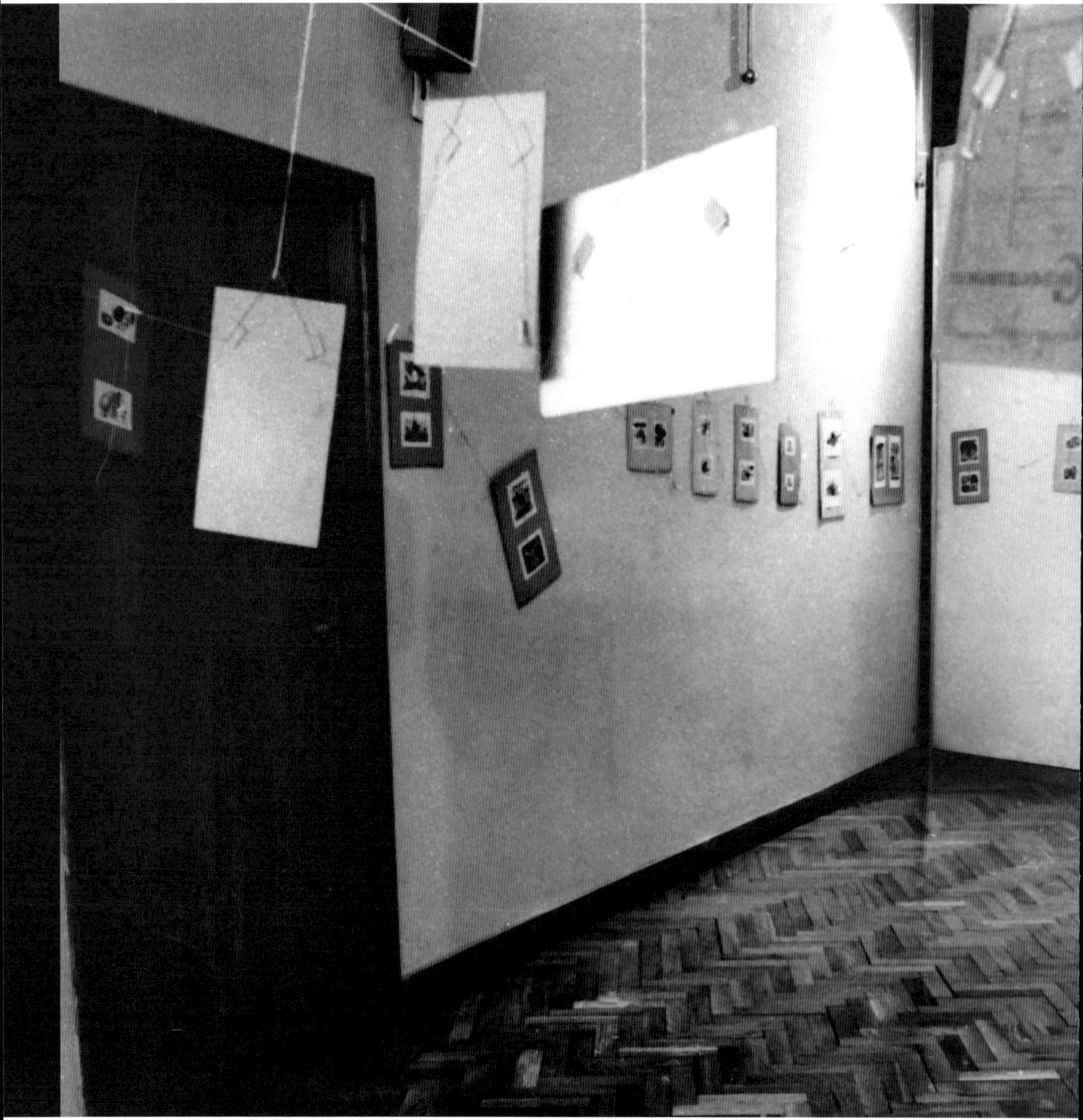

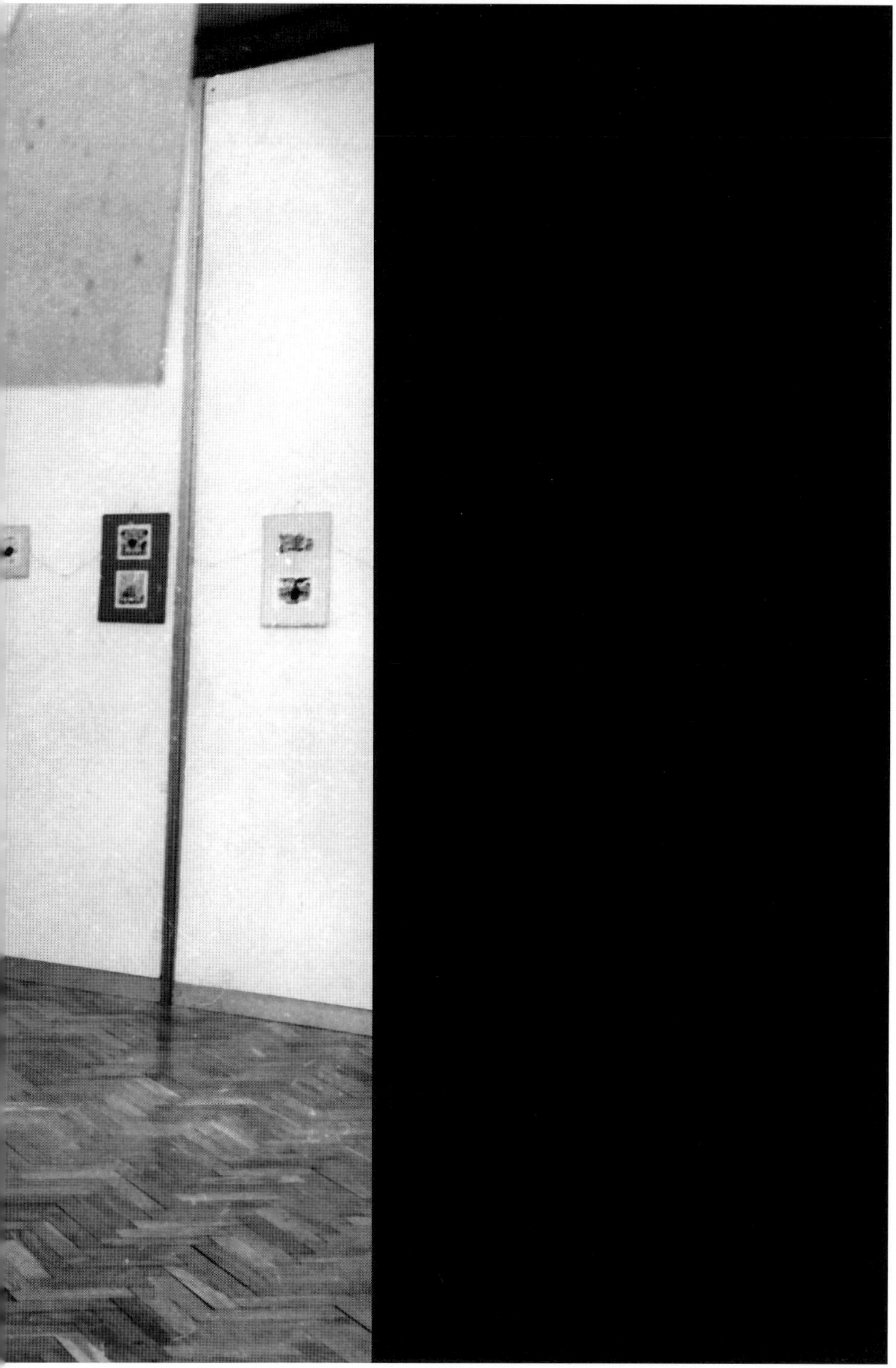

12.1
Installation view of Ilya Kabakov's *Transmission of Energy,* at the exhibition "Expensive Art," Palace of Youth, Moscow, 1989.

referential context (figs. 12.1, 12.2). At present, when answering the question, "What is this artist's purpose and what do his works point to?" the enlightened spectator in New York, Frankfurt, or London goes back mentally not to the mysterious context of Russia, but to Kabakov's earlier exhibitions in the West. In other words, the "Ur-scene" or the "Ur-text" now is not Russia itself but its image created in Kabakov's early installations of the late 1980s and early 1990s. Such is the final balance sheet of the exhibition marathon that made it possible for the artist to succeed at what could be called the *cloning* of the referent. This has given his art and his exhibitions in the West a diachronic dimension that visiting artists from Russia rarely have the time to establish.

12.2
Ilya Kabakov shows his works to other conceptual artists, Kabakov's studio, Moscow, 1980. Photo Georgii Kizeval'ter.

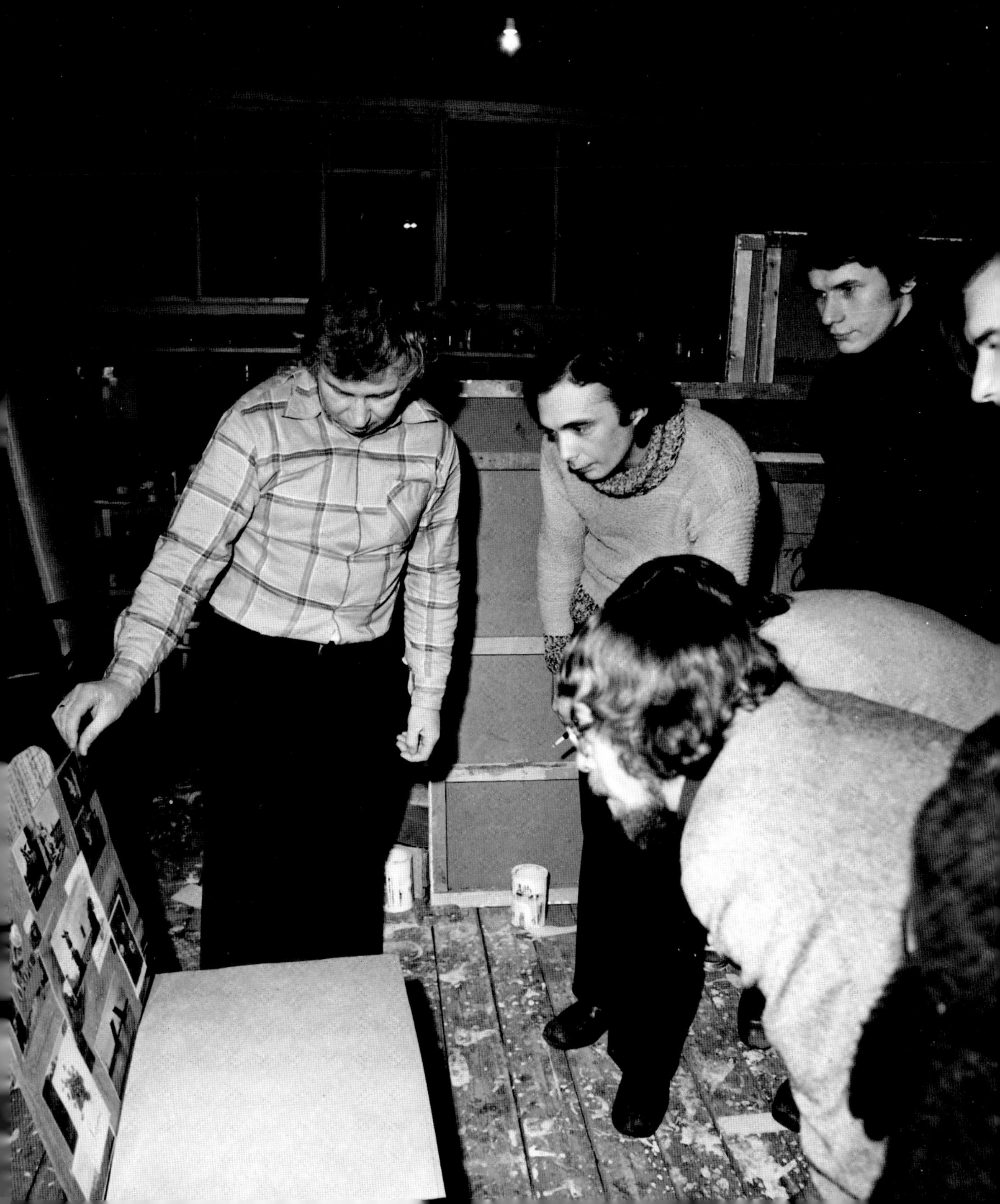

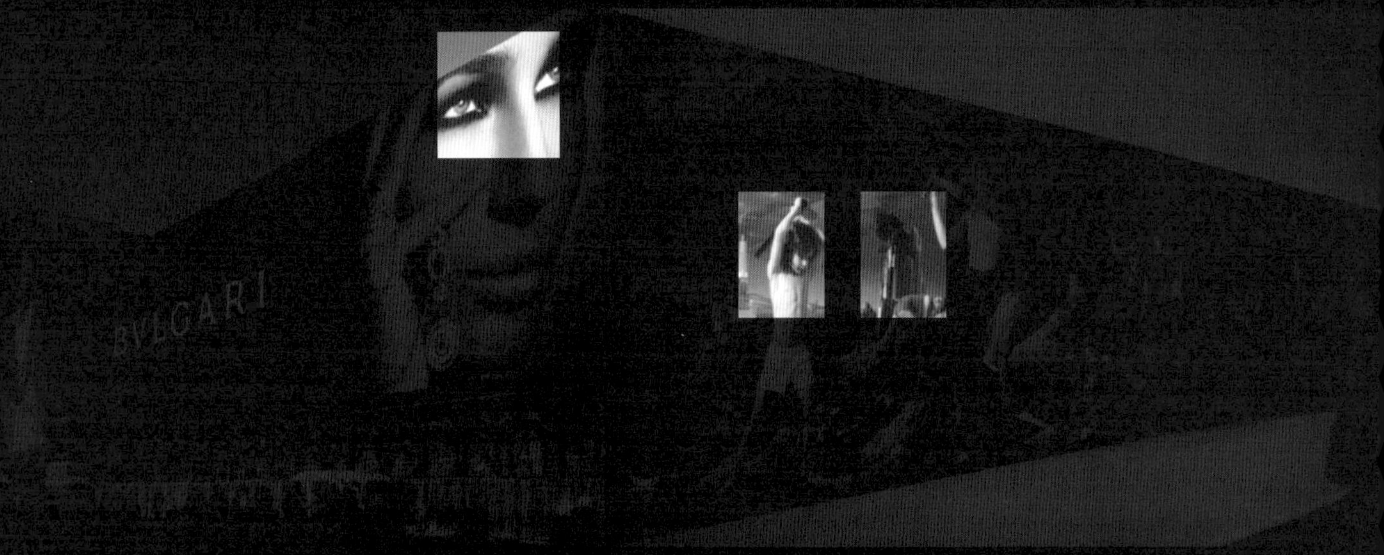
BVLGARI

CHAPTER 13

Rublevskoe Chaussée[1]

1. THROWING ROSEMARY'S BABY OUT WITH THE BATH WATER

The reference to Roman Polanski's 1968 film reflects the attitude toward alternative Russian art on the part of key Western intellectuals, who, since the emergence of this art in the late 1950s, have perceived it as "impure," highly suspicious, and the unwanted offspring of the revolutionary avant-garde (the prey) and socialist realism (the perpetrator). Now, at a time when Russian orphanages are wide open for the flood of desperate adoptive parents from all over the world, it seems that "Rosemary's baby" has finally passed its legitimation crisis, and therefore no longer requires supervision or protective custody.

The First Moscow Biennale of Contemporary Art featured many exhibitions, sharing in common at least one thing—they were all physically accessible.[2] The former Lenin Museum was the main building to host the Biennale. Adjacent to the Red Square, it carries symbolic weight and underscores the condition under which global capitalism and its culture industry can finally harmonize with something that defies reification. I am referring to the "specter of Communism" in an age of regained spectrality. By returning to its initial, spectral (read: de-reified) state in the early 1990s, the communist culture industry paved the way for its capitalist counterpart to follow suit. If this was the agenda that the First Moscow Biennale curators meant to pursue, they should definitely be praised and encouraged.

As is known, societal spectacles and public events of considerable importance have often been used to manipulate people's consciousness. The pope's funeral, the royal wedding, and Terri Schiavo's ordeal are illustrations of this rule. In this respect, crossing the line between art culture and mass rituals (as occurred in Russia soon after the revolution) is more than the organizers of Biennales, Documentas, or Manifestas can afford.[3] And yet the scope of their ambitions can be measured by the size of an exemplary exhibition space designed to present an *overall picture* of contemporary art. Even if such a picture were a displayable concept, it would still require a different means of presentation. Equally, unless we alter our perception of exhibition spaces that are suitable for hosting international art events, such spaces may well be regarded as culture industry showrooms.

In the Lenin Museum my attention was captured by David Ter-Oganian's work *This Is Not a Bomb*, consisting of several suspicious objects with canned vegetables, ticking clocks, and exposed wires spread around many locations (fig. 13.1).[4] Each of these "weapons" silently undermines the label "This Is Not a Bomb," for it actually is one. The piece also undermines the Biennale's claim that the general picture of what is happening in art today can be constructed out of small and statistically unreliable samples endowed with an exaggerated sense of universality.

Santiago Sierra's *Spraying of Polyurethane over 18 People* (2002) featured eighteen young prostitutes, "mainly of Eastern European descent, placed inside an empty medieval church and sprayed with polyurethane on their genitals in two different positions—from the front and from the back."[5] The entire process was videotaped and exhibited in the Lenin Museum, along with remnants of the orgy—spermlike clouds of foam and phallic-shaped containers of polyurethane brought to Moscow from Lucca, Italy. Despite the "position" that this Western artist assigned to his Eastern European counterparts, Sierra's piece can be interpreted as yet another representation of the immaculate conception. While in Sandro Botticelli's painting we notice a strip coming out of the Archangel Gabriel's mouth (directed toward the Virgin Mary) with the text of the Annunciation written on it, in Sierra's case, the annunciation is no longer textual: it is bodily and formless ("informe," to use Bataille's terminology).[6]

Departing from the Lenin Museum, I encountered a group of aging Stalinists standing near the entrance with red banners and portraits of dead leaders (including Lenin). To my surprise, they knew nothing about the First Moscow Biennale. However, if they had, it would have been very painful for them to learn that the former Lenin Museum was now being subjected to this kind of "sacrilege." At any rate, their display of flags and political portraiture proposed no alternative to the Biennale, nor did it seize the moment to form a binary opposition, which we all tend to dwell upon.

My next destination, the Shchusev State Museum of Architecture, was under reconstruction. Its naked interior, dressed up for the occasion by Christian Boltanski, reinforced my respect for this artist, whose addiction

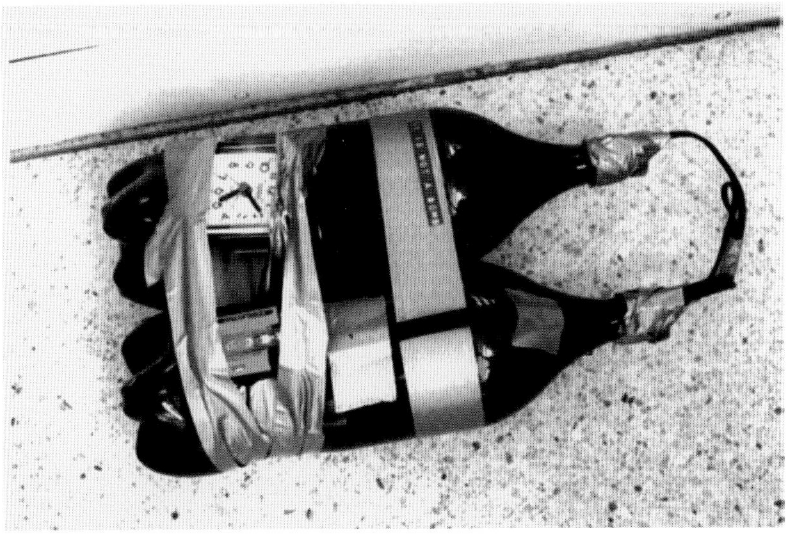

13.1
David Ter-Oganian, *This Is Not a Bomb*, 2005.

to tautology (especially in the last decade) has been overwhelming.[7] His installation's title was *Odessa Ghosts* (2005); it consisted of countless frozen overcoats suspended from the ceiling in such a way that the whole space looked and even felt haunted. This impression was exacerbated by the dreary light of bulbs descending from the top to the first and second floors. Stripped bare, the museum had only temporary passages, made out of wood and laid on the second (but barely existing) floor, thus enabling the viewer to observe the installation from the top floor. Half an hour later, and already outside, I felt the urge to repress what I had seen in the Shchusev Museum. Nothing seemed more alarming than art's ability to make the ordinary look like Auschwitz or Gulag.

Bill Viola's video work *The Greeting* is a slow-moving animation of the encounter between Elizabeth and Mary in Jacopo Pontormo's mannerist painting.[8] Its placement in the "sanctuary" of the Pushkin State Museum of Fine Arts proved to be as smart as Boltanski's choice to "haunt" the Shchusev Museum. Luckily, Viola showed his work parallel to an ambitious exhibition of religious art (religious in a figurative sense as well as literally), held in the same building. Titled "Russia and Italy through the Ages: From Giotto to Malevich," it reflected the influence of those Russian scholars who choose to interpret Malevich as a mystic.[9] In this context, Viola's secular optic served as an alternative to the clerical vision that has gained momentum in recent years all over the world, including the United States.[10] In Russia, where the religious right attempts to institute control over art and literature, it has partially succeeded in blocking frivolous (read: unsanctioned) interpretations of the Holy Scripture.

Anatolii Osmolovskii's show, titled "The Way Political Positions Turn into Form," introduced several series of abstract works from 2004. All of them are formally undersigned *Untitled,* because, in the opinion of the artist (quoted in the press release), "this very word usually accompanies truly avant-garde work." At the same time, however, Osmolovskii refers to a series of black sculptures as "Bugs," pink ones as "Pieces," grey ones as "Finger Nails," and yellow ones as "Details." The artist believes that "any artworks, regardless of how silent and formal they may be, will always be loaded with some political content." Curiously, Osmolovskii's "Bugs," "Pieces," and "Finger Nails" bear resemblance to Paul McCarthy's objects, made from silicon and painted brown, most notably, *Penis and Vagina* (1998–2000). Their different "political" content brings to mind Nicolas Cage and John Travolta in the 1997 film *Face/Off,* where contents (the characters' personalities) become as interchangeable as their appearances. René Magritte's *The Treachery of Images* and Duchamp's *Fountain* have long warned us against a lifetime enslavement of one stereotype to another, of a semantic cliché enslaving a visual one. The difficulty, however, is that treating these clichés as free agents makes them incessantly available for political manipulation. Whether this sinister economy of the sign will ever help critically engaged artists like Osmolovskii get their message through is yet to be seen.

It was very cold in Moscow. Given the Biennale's physical dispersal, getting from one place co-hosting the show to another was quite a miserable experience. That is why, as a detour from the temperature, I took refuge in the State Tret'iakov Gallery (on the Krymskaia embankment) on the third day of my stay in the city. The exhibition I intended to see was "Accomplices: Collective and Interactive Work in Russian Art of the 1960s–2000s." It featured an already familiar repertoire of aesthetic activities—most of it had already been exhibited under the same roof, even though the title was different. As in earlier presentations of this material, the conceptual and performance artists looked better than the others. Their advantage is that they can easily duplicate their "factography"—make reprints from original negatives, copy texts, and sell the "additions" to the museum.[11] As for the rest of the participants working in more traditional media, their share in the State Tret'iakov Gallery collection of ex-unofficial art consists, for the most part, of leftovers. The best works were sold in the 1970s and 1980s to foreigners, American or Western European diplomats and reporters who were determined to bring back exotic souvenirs from the "Evil Empire." Perhaps they will one day be willing to resell them to some Russian oligarchs interested in retrieving the best examples of domestic art in order to donate them to museums (preferably, new ones). In fact, the entire history of art can be viewed through the prism of the generosity that results from a guilty conscience.

In the Central House of Artists (adjacent to the State Tret'iakov Gallery), I happened upon two more exhibitions—"Human Project" and "Russia-2." There, I found several artworks (an installation, a sculpture, and a mural) dealing with the issue of terrorism and the Chechen War: Oleg Kulik's *Madonna* (2004), Vasilii Tsagolov's *Fountain* (2004), and Aleksei Kallima's *Metamorphoses* (2005). Executed in the style of Hirst, these pieces catch your eye right away but then, in a matter of minutes, leave you feeling ashamed for being such a "good customer" and compliant recipient of such predatory optics. The duo of Aleksandr Vinogradov and Vladimir Dubossarskii aroused even less enthusiasm, even though their oversized paintings—paintings in form, cartoons in content—have become a source of amusement for some museum curators in the West. From the Krymskaia embankment I went to the newly opened National Center for Contemporary Arts, the best exhibition space in Russia—at

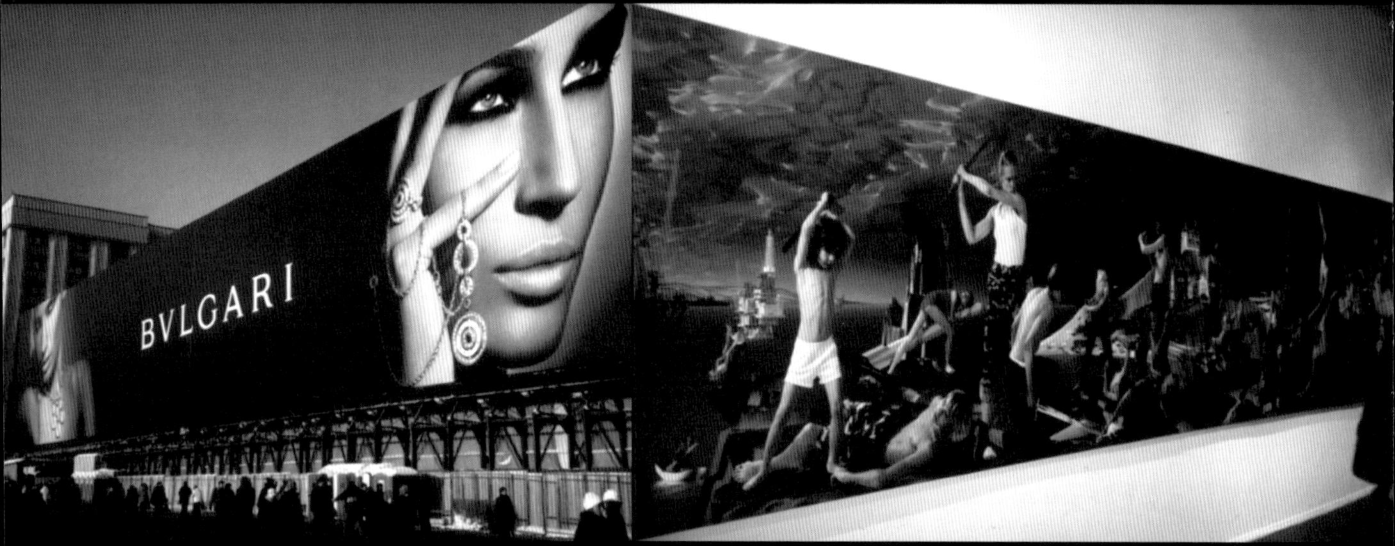
BVLGARI

13.2
Left: Bulgari billboard; right: AES+F group's *Last Riot,* 2005.

least for "current developments" in visual culture. I could not miss the chance to see Mikhail Roginskii's posthumous exhibition "My Other Self," consisting of painterly works I had first enjoyed twenty years earlier in the artist's studio in Paris.

The next day I attended three shows at the Multimedia Complex for Actual Arts: "Last Riot" (2005), authored by the group AES+F; Mikhal' Rovner's *Order,* a 2003 minimalist paraphrase of Nishat Shirin's video work; and Robert Mapplethorpe's photographs mingled with mannerist etchings of the old masters[12]—a banal idea, regardless of how little Russians know about Mapplethorpe and his aesthetics. To label it "mannerist" was beyond the point. First of all, mixing deferred and spatially dislocated contexts is counterproductive unless you do horoscopes or make fortune cookies. Secondly, Mapplethorpe's politics of the signifier has been fully explored and written about. In my view, putting his oeuvre alongside work by artists and photographers of the 1930s would be a far more challenging project.[13]

I was not moved by the five-meter-long canvas covered with jet-printed imagery that was produced by AES+F;[14] it seemed to me a decadent reappropriation of Orwell's *Animal Farm.* But the artists' text is a different matter, because it accommodates the notion of the free agent, mentioned earlier in relation to Osmolovskii. AES+F write, "The virtual world, generated by the real world of the past twentieth century, is a test-tube organism, expanding, leaving its borders, and grasping for new zones that absorb its founders and mutate into something absolutely new. In this new world, real wars look like a game on americasarmy.com, and prison tortures resemble the sadistic exercises of the modern valkyries. The heroes of the new epos have only one identity, the identity of the rebel of the last riot. The last riot is where all are fighting against all, and against themselves; where there is no longer any difference between victim and aggressor, male and female. This world celebrates the end of ideology, history, and ethic."[15]

This text's ability to touch base with nearly everything makes it applicable to a variety of unrelated images, including the ones I saw across the street from the Lenin Museum, on an immense advertising board with "modern valkyries" wearing Bulgari jewels (fig. 13.2). (If this was not a riot, then what is?)

To conclude, I will soften my critique of the Biennale as reckless recontextualization—not because it is untrue, but because art itself is the most powerful (and equally reckless) recontextualizing metaphor. Even if the curators of international exhibitions are guilty of tearing art away from its sources and placing it, at least for the duration of the show, in an orphanage (like the Lenin Museum), they unconsciously imitate artists. The analogy can be extended (albeit regressively) to the law of sign formation: repression of the signified, neglect of contextual referents, and so forth. This law manifests itself indiscriminately, sparing neither artistic nor curatorial work. Artists act as curators, and curators as artists, in relation to their respective projects. The work of curatorial art utilizes contributions of group show participants the same way artists use raw materials. From the artists' standpoint, the entire group show (including the curator's concept, the wall text, and so forth) is an extended frame around their own pieces, and the bigger the exhibition, the more baroque it may seem as a frame. The point, however, is that our understanding of the endless game of recontextualization as a distinctive trait of human experience should not be used as an ideological alibi. The suspicion that *Homo sapiens* is a recontextualized ape does not exempt us from loving our neighbors.[16]

2. RUSSIA?

Any exhibition at the Guggenheim is structured a priori by its architecture, which is conducive from the beginning to a mix of languages, contexts, and aesthetic and political aspirations. In this respect, the exhibition "Russia! Nine Hundred Years of Masterpieces and Master Collections" is no exception—particularly since it covers a vast historical range, from the Middle Ages to our own time.[17] The exhibition could be more properly called "Russia through the Eyes of the New Russians"—in the sense that the imposition on the West of the (post-) Soviet historical vision, the vision of the nouveaux riches and the profiteers from the "shadow economy," fits well with the predatory leveling of contextual, temporal, or other distinctions by turning them into different regimes of spectacle.

In this context, one may recall Fellini's film *Satyricon,* which many of my compatriots—especially in the 1970s—regarded as the outer limits of genius. What shocked me upon a recent viewing of this film was not so much the theatricality of kitsch, as the underlying vision of history: history is depicted as total theater, where temporality is attributed to the "imperfection" of our vision, and where the movement of time is perceived as a result of instant changes in costumes or sets. But if everything is spectacle, the protest against spectacularized politics, or reconciliation with power, becomes just as much of a spectacle. Is indifference the only thing that can preserve the status of the nonspectacle? In other words, once again we have "vertical" time, a proto-totalitarian aesthetic, the coextensivity of past and future.

The alienation of spectacle time from the perceptual does not in any way contradict the imperial politics of representation adopted by the Guggenheim. The museum website says, "The Guggenheim isn't just a museum—it's an international empire." This imperial twist of the Guggenheim spiral gives us an idea of the trajectory followed by the American culture industry. While viewing the exhibition, I could not rid myself of the feeling that it was organized on the principle of a roller coaster, which is based on a rapidly moving gaze that clings, not to the objects speeding by, but to the possibility of staying on top of the spiral that serves as the observation point, the way it happens on roller-coaster rides at amusement parks.

If one compares this Russian exhibition to the previous one, "The Great Utopia" in 1992, the distinctions between them are by no means limited to the fact that in 1992 the Guggenheim paid for everything, while today the Russian side bears most of the financial burden. While "The Great Utopia" limited itself to a more or less homogeneous horizon of avant-garde aesthetics, the 2005 exposition offers the audience a heterogeneous picture of the Russian cultural heritage in all its totality, a sort of "crash course" for the uninitiated culture-snatcher. The quality of the articles in the catalogue has changed accordingly. The curators of "Russia!" are no longer experts but functionaries, and this "powerful and rotting stench" (to quote the Russian poet Aleksandr Blok) of bureaucratic mediocrity is reflected not only in the expositionary discourse but in the texts as well. I should note that my attitude toward cultural functionaries and apparatchiks—whether they are representatives of the unsinkable American *nomenklatura* or of the corrupt Russian elite—is fundamentally different from that of a number of American intellectuals. For example, in his review "Back to the Future: The New Malevich,"[18] Yve-Alain Bois respectfully quotes the managerial gems of Petrova, deputy director of the State Russian Museum, as if this Brezhnev-era fossil could formulate anything other than clichés. As for Bois, his lack of critical negativity toward Petrova as well as a number of other individuals makes me wonder why he needs this alliance.

Contemporary art is represented in "Russia!" by a small number of works. In the original project, there were even fewer: only Kabakov and Komar and Melamid (all three are U.S. citizens). However, as a result of the lobbying of the exhibition organizers, backstage fighting, and the use of government connections, this list was expanded to more than twenty artists. The fact that half of them are émigrés is unimportant: many of them travel regularly to Russia, exhibit artworks there, and sell their production to influential new Russians; their presence in the post-Soviet culture industry is becoming more and more visible. What remains spectral is their critical stance—a concept extremely unpopular with most Russian artists.

Deserving of mention, too, are certain promotional phrases, both in the catalogue and in the press release—such as "masterpieces of socialist realism." The meaning of this phrase is mystifying, considering the contamination of the authorial by the authoritarian. The Stalin slogan—"national in form, socialist in content"—meant that the patent on form was held by the entire nation, and the patent on content by the socialist system (i.e., by party functionaries). The artist was reduced to the role of an inspired follower of instructions from above. From this perspective, socialist realism is a parody of icon painting, the difference being that in icon painting, the role of coauthors was given to Church and God.

Nonetheless, the most depressing aspect of "Russia!" is the exhibition's tendency toward defragmentation, that is, toward leveling the aesthetic and sociocultural distinctions that, in the 1970s and 1980s, separated official artists (those loyal to the regime) from the unofficial or alternative art world. The attempt by the Russian side to create some sort of unified (artistic and, simultaneously, historical) image of Russian culture, including its contemporary art, is pure ideology that can be seen as "false consciousness" and false self-reflection. Starting in 1980, exhibitions of Soviet and, later, post-Soviet art in the West have been oriented toward some homogeneous context, whether the "unofficial" painting of the 1960s, "Moscow communal conceptualism," sots art, apt art, etc.[19] In those instances, the fragmentation was based on a desire to "clutch at the straw" of context, which seemed at the time to offer salvation from the superficial, touristic, spectacularized perception of art. That is precisely the perception that has triumphed at the Guggenheim, and in this sense, the "Russia!" exhibition is nothing but yet another pseudo-historical Thermidor.

The spectacularist tendencies usually mentioned with regard to the Young British Artists (Hirst, the Chapman brothers, etc.) were represented in the exhibition by the works of Kulik and Dubossarskii and Vinogradov. Their ability to shock (and simultaneously entertain) the viewer is not in doubt. The problem lies elsewhere: in Russia, spectacularist art entertains mostly the new bourgeoisie, which grew rich during the period when national resources could be plundered with impunity. The pseudo-negativity of *art-as-spectacle* is yet another charge leveled against such work. When opponents of spectacle culture speak of it as a totalitarian or "proto-totalitarian" phenomenon, this attests to the fact that stand-up comedy is unable to compensate for the paucity of negativity and, in particular, the paucity of critical reflection. In any case, the identification of the artist with a dog (Kulik), or Stalin with Malevich (Groys),[20] and so on is a result of the "spectacularization" of our consciousness (particularly since, thanks to the mass media, spectacle and kitsch now metastasize on an unprecedented scale).

If we think of the past as a utopia, then history has to appeal to something unattainable, something that is denied the possibility of appearing to us the way it really was. It is obvious that the desire for complete knowledge makes historical discourse more and more adequate to the *object* of study—the past. The paradox is that at the moment when it becomes most adequate to this utopian object, history itself becomes utopia. However, there are different kinds of wishful thinking. One such possibility ("institutional") was realized by the organizers of *Russia!* while another ("contractual") was carried out by the artist Vadim Zakharov in his installation *The History of Russian Art from the Avant-Garde to the Moscow Conceptual School* (2003). In both cases, history—despite manipulation and arbitrariness—"enters directly into the heart of utopia, into the heart of nowhere."[21]

Before returning to the Guggenheim spiral, I will mention Robert Smithson's project *Floating Island* realized by the Whitney Museum at the same time.[22] But what does Smithson have to do with the Guggenheim's architecture? After all, it's perfectly obvious that his *Spiral Jetty* (1970) is a two-dimensional configuration, while Frank Lloyd Wright's building is a three-dimensional one. The connection, however, is precisely that the *Spiral Jetty* can be interpreted as a trace left by the Guggenheim at the moment of its collapse. In my own mind this has already happened; therefore, I would like to refer the reader to Komar and Melamid's work *Scenes from the Future: Guggenheim Museum* (1974): it depicts the ruins of the Guggenheim Museum, a reality that was once difficult to believe (fig. 13.3).

3. THE MAN IN THE IRON MASK

Erik Bulatov's 2006 retrospective at the State Tret'iakov Gallery in Moscow was organized and paid for by Vladimir Semenikhin, who, unlike other, less fortunate Russian oligarchs, managed to rechannel his ambitions away from politics into a much safer place—art.[23] His protégé, Bulatov (already discussed in chapters 2 and 4), belongs to the first generation of Soviet "alternative" artists who emerged in the late 1950s, at the time of Khrushchev's thaw. The most interesting (if not the only interesting) part of this artist's oeuvre is the body of works produced in the period from 1972 to 1991 (see figs. 2.10, 4.3).

In 1981, in an essay titled "Two Railwaymen," Kabakov reveals the circumstances under which the railroad crossing sign "Dangerous," a warning against looming trains, defined Bulatov's poster-style approach to the

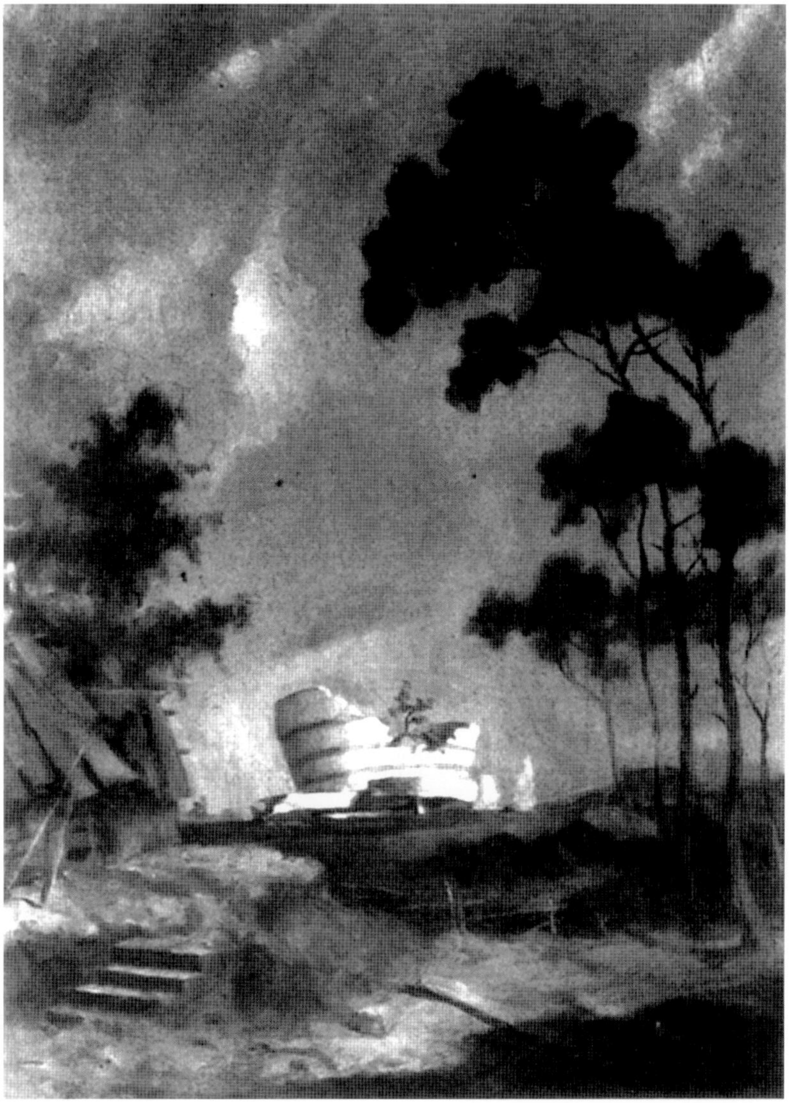

13.3
Vitaly Komar and Aleksandr Melamid, *Scenes from the Future: Guggenheim Museum*, 1974.

medium of painting. In paintings such as *Caution* (1973) and *Not to Be Leaned On* (1987), the way Bulatov incorporates within pictorial space the performative language of commands and warnings echoes the didactics of railroad posters: beware of high platforms, do not walk on the tracks, do not jump from the footboard, don't ride on the roof, etc.

In Bulatov's portrait of Brezhnev, the alternative artist recreated in his own home a poster that was hanging in a public place (see fig. 4.3). A socialist realist icon was displaced from the sphere of affirmative perception to that of alienated optics. Having wound up in the studio of an "alienated" artist, Brezhnev's portrait thus became a work of alienated art. And, in some sense, as I commented in chapter 4, Brezhnev was also alienated from himself.

What Bulatov's retrospective brings to light is that the imperial ulterior of this artist's career has always been mediated by the discourse of power, and it comes as no surprise that, in the post-Soviet era, all previously submerged codes and signs of authority have finally come to the surface.[24] However exaggerated, the confrontation between Bulatov's negatively charged painting of the 1970s or 1980s and the affirmative art of socialist realists invokes the two royal brothers in Alexandre Dumas's *The Man in the Iron Mask:* the ruler and his less fortunate contender, who in spite of everything aims at reversing his luck. Another example is Sergei Mikhalkov's national anthem: Stalinist in form and content, it was retouched in 2000 by its elderly author to meet the demands and conditions of the post-Soviet spectacle. The same is true of the overall situation in Putin's Russia, where today's cultural and political establishment coexists (quite harmoniously) with the old one under the banner of renewed imperial aspirations.[25]

But when Bulatov relocated to New York in 1991 (and, a year later, to Paris), he entered a state of tranquility—that is, an imaginary bubble with zero-degree alienation. The loss of negativity as a state of mind[26]—advocated by a number of critically engaged artists of his generation—was a side effect of Bulatov's fascination with Western spectacle. As this artist admitted in an interview at the time, he watched it "with the superficial eyes and naïve enthusiasm of a tourist," so that his work assumed a kind of "beyond-good-and-evil" dimension.[27] For the next seven years, his paintings were eligible for look-alike contests with promotional posters, sightseeing ads, and other "life-celebrating" items, and the artist was virtually forgotten by his admirers, Russian and Western alike.

Since 1999, Bulatov has been inserting lines of poetry by his friend Vsevolod Nekrasov into the same illusionist space he used decades before. His painterly techniques have long been adjusted to poster-style execution, and he spends time (up to several months!) primarily on preliminary sketches, while the actual process of painting usually takes only a few hours. Even with the familiar countrysides, urban landscapes, and cloudy skies, the results resemble constructivist book designs, with the texts narrowing at angles; but Bulatov's use of diagonals in such "timeless" compositions as *The Way the Clouds Move—the Way Things Are Going* (2001) has little to do with what the constructivists can be credited with: a compromise between two (di-) contests (agons)—utopian and historically specific. Regardless, this series partially fulfills its author's desire to move away ("the way the clouds move") from the social in order to stake out a more "universal" place for his melancholically detached paintings. The problem, however, is that the point of destination has turned out to be Bulatov's own mind, or rather, the "theater of the mind," to use Mallarmé's phrase. Perhaps nothing is more theatrical than our chronic dependence on binary oppositions, considering that the ubiquitous "play [read: mise en scène] of differences" is a modus operandi of "spectacle culture" and the "condition of spectacle."

4. SUDDEN GUST OF "DARKNESS"

In May 2006, I traveled to Moscow to attend my book presentation at the local art fair called Art Moskva. This fair turned out to be more modest in size than the International Fair for Contemporary Art (FIAC) or the Cologne Art Fair, but nearly as bad in terms of quality. And yet there were some interesting works—particularly those by Andrei Molodkin, a Russian artist who splits his time between Moscow, New York, and Paris. He is best known for his three-dimensional pieces consisting of oil barrels and pipes connected to transparent acrylic boxes: each has a hollow sculpture or phrase inside—half-filled with crude Chechen or Iraqi oil. The phrases (for example, "Support our troops," "Democracy," "Human rights") are subversive, provided that, in the "court" of art, official demagoguery cannot "take the Fifth" in order to be exempt from testifying against itself (fig. 13.4). Although the images tend to be deconstructive, they nonetheless skillfully combine anarchy with order, or defiance of the status quo with aesthetic standards, thereby turning the opposites into connected vessels.

On the one hand, oil is the most ancient of resources; on the other hand, there is nothing more in demand by modernity than oil. It is an "ideal model" for art, which aspires to something *always already* existing and yet at the same time is modern. The sign of our times is the "demographic explosion" of vacant forms easily filled with equally vacant content, including any ideology or any discourse, and provided that an empty form is a prop for mimesis. In Molodkin's work, the empty form is "a

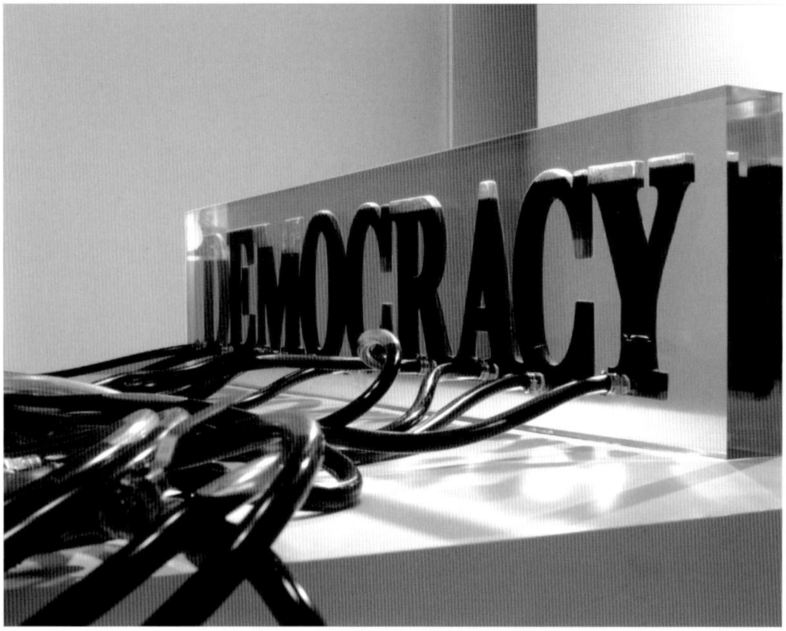

13.4
Andrei Molodkin, *Democracy*, 2005.

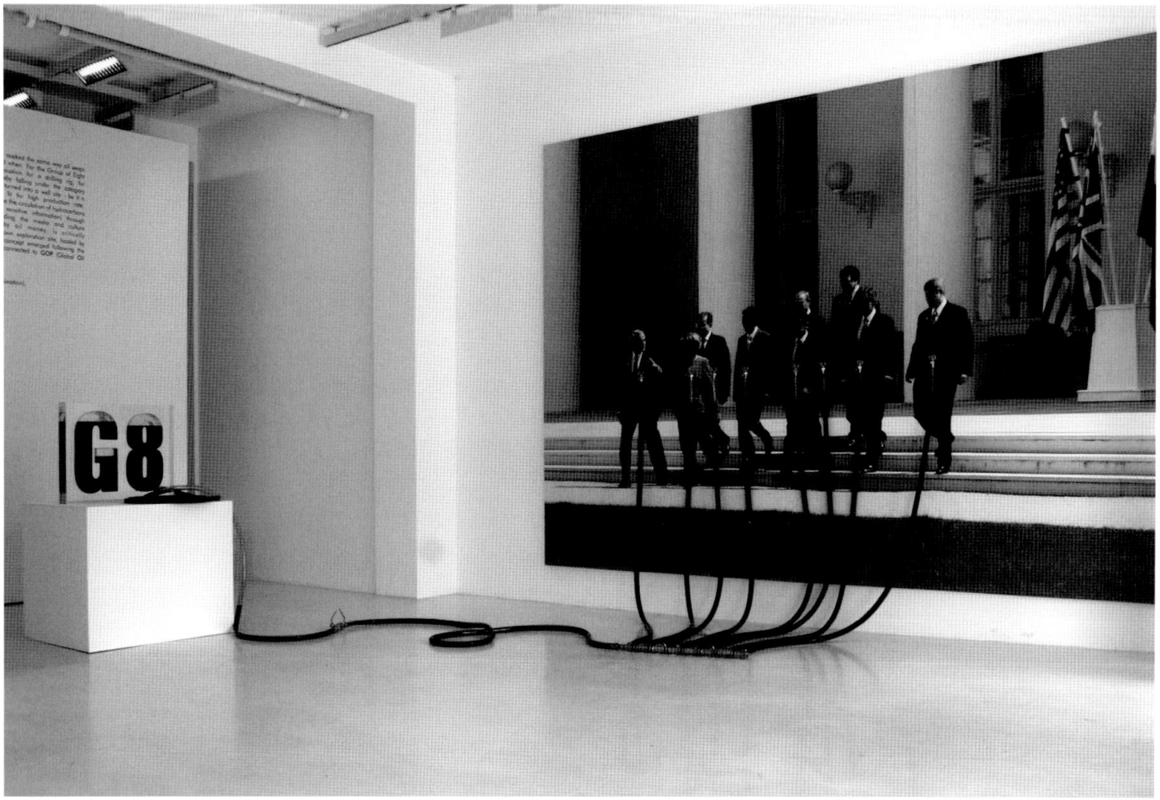

13.5
Andrei Molodkin, *G8*, 2007.

hollow matrix that you can fill with oil." For him, "culture is an emptiness we have to fill and affirm with economics."[28] Hence, it comes as no surprise that, in order to reaffirm the value of Kazimir Malevich's *Black Square,* Molodkin chooses to pump oil into "*it.*"

Molodkin's recent series, *Cold War II,* consists of photographs he took while working on a project in Russia's oil-producing northern region. The artist refers to oil as the newly reinvented "apple of discord," rife with competition (and possibly confrontation) between the West and the East. Another series, titled *G8* (2007), is about people "being soaked the same way oil seeps through a pipe, regardless of where or when" (fig. 13.5).[29] For the Group of Eight (G8), each of us is the perfect location for a drilling rig, for everyone can drill or be drilled, thereby falling under the category of supply and demand. Anyone can be turned into a well site—be it a hand-dug hole or a rich reservoir—fit for a high production rate. Hence, *G8* acts as a pump jack, safeguarding the circulation of hydrocarbons and their "byproducts" through various communicating vessels, including the media and culture industry. Their rhetoric, tainted by oil money, is critically challenged by the artist.

Today, politically engaged art is highly unpopular in Russia. This is particularly true of the "unauthorized" fusion of art and politics—unauthorized by those for whom visual culture is a variety of oil, which can be used as a political weapon only if they themselves choose to use it that way. Because all the national resources were privatized during Yeltsin's reign, and then redistributed by his successor, art has finally earned the attention of the nouveaux riches as the only resource left unclaimed. Oil tycoons and other wealthy Russians, who felt "underwhelmed" by their lack of access to political power or the media,[30] began to rechannel their "sweet crude" fantasies into the "art of controlling art," that is, into sponsoring, collecting, and imposing their tastes on both individuals and institutions. By positing the sublime as the sublimated, sized up for any "*objet a,*" they compensate (albeit symbolically) for being cut off from it.[31]

Among the outcomes are successful Russian sales at Sotheby's, Christie's, and Phillips; each of these auction houses has become a psychodrome for competing buyers who raise prices on insignificant artworks at the expense of good ones in order to impose (money-wise) their vision of "who is who" in contemporary Russian art. Some of them have already housed their acquisitions in the newly established private museums and foundations. Predictably, these institutions are run by the collectors themselves.

The influx of big money, combined with access to the nouveau riche lifestyle, has made the art world "glamorous" to the extent that, while entertaining wealthy art lovers on Rublevskoe Chaussée, one can also enlist their support and commitment. What these liaisons usually result in is personified by Iuliia Mil'ner, an immature artist whose participation in the 2007 Venice Biennale was secured by her husband—a sponsor of the Russian pavilion.[32] Thus, alongside the new political and financial class, there have emerged a new official art capable of satisfying its customer.[33]

In January 28, 2007, Moscow's Vinzavod (formerly a wine factory) hosted the "I Believe" Project, which aimed at the resumption of communal activities and communal participation.[34] In his installation *Darkness*, Andrei Monastyrsky mounted a typewritten text on the wall, opposite the entrance. The space in between was large enough to ensure that the viewer could not possibly read the text without standing in close proximity to it. But any attempt to approach the wall made the lights automatically go off, thus plunging viewers into a sudden darkness and prohibiting them from reading the text.[35] Having heard about this dilemma prior to my visit to Vinzavod, I brought a pair of binoculars with me and managed to decipher the "crypt" without approaching it. Weeks later, I admitted my guilt to Monastyrsky and promised not to reveal the content of the text. So, I will conclude this last chapter by keeping my promise.

NOTES

INTRODUCTION

1 Jacques Derrida, *Edmund Husserl's Origin of Geometry: An Introduction* (Lincoln: University of Nebraska Press, 1989), p. 81.
2 Ibid.
3 Ibid., p. 82.
4 Sots art emerged in Moscow in 1972 as a result of socialist realism's small-scale relocation from the sphere of affirmative perception to the sphere of alienated optics.
5 Following the death of Lenin in 1924, city apartments in Russia became overcrowded to the extent that families of every variety, belonging to various social, national, and cultural-ethnic groups, were forced to cleave together in a single communal body.
6 In communal life, everything (including vision) was ruled by speech rituals. In short, as I wrote in the preface, communal vision can be defined as seeing through the eyes, or on behalf, of the "collective *other.*"
7 The New Economic Policy (1921–ca. 1929) began in Lenin's time and was ended by Stalin.
8 See Aleksei Gan, "Da zdrastvuet demonstratsiia byta!", quoted in Margarita Tupitsyn, *El Lissitzky: Beyond the Abstract Cabinet* (New Haven: Yale University Press, 1999), p. 32.
9 Susan Buck-Morss, *The Dialectics of Seeing: Walter Benjamin and the Arcades Project* (Cambridge, Mass.: MIT Press, 1991).
10 See "Beseda s Zhakom Derrida," in *Zhak Derrida v Moskve: Dekonstruktsiia puteshestviia* (Moscow: Ad Marginem, 1993), p. 168.

CHAPTER 1

1 Jacques Derrida, *Edmund Husserl's Origin of Geometry: An Introduction* (Lincoln: University of Nebraska Press, 1989), p. 105.
2 The term "psychedelic commodity," which alludes to the overproduction of "paradisiacal" propaganda (Soviet-style), can be referred to Julia Kristeva's notion of "visual representations, fixing . . . an hallucinatory and untouchable *jouissance.*" See Julia Kristeva, *The Kristeva Reader,* ed. Toril Moi (New York: Columbia University Press, 1986), p. 227.
3 Biologists who study cells know that a substantive advantage can sometimes be gained through shifting attention from nucleus to cytoplasm, from the "core" of the problem to its margins. In a similar way, this chapter aims at switching priorities in our examination of the case study concerning the relationships between socialist realism and its "dangerous supplement," the Communal.
4 In the later work of Lacan the term *plaisir* is used as the restricted notion of phallic *jouissance.* See Jacques Lacan, *Écrits* (Paris: Édition du Seuil, 1966), p. 835.
5 *Écrits,* p. 249. If *jouissanse* without alienation is a synonym for paradise achieved at the cost of the disappearance of the *body,* the works of socialist

realists attest not to the loss, but to the repression of *it*. Repression of the *body*, of its physical needs and functions, is a distinguishing characteristic of socialist realist representation. The goal of socialist realism as a cultural text is to prevent the alienation of its own meaning, i.e., to avert (or annul) what Derrida defines as *la différance*. One precondition for such prevention is the confessional-cathartic joining of the trace and the deferred referent which, as a result of this magical operation, ceases to be deferred and to elude presence. Such is the logocentric reverie of socialist realism.

6 Ilya Kabakov, quoted in Victor Tupitsyn, "From the Communal Kitchen: A Conversation with Ilya Kabakov," *Arts* (October 1991): 51.

7 Il'ia Kabakov and Victor Tupitsyn, "Za predelami kommunal'noi rechi," *Tvorchestvo*, no. 1 (1992): 23.

8 Michel Foucault, *The History of Sexuality*, vol. 1 (New York: Vintage Books, 1980), p. 6.

9 The explanation can be based on the Lacanian distinction between the instincts (e.g., sexual drive) and the "family complexes," given that the *ideological orgasm* fits into the latter category. Apparently, it is rather difficult to tame the instinctual, especially with forces of a different nature. Cathartic vision (which is an example of such an alien force) is, nonetheless, quite compatible with unconscious representations (*imagoes*) linked to the "intrusion complex." This is the operative force beneath the subject's "realization that his/her identity is inescapably bound up with the identity of others" and, in particular, with "fraternal *imago*." See Jacques Lacan, *Les complexes familiaux dans la formation de l'individu: Essai d'analyse d'une fonction en psychologie* (Paris: Navarin, 1984), pp. 22–24 and 33–46.

10 See Emmanuel Levinas, "Language and Proximity," in *Collected Philosophical Papers* (Dordrecht: Martinus Nijhoff, 1987), pp. 118–120.

11 In Antonin Artaud's opinion, the tongue should be credited as a sexual organ, and not only in relation to oral sex but chiefly for its ability to perform speech acts.

12 Kabakov, quoted in Tupitsyn, "From the Communal Kitchen," p. 51.

13 Ideological objectification in the USSR can be regarded as analogous to sexual objectification in the West, taking into account the fact that ideological objectification (Soviet style) was generally a prerogative of the communal vision—the vision that allowed the individual "I" to look at the world through the lens (or on behalf) of "we."

14 See, for example, Christina Kiaer, "Rodchenko in Paris," *October*, no. 75 (Winter 1996): 3–35.

15 Some of these sign-objects combined symbolic and indexical dimensions.

16 Aleksei Gan, "Da zdravstvuet demonstratsiia byta!," cited in Margarita Tupitsyn, *El Lissitzky: Beyond the Abstract Cabinet* (New Haven: Yale University Press, 1999), p. 32.

17 This gave way to a buildup of communal ego and a decrease of what Husserl called "I-presentation."

18 See the discussion of "solar myth" in Richard M. Dorson's "The Eclipse of Solar Mythology," in *Myth: A Symposium*, ed. T. A. Sebeok (Bloomington: Indiana University Press, 1958), pp. 25–63. The role of heliotropic metaphors in theoretical discourses is illuminated by Jacques Derrida in his *Margins of Philosophy*, trans. Alan Bass (Chicago: University of Chicago Press, 1982). "Unceasingly, unwillingly," writes Derrida, "we have been carried along by the movement which brings the sun to turn in metaphor.... Insofar as it structures the metaphorical space of philosophy, the sun represents what ... should always lead us back ... to a certain history of perception" (*Margins of Philosophy,* pp. 250–251). In Derrida's opinion, "the tenor of the dominant metaphor will return always to this major signified of ontotheology: the circle of the heliotrope" (*Margins of Philosophy,* p. 266).

19 Goethe, cited in Rudolf Magnus, *Goethe as a Scientist* (New York: Henry Schuman, 1949), p. 141.

20 Max Müller, the leading Sanskrit scholar of the Victorian epoch (who came to Oxford from his native Germany as a youth of twenty-six), published a number of books and essays on solar mythology, in which he insisted that "ancient Aryans had many solar myths" (cited in Dorson, "The Eclipse of Solar Mythology," p. 32). In 1870 George W. Cox, Müller's disciple, produced two large volumes on *The Mythology of the Aryan Nations.* Throughout these books, all the Aryan legends and fairy tales are reduced to the contest between the sun and the night. Similar "solarism" is overwhelmingly present in W. Schreder's *History of German Literature,* ed. Müller and published in Germany in 1906. For Hitler, whose obsession with the word "Aryan" is well known, the choice of the swastika as the Nazi emblem was not accidental: "The swastika—originally a Sanskrit word meaning 'all of all'—was long a symbol of Teutonic Knights. For centuries it had represented not only for Europeans, but also for certain North American Indian tribes the wheel of the sun." John Toland, *Adolf Hitler* (Garden City, N.Y.: Doubleday, 1976), p. 105. Hitler admired Wagner's *Ring des Nibelungen,* and it is no surprise that the name of the Aryan sun goddess was Brunhild (formerly Sindgund), whereas the name of the heaven god was Siegfried.

21 On the one hand, socialist realist mythos is synonymous with an inventory of heroic clichés; on the other, it fits the definition of etiological myth. This serves as an interpretative enterprise in relation to its own heroic canon, imposing an identity frame on artists by separating "those who are with us" from "those who are not." It also celebrates the origin's "eternal return" (on the wings of the Great Terror or, for example, in the guise of Lenin's heart, which, according to Vladimir Mayakovsky, "will thunder in the revolution's chest until the end of time"). In combination, the two mythological hypostases constituted a huge metalinguistic system, known as socialist realism. (See Vladimir Mayakovsky, *Vladimir Il'ich Lenin* [Moscow, 1924].)

22 See, for example, Herbert Marcuse, *Negations* (Boston: Beacon Press, 1969), 120.

23 See Vladimir Papernyi, *Kultura 2* (Ann Arbor: Ardis, 1985), p. 83.

24 As is known, some of Le Corbusier's architectural projects were not only modernist in form but also communal in content, in the sense that they were meant for communal dwelling.

25 *Uplotnenie* is the reduction of space per person in living accommodation.

26 Papernyi, *Kultura 2,* p. 83. Communalization was praised by Anatolii Lunacharskii in his film *Uplotnenie,* which was produced soon after the revolution.

27 Kabakov, quoted in Tupitsyn, "From the Communal Kitchen," p. 51.

28 "Underground is better than above ground"—that was how the artist Valentina Kulagina (Gustav Klutsis's wife) responded to the 1935 opening of the first line of the Moscow metro in her diary. In the words of the

Commissioner of Transportation, Lazar' Kaganovich, "This is why, comrades, we built such a subway, where a person ... can feel as if he is in a palace right in the middle of working Moscow" (information in Rossiskii Gosudarstvennyi Arkhiv Literatury i Isskusstva; dated May 15, 1935).

29 VSKhV (The All-Union Agricultural Exhibition) opened in August 1939. Situated on a six-hundred-acre site north of Moscow, the exhibition included pavilions representing the agricultural achievements of each of the republics. It was renamed Permanent Exhibition of Soviet Economic Achievements, or in Russian, Vystavka Dostizhenii Narodnogo Khoziaistva (VDNKh), in 1959.

30 See Jacques Derrida, "Back from Moscow, in the USSR," in *Zhak Derrida v Moskve: Dekonstruktsiia puteshestviia* (Moscow: Ad Marginem, 1993), p. 50. Also see my review of this book in *Parallax*, no. 3 (1996): 146–149.

31 This entire set of architectural codes was meant to attest to the indestructibility of the Civitas Solis (Soviet-style). Due to their immense metaphorical weight, such "solarly engaged" mental constructs, as opposed to stone or concrete constructions, were unprecedented. On the level of the signifier, this "symbolic" architecture can be viewed as "proto-postmodernist," for it resembles what Federico Fellini once called "the hallucination of a drunken pastry chef."

32 Kabakov, quoted in Tupitsyn, "From the Communal Kitchen," p. 50.

33 Gilles Deleuze, "Coldness and Cruelty," in *Masochism* (New York: Zone Books, 1991), p. 55.

34 In 1925, Georges Bataille cotranslated *L'idée de bien chez Tolstoi et Nietzsche,* a book written by the Russian philosopher Lev Shestov, whom he knew personally. Given that some of Bataille's essays (saturated with solar-centric metaphors) are focused on the intensity of the communication of anguish in collective bodies, it seems justifiable to suggest that the notion of *sobornost'* (i.e., an orthodox version of ecclesiastical communality) was communicated to the French writer through Shestov and his circle in France.

35 Richard Stites, *Revolutionary Dreams: Utopian Vision and Experimental Life in the Russian Revolution* (New York: Oxford University Press, 1989), p. 207.

36 OSA was founded at the end of 1925 and included Aleksandr and Viktor Vesnin, Moisei Ginsburg, and Il'ia Golosov. See Selim O. Khan-Magomedov, *Pioneers of Soviet Architecture* (New York: Rizzoli, 1987), pp. 594–598.

37 Anatolii Lunacharskii, cited in Stites, *Revolutionary Dreams.*

38 Ibid., p. 241.

39 This case perfectly fits Lacan's definition of the "discourse of the master." See, for example, Fredric Jameson, "Imaginary and Symbolic in Lacan," in *The Ideologies of Theory,* vol. 1 (Minneapolis: University of Minnesota Press, 1988), p. 113.

40 Peter Sloterdijk, *Critique of Cynical Reason* (Minneapolis: University of Minnesota Press, 1987), p. 70. Here, Sloterdijk points out that "proletarian existence is defined negatively: to have nothing besides offspring and to remain excluded from better chances and the riches of the life. . . . Only in the revolutionary Prolet-Cult, which blossomed in Russia shortly after the October Revolution, was there something like a *direct* class narcissism, a self-celebration of the proletariat that soon had to wither" (ibid.).

41 In my conversation with the artists Vitaly Komar and Aleksandr Melamid, they argued that "the language of power is echoed in the visual language of

the communal apartment. One example is the Mausoleum in Red Square.... If we compare the Mausoleum and a pile of shit in any communal apartment, the formal resemblance is quite obvious: the pile of shit is shaped like a pyramid. The same can be said of the Tatlin's tower. The tragedy of the Russian revolution is that no other, nonpyramidal form of society was found. In 1905, a rather popular cartoon was published depicting society as a pyramid: the workers below, then soldiers, and the government at the top. Those who looked at the Mausoleum at the time of the May Day celebrations observed the same picture: the people below, then, at the entrance, soldiers, and the government at the top." See Victor Tupitsyn, "*Drugoe*" *iskusstva* (Moscow: Ad Marginem, 1997), pp. 174–175.

42 Most of these theories rest upon the assumption that the experience of human subjects is essentially shaped by the language they speak. In this respect, one can mention Hegel's "word-concept," Heidegger's claim that "language speaks, not men," or Lacan's "the world of words that creates the world of things," and "man speaks ... because the symbol has made him man," in Jacques Lacan, *Écrits: A Selection,* trans. Alan Sheridan (New York: W. W. Norton, 1977), p. 65. Even Philippe Sollers, for whom "writing is the continuation of politics by other means," compares the revolution with a "red text," thereby attesting to the fact that nothing—whether politics or revolution or even the color red—is text-free. See Sollers's "Ecriture et révolution," in *Tel Quel: Théorie d'ensemble* (Paris: Seuil, 1968), pp. 78–79.

43 Kabakov, quoted in Tupitsyn, "From the Communal Kitchen," pp. 51–52.

44 Theodor W. Adorno, *Negative Dialectics* (New York: Continuum, 1973), p. 147. I do not share Adorno's opinion (expressed in his *Aesthetic Theory*) that the language of art is "speechlessness." And yet there is always a vacancy for external messages—commercial, political, etc.—a slot to be filled when art becomes integrated into the culture industry. Depending on the sociocultural context, this industry assumes different forms and, consequently, different modes of objectification.

45 According to Vygotsky, "Inner speech is not the interior aspect of external speech—it is a function in itself.... But while in external speech thought is embodied in words, in inner speech words die as they bring forth thought. Inner speech is to a large extent thinking in pure meaning. It is [a] dynamic, shifting, unstable thing, fluttering between words and thought." See L. S. Vygotsky, *Thought and Language,* ed. and trans. Eugenia Hanfmann and Gertrude Vakar (Cambridge, Mass.: MIT Press, 1966), p. 149. Vygotsky (1896–1934) was the leading Soviet psychologist and one of the founders of psycholinguistics.

46 Ibid., p. 145.

47 Ibid., p. 141.

48 Ibid., p. 136.

49 Félix Guattari argues that "subjectivity in the end is nothing else but a collective accommodation of utterances. As such, in certain social and semiological contexts ... subjectivity becomes collective." See Guattari, "Des subjectivités, pour le meilleur et pour le pire," *Chimères,* no. 8 (May 1990): 25–28. Dwelling upon the early ideas of Mikhail Bakhtin, Guattari speaks of channeling the flow of subjectivity between the author and a beholder. As a result, "the beholder becomes, in a way, a co-creator." Thus, instead of identifying with the personage who might—quite literally—be excluded from the realm of the representation, the viewer can choose to identify with the author's desire to break the chain of iconic signifiers. Among other issues discussed in this essay are the "means of production of polyphonic subjectivity." Incidentally, Guattari's position regarding "the vicissitudes of subjectivity" is not in disagreement with Lacan's statement that "the subject goes well beyond what is experienced 'subjectively' by the individual" (Lacan, *Écrits,* p. 55).

50 Describing the case of Billy Milligan, a criminal with multiple personalities, Samokhvalov writes: "This is the most famous case of multipersonality disorder since the diagnosis was made by American psychiatrists during the course of a forensic examination (D. Keyes, 1981). Billy was arrested in 1977 on suspicion of serial murders, child abduction and robbery. It was established that Billy had twenty-four personalities, which varied according to age and gender; among these two were dominant. The first was Arthur, an Englishman: he spoke with a British accent and dominated in calm situations; he was a capitalist and atheist, knew physics and medicine, spoke and wrote Arabic. The second was Ragen Jadaskovinich—'the keeper of the hat'; a Yugoslav who spoke English with a Slavic accent and knew Serbo-Croatian; a Communist skilled in karate and use of weapons; he dominated during moments of danger. When necessary the dominant personalities were able to turn other personalities off or on; each of these had its own anamnesis, memory and interests. In the given pathology, the personalities were marked not only by different behavior and memories, but by different EEGs and even cutaneo-galvanic coefficients: all of this may witness to the fact that a human being functions in ways similar to an orchestra: different personalities (enclosed within one's 'I') act like musical instruments. The result of a psychodrama and skill in acting are considered models of this illness (J. Bears, 1982)." (Excerpted from Samokhvalov's paper "Mnogolichnostnye problemy i futurologia lichnosti,"presented at the conference in St. Petersburg, May 1997. I received a copy of the text from the conference organizer, Viktor Mazin.)

51 Lacan's conception of the unconscious as "the discourse of the other" (*Écrits,* p. 55) is as notorious as his assertion that "the unconscious is structured in the most radical way like a language" (ibid., p. 234).

52 Vygotsky, *Thought and Language,* p. 135.

53 Keeping thoughts to oneself that are "mandated" to be shared—communal—is sabotage of speech. The silent person is suspected of privatizing language, or running a capitalist verbal enterprise, which is a breach of faith in the communal world order. There is no room in the communal for the idiosyncratic word.

54 As a degenerate form of social speech, communal speech is overwhelmed by the "traces" of egocentric speech and endophasy.

55 Kabakov, quoted in Tupitsyn, "From the Communal Kitchen," pp. 53–54.

56 In the view of the art historian Paul Wood, a similar attitude toward life was also typical of the leading representatives of the postrevolutionary avant-garde: while serving the ideal of liberating humanity, they nonetheless showed little interest in its actual living conditions. See Paul Wood, "The Politics of the Avant-Garde," in *The Great Utopia* (New York: Guggenheim Museum, 1992), pp. 1–37.

57 In the late 1940s, Mikhail Zoshchenko (along with the poet Anna Akmatova) became a target of the Zhdanovian bashing of the creative intelligentsia.

58 See, e.g., Nicolas Abraham and Maria Torok, *The Wolf Man's Magic Word: A Cryptonymy* (Minneapolis: University of Minnesota Press, 1986).

59 Osip Mandel'shtam, *The Complete Poetry of Osip Emilevich Mandelstam,* trans. Burton Ruffel and Alla Burago (Albany: State University of New York Press, 1973).

60 Pasternak's vision of "sister life" brings to mind Antigone in Sophocles' tragedy. See Boris Pasternak, *My Sister, Life and Other Poems* (New York: Harcourt Brace Jovanovich, 1976).

61 The unconscious can be compared to a zoo where "white wolves" are in the state of "pure potentiality," being unable escape from their enclosure. At the same time, it is clear that they cannot be kept there forever. Therefore, when we get married or enter a long-term relationship, we engage, as it were, in subterfuge, hoping that when the wolves finally succeed in breaking free, we will be able (unconsciously?) to throw the person we love in our place.

62 *Sis-tierka* is a playful variation of the word *siestra* ("sister" in Russian).

63 Woody Allen's film *Husbands and Wives* (1992) shows many signs of this "confessional/cathartic communality." Another example is Werner Fassbinder, who could rarely begin filming anything at all without first engaging his crew and actors in a nerve-racking communal experience. Also see Theo Altenberg, "Wiener Aktionismus und AA Kommune," *Texte zur Kunst,* no. 10 (1993): 121–127.

64 G. W. F. Hegel, introduction to *Lectures on the Philosophy of History* (New York: Colonial Press, 1900), pp. 109–110.

65 For details, see Edward Said, *Orientalism* (New York: Pantheon Books, 1978).

66 Decommunalization took place also at the level of the everyday; for example, in the sweep of Khrushchev's building programs, which were charged with the resettling of people from the communal apartments of Stalin's time. See chapter 2.

CHAPTER 2

1 Among the most influential cultural events were the exhibition of Picasso's works in fall 1956 (organized with the cooperation of Ilya Ehrenburg, a friend of the artist); the international open-air exhibition in Moscow's Gorky Park under the aegis of the Sixth World Festival of Youth and Students, in summer 1957; the "National American Exhibition" in Sokol'niki Park in summer 1959, which displayed works by Jackson Pollock, Willem de Kooning, Adolph Gottlieb, Mark Rothko, and William Baziotes; and on the same site, the "French National Exhibition" opened in summer 1961, and presented work by artists affiliated with the School of Paris. For more on this period, see Margarita Tupitsyn, "Avant-Garde and Kitsch" in her *Margins of Soviet Art: Socialist Realism to the Present* (Milan: Giancarlo Politi Editore, 1989), pp. 23–37; and Margarita Tupitsyn, *Against Kandinsky* (Cologne: Hatje Cantz, 2006), pp. 163–167.

2 "Alternative" artists, who were institutionalized under the aegis of MOSKh, usually abstained from confrontations with the institutional power for fear of losing their privileges, such as studios and small commissions.

3 The Leningrad "Barracks School" is associated with Sholom Shvarts, Rikhard Vasmi, Vladimir Shagin, and Aleksandr Aref'ev.

4 Sots art is discussed in the second part of this chapter and, in more detail, in chapter 4.

5 This project was initiated in 1919–1920 by female avant-gardists Liubov' Popova and Varvara Stepanova.

6 The term "dissident modernism" was coined by Margarita Tupitsyn in the early 1980s. Other similar terms are "nonconformism," "underground" (or "unofficial") culture, "alternative art," etc.

7 Quoted in Leonid Talochkin and Irina Alpatova, ed., *Drugoe Iskusstvo: Moskva 1956–76*, vol. 1 (Moscow: SP "Interbuk," 1991), p. 83.

8 Ilya Kabakov, quoted in Victor Tupitsyn, "From the Communal Kitchen: A Conversation with Ilya Kabakov," *Arts* (October 1991): 53.

9 See M. M. Bakhtin, *The Dialogical Imagination: Four Essays by M. M. Bakhtin*, trans. Carl Emerson and Michael Holquist (Austin: University of Texas Press, 1981).

10 This pessimistic evaluation comes as no surprise, considering that socialist realism was perceived as the epitome of the Soviet identity, which "dissident modernists" did not want to be associated with.

11 See Rosalind E. Krauss, *The Originality of the Avant-Garde and Other Modernist Myths* (Cambridge, Mass.: MIT Press, 1985).

12 When, in the 1980s, Iakovlev's relatives had him institutionalized, the artist's colleagues (Nemukhin and others) visited him regularly. His release from the hospital could not be arranged until the early 1990s.

13 However tempting the comparison may be, this ship should not be confused with the *Titanic:* its itinerary was different and there were hardly any icebergs around.

14 For a detailed overview of Western artists' fascination with, or knowledge of, the Russian avant-garde, see Maurice Tuchman, "The Russian Avant-Garde and the Contemporary Artist," in *The Avant-Garde in Russia, 1910–1930: New Perspectives* (Los Angeles: Los Angeles County Museum of Art; Cambridge, Mass.: MIT Press, 1980), pp. 118–121. The kinship between American minimalism and Russian constructivism and suprematism has been a subject of a number of studies and continues to inspire more. Less analyzed is the influence of Ivan Dabrowsky (Dan Graham) on Jackson Pollock, or of Aleksei Brodovich on American photography and design. Published in 1962, Camilla Gray's *The Great Experiment: Russian Art, 1863–1922* (London: Thames and Hudson) had a great impact on American postexpressionist abstraction. In 1967, George Rickey's *Constructivism: Origins and Evolution* (New York: G. Braziller) claimed that a number of postwar sculptors inherited Soviet constructivist precepts. As Margarita Tupitsyn points out, "discussions of the Soviet avant-garde [in relation to postwar art] were generally motivated by a desire to give more historical weight to American Minimalism" (*Against Kandinsky*, p. 172, n. 29). On American minimalism and the Russian avant-garde, see Hal Foster, "Some Uses and Abuses of Russian Constructivism," in *Art into Life: Russian Constructivism, 1914–1932* (New York: Rizzoli, 1990), pp. 241–253; and Benjamin H. D. Buchloh, "Constructing (the History of) Sculpture," in *Reconstructing Modernism*, ed. Serge Guilbaut (Cambridge, Mass.: MIT Press, 1989), pp. 85–110. Also see Donald Judd's review of Malevich's exhibition at the Guggenheim Museum in *Art in America* (March-April 1974): 52–58, and Frank Stella's essay "About Kandinsky," in the exhibition catalogue

Kandinsky: Hauptwerke aus dem Centre Georges Pompidou, Paris (Paris: Centre Georges Pompidou; Tübingen: Kunsthalle, 1999), pp. 220–227.

15 Talochkin and Alpatova, *Drugoe Iskusstvo,* p. 9.

16 Three days after Khrushchev's visit to the Manezh, the show's organizers were officially censured for "permitting" formalism; some of its participants were reprimanded.

17 Quoted in P. Sjeklocha and I. Mead, *Unofficial Art in the Soviet Union* (Berkeley: University of California Press, 1967), p. 94; and in P. Johnson and L. Labedz, eds., *Khrushchev and the Arts: The Politics of Soviet Culture* (Cambridge, Mass.: MIT Press, 1965), pp. 102–103. (A comparison with the U.S. Congress comes to mind, specifically their reaction to the work of Robert Mapplethorpe and Andres Serrano.)

18 Ilya Kabakov, quoted in Victor Tupitsyn, *Glaznoe iabloko razdora: Besedy s Il'ei Kabakovym* (Moscow: NLO, 2006), p. 26.

19 See Slavoj Žižek, *For They Know Not What They Do: Enjoyment as a Political Factor* (London: Verso, 1991), p. 134. In Shteinberg's letter, Malevich is addressed as a prophet, which is typical of those individuals (Russian and Western alike) who cannot distinguish metaphysics from mysticism. For details, see my "Incitement and Thought," in Margarita Tupitsyn, *Malevich and Film* (New Haven: Yale University Press, 2002), pp. 125–146.

20 Similarly, in 1995, American art historian Moira Roth set up a fictional correspondence with Marcel Duchamp, who had died in 1968.

21 Quoted in Victor Tupitsyn, *Kommunal'nyi postmodernism* (Moscow: Ad Marginem, 1998).

22 Here, I am citing Roginskii's words from our conversation in Paris in 1985.

23 Yve Alain Bois, "From $-\infty$ to $+\infty$: Axonometry, or Lissitzky's Mathematical Paradigm," in *El Lissitzky* (Eindhoven: Municipal Van Abbemuseum, 1990), p. 29.

24 This orator is a party leader giving a speech in a Kremlin assembly hall. The image was printed on the cover of the magazine *Ogonek,* which served as the point of departure for Vasil'ev's painting. In it, a "speech-vision," inherent to socialist realism, is supplanted by "pure visuality" (a gaze, inattentive to the tuning fork of voice).

25 See the interview with Ivan Chuikov in Victor Tupitsyn, *"Drugoe" iskusstva* (Moscow: Ad Marginem, 1997), pp. 75–77.

26 Ibid.

27 See Erik Bulatov, "O kartine," *Flash Art* (Russian edition), no. 1 (1989): 139.

28 According to Kabakov and Bulatov, both of them were fond of railroad posters in the early 1970s. The railroad crossing sign "Dangerous," which warned against the approach of trains, was the prime source for Bulatov's painting *Dangerous.* Kabakov wrote an essay on the subject, titled "Two Railwaymen" (1981; unpublished text in Margarita and Victor Tupitsyn Archive, New York and Paris).

29 Besides Kabakov, and of course Komar and Melamid, Irina Nakhova is one of the pioneers of the installation medium in Russia. Her first installation, *Room no. 1,* was realized in 1983 in her Moscow apartment.

30 An example of this is Pivovarov's album *Don't You Recognize Me?* (1981), in which a communal character faces everyday objects.

31 Jacques Derrida, *L'écriture et la différance* (Paris: Editions du Seuil, 1967), p. 289.

32 Here, I cite Komar and Melamid's ironic self-definition, which was inscribed on their *Double Self-Portrait* (1972–1973).

33 During the performance, Komar and Melamid were shredding pages of the newspaper *Pravda.*

34 This is how Jacques Derrida defines deconstruction in "Signature Event Context," in *A Derrida Reader: Between the Blinds,* ed. Peggy Kamuf (New York: Columbia University Press, 1991), p. 108.

35 "Speech-vision" is a term coined by the Moscow philosopher Mikhail Ryklin. See chapter 9, note 13.

36 In Kabakov's installations, the extracommunal *sur-moi* (i.e., the state) became an object of critical reflection only in the beginning of the 1990s. During the same period, Komar and Melamid began to pay attention to the communal *moi:* in 1993, they produced two paintings, *America's Most Wanted* and *America's Most Unwanted,* based on "collective responses" obtained through a "scientific poll of American tastes in Art."

37 If one accepts this interpretation, it would seem to apply to the work of Kosolapov, Sokov, and Boris Orlov, but by no means to that of Komar and Melamid or Bulatov.

38 A toy that had its American heyday in the 1970s, as in "weebles wobble but they won't fall down."

39 In 1982, Iurii Andropov succeeded Leonid Brezhnev as the Secretary General of CPSU.

40 "Unauthorized" photographs are those which have not been commissioned or approved by the authorities.

41 See Margarita Tupitsyn, *Sots Art* (New York: New Museum of Contemporary Art, 1986).

42 See *Poezdki za gorod* (Trips outside the city) (Moscow: Ad Marginem, 1998).

43 Quoted from Victor Tupitsyn and Il'ia Kabakov, "Serebrianyi dvorets," *Kh/Zh,* no. 42 (2002): 10–14.

44 Letter from Andrei Monastyrsky to Victor Tupitsyn, spring 1980, Victor and Margarita Tupitsyn Archive.

45 In September of the same year, an exhibition at the VDNKh (House of Culture) included 522 works by 145 artists.

46 Michel Foucault, *La volonté du savoir,* vol. 1 of *Histoire de la sexualité* (Paris: Gallimard, 1976), 126; translation mine.

47 Petr Miturich's *Graphic Dictionary* (1919) was a visual interpretation of Velimir Khlebnikov's "Starry Alphabet."

48 Among those who emigrated were Mikhail Chernyshov, Mikhail Grobman, Iurii Kuper, Mikhail Kulakov, Genrikh Khudiakov, Vagrich Bakhchanian, Aleksandr Kosolapov, Lidiia Masterkova, Valentin Vorob'ev, Vitalii Dlugi, Oleg Kudriashov, Oleg Prokof'ev, Vasilii Sitnikov, Lev Nussberg, Grigorii Perkel', Sergei Esaian, Aleksei Khvostenko, Mikhail Roginskii, Vitaly Komar, Aleksandr Melamid, Oleg Tselkov, Igor' Shelkovskii, Ernst Neizvestnyi, Rimma and Valerii Gerlovin, Leonid Sokov, Aleksandr Driuchin, Mikhail Odnoralov, Leonid Lamm, and many others.

49 A similar decree was later issued to deprive Igor' Shelkovskii, editor of the journal *A-Ya,* of his Soviet citizenship.

50 The use of such a term as "maternal" in the case of communal speech is not accidental here. Likewise, Gilles Deleuze, in his "Coldness and Cruelty," in *Masochism* (New York: Zone Books, 1991), identifies hegemony of speech

as immanent to agrarian sects and collectives (the "Law of the Commune") with the so-called oral mother.

51 See V. Tupitsyn and M. Tupitsyn, *Moskva–N'ui-Iork* (Moscow–New York) (Moscow: WAM, 2006), pp. 124–254.

52 Letter from Andrei Monastyrsky to Victor Tupitsyn, July 19, 1981, Victor and Margarita Tupitsyn Archive; printed in Tupitsyn and Tupitsyn, *Moskva–N'ui-Iork,* p. 181. The action *Pour* took place July 7, 1981, in Moscow.

53 This thought is borrowed from Margarita Tupitsyn, *Margins of Soviet Art,* p. 100.

54 Apt art exhibitions were reconstructed in America by the present author in several exhibition spaces between 1983 and 1986. I curated the last one along with Margarita Tupitsyn at the New Museum of Contemporary Art in New York in 1986.

55 See Victor and Margarita Tupitsyn, "At the Studios on Furmannyi Lane," *Flash Art,* no. 142 (1988).

56 Letter from Nikita Alekseev to Victor Tupitsyn, February 18, 1983, Victor and Margarita Tupitsyn Archive; printed in Tupitsyn and Tupitsyn, *Moskva–N'ui-Iork,* p. 230.

57 From 1985 to 1986, the Kindergarden group hosted exhibitions of works by Igor' Kopystianskii and Svetlana Kopystianskaia, Sergei Shutov, Sergei Volkov, Vladimir Naumets, and Alekseev.

58 Champions of the World, initially under the influence of Zvezdochetov, enticed such occupants of the Furmannyi Lane Studios as Igor' Zaidel' and Vadim Fishkin into their orbit.

59 Among such exhibitions were "The Object in Contemporary Art" (Ob'ekt), Gorkom of Graphic Artists, Moscow, 1987; "The Retrospective, 1957–1987" (Retrospektsiia, 1957–1987), Hermitage Society, Moscow, 1987; "Iskunstvo," Berlin, 1988; three exhibitions sponsored by the Avant-Gardists' Club (1987–1989); "Expensive Art" (Dorogoe iskusstvo), Youth Palace, Moscow, 1989; "The Photo in Painting" (Foto v zhivopisi), Pervaiia Galereia, Moscow, 1989; "From Unofficial Art to Perestroika," Exhibition Pavilion at the Pier, Leningrad, 1989; "The Green Show," Exit Art, New York, 1989; "The Work of Art in the Age of Perestroika," Phyllis Kind Gallery, New York, 1990; "Between Spring and Summer: Conceptualism in the Era of Late Communism," Institute of Contemporary Art, Boston, 1990; "Toward the Object" (V storonu ob'ekta), Tsaritsyno Museum, near Moscow, 1990; "Schizo-China: Hallucination in Power" (Shizo-Kitai: Galutsinatsiia u vlasti), the Avant-Gardists' Club, Moscow, 1990.

60 The Russian issue of *Flash Art,* compiled and edited by Victor and Margarita Tupitsyn, was distributed in Moscow and Leningrad.

61 This has become possible through the efforts of several people, including Margarita Tupitsyn and me (in the United States), as well as some other ex-Soviet scholars and theorists.

62 Among such exhibitions were "Geopolitics" (Geopolitika), Ethnographic Museum, St. Petersburg, 1991; "Another Art" (Drugoe iskusstvo), State Tret'iakov Gallery, Moscow, 1991; "Perspectives of Conceptualism," Clock Tower, P.S. 1, New York, 1991; "Topography" (Topografiia), Galereia *L,* Moscow, 1993; "From Malevich to Kabakov," Ludwig Museum, Cologne, 1993; "After Perestroika: Kitchenmaids or Stateswomen," Independent Curators Inc., New York, 1993; "Collective Actions," Exit Art, New York,

1997; "Kabinet," Stedelijk Museum, Amsterdam, 1997. For more details, see my article "Semnadtsat' let spustia," NLO (*Novoe literaturnoe obozrenie*), no. 83 (2007): 680–684.

63 Two years before the collapse of the USSR, the group *Eti* (These) had also held a "test action" in Red Square. On April 19, 1991, Osmolovskii and other members of the group lay down on the pavement in front of the Lenin mausoleum so that their bodies formed the word *khui* (prick).

64 Gilles Deleuze, "Becoming-Animal," in *The Deleuze Reader,* ed. Constantin V. Boundas (New York: Columbia University Press, 1993), p. 121.

65 Ibid.

66 In June 1995, the artist Haralampi Oroschakoff organized the project *Kräftemessen* at Künstlerwerkstatt Lothringerstrasse, Munich. It aimed at a comprehensive examination of Russian art of the 1990s. The curators, Margarita Tupitsyn, Boris Groys, and Viktor Misiano, provided three different interpretations of post-Soviet visual culture. In the first exhibition, "Damaged Utopia," Tupitsyn used the indispensable tools of distancing and nostalgia to communicate her message—farewell to the Utopian. See *Kräftemessen,* ed. Haralampi G. Oroschakoff (Ostfildern: Cantz, 1995). Texts in English, German, and Russian.

67 "Zone of nondifferentiation" is one of Monastyrsky's key concepts adopted by the Collective Actions group (CA). This is the zone to which viewers are navigated by the performance's organizers so that they can experience the phenomenon of an ambiguous reading, with the impossibility of differentiating between representation of the fact and the fact of representation.

CHAPTER 3

1 *The Poems of Mao Tse-tung,* trans. Willis Barnstone (New York: Bantam Books, 1972).

2 However different, writing between the ruins does not exclude Adorno's "writing of the ruins." See, for example, James Martin Harding, *Adorno and "A Writing of the Ruins": Essays on Modern Aesthetics and Anglo-American Literature and Culture* (Albany: State University of New York Press, 1997).

3 Whereas Joseph Kosuth prefers the term "art-as-idea," Bernar Venet emphasizes "art-as-knowledge," and Douglas Huebler—"art-as-documentation." As for Terry Atkinson, Ian Burn, Mel Ramsden, and some other members of the Art-Language group, "the redefinition of artwork as syntactical" turns conceptual art into a metalinguistic enterprise.

4 The Collective Actions group originated in 1976 and consisted (along with Monastyrsky) of such artists as Nikita Alekseev, Nikolai Panitkov, Georgii Kizeval'ter, Igor' Makarevich, Elena Elagina, and the philologists Sergei Romashko and Sabina Haensgen.

5 On the Medical Hermeneutics group, see Victor Tupitsyn, "The Inspection of Inspectors," *Flash Art,* no. 148 (October 1989); and also Victor Tupitsyn and Ilya Kabakov, "Parallels Lebe oder Leben im Kanon," *Neue Bildende Kunst,* no. 6 (December 1999). In reference to Mukhomor and SZ, see Victor and Margarita Tupitsyn, "The Studios on Furmannyi Lane in Moscow," *Flash Art,* no. 142 (October 1988). The Champions of the World were featured in the Russian edition of *Flash Art,* guest-edited by Victor and Margarita Tupitsyn, 1989.

6 Ilya Kabakov, quoted in Victor Tupitsyn, "From the Communal Kitchen: A Conversation with Ilya Kabakov," *Arts* (October 1991): 50.

7 Ibid., p. 51.

8 Ibid., p. 49.

9 Ibid.

10 Terry Eagleton, *Walter Benjamin, or Towards a Revolutionary Criticism* (London: Verso, 1981), p. 92.

11 This term combines Benjamin's concept of the artist as a producer with Deleuze and Guattari's vision of deterritorialized subjectivity in *L'Anti-Oedipe* (1972) and in *Mille plateaux* (1980).

12 Kabakov, quoted in Tupitsyn, "From the Communal Kitchen," p. 55.

13 Ilya Kabakov and Victor Tupitsyn, "The Piper of Disaster: Boris Mikhailov's 'Calm' Photographs," in *Boris Mikhailov: Case History* (Zurich: Scalo Verlag, 1999), pp. 473–478.

14 Harold Bloom, *Poetry and Repression: Revisionism from Blake to Stevens* (New Haven: Yale University Press, 1976), p. 18.

15 Ibid., p. 4. "Creative misreading" echoes Claude Lévi-Strauss's reference (in his *The Elementary Structures of Kinship*) to "a misuse of language" among the Andaman Islanders. In part, these notions seem to be synonymous with what Jacques Lacan referred to as the function of *méconnaissance* (misrecognition). See Lacan, *Écrits* (Paris: Editions du Seuil, 1996), p. 99.

16 To a degree, abbreviational optics characterizes any reading and any remembrance.

17 See, for example, L. S. Vygotsky, *Thought and Language,* ed. and trans. Eugenia Hanfmann and Gertrude Vakar (Cambridge, Mass.: MIT Press, 1966). Vygotsky's writings are discussed and applied in chapter 1.

18 Kabakov, quoted in Tupitsyn, "From the Communal Kitchen," p. 53.

19 Bloom, *Poetry and Repression,* p. 7.

20 Kabakov, quoted in Tupitsyn, "From the Communal Kitchen," p. 55.

21 Bloom, *Poetry and Repression,* p. 26.

22 See, e.g., Nicholas Abraham and Maria Torok, *The Wolf Man's Magic Word: A Cryptonymy,* trans. Nicholas Rand (Minneapolis: University of Minnesota Press, 1986).

23 Vladimir Nabokov, *The Gift,* trans. Michael Scammel (New York: G. P. Putnam's Sons, 1963), p. 30.

24 It is actually both phono- and audioclastic, i.e., *phonaudioclastic.*

25 "Mythical speech" is the term used by Roland Barthes in his *Mythologies,* trans. Annette Lavers (London: Vintage, 1993).

26 Besides the indistinguishable nature of these images, it was obviously impossible to develop film and print photographs in a snowy field near Moscow.

27 These are two fictional characters that Komar and Melamid introduced in a series of works executed in the 1970s. See Carter Ratcliff, *Komar & Melamid* (New York: Abbeville Press, 1988), pp. 68–75.

28 Foucault's "Archive" is a quasi-historicist version of what I call the "abbreviarium"—a mnemonic landscape structured by "symbolic ruins." The abbreviarium is also an allusion to "verbarium," the neologism coined by Nicholas Abraham. (See Abraham and Torok, *The Wolf Man's Magic Word.*)

29 *Trips outside the City* (Poezdki za gorod), a documentation of CA performances, was printed in Moscow by Ad Marginem (1998).

30 In the late 1970s and early 1980s, sots artists' reaction toward Kabakov's sensibility oscillated between two prefixes, non- and anti-. The latter (the antithetical mode) reached its peak when open polemics took place. See *Beseda* (Paris), ed. T. Goricheva, no. 3 (1985) and no. 4 (1986).

31 From a conversation between Monastyrsky and the present author, recorded in 1979 and printed in 2005. See Victor Tupitsyn, "Kontseptual'nyi khudozhnik: Sektant ili litsedei?" (Conceptual artist: A sectary or a guisard?), *Kh/Zh*, no. 60 (2005): 23–25.

32 One needs to read all five volumes of *Trips outside the City* (Poezdki za gorod) to figure out whether the third path chosen by CA will ever prove to be a way to cure artistic language, a form of linguistic neurosurgery.

33 Kabakov, quoted in Tupitsyn, "From the Communal Kitchen," p. 55.

34 Although Mikhailov lived in Kharkov (Ukraine), he would frequently come to Moscow to show his new work to Kabakov who (for many years) was his only audience. See my conversation with Mikhailov in Margarita and Victor Tupitsyn, *Verbal Photography: Ilya Kabakov, Boris Mikhailov, and the Moscow Archive of New Art* (Porto: Museu Serralves, 2004).

35 See Mikhailov's series *Unfinished Dissertation* (1980s) and *Viscidity* (1982) in Margarita and Victor Tupitsyn, *Verbal Photography.*

36 See M. M. Bakhtin, *The Dialogical Imagination: Four Essays by M. M. Bakhtin,* trans. Carl Emerson and Michael Holquist (Austin: University of Texas Press, 1981).

37 Kabakov uses this term to characterize his re-creations of Soviet communal *faktura* in a museum space.

CHAPTER 4

1 Benjamin first used this term in 1931. See Walter Benjamin, "Small History of Photography," in *One-Way Street,* trans. Edmund Jephcott and Kingsley Shorter (London: New Left Books, 1979).

2 Reflecting on the sources of the Cartesian visual paradigm in the context of Soviet history, one has to note that in order to steer clear of bourgeois "new" forms that "only mask the old bourgeois content," the socialist realists rejected the Baudelairian (i.e., modernist) conception of style in favor of the Cartesian concept of "method." The first Congress of the Soviet Writers' Union in 1934 called upon those working in the sphere of culture to "truthfully depict . . . reality in its revolutionary development. Here, the truthfulness and historical specificity of artistic representation must be in accord with the task of ideological reconstruction and of educating workers in the spirit of socialism. This method of literary fiction and literary criticism is what we call the method of socialist realism" (*The First All-Union Congress of Soviet Writers,* transcript [Moscow, 1934], p. 4). Stalin defined socialist realism as art that is "national in its form, socialist in its content." Zhdanov transformed Stalin's definition into a theory of the dialectical unity of "folkishness" and *partiynost* (party-ness). Armed with these formulas, the practitioners of socialist realism created a system of key mythological plots and narratives, adapted for the purpose of repeated didactic representation of the revolutionary past and the equally revolutionary present. "The civil war in art continues": in this remark made by Kazimir Malevich, one could substitute for "art" any other sphere of activity, any other *front* of socialist change.

The phenomenon of the metonymic inheritance of the metaphor of revolution ensured the continuity of terror, transported from the field of revolutionary battles to the field of revolutionary construction.

3 Sots art is described in chapter 2. This unofficial art movement is associated with former Soviet painters and sculptors such as Vitaly Komar and Aleksandr Melamid; Leonid Sokov; Boris Orlov; Rostislav Lebedev; Aleksandr Kosolapov; the Kazimir Passion group; and the photographers Boris Mikhailov, Vladimir Kupriianov, and Igor' Mukhin. Sots art has also been on the minds of D. A. Prigov, Erik Bulatov, Ilya Kabakov, Eduard Gorokhovskii, Oleg Vasil'ev, Grisha Bruskin, Sergei Mironenko, and a number of other artists.

4 The same is true of China or North Korea. However tempting, recontextualization of authoritarian imagery eliminates some of its functions and changes its perception. It suffices to mention Pablo Picasso's "scandalous" Stalin sketch, printed in *Les Lettres Françaises* in 1953, and Andy Warhol's *Mao,* produced in 1972 (coincidentally, the year that sots art began).

5 "Transreferential" is a combination of "transferential" and "referential," for it transfers and refers at the same time.

6 With verbal maturation, the transition is made from the mirror stage to the territory of *je,* to the "Symbolic order," which has to do with an identity constructed at the demand of the Other, and differs from the "Imaginary order" in that the identificatory function can be transferred from image to image, from picture to word, etc. The third Lacanian register—*le réel*—cannot be confused with reality, which (in Lacan words) represents "its grimace." *Le réel* is manifested in inconsistencies, lapses and breaks in which the Symbolic order abounds. Here, *le réel* turns out to be a mediator in the relationship between the Imaginary and the Symbolic. See Jacques Lacan, *Écrits* (Paris: Édition du Seuil, 1966), pp. 793–827. Also see Lacan's "Television," trans. Denis Hollier, Rosalind Krauss, and Annette Michelson, *October,* no. 40 (1987): 5–50.

7 Aleksei Khomiakov (1804–1860), eminent Slavophile philosopher; Vladimir Solov'ev (1853–1900), major Russian religious philosopher; Lev Karsavin (1882–1952), religious philosopher.

8 For a closer examination, see Slavoj Žižek, *For They Know Not What They Do: Enjoyment as a Political Factor* (London: Verso, 1991), pp. 233–277. Also see Hal Foster, "Death in America," *October,* no. 75 (Winter 1996): 37–59.

9 This condition can be referred to as ideological *jouissance.*

10 Here, this means the ideological "object of desire."

11 The distinctions between the substages of the mirror stage can be defined in the Freudian terms, "*Fort! Da!*"—where "*Da!*"corresponds to the first substage and "*Fort!*" to the second.

12 The Soviet regime, which tried to prevent the accumulation of large doses of collective (rather than individual) alienation, always gave preference to group (rather than personal) perception. That is why the *kommunalka* (the communal ghetto in Stalin's Russia), with its confessional-cathartic response to authoritarian iconography, should be regarded as the Stalinist analogue of the first substage of the mirror stage.

13 Margarita Tupitsyn, *Kriticheskoe opticheskoe* (Moscow: Ad Marginem, 1997), p. 192.

14 What *Brezhnev in Crimea* brings to light is that Bulatov's career has always been mediated by the discourse of power, which is particularly true of the "dialogue" between his negatively charged painting of the 1970s or 1980s and the affirmative art of socialist realists.

15 Victor Tupitsyn, "Beseda s Komarom i Melamidom: vtoroi razgovor," in "*Drugoe*" *iskusstva* (Moscow: Ad Marginem, 1997), p. 174.

16 Claude Lefort, *Democracy and Political Theory* (Minneapolis: University of Minnesota Press, 1988), p. 244.

17 This rudiment or remnant of the identificatory function echoes the notion of the "trace" (in Derrida's terminology).

18 Jacques Lacan, "The Neurotic Individual's Myth," *Psychoanalytic Quarterly* 48 (1979): 422–423.

19 Genrikh Sapgir (1928–2004), an alternative Russian poet.

20 The mirror stage and the theory of the *moi* were articulated in Jacques Lacan's 1949 paper on "The Looking-Glass Phase," delivered at the sixteenth international congress of the International Psychoanalytic Association in Zurich.

21 According to Adorno, "identity is the primary form of ideology," and "any definition is identification." See Theodor W. Adorno, *Negative Dialectics* (New York: Continuum, 1973), pp. 148–149.

22 Identity corrupts. Nevertheless, to reject identification would be analogous to fish bailing themselves out of water.

23 Adorno, *Negative Dialectics,* p. 147.

CHAPTER 5

1 This campaign was led by Andrei Zhdanov, Nikolai Ezhov, and Platon Kerzhentsev.

2 Jean-François Lyotard, *The Postmodern Condition: A Report on Knowledge* (Minneapolis: University of Minnesota Press, 1979), p. 74.

3 Such a reaction to the genre of photography by the powers that be goes back to the times of romanticism and symbolism, when it seemed to many that photography's connotative potential was below its denotative possibilities. Authors who wrote about the first daguerreotypes in 1840 outdid themselves inventing synthesizing terms such as solar agency, "heliography" (Samuel Morse), or "pencil of nature" (Fox Talbot). For a closer examination, see, for example, Allan Sekula, "On the Invention of Photographic Meaning," in *Thinking Photography,* ed. Victor Burgin (London: Macmillan, 1990), pp. 86–87.

4 On this point Adorno totally disagreed with Benjamin. Unlike the author of *Illuminations,* he did not think that photography and the film provide the most suitable means for "deritualization of art." For details, see Walter Benjamin, "The Work of Art in the Age of Mechanical Reproduction," in *Illuminations* (New York: Schocken, 1969).

5 Jürgen Habermas, *The Structural Transformation of the Public Sphere* (Cambridge, Mass.: MIT Press, 1989), p. 201.

6 The first effort to make color photography was in connection with the Soviet Pavilion at the New York World's Fair in 1939. One year later, however, *Soviet Photo* reported that this experiment remained largely unsuccessful and that prints used in exhibition designs were hand-colored

with oil bromide. See Margarita Tupitsyn, *Glaube, Hoffnung, Anpassung, 1928–1945* (Essen: Museum Folkwang, 1995), p. 160.

7 I am referring to Fedor Antonov's 1938 painting *Disclosure of the Enemy in the Workshop* (Archive of the Ministry of Culture of the Russian Federation).

8 Walter Benjamin, "Moscow Diary," *October,* no. 35 (1985): 6–7.

9 Serebriakova used photographic readymades, i.e., found or archival photographs.

10 Nikolai Chuzhak, ed., *Literatura fakta* (Moscow: Federatsiia, 1929), p. 21.

11 Mikhail Bakhtin, *Toward a Philosophy of the Act,* ed. Vladimir Liapunov and Michael Holquist (Austin: University of Texas Press, 1993), p. 47.

12 Ibid., p. ix.

13 In Jacques Derrida's view, the insistence on factography is a symptom of metaphysical and/or phenomenological orientation, peculiar to Benjamin's writings of the late 1920s (specifically, "Moscow Diary"). In *Zhak Derrida v Moskve,* Derrida unfolds the metaphysical dimension of what he calls "being-in-construction," which—according to Benjamin—can "be formulated . . . only on the basis of economic facts" (Benjamin, "Moscow Diary, pp. 6–7); Derrida, *Zhak Derrida v Moskve: Dekonstruktsiia puteshestviia* (Moscow: Ad Marginem, 1993), p. 50. Also see *Soviet Factography: A Special Issue,* ed. Devin Fore, *October,* no. 118 (Fall 2006).

14 Bakhtin, *Toward a Philosophy of the Act,* p. 47.

15 Under Stalin, taking photographs of streets, squares, or industrial sites (even if intended for limited circulation) required special permission.

16 "Damaged Utopia" was curated by Margarita Tupitsyn and realized within the *Kräftemessen* project. This exhibition took place at Künstlerwerkstatt Lothringer Strasse, Munich, Germany, June 1–July 30, 1995.

17 *Murk* is somewhat closer to the Russian title of this series, *Sumerki,* which means "submurk," the state of submerging into darkness.

18 See Benjamin H. D. Buchloch, "From Faktura to Factography," *October,* no. 30 (Fall 1984): 81–118.

19 "Being-toward-death" is the term coined by Martin Heidegger in *Sein und Zeit* (1927).

20 Jacques Derrida, "Back from Moscow, in the USSR," in *Zhak Derrida v Moskve,* p. 58.

21 See Benjamin, "Moscow Diary," 6–7.

22 Derrida, "Back from Moscow, in the USSR," p. 55.

23 CA members took part in the earlier performance and were the people actually shown in the photographs.

24 Michel Foucault, *The Archaeology of Knowledge and The Discourse on Language,* trans. Sheridan Smith (New York: Pantheon Books, 1972), p. 127. In Hiroshi Sugimoto's "Portraits," the same vacancy is filled by the figures of famous people in wax museum.

25 The light pressure of *heliocracy* is analogous with "white mythology," as Derrida terms it in *Margins of Philosophy* (Chicago: University of Chicago Press, 1982).

26 Nietzsche quoted in "Spurs: Nietzsche's Styles," in *A Derrida Reader: Between the Blinds,* ed. Peggy Kamuf (New York: Columbia University Press, 1991), p. 375 (n. 4).

27 Lyotard attributes this "lack of reality" to the "aesthetic of the sublime," which—among other things—"makes it possible to subordinate thought to the gaze and to turn it away rom the unpresentable" (*The Postmodern Condition,* p. 79). Later, in "Glose sur la résistance," *Le postmoderne expliqué aux enfants* (Paris: Galilée, 1986), pp. 137–151, Lyotard's position became equitable with that of Claude Lefort, who claimed that "lack of reality" is caused by the totalitarian power of metanarrative. See Claude Lefort's essay on Orwell in *Ecrire, à l'épreuve du politique* (Paris: Calmann-Lévy, 1992).

CHAPTER 6

1 A Vrubel retrospective was on view at the Kunsthalle Düsseldorf (January 25–April 13, 1997) and the Haus der Kunst München (May 8–July 20, 1997).

2 These two works were included in this particular exhibition. Larisa Zvezdochetova, Mariia Serebriakova, and Svetlana Kopystianskaia did not participate in the show because they were either traveling or working abroad.

3 Among those who focus on various aspects of female sexuality are Bella Matveeva, a painter from St. Petersburg, and the photographers Vita Bujvid and Tanya Liberman.

4 For the details, see Margarita Tupitsyn, *After Perestroika: Kitchenmaids or Stateswomen* (New York: Independent Curators Inc., 1993).

5 Nonverbal vision is the romantic fantasy of a number of modern theorists comparable to the fantasy of feminine chastity.

6 Elagina executed this installation in collaboration with Igor' Makarevich.

7 Elena Elagina, quoted in Victor Tupitsyn, "Utopia as Utoplennik: Russian Artists Speak for Themselves," in *Kräftemessen,* ed. Haralampi G. Oroschakoff (Ostfildern: Cantz, 1995), p. 205.

8 It's worth mentioning that some important exhibitions of sots art, apt art, Moscow conceptualism, and Russian women artists took place in Western art museums long before perestroika. The same is true of the discourse on Russian visual culture—contrary to the position taken by some post-Soviet art publications, in which perestroika is (practically) equated with *l'origine du monde.*

9 Svetlana Kopystianskaia, quoted in my "Beseda so Svetlanoi i Igorem Kopystiankimi." See Victor Tupitsyn, "*Drugoe*" *iskusstva* (Moscow: Ad Marginem, 1997), p. 187.

10 Ibid.

11 Anasemia is a "process of problematizing the meaning of signs in an undermined way." See Nicolas Abraham and Maria Torok, *The Wolf Man's Magic Word: A Cryptonymy (*Minneapolis: University of Minnesota Press, 1986), p. 117 (n. 1).

12 An "allosemic double" is a quasi-synonym associated with some cryptic word, either semantically or phonetically. Ibid., pp. xi–xiii.

13 The first discussion of homosexuality in relation to Russian art can be found in Victor and Margarita Tupitsyn, "Timur and Afrika," *Flash Art,* no. 151 (March-April 1990): 122–125.

14 In this sentence I deliberately "misrecognize" art as a woman in order to demonstrate the inner working of the patriarchal unconscious (e.g., the synchronic system of the signifier).
15 Even very serious and fairly professional television newscasters in Moscow would never miss their chance to make a dismissive comment about feminists' activities in the West.
16 In 1996, I witnessed an enthusiastic endorsement of pornography on Moscow television. The event was sponsored by a bunch of "wild capitalists" who looked as fearsome as their bodyguards. The presentation reached its climax when topless women were encouraged to eat chocolate penises while sitting on the sponsors' laps.
17 See note 18. Orality goes back not only to the practice of breast-feeding, or to the experience of learning about the world by stuffing various objects in one's mouth as small children do, but also to the acts of speaking and repeating spoken words. In this case, the reference is to "feeding" with the mother's milk of communal speech.
18 Gilles Deleuze, "Coldness and Cruelty," in *Masochism* (New York: Zone Books, 1991), pp. 128–129.

CHAPTER 7

1 The pushmi-pullyu, which "had no tail, but a head at each end, and sharp horns on each head," is an invention of Hugh Lofting, in the children's book *The Story of Doctor Dolittle* (Philadelphia: J. B. Lippincott, 1920), p. 77.
2 "Communal salvation" concerns not only artists' careers, but also the sensibility that these individuals share. The exhibition was curated by Geurt Imanse, Viktor Mazin, and Olesia Turkina.
3 The door was also shown in the exhibition at the Stedelijk Museum.
4 See Gilles Deleuze's analysis of Leopold von Sacher-Masoch's *Venus in Furs* in "Coldness and Cruelty," in *Masochism* (New York: Zone Books, 1991).
5 This iconic sculptural composition was disassembled in 2003.
6 *Znaika* and *Neznaika* are the main characters of Nikolai Nosov's *The Adventures of Neznaika and His Friends* (1954).
7 When I met Afrika in 1988, I spent hours listening to tales about imaginary pigs he had contemplated in the backyard of an abandoned Buddhist temple in St. Petersburg, about Gaussian curves collapsing (as a result) toward a negative vertical (and thus rehabilitating the "concept" of negative probabilities), about secret laboratories to detect geopolitical anomalies, or about ideology viruses from outer space inhabiting test tubes and jars welded into chunks of meteorites. Listening to all that, I had the vague feeling that a goblinesque act was being played out on me, and that I was being tested to see if I qualified as a *Znaika* or a *Neznaika*. Like any consistent goblin, Afrika rather successfully uses a spectrum of various *Znaikas,* who include—besides critics, philosophers, and art scholars—an entire array of scientists: physicists, mathematicians, and representatives of other exact and "inexact" sciences.
8 The injection of "not" means negation of all already existing "nots" in the sentence.
9 Given its shyness and lack of self-confidence, the pushmi-pullyu can be contrasted with an androgynist construct of *The Worker and the Female*

Collective Farmer. While the notion of androgyny is offered here as a symbolic fulfillment of a utopian drive toward wholeness, the hermaphroditic libido (read: pushmi-pullyu) fails to become invested in itself due to its never-ending "identity crisis." (Also, see chapter 6, "If I Were a Woman.")

10 Theodor W. Adorno, *Negative Dialectics* (New York: Continuum, 1973), p. 149. In Adorno's words, "The spread of the [identity] principle imposes on the whole world an obligation to become identical, to become total" (p. 146).

11 Mikhail Ryklin, *Iskusstvo kak prepiatstvie* (Moscow: Ad Marginem, 1998). Ryklin is referring to Boris Groys's book, *The Total Art of Stalinism: Avant-Garde, Aesthetic Dictatorship, and Beyond* (Princeton: Princeton University Press, 1992), which—regardless of (or perhaps due to) its apocalyptic tone—generates conflicting opinions. Although inventive, this book is a fiction: its author was clearly unaware of the fact that there had been many avant-gardes in postrevolutionary Russia—all disagreeing with one another, which among other reasons makes it impossible to fit them within the identity frame of "Stalin's precursors." While the genre of fiction cannot easily be debated issue-wise or in terms of belief systems, some scholars find it necessary to reproach Groys for "scapegoating the artists," as T. J. Clark did in response to a question from the audience at the Getty Research Center in 1998.

12 Curiously, Lacoue-Labarthe's views (reiterated in his lectures and conversations with Russian intellectuals in the mid-1990s) resolves the telephone "debate" between Pasternak and Stalin in favor of the latter.

13 Adorno, *Negative Dialectics,* p. 145.

14 T. S. Eliot, "Sweeney Erect" (1920), in *T. S. Eliot: The Complete Poems and Plays, 1909–1950* (New York: Harcourt, Brace and Company, 1952), p. 4.

15 My description of this reductionist scheme does not constitute agreement (or disagreement) with it.

16 See Paul de Man, *Blindness and Insight: Essays on the Rhetoric of Contemporary Criticism* (London: Oxford University Press, 1971).

17 Goethe, cited in Rudolf Magnus, *Goethe as a Scientist* (New York: Henry Schuman, 1949), p. 141.

CHAPTER 8

1 "Telesniks" are those who embrace *telesnoe,* i.e., the bodily (in Russian).

2 Reductionism, in this case, means body-seeking that alludes to the possibility of perceiving the body as a nonartificial authenticity. The paradox is that, in the philosophical circles in Moscow, body-seeking coexists with the vogue for deconstruction, which has always targeted reductionism.

3 The Russian version of Darwin's ape is, of course, Pavlov's dog. Lacan sarcastically describes Pavlov's experiments as the "attempt to obtain [from the dog] information about our own perceptions, while remaining completely ignorant of the supposed soul of the unfortunate animal." See Jacques Lacan, *The Four Fundamental Concepts of Psycho-analysis* (New York: W. W. Norton, 1977), p. 228.

4 "Well-tempered autochthony" is probably the right way to define Osmolovskii's work.

5 Kulik's fascination with Steven Spielberg's film *Jaws* (1975) hints at the possibility that in his biting spree he mistook himself for a dog or used this image as a cover-up for his crypted identity—"Vagina Dentata."

6 Long before Brener defecated in the Pushkin Museum in Moscow, the same institution rejected a Kabakov exhibition on the grounds that, as he told me, Kabakov was capable of soiling the Temple of Art by "turning it into a toilet." He also (yet again) "anticipated" Brener by building a toilet at Documenta IX in Kassel.

7 The Stedelijk Museum curator, Geurt Imanse, at whose invitation I visited Amsterdam in February 1997, showed me the damaged canvas. Despite all efforts of the conservators, the "indelible" dollar sign is still visible.

8 See Aleksandr Brener trial report, www.kinetconpictures.

9 See Marcel Mauss, *Sociologie et anthropologie* (Paris: Presses Universitaires de France, 1966), and Jean-Joseph Goux, *Symbolic Economies: After Marx and Freud* (Ithaca: Cornell University Press, 1990).

10 "Affirmative" is understood in this text in the Adornian sense as the opposite of critical and negative.

11 Guattari told me about his and Negri's troubles with Politi in New York in 1988, shortly after the publication of "An Eye on the East," *Flash Art* (Fall 1987), to which both of us contributed.

12 Quoted in Victor Tupitsyn, "*Drugoe*" *iskusstva* (Moscow: Ad Marginem, 1997), p. 278.

CHAPTER 9

1 Association of Artists of Revolutionary Russia (AKhRR, 1922–1928) and then Association of Artists of the Revolution (AKhR, 1928–1932). Its members opposed the avant-garde and, in this sense, preceded socialist realism.

2 See Louis Althusser and Etienne Balibar, *Reading Capital* (London: Verso, 1979), pp. 243–247.

3 Ilya Kabakov, quoted in Victor Tupitsyn, "*Drugoe*" *iskusstva* (Moscow: Ad Marginem, 1997), p. 106.

4 Admirable in theory, multiculturalism (American-style) has never been realized on a serious level, beyond the talk show medium or any other situation in which many people talk simultaneously in sound bites that prevent everyone from presenting actual issues.

5 *Telesnoe* (Russian for "the bodily") is often oppressive or even reactionary—unless it represents the minority's resistance against the majority, that is, the bodily as a form of protest or gesture against the grain.

6 A term coined by Antonen Artaud and later appropriated by Gilles Deleuze and Félix Guattari in *L'Anti-Oedipe* (1972).

7 Cornel West, "The New Cultural Politics of Difference," in *Modern Art and Society,* ed. Maurice Berger (New York: Icon Editions/HarperCollins, 1994), pp. 1–24. With all due respect to Cornel West, one may recall that Soviet art was defined (by Stalin) as "socialist in content and national in form."

8 These terms are attributed to Viktor Shklovskii and Bertolt Brecht, respectively.

9 Differences between androgynes and hermaphrodites as metaphoric constructs have been discussed by Plato, Aristophanes, Ovid, Friedrich Schlegel, Freud, and Lacan.

10 Hermaphroditism can be defined as procrastinated androgyny. On the border between them are located the two-sex images of the three-eyed builders of a new life. See El Lissitzky's poster for the "Russian Exhibition" in Zurich

(1929) or Gustav Klutsis's poster design (also ca. 1929) *We Will Build Our Own New World* (fig. 6.1).

11 An excerpt from my conversation with Ilya Kabakov about "Medical Hermeneutics," printed in *Mesto pechati,* Moscow, no. 11 (May 1998): 88–96, and in *Neue Bildende Kunst,* Berlin (December 1998): 60–64.

12 Unlike maturation, which takes place as we move from one social layer to another, infantilism is associated with social immobility and stagnation.

13 See Mikhail Ryklin, *Terrorologiki* (Tartu and Moscow: Eidos, 1992). In his book, Ryklin thanks me for "hinting at some intellectual strategies during our conversations in Moscow, in 1988–89" (p. 95). Although our interpretations of these (and many other) strategies are quite different, I am equally grateful to Ryklin for sharing his thoughts with me, particularly on the subject of "speech-vision."

14 Jacques Lacan, *Écrits: A Selection,* trans. Alan Sheridan (New York: W. W. Norton, 1977), p. 15.

15 Ibid., p. 16.

16 Viktor Misiano's letter defending Aleksandr Brener's destruction of his colleague's work at the 1996 Interpol exhibition can be regarded as advocacy for accident. See *Flash Art,* no. 188 (May-June 1996): 46. That same year, Brener performed yet another "accident" by drawing a dollar sign on Kazimir Malevich's painting *Suprematism (White Cross)* in the Stedelijk Museum (for details, see chapter 8 of this book).

17 Some of these people (better known as oligarchs) have already "legitimized" themselves by collecting art, subsidizing cultural institutions, and by being extra loyal to the ruling elite.

18 See André Gide, *Return from the USSR* (New York: Alfred A. Knopf, 1937); Walter Benjamin, "Moscow Diary," *October,* no. 35 (1985); and Louis Althusser, *L'avenir dure longtemps, suivi de Les faits* (Paris: Editions Stock/IMEC, 1992). As for René Etiemble, who visited Russia in 1934 and 1958, his enthusiasm for Soviet life had given way to indignation: in 1989, Etiemble published the book *Le meurtre du petit père: Naissance à la politique,* in which he criticized himself for his former uncritical attitude toward Stalin's regime.

19 What Polyphemus *actually* said was: "Nobody has tricked me, Nobody has ruined me." See Homer, *The Odyssey,* trans. Robert Fitzgerald (New York: Farrar, Straus and Giroux, 1998).

20 Peter Sloterdijk, *Kritik der zynischen Vernunft* (Frankfurt am Main: Suhrkamp, 1983).

21 In Plato's *Cratylus,* Socrates insists on the capacity of the name to reveal the "essential being" of the named. In his deconstruction of Plato, Derrida treats names as "sites of plurality."

22 This double jeopardy requires the redefinition (or de-procrastination) of the basic functions of visual art, including its critical function.

CHAPTER 10

1 See Karl Jaspers, *The Great Philosophers: The Foundations,* ed. Hannah Arendt, trans. Ralph Manheim (New York: Harcourt, Brace & World, 1962).

2 Although in his book Jaspers uses another word, "exposition," its museological lineage reveals itself as the philosopher describes "expositions" in terms of "a history of art." Ibid., p. 5.

3 Michel Foucault, "Of Other Spaces"(1967), translated by Jay Miskowiec and reprinted in *Thessaloniki Biennale 1 of Contemporary Art* (Thessaloniki: State Museum of Contemporary Art, 2007), p. 24.

4 See Ilya Kabakov, *Shestidesiatye i semidesiatye gody* (The '60s and '70s) (Vienna: Wiener Slawitscher Almanach, Sonderband 47, 1999). Also see Mark Ural'skii, *Nemukhin's Monologues* (Moscow: Bonfi, 1999); Igor' and Svetlana Kopystiansky, *Dialog* (Stuttgart: Institut für Auslandsbeziehungen, 1999); and *Leonid Sokov: Sculptures, Paintings, Objects, Installations, Documents, Articles* (St. Petersburg: State Russian Museum and Palace Edition, 2001). The Moscow performance group Collective Actions is discussed in chapter 3.

5 The museological function makes possible the transfer of the instinct of self-preservation from the individuals' physical bodies to the fruits of their labor, their merits, and their achievements in culture, science, etc.

6 I am referring to Piaget's description of the "egocentric speech" detectable in every creative gesture or event, including the results and traces of one's artistic quest—archival photographs, letters, drafts, early versions, and fragments.

7 Before the fall of the Soviet Union, its alternative artists had lived and worked for many years in a country that had no interest in experimental art.

8 Here, "deviant" can mean opposite to signification, or perpendicular to it, or heading the same way, but with a delay (deferred signification). Although egocentric reading usually takes an orthogonal attitude to signification, one should be informed that things horizontal in one cultural context may turn vertical in another.

9 Foucault was right when he defined the author as "a certain functional principle by which in our culture, one limits, excludes, and chooses." For him—unlike for Barthes and Derrida—the author is not an anonymous figure, and thus cannot be separated from the ideological function he or she performs. See Michel Foucault, "What Is an Author?" in *The Foucault Reader,* ed. Paul Rabinow (New York: Pantheon Books, 1984), pp. 118–119.

10 Moira Roth, *Difference/Indifference: Musings on Postmodernism, Marcel Duchamp and John Cage,* with commentary by Jonathan D. Katz (Amsterdam: GB Arts International, 1998), p. 30.

11 Duchamp's desire to museify his image is comparable with Marcel Broodthaers's "self-museologizing." The latter—in the words of Rosalind Krauss—was "a way in which he [Broodthaers] conducted a form of *détournement* on himself." See Rosalind E. Krauss, *"A Voyage on the North Sea": Art in the Age of the Post-Medium Condition* (London: Thames & Hudson, 2000), p. 34.

12 Clement Greenberg, "The Situation at the Moment," *Partisan Review* 15 (January 1948): 82.

13 See Greenberg's article "Irrelevance versus Irresponsibility," *Partisan Review* 15 (May 1948): 577.

14 In museums, heterochronic events take place simultaneously, contemporaneity becomes aged, and Clio gets a face-lift.

15 The key factors in this comparison would be the deficit of signification in contemporary Russian art and its overabundance in the West. As for Richter, his *Atlas* is in equilibrium between (a) egocentric speech of the signified, and (b) the image of an institutionally accepted artist, canonized during his lifetime.

16 Ilya Kabakov and Victor Tupitsyn, "The Piper of Disaster: Boris Mikhailov's 'Calm' Photographs," in *Boris Mikhailov: Case History* (Zurich: Scalo Verlag, 1999).

17 One such museum is the Moscow Museum of Modern and Contemporary Art (MMSI), founded in 2000 and based on the art collection of the sculptor Zurab Tsereteli. However, MMSI is a museum in appearance (or in outer crust) only. The same is true of Art4.Ru, established at the end of 2007 and based on the collection of Igor' Markin.

18 In the West, an "exemplary" art museum is no longer a temple, but a culture-industry showroom.

19 Later, as a result of the Stalinist cultural revolution, socialist modernism was replaced by socialist realism.

20 In spring of 2007, a display of contemporary Chinese paintings (executed in a mock-heroic style) took place in Moscow at the State Tret'iakov Gallery. The success of this art in Russia and in the West brings to mind Andrei Tarkovsky's film *Solaris* (based on Stanisław Lem's novel). On the one hand, Solaris is a planetary brain capable of capturing every "imago" (unconscious representation)—fears, perversions, taboos, remorse, and phobias—of the heroes, with the aim of embodying them in life. On the other hand, it's the most effective mode of production, for it combines psychomimetic reciprocation with instant reification. As for the personages of the novel, Solaris arranged for a rendezvous with their unconscious: the main hero with his lover who had died by his fault; and Gebarian (another scientist who was working in the laboratory) with the fruit of his imagination—a gigantic black woman, a hetaera and mother in one person. And while this monumental African goddess was coming to him, he committed suicide in horror. This is how signals sent by the consumers of the culture industry return to them. On its delivery, each "item" looks seamless to the extent that we rarely know whether it is "real" or cloned in the likeness of our museological "imagos." In this respect, the receptiveness of a Chinese "Solaris" is yet to be matched. Among the examples are Shi Xinning's *Mao and Marilyn Monroe,* 2005, and Yue Minjun's portrayal of smiling Chinese citizens with oversized jaws (*Cynical Realism,* 1999–2005). The latter evokes the nightmares, linked to castration anxiety, and aptly illustrates the phenomenon of "Solarisation," which can be defined as an instant psychomimetic reciprocation between capitalist culture industry and its socialist counterpart.

21 The photographer Boris Mikhailov once compared himself to "a dog who is forced to sniff the worn-out soles of an era" in order to recreate the era from the "smell." The same is true with the museological unconscious: whenever its symptoms are available for "sniffing," we should think twice before we dismiss them as mere jokes and gossip, fantasies, and paradoxes.

22 In Foucault's view, "The heterotopia is capable of juxtaposing in a single real place several spaces, several sites that are in themselves incompatible. . . . Heterotopias are most often linked to slices in time—which is to say that

they open onto what might be termed, for the sake of symmetry, heterochronies." Foucault, "Of Other Spaces," pp. 26–27.

23 I learned about this episode while writing an introduction to Nemukhin's *Monologues.*

24 This story was "leaked" to me by Pierre Restany in the 1990s.

25 The child's passion to retain feces and delay the process of evacuation in order to receive greater pleasure while performing it, turns, in the adult (whose anal eroticism is displaced into the unconscious), into the passion to retain and accumulate gold (money), which resembles feces in color. In this context, the promise of a golden toilet, on which everyone was going to sit in the future, confirms the anal nature of a number of social utopias.

26 Unconscious (or predicative) optics are a visual analogue of "inner speech," of which Lev Vygotsky wrote. For details, see chapter 1, note 45.

27 "Spectacular order" is an allusion to Guy Debord's "Society of the Spectacle." See, for example, Guy Debord, *Society of the Spectacle and Other Films,* ed. Richard Parry (London: Rebel Press, 1992).

28 See T. W. Adorno, *Aesthetic Theory* (New York: Routledge, 1984), p. 163.

29 See Robert Smithson, *The Collected Writings,* ed. Jack D. Flam (Berkley: University of California Press, 1996).

30 Adorno, *Aesthetic Theory,* p. 6.

31 Psychoanalysis has long ceased to be an idiom for reducing art to an absolutely subjective system of signs. In this respect, Adorno's dismissal of psychoanalytical theory (as too individualistic, nonnegative, and uncritical) is what largely contributed to the short-sightedness of his analysis of the relationship between art and the culture industry. In effect, it prevented him from facing the austerity of the situation and from foreseeing its further development. (For details, see "On the Critique of the Psychoanalytical Theory of Art" in *Aesthetic Theory.*)

32 Slavoj Žižek, *The Sublime Object of Ideology* (London: Verso, 1989), p. 50.

33 This action, titled *Exposing the Foundation of the Museum,* was performed at MOCA, Los Angeles, 1988.

34 In the second substage, the joyous affirmation of bodily wholeness in a visual image, inherent to the first substage, gives way to alienation.

35 Gilles Deleuze, "Coldness and Cruelty," in *Masochism* (New York: Zone Books, 1991), p. 131.

36 To wander around a museum from hall to hall is like leafing through the pages of an album, and this, in principle, is an act of art. Not everyone understands that art is not the works themselves, but our interrelationship with them. Art is a reaction to art in order to prevent it from becoming its own sepulchral monument.

37 Foucault, "Of Other Spaces," p. 24.

38 Adorno, *Aesthetic Theory,* p. 25.

39 This term is often used by the Moscow philosopher Valerii Podoroga.

40 The effect of fractionality is also discussed in chapter 12.

41 See Jacques Derrida, introduction to *Edmund Husserl's Origin of Geometry* (Lincoln: University of Nebraska Press, 1989), p. 124.

42 The problem of wholeness (wholeness versus fractionality) brings to mind phenomenology, particularly the concept of the universal a priori, without which whole objects cannot appear in "pure experience."

43 "Expanded field" is Rosalind Krauss's term in *The Originality of the Avant-Garde and Other Modernist Myths* (Cambridge, Mass.: MIT Press, 1985); "extended vision" was advocated by Mikhail Matushin and (later) by Herbert Bayer.

44 When images of the artworks circulate in the media, turning museum collections into traveling exhibitions, they end up being additionally mythologized and museified. To put it differently, the media temporarily set free fixed (capitonnized) signifiers in order to secure surplus museification on their way home.

45 Art and democracy are similar in that they are equally unattainable. Even though their promise will not be fulfilled, our participation in each is still crucial. One should think twice before disengaging from this process, for the only way to experience art and democracy (especially in the consumer society) is to never stop reinventing them, even if our participation is under threat of being fetishized.

46 The same is true of media icons, e.g., famous athletes and fashion models who tend to display bodily "artifacts" rather than "lexical" ones.

47 See Jean Baudrillard, *Utopia Deferred: Writings from Utopie (1967–1978)*, trans. Stuart Kendall (New York: Semiotext(e), 2006), p. 215.

48 The shark's metamorphosis seems analogous to the wrinkling of upholstery in the places (*points de capiton*, as Lacan terms them) where it is pinned to a furniture frame. Given that in the symbolic network, signifiers are pinned (or "capitonnized") in the same way, it is safe to suggest that our psychic upholstery may also wrinkle around *points de capiton*, thereby providing (in its folds) an opportunity to shelter "presymbolic intention" (Δ in Lacan's terminology). See Jacques Lacan, "Subversion of the Subject and Dialectics of Desire," in *Écrits: A Selection*, trans. Alan Sheridan (New York: W. W. Norton, 1977).

49 Lunacharskii borrowed this term from the German philosopher Richard Avenarius (1843–1896).

50 See Pavel Pepperstein, "Filosofstvuiushchaia gruppa i filosofskii muzei," *Mesto pechati*, no. 11 (Moscow: Obscuri Viri, 1998), pp. 73–79.

51 Ibid., p. 78.

52 Ibid.

CHAPTER 11

1 See Clement Greenberg, "Irrelevance versus Irresponsibility," *Partisan Review* 15 (May 1948).

2 "Globalization" comprises not only the sphere of visual representation (the so-called "international style"), but other spheres as well—the economy, politics, sex, etc.

3 The atrocities committed by Serbs in Kosovo are overwhelming. But in the eyes of many East Europeans, NATO is not a peacemaker either.

4 Along with the display at the State Tret'iakov Gallery and the opening of the MAD exhibition, one must also take note of Irina Nakhova's installation *Big Red* (at the XL Gallery) as well as the performance of the CA group on the Kievogorskoe field near Moscow (March 31, 1999).

5 For details, see Victor Tupitsyn, "Romancing the Negative: Boris Mikhailov's New Photographs," in *Boris Michailov: Les Misérables* (Hannover: Sprengel Museum, 1998), unpaged.

6 Pierre Klossowski, *Un si funeste désir* (Paris: Gallimard, 1963), pp. 126–127.

7 It is worth looking at the idea of the panic state and panic consciousness from an etymological point of view. As a concept, "panic" comes from the word "Pan." Pan was a minor ancient Greek deity with hooves and horns, whose playing on a reed pipe inspired panic. In some old verses I read in my youth, he was described as "the piper of disaster." On the other hand, as one of the companions of Dionysus, Pan belongs to the orgiastic and carnival element. As part of Dionysus's retinue, Pan panicked at the sight of Apollo. The sources of this "Pan-theistic panic" are illuminated in Nietzsche's *The Birth of Tragedy out of the Spirit of Music.*

8 Ilya Kabakov and Victor Tupitsyn, "The Piper of Disaster: Boris Mikhailov's 'Calm' Photographs," in *Boris Mikhailov: Case History* (Zurich: Scalo Verlag, 1999), pp. 473–474.

9 When saving infants from slaughter, God distinguished between "his own" (children) and others by palpating their sexual organs.

10 This painting is now in Musée d'Orsay, Paris.

11 See, for example, the special issue of *Kh/Zh* (*Khudozhestvennyi Zhurnal,* Winter 1998–1999), published in Moscow and dedicated to the problems of East European identity.

12 Positive and negative affections (*positiv affektsional* versus *negativ affektsional*) are discussed in chapter 10.

13 In *Aesthetic Theory* (1970), Adorno posits the existence of a negative dialectic of art that resists unities and syntheses embraced by historical dialectics. See T. W. Adorno, *Aesthetic Theory* (New York: Routledge, 1984).

14 Here, I am referring to the philosopher Andrew Benjamin, who expressed this opinion in our conversation in New York (Fall 1997).

15 The term "de-framer" alludes to Deleuze's deframing. See Gilles Deleuze, *Cinema 1: The Movement-Image* (Minneapolis: University of Minnesota Press, 1986), p. 15. An example of such a de-framer (or schizo-intellectual) is Kabakov, whose authorial "I" splits into a multitude of personages, some of whom are passionate and eager to be identified whereas others are critical and alienated.

16 In *Anti-Oedipus* (1972), desire is posited as the only revolutionary force, which partially attests (especially after the failure of May 1968 events) to the state of disillusionment among young radicals, and to their consequent social disengagement. See Gilles Deleuze and Félix Guattari, *Anti-Oedipus: Capitalism and Schizophrenia,* trans. Robert Hurley et al. (New York: Viking, 1977).

17 Filmmaker Michael Moore seems to have been able to promote serious issues in a funny and relaxed way while dealing with an audience addicted to entertainment.

18 Examples are Derrida, Lacoue-Labarthe, and Nancy in France; Michelson, Krauss, Bois, Buchloh, and Foster in the United States (*October* magazine); Podoroga, Ryklin, Mikhail Iampolskii (before he moved to New York), and Elena Petrovskaia in Russia (Moscow Institute of Philosophy). Internal friction within some of these groups attests to the ephemeral nature of intellectual alliances.

19 Sorokin shared this opinion with me in Munich (1995). Similar thoughts are expressed in his *Collection of Writings,* vol. 1 (Moscow: Ad Marginem, 1998), p. 9.

20 "Motherland and Death" is an example of these tendencies. As Komar and Melamid admitted in a conversation, "Parallel to our American life, there are Russia and Russian history. Here, a lowly personal life; there, a heroic Russian death, which is also immortality. As for our place, it is somewhere between Russian immortality and American death." Quoted in Victor Tupitsyn, "Excerpt from a Conversation with Vitaly Komar and Alexander Melamid," in *Kräftemessen,* ed. Haralampi G. Oroschakoff (Ostfildern: Cantz, 1995), pp. 206–208.

21 Kabakov and Tupitsyn, "The Piper of Disaster," p. 477.

CHAPTER 12

1 All quotations in this section are from that trialogue (translations by Cathy Young). See Victor Tupitsyn, *Glaznoe iabloko razdora: Besedy s Il'ei Kabakovym* (Moscow: NLO, 2006), pp. 106–128.

2 The concept of fractionality is developed in my other articles; see, for example, Victor Tupitsyn, "Shock Identities," in "Post-Soviet Russia," ed. Victor Tupitsyn, special issue, *Third Text* 17, no. 65, issue 4 (December 2003): 369–377, and "Alienation De-realized/ Alienation Carnivalized," in *Parachute,* no. 122 (2006): 121–128.

3 "Theories, Models, Methods, . . ." attests to its author's desire to appropriate everything that was traditionally the prerogative of the spectator or the critic. Along the way, he usurps every possible angle of vision, including that of the retrograde.

4 In Adorno's time, "the consumer [was] allowed to project his . . . mimetic residues on to anything he please[d], including art." See T. W. Adorno, *Aesthetic Theory* (New York: Routledge, 1984), p. 25. Today, such "mimetic residues" can be characterized as either an "afterimage," or a "counterimage" of culture industry.

5 This and subsequent quotations are from Tupitsyn, *Glaznoe iabloko razdora,* pp. 106–128. In the trialogue "Vzryvnye raboty," Kabakov said he believes that "some artists switch from art to design, under the pretext that fashion today is on the cutting edge while art is a geriatric phenomenon." In response, Margarita Tupitsyn pointed out that "often, we fail to recognize the importance of the development of a process and react solely to its culmination. Thus, the takeover of art by design and the competition between them is a fairly old story. In New York, this began in the mid-1980s, with the opening of such shops as Comme des Garçons and Yohji Yamamoto. Visiting these shops was sometimes more interesting than visiting galleries, and even the well-known architect Peter Eisenman made an installation in Comme des Garçons which was featured in an issue of the journal *October.* In a sense, he declared this space to be more modern than the traditional premises of an exhibition. Then, many art galleries moved to Chelsea and began to impress not with their art but with their space and design. Curiously, Comme des Garçons is the only shop that also moved from SoHo to Chelsea. In other words, all this developed over a fairly long period of time. And if we're going to talk about the historical aspect of the relationship between design and art, one has to remember the Russian avant-garde, and Bauhaus. As Baudrillard put it, 'The mortal enemy of design is kitsch. Ostensibly destroyed by Bauhaus, it nevertheless rises from its ashes.' When

I curated the exhibition 'Bauhaus: Dessau, Chicago, New York,' I put this statement up on the wall at the end of the exposition. Upon leaving it, the visitor entered the museum shop, which sold modern kitsch made in the Bauhaus style. The culmination of this process took place not in the zone of art but outside it."

6 To follow up on the theme of confusion, I will add that something similar is happening now in Russia, where the right is labeled "left" and vice versa. That is why the philosopher Richard Rorty, who does the same thing, is so popular in Russia. Rorty chides American leftists for their eschatological mindset, since, in his view, they are unwilling to forgive their country's sins. If one agrees with Rorty, the presumption of irredeemable sin is an empty center around which the planetary system of leftist discourse revolves. Curiously, Rorty's field of vision omits the fact that his own attempt to refashion the concept of leftism and thus to take away the left's "primogeniture" (with which, along the way, he invests his predecessors Dewey and Whitman) is a typical eschatological enterprise. Here, I am referring to the serious of lectures given by Rorty at the Stanford Humanities Center in 1996–1997 under the title "Politics of the Left in Twentieth-Century America."

7 See J.-F. Lyotard, *Le différend* (Paris: Éditions de Minuit, 1983).

8 This is precisely the case of Hirst. Ironically, Kabakov has been accused of the same "crime" by some of his younger compatriots, including Anatolii Osmolovskii and Dmitrii Gutov.

9 Derrida's assertion that everything is Text invalidates the concept of critical distance (Brecht's "alienation effect"), because in such an environment nothing can transcend its textual identity or attain the position exterior to something else. This applies to both critical discourse and to what it criticizes (for as long as they are equally doomed to be textual phenomena).

10 In the 1960s, the term "aesthetics of indifference" was associated with Marcel Duchamp and his younger American colleagues and admirers, including John Cage.

CHAPTER 13

1 "Chaussée" (in French) is the same as "Shosse" (in Russian) or "highway" (in English). To explain what Rublevskoe Chaussée is, I will offer an anecdote about an art critic whose car breaks down while he's on the Rublevskoe Chaussée, leading to many villas inhabited by the nouveaux riches. As he hitchhikes at the side of the road, a car pulls up and the driver asks, "Are you in the oil business?" "No," says the critic. And the driver zooms off. This exasperating conversation continues to repeat itself with other drivers, so when a Mercedes driven by a leggy, glamorous blonde pulls up, and she asks the same question, he answers, "Yes, I work in the oil business." She opens the door, moves over to the passenger seat, lets the guy drive her Mercedes, and starts giving him a blow job. In the process, he receives a phone call from a friend, asking if he's still working as an art critic. "No," he replies, "I'm working in the oil business now." "Oh, how long have you been doing that?" inquires his friend. "Ten minutes, and it's so much fun."

2 The curatorial team of the First Moscow Biennale (January 28–February 28, 2005) consisted of Joseph Bakshtein, Daniel Birnbaum, Nicolas Bourriaud, Iara Boubnova, Rosa Martinez, and Hans Ulrich Obrist.

3 Otherwise, registering these activities as "art-into-life" or "life-into-art" would be well publicized.

4 David Ter-Oganian's objects are reminiscent of those produced by his compatriots, the Peppers (Oleg Petrenko and Mila Skripkina), in the late 1980s and early 1990s.

5 Quoted from the wall text in the former Lenin Museum.

6 See Georges Bataille, "Informe," *Documents* 1, no. 7 (1929).

7 Unlike most of the Biennale's participants, Boltanski managed to come to Moscow in advance, chose the space very carefully, and paid attention to the local context, which, in the end, became his coauthor.

8 Viola's piece (which, by the way, echoes Chris Burden's 1974 performance *The Visitation*) is not animation in a literary sense. What it animates is the act of mimesis based on Pontormo's painting of 1528–1529.

9 These scholars should be reminded of Gustav Shpet's argument in *The Problems of Modern Aesthetics* that "Vulgar nomenclature mixes up metaphysics and mysticism." Shpet (1879–1937) was a prominent Russian philosopher, executed during the Great Terror.

10 Viola's stance is that of an enlightened pagan of the Wagnerian type. Perhaps he is a moderate Wagnerian, who prudently trimmed his fangs, manicured his claws, and embraced elemental spirituality as a prerequisite for his involvement in a new and ambitious staging of *Tristan and Isolde.*

11 Conceptualism's gains are inseparable from its losses. Among the "endangered species" is the principle of negativity manifested in the early stages of conceptualism in its characteristic *faktura*-clastic pathos. Today, interest in the object has been revived, the sole difference being that now it is not space itself that is objectified, but the figures of orientation within space. Generally speaking, nostalgia for the lost object is a typical feature of late conceptualism.

12 The title of the show was "Robert Mapplethorpe and the Classical Tradition: Photographs and Mannerist Prints."

13 I am referring to a variety of styles and tendencies prevalent in art and design of the 1930s, most notably neoclassicism and art deco.

14 These are the initials of (Tat'iana) Arzamasova, (Lev) Evzovich, (Evgenii) Sviatskii, + (Vladimir) Fridkes.

15 Taken from the artists' text, AES+F, "Last Riot" (2005), distributed by the organizers of the show.

16 This is a paraphrasing of Vasilii Rozanov's skeptical reaction to Darwin: "Great news: we descended from apes, therefore let's love each other." Rozanov (1856–1919) was a Russian writer and religious philosopher.

17 Solomon R. Guggenheim Museum, September 16, 2005–January 11, 2006.

18 Yve-Alain Bois, "Back to the Future: The New Malevich," *Book Forum,* Winter 2003.

19 Sots art and apt art are discussed in chapter 2.

20 I am referring to one of the catalogue contributors, Boris Groys, whose book *The Total Art of Stalinism: Avant-Garde, Aesthetic Dictatorship, and Beyond* (Princeton: Princeton University Press, 1992) cannot be regarded as anything other than a spectacularist project (see chapter 7, note 11).

21 Jean Baudrillard, *The Conspiracy of Art,* trans. Stuart Kendall (New York and Los Angeles: Semiotext(e), 2005), p. 44.

22 Robert Smithson's *Floating Island to Travel around Manhattan Island.*

23 Semenikhin also sponsored a display of Bulatov's paintings in a foyer of the Musée d'Art Moderne de la Ville de Paris in the summer of 2007.

24 For viewers, Bulatov's exhibition presented a chance to realize that authoritarian intertexts (buried alive underneath any cultural heritage) are powerless without the "corrupt eye" of the beholder. For details, see Victor Tupitsyn, "Eric Bulatov: State Treatiakov Gallery, Moscow," *Artforum* (January 2007): 244, 276.

25 In an interview with a Moscow newspaper, the State Tret'iakov Gallery curator Andrei Erofeev said that the currently vacant role of art leader in Russia should be filled by Bulatov, whose painting(s) would then accompany Putin in his trips abroad, thereby enabling him to demonstrate Russia's strength in visual arts at G8 summits. Traditionally, imperial aspirations have been matched by decadence and "glamour," and this is precisely the case of many exhibitions organized by the New Russians, both inside and outside of Gazprom's sphere of competence.

26 In "Something's Missing," Ernst Bloch and Theodor W. Adorno argued that "the function of utopia is a critique of what is present" (Bloch) and that "utopia is essentially in the determined negation of that which merely is" (Adorno). See Ernst Bloch and Theodor W. Adorno, "Something's Missing," in *The Utopian Function of Art and Literature: Selected Essays by Ernst Bloch,* trans. Jack Zipes and Frank Mecklenburg (Cambridge, Mass.: MIT Press, 1988), p. 12. Another approach to negativity was outlined by Alain Badiou in an interview (*Artforum,* October 1994): "Only a fidelity offers the possibility of betrayal."

27 Erik Bulatov, quoted in Victor Tupitsyn, "Beseda s Erikom Bulatovym," in "*Drugoe*" *iskusstva* (Moscow: Ad Marginem, 1997), p. 69.

28 *Andrei Molodkin: Cold War II,* ed. Victor and Margarita Tupitsyn (Zurich: Kashya Hildebrand Gallery, 2007), p. 30.

29 Quoted from the wall text for Andrei Molodkin's *G8* exhibition at Kashya Hildebrand Gallery.

30 This access was blocked by Putin soon after he came to power. In due course, mainstream media and political discourse have been "putinized."

31 Being in charge of arts (in charge of the "sublime") is a sublimation of one's self-image (or identity) as a power broker.

32 Mil'ner's contribution was the phrase "I hope," featured on the facade of the Russian pavilion and repeated in many languages.

33 In today's Russia, "new official art" is epitomized by the work of Kulik, Vinogradov and Dubossarskii, and the AES+F group.

34 Curated by Kulik, this exhibition was part of the Second Moscow Biennale of Contemporary Art. The entire "I Believe" project was clouded by mysticism—a concession to the religious right and to those conservative politicians who want to exercise control over culture.

35 This ending bears resemblance to a CA group action in Iakutiia, *For G. Kizeval'ter (The Slogan—1980),* described in chapter 2 (see fig. 2.20).

INDEX

Page numbers in boldface type indicate figures.